D1327499

German Course

Handbook

**Instructions
Explanatory Notes
Vocabularies**

The Linguaphone Institute

Linguaphone Institute Limited
209 Regent Street
London W1R 8AU

First published 1972
11th edition 1984

LSN NGEENH10

Printed and bound in Great Britain by
Hazell Watson & Viney Limited,
Member of the BPCC Group,
Aylesbury, Bucks

Course validated by:	Professor Dr. Heinz Fischer, formerly Associate Professor of German, University of Waterloo (Ontario), Canada.
Compiled by:	Ingrid K. J. Williams, M.A. (Munich), Senior Lecturer, Ealing College of Higher Education, (formerly Lecturer in German for Foreigners, University of Munich).
Under the direction of:	Una McNab, M.A., Lecturer in German, Brunel University.
Recorded by:	Heinz Fischer Corinna Schnabel Andrew Sachs Sabina Michael Paul Hansard Maria Warburg Henry Imberg Hannah Norbert-Miller Michael Wolf
Under the supervision of:	Professor Dr. Heinz Fischer and Ingrid K. J. Williams.

The Linguaphone Academic Advisory Committee:	Professor A. C. Gimson, B.A., Professor of Phonetics, University College London. (Chairman)
	Monsieur André Martinet, Professeur à l'Université de Paris (Sorbonne), Directeur de l'Institut de Linguistique.
	Professor Randolph Quirk, CBE, DLitt, FBA, Vice-Chancellor, University of London; formerly Quain Professor of English, University College London; Hon. Fil. Dr. (Lund, Uppsala), Hon. Doct. d'Univ. (Paris, Liège), Hon. LLD (Reading), Hon. DLitt (Leicester); Fellow of the Royal Belgian Academy of Sciences.
	Professor Albert Sonnenfeld, Ph.D., Officier, Ordre des Palmes Académiques, Professor of French and Comparative Literatures, Chairman, Department of Romance Languages and Literatures, Princeton University.
	Graham Till, M.A., Head of Course Planning and Research, The Linguaphone Institute. (Secretary)

Contents

Learning with Linguaphone
(Deutscher Kursus)

Your Linguaphone Course has been carefully constructed in the most up-to-date scientific way to build up the language you are learning from an absolute beginning to the point where, if you have followed the instructions, you will be able to speak, read and write the language and to understand it when it is spoken. You will be able to cope confidently with everyday situations in the country where the language is spoken.

Instructions

Regular study and practice with this course is much more efficient than attempting large amounts at irregular intervals. 'A little and often' is preferable to 'a lot but seldom'. For the Introduction and each lesson:

1 **Recording** Listen to the recording of Part 1 once. Don't try to understand at this stage. Just listen to the sounds of the language.

2 **Handbook** Read the section 'what happens'. This will give you an idea of what happens in the lesson and in Part 1. (For the Introduction only, you have a complete translation.)

3 **Recording** Listen to the recording of Part 1 several times more. You will now begin to associate the sounds with what happens. You will find that you are becoming accustomed to the sounds of the language.

4 **Recording   Illustrated book (*Deutscher Kursus*)** Listen to the recording of Part 1 and follow the text in the book several times. You will now be able to relate what you hear to what you see written. At the same time, the pictures will help you to understand a little more.

5 Handbook Work out the meaning. Use the word list and notes. (For the Introduction only, you have a complete translation.) Try to understand first of all the meaning of the phrases, and then of whole sentences.

6 Recording Listen to the recording again now that you understand the meaning. Continue to listen until you can understand everything as you hear it.

7 Recording Illustrated book (*Deutscher Kursus*) Read the text to yourself and then read it aloud several times. If you have any doubts about the pronunciation of any word or phrase listen to that part of the recording again. You can also listen to the recording of the sounds of German (*Die deutschen Laute*).

8 Now repeat instructions 1–7 for Part 2 and then for Part 3.

9 Written exercises (*Schriftliche Übungen*) Do the exercise "*Verstehen Sie die Lektion?*" (Do you understand the lesson?) to see if you have fully understood the lesson.
  i   Read the four sentences a, b, c and d.
  ii   Write down the letter which is alongside the one correct sentence. The other sentences are wrong. Do the whole exercise like this. Then:
  iii Check with the answers at the end of the book.

NB Write your answers on a separate sheet of paper, not in the book.

10 If you have made no more than one mistake in the exercise, go on to instruction 11. If you have made more than one mistake, go back to instruction 4 and work through the lesson again.

11 Written exercises (*Schriftliche Übungen*) Do the written exercises on a separate sheet of paper, not in the book.
  i   Read the examples: they show you what you have to do.
  ii   Write out each sentence in full, including the first two or three, which are the same as the examples.
  iii Check your sentences with the answers at the end of the book.
  iv   If you have made a mistake and cannot understand why, refer to the text again and check with the appendix.
  v   If you have made more than two mistakes in one exercise, do the exercise again, but study the lesson first.

12 Begin the next lesson.

The Books and the Recordings

The Illustrated Book (Deutscher Kursus)

The Introduction introduces you to some elementary sentence patterns and to the sounds of the language.

Each of the thirty lessons has three separate parts so that, once you have understood the Introduction, you have ninety carefully graded, easily paced stages to work through. Each stage is long enough to give you meaningful language practice and short enough for you to understand everything in it in a single study period.

Part 1 is a monologue which brings in the main teaching points of the lesson. This means that you have only one voice to listen to while you absorb the new language.

In *Part 2* you will hear the characters of the story using the new language in everyday situations.

In parts 1 and 2 you will meet a family and their friends in everyday life. We hope you will become their friend and learn to speak their language as well as they do.

Part 3 consists of conversations set in different situations. This part is based on the language you have learned in Parts 1 and 2 and gives you the chance to practise it in varied situations.

The illustrations to the lessons are there to show you at a glance what is happening in the story and to enable you to see without delay the meaning of individual words and phrases.

The Recordings

The Introduction and all the lessons are recorded. The professional speakers have been carefully selected for their correctness and clarity of speech. The early lessons have been recorded as slowly as possible without distorting the language. Gradually, the speed of speech is increased through the course. There is a separate section on the sounds of the language designed to enable you to recognise and practise the key sounds. Refer to this section regularly throughout the course. Remember that different languages often pronounce the same letters or combination of letters in quite different ways. Practice makes perfect.

This Handbook

After this section you will find a translation of the Introduction and then a guide to each lesson which gives you:

1. i) A short account of what happens in the lesson.
    ii) A list of the new words used in the lesson. This is arranged in groups of words which have a similar grammatical function. By seeing them grouped this way you will learn them more quickly. For easy reference, each group is given in alphabetical order.
    iii) Notes on the meaning of the lesson, with the language points carefully explained; these notes progressively build up to give an understanding of the whole language.

2. Appendices which list useful categories of language, such as irregular verbs, which you will have met in the course.

3. Two alphabetical vocabularies which give you the meaning of each word as it is used in the course. In the German-English vocabulary the numbers in front of the English meaning(s) for each German word or phrase refer to the lesson in which it first occurs with that meaning. The English-German vocabulary gives you an alphabetical list of the English words and phrases contained in the German-English vocabulary with their meanings in German.

The Exercise Book (Schriftliche Übungen)

This book enables you to practise writing the language you have learned.

Introduction

Part one

Good morning!
Listen, please.
I'm Dieter Klein.
I'm a teacher.

I'm German.
I speak German.
You are learning German.
You are a student.

This is a book.
This is a tape.
This is a cassette.
This is a record.

Part two

Herr Klein	Good morning!
Student	Good morning, Herr Klein!
Herr Klein	How are you?
Student	Fine, thank you.
	And you?
Herr Klein	Very well, thank you.
	Are you a student?
Student	Yes, I am.
Herr Klein	Are you German?
Student	No.
Herr Klein	Are you learning German?
Student	Yes.
Herr Klein	Have you got a book?
Student	Yes.
Herr Klein	Good. Where is it?
Student	Here it is.

Part three

Herr Kühn	Good morning!
	I'm Walter Kühn.
	I'm a sales engineer.
	This is my wife, Lore.
Frau Kühn	Good morning!
	I'm Lore Kühn.
	I'm German.

Herr Kühn	This is my daughter.
Renate Kühn	Good morning!
	I'm Renate.
	I'm fifteen.
	I'm a schoolgirl.
	I'm also German.

Herr Kühn	And this is my son.
Herbert Kühn	Good morning!
	I'm Herbert.
	I'm German.
	I'm twenty-three.
	I'm a student.
	And this is my girl-friend, Eva.

Eva Schultze	Good morning!
	I'm Eva.
	I'm a kindergarten teacher.

Frau Pfaffinger	I'm Grete Pfaffinger.
	I'm Walter's sister.
	I'm a housewife.
	And this is my husband, Max.

Herr Pfaffinger	Good morning!
	I'm Max Pfaffinger.
	I'm Walter's brother-in-law.
	I live in Germany, in Munich.
	I'm a carpenter.

2

Lektion eins   Rhein-Main-Flughafen, Frankfurt

Lesson one   Rhein-Main Airport, Frankfurt

What happens

In this lesson you will meet Walter Kühn, his wife Lore and their daughter Renate. Herr Kühn is a business-man, a senior technical sales executive with a German firm which manufactures electrical goods. For some years he has been working in Rio and he is now coming home to Germany on six months' leave.

In Part 1 Heinz Schmidt, a colleague of Herr Kühn's, who has come to the airport to meet him, tells you something about Herr Kühn.

In Part 2 the Kühns pass through customs and immigration, Herr Schmidt is introduced to Frau Kühn and Renate, and he drives them all to their hotel.

In Part 3 of each lesson there are short dialogues demonstrating the use of the language introduced in Parts 1 and 2 but in different situations.

Words in this lesson

der, die, das the
ein, eine a
mein, meine my
Ihr, Ihre your
ihr, ihre her

ich I
er he, it
sie she, it
es it
wir we
Sie you
sie they
Ihnen you (dat.)

was? what?
wer? who?
wo? where?

alle all (plural)
das that
eins one

etwas something, anything
nichts nothing

der Alkohol alcohol
der Flughafen airport
der Gepäckträger porter
der Geschäftsmann businessman
der Herr gentleman
Herr Kühn Mr. Kühn
der Koffer suitcase
der Kognak brandy
der Kollege colleague
der Paß passport
der Paßbeamte passport official, immigration officer
der Reisepaß passport
der Tabak tobacco
der Teil part
der Urlaub holiday
der Wein wine
der Zollbeamte customs officer

3

1

die Begrüßung welcome
die Dame lady
die Flasche bottle
die Frau woman, wife
Frau Kühn Mrs. Kühn
die Lektion lesson
die Paßkontrolle immigration, passport
  control
die Reisetasche travelling bag
die Tochter daughter
die Zollkontrolle customs control

das Auto car
(das) Brasilien Brazil
(das) Deutschland Germany
das Flugzeug plane
das Fräulein young lady
Fräulein Kühn Miss Kühn
das Gepäck luggage
das Parfum perfume

Deutsche German (people)
Zigaretten cigarettes

(haben) (to have)
ich habe I have
er hat he has
wir haben we have
Sie haben you have

(sein) (to be)
ich bin I am
er ist he is
wir sind we are
Sie sind you are
sie sind they are

(arbeiten) (to work)
er arbeitet he works, he is working
(fahren) (to drive)
wir fahren we drive, we are driving
(heißen) (to be called)
ich heiße my name is, I am called
Sie heißen you are called
er heißt he is called
(kommen) (to come)
Herr Kühn kommt Herr Kühn is coming

(landen) (to land)
das Flugzeug landet the plane lands,
  is landing
(machen) (to do)
Sie machen you do, you are doing
(wohnen) (to live)
Sie wohnen you live, you are living
wir wohnen we live, we are living

braun brown
erste first
gut good
richtig right
schön nice, beautiful
schwarz black

auf on
aus from
in in
nach to
von of

gerade just
heute today
jetzt now
sofort at once

dort there
draußen outside
hier here

auf Urlaub on holiday
aus Brasilien from Brazil
aus München from Munich
in Deutschland in Germany
in Ihr Hotel to your hotel
nach Deutschland to Germany
von Walter Kühn of Walter Kühn

aber but
auch also
nicht not
und and

ah! ah!
aha! aha! (I see!)
ah gut oh good
bitte please
bitte schön! please!
da sind Sie ja well, there you are

danke thank you
danke schön thank you very much
das bin ich that's me
das ist doch but that is
guten Tag good morning,
   good afternoon, how do you do?
haben Sie etwas zu verzollen? have you
   anything to declare?
hallo! hey! I say!
in Ordnung that's fine

ja yes
mein Herr sir
nein no
nicht wahr? isn't it?
richtig that's right
sehr gut very well
vielen Dank thank you very much
wie geht es Ihnen? how are you?
wie heißen Sie? what is your name?
zweihundert two hundred

Notes

Part one

1 **Guten Tag!** This is an everyday greeting used by people who
   know each other, as well as on occasions when we would say,
   "How do you do?" It serves for any time of day except evening.

2 **Ich bin Heinz Schmidt.** *I am (I'm) Heinz Schmidt.*

3 **Ich bin ein Kollege von Walter Kühn.** *I'm a colleague of Walter
   Kühn's.*

a **ein Kollege** All German nouns are written with an initial
   capital letter.

b **von Walter Kühn** **Von** doesn't always mean *of*, but before
   someone's name it usually does.
   ü The two dots above the **u** are called an UMLAUT and change the
   normal sound, spelt **u** in German (very like the sound spelt *oo* in
   English) to a sound which doesn't exist in English but is very
   common in German. To say it, try pursing your lips, as for
   whistling. Listen to it again and try to say it. If you have
   difficulty, position your lips ready to make the *oo* sound, but
   instead say *ee* (as in *been*).

4 **Herr Kühn kommt heute aus Brasilien.** *Mr. Kühn is coming from
   Brazil today.*

a **Herr Kühn** **Herr** before a name is the equivalent of *Mr.*

b **kommt** As in English, German verbs (action words) show
   changes according to the doer of the action, who is called the
   SUBJECT – *I come* but *he comes*. **-t** is the usual ending when the
   subject is not the speaker (*I*), not the person(s) spoken to (*you*),
   but someone (or something) being spoken about (*he, she, it,
   Walter, Lore,* etc.) – in this case Herr Kühn.
   Kommt means either *is coming* or *comes*. It is very important to

1

remember this, as you may think you need two words for expressions such as *is coming, is doing*.

c heute aus Brasilien: *from Brazil today*   Note the order in German, which is not optional. Expressions of time normally precede those of place. **Eu** is pronounced like *oy* in *boy*.

d aus Brasilien   To come *from* a country or a town requires **aus**.

5 Er arbeitet dort. *He works there.* **Arbeitet** is a form similar to **kommt** (**L1, N4b**), but this time the appropriate English is *works* rather than *is working*.

You may have sensed that although **arbeitet** is the same part of the verb as **kommt,** there is something slightly different about it. The part of the verb that describes the action is called the STEM. That is, as soon as we hear **komm-** we know that we're talking about someone *coming*, but without the appropriate ending we don't know who. Endings, then, are attached to the stem. When we are talking about *working*, **arbeit-** is the stem. When the required ending is **-t** we have a problem, because there is a **t** there already. Adding another **t** won't solve it because **tt** sounds the same as **t**. To show that the **-t** ending is there, we must insert a sound between the **t**'s, spelt **e**, giving **arbeitet**. This happens with any German verb whose stem ends in **t** or **d**.

6 Er ist Geschäftsmann. *He's a businessman.* There is no need to include the word for *a* when stating one's trade or profession.
ä When there is an Umlaut on an **a** it is pronounced rather like the *e* in English *left*.

7 Er kommt nach Deutschland, nach Frankfurt   *He's coming to Germany, to Frankfurt.*
To all towns and most countries is rendered by **nach**.

8 Frau Kühn und ihre Tochter, Fräulein Kühn, kommen auch nach Frankfurt. *Mrs. Kühn and her daughter, Miss Kühn, are also coming to Frankfurt.*

a ihre   *Her* is **ihr** and when it occurs before a so-called feminine noun an **e** is added.

b Fräulein Kühn   **Äu,** the combination of **a** and **u** with an Umlaut on the **a,** is pronounced rather like the *oy* in *boy*.

c kommen: *are coming*   This time we have a different ending on **komm-**. The ending indicates that more than one person is coming, here Frau Kühn and her daughter.

d kommen auch: *are also coming*   **Auch** is placed immediately after the verb.

6

e auch The **au** is pronounced like *ow* in *how*. The **ch** is pronounced like the *ch* in the Scottish word *loch,* not like a *ck.*

9 Ein Flugzeug aus Rio landet gerade. *A plane from Rio is just
landing.*

a landet The stem of the verb (**land-**) ends in **-d,** so the ending is
-et and not just **-t** (L1, N5).

b landet gerade: *is just landing* **Gerade** is placed after the verb.
Note that there are no silent **e**'s in German. Many German
words end in **-e** and the **e** must be heard, e.g. **heute, Kollege.**

Part two

Paßkontrolle *Passport control*

10 der Paßbeamte *Immigration officer*

a A person employed in a Government department is called
Beamte in German. The particular department is indicated by the
first part of his 'title', e.g. **der Paßbeamte:** *passport officer.*
Beamte You will hear the pronunciation of this word in Lesson 5.
Meanwhile note that it has three syllables: **Be-am-te.**
Note that the two nouns are joined together to make a compound
noun. The word for *the* depends on the second component.

b ß This is the only writing symbol (apart from the Umlaut) which
is unfamiliar to you. It is always sounded like the *ss* in *hiss.* You
do not have to use it yourself (you can write **ss**), but you must
be able to recognize it when you see it.

c der Paßbeamte **Der** is the word for *the* before all so-called
masculine nouns. Here is your first shock: there is not just one
word for *the* in German. German nouns are of three kinds or
classes, which, for want of better terms, are named masculine,
feminine and neuter. The German word for *the* before a noun
depends on the class to which the noun belongs. The best way to
remember which class new nouns belong to is to learn the right
word for *the* along with them, and the lesson vocabularies have
been arranged in such a way as to make this as easy as possible
for you. Beware of confusion with English, however, which uses
masculine, feminine and neuter to distinguish between male and
female beings and inanimate objects. You will discover that in
German, things can be any one of the three!

11 Wo ist Ihr Paß, mein Herr? *Where is your passport, sir?*

a Ihr Paß **Ihr:** *your* is always written with a capital **I** – a sign of

7

the formal courtesy it implies. As with *a* and *the*, words like *your* and *my* change according to the class of the following noun. This seems complicated, but you will see that the changes follow a pattern. **Ihr** is used before MASCULINE or NEUTER nouns.

b **mein Herr** Herr can mean *gentleman* as well as *Mr*. **Mein** is the word for *my* before masculine or neuter nouns. The expression **mein Herr** is used on occasions when we would say *sir*. Such expressions are only used by waiters, porters, officials, etc.

12 **Hier, bitte.** *Here you are*. The conventional English phrase, inviting the person addressed to *help yourself*. **Bitte** really means *please*, but is also used when you are offering someone something.

13 **Hier ist mein Reisepaß.** *Here's my passport* (*travel pass*). It is quite in order to shorten **Reisepaß** to **Paß**. Remember the class of a compound noun is the class of its last component, so **die Reise + der Paß = der Reisepaß** (L1, N10a).
   mein Reisepaß Remember **mein** is the word for *my* before masculine or neuter nouns (**L1, N11b**).

14 **Sie heißen Kühn, nicht wahr?** *Your name is Kühn, isn't it?*

a **Sie heißen Kühn** **Heißen** is a verb which has no exact equivalent verb in English. The nearest is *are called*, in this instance *you are called*, but the only acceptable translation is *your name is...*

b **Sie heißen** -en is the ending for a verb when the subject is the person (or persons) being spoken to, i.e. *you*. **Sie** meaning *you* is always written with a capital **S**.

c **nicht wahr?**: *not true?* This is a pleasant surprise for a change, since it is a most useful phrase for requesting confirmation from the listener. It is very much easier to use than the equivalent English phrases. **Nicht wahr?** serves for any phrase like *isn't it?*, *aren't you?*, *don't we?*, *can't they?*, etc.

15 **Ja, ich heiße Walter Kühn.** *Yes, my name is Walter Kühn.* (L1,N14a)
   ich heiße -e is the usual ending on the verb when the speaker is referring to himself, that is, the ending which goes with **ich**: *I*. When **ich** is not the first word in a sentence it is written with a small **i**.

16 **Hier, bitte schön!** Used in this sense, **bitte schön** is just an elaboration of **bitte** (L1, N12).
   ö Listen to this sound again. There is no English equivalent.

17 **Die Dame heißt auch Kühn.** *The lady's name is also Kühn.*

a **die Dame** **Die** is *the* before all feminine nouns (L1, N10c).

b **heißt** (L1, N14a) -t is the usual ending, remember, when the subject is someone being spoken about, in this case **die Dame**.

18 Sie ist meine Frau. *She is my wife.*

a **Sie** has a capital S here only because it begins the sentence. Otherwise **sie**: *she* has a small **s**. In speech, there is no danger of confusion between **Sie**: *you* and **sie**: *she*, because of the verb form.

b **meine Frau Frau** means *wife* as well as *Mrs*. **Meine** is the word for *my* before any feminine noun (**L1, N11b**).

19 Und wer ist das Fräulein hier? *And who is the young lady here?*

a **wer?** *who?* (NEVER *where*, as you might think). Except with the verb "to be" (see title, Part 3), **wer** takes the singular verb ending even if it refers to several people: **Wer kommt?** *Who is coming?*

b **das Fräulein Das** is *the* before all neuter nouns (**L1, N10c**). **Fräulein** means *young lady*, as well as *Miss*. **Fräulein** is a neuter noun. This seeming absurdity has a purely grammatical explanation. All diminutives (a word formed from another to express smallness or affection such as *flatlet* and *doggy* in English) in German, irrespective of meaning, are neuter. **Fräulein** (*little woman*) has a diminutive ending **-lein** and any word ending in **-lein** is neuter.

20 Das Fräulein ist meine Tochter Renate. *The young lady is my daughter, Renate.*

Remember, **meine** is *my* before any feminine noun (**L1, N18b**).

Das Gepäck *The luggage*

21 Das bin ich. *That's me.* (*That am I.*) The verb form matches the person being identified in such expressions. **Das** can mean *that* or *this*, as well as *the*.

22 Ist das Ihr Koffer? *Is that/this your suitcase?* Questions like this are quite easy; the word order is exactly the same as in English. **Ihr Koffer Ihr** is *your* before masculine or neuter nouns.

23 Nein, das ist nicht mein Koffer. *No, that isn't my suitcase.* **Nicht** (*not*) is generally placed immediately after the verb *to be*.

24 Der Koffer hier ist braun. *This suitcase here is brown.* **Der** does not mean *this*, but when **hier** is used after the noun, it can be translated *this*.

25 Das ist doch mein Koffer. *That's* MY *suitcase.* **Doch** would be rendered in English simply by a tone of protest in the voice.

26 Aber wo ist mein Gepäck? *But where is my luggage?* **Mein** is *my* before neuter as well as masculine nouns.

27 Es ist hier, mein Herr. *It's here, sir.* **Es** is *it*, when referring to a neuter noun, (i.e. a **das** noun) and only then. **Er** and **sie** (*he* and *she*) also mean *it* when they refer to a thing which happens to be masculine or feminine in German.

28 Ein Koffer und eine Reisetasche. *A suitcase and a travelling bag.*

a ein Koffer **Ein** is *a* or *an* before masculine or neuter nouns. Compare this with **mein Koffer** and **Ihr Koffer**. **Mein** and **Ihr** follow the **ein** pattern, that is, no ending before masculine and neuter nouns.

b eine Reisetasche **Eine** is *a* or *an* before a feminine noun. Compare this with **meine Frau** and **meine Tochter** (**L1, N18b** and **20**). Words like **mein,** which follow the **ein** pattern, end in **-e** before a feminine noun.

29 Hier sind sie. *Here they are.*

a The German word order is surprising, but very common. **Sie sind hier**: *they are here* gives the same information, only the subject of the sentence, *they:* **sie** is placed first. In English, when any item other than the subject occupies position 1, everything just moves along:

they	*are*	*here*
here	*they*	*are*

In German, the verb cannot be shifted from position 2, so if any other word or phrase begins the sentence, the subject moves to position 3:

sie	**sind**	**hier**
hier	**sind**	**sie**

b sie Here is a third meaning for **sie**, namely *they*. It can also mean *you,* spelt with capital **S** or *she* (**N14b** and **18a**). Although the verb form used with **Sie**: *you* and **sie**: *they* is the same, confusion rarely occurs, because it is usually clear from the context whether the speaker means *you* or *they*.

30 Hallo! Renate! *Hey – Renate!* **Hallo** in German is only used to attract someone's attention or on the telephone.

31 Ich komme. *I'm coming.* Remember **-e** is the usual ending when the speaker is referring to him/herself (**L1, N15**).

Zollkontrolle *Customs control*

32 Das Gepäck, bitte! *Your luggage, please!* It is quite often enough to say *the* instead of *your* in German when ownership is obvious.

33 Haben Sie etwas zu verzollen? *Have you anything* (*something*) *to declare?*

a **Haben Sie?** The verb normally ends in **-en** when the subject is **Sie.** Remember **Sie:** *you* always has a capital **S.**

b **zu verzollen:** *to declare* **Verzollen,** though similar in ending to other verb forms you have already met, is a new form. It is the form of the verb which describes the action alone without any reference to anyone in particular doing it. The action is not, therefore, limited or confined by a subject or doer. This is implied in the name given to it – the INFINITIVE. The infinitive of any verb is the convenient basis to work from. It is the form you will find listed in dictionaries. **Zu** very often precedes it in phrases where *to* is used in English.

34 **Ich habe eine Flasche Kognak** *I have/I've got a bottle of brandy*

a **Ich habe** Remember **-e** is the usual ending with **ich.**

b **eine Flasche Kognak** *a bottle of brandy* *Of* is missed out in expressions of quantity in German.

c **eine Flasche** Remember **eine** is *a* or *an* before feminine nouns.

35 **200 (zweihundert) Zigaretten** *two hundred cigarettes*

a **zweihundert** Note that this is one word in German.

b **Zigaretten** The singular is **(die) Zigarette.** Feminine nouns form the plural by adding **-n** or **-en** to the singular.

36 **Hat die Dame etwas?** *Has the lady (got) anything?*
Hat This follows the usual pattern of **-t** endings for someone or something being spoken about (**L1, N4b** and **17b**).

37 **Wir haben nichts.** *We haven't (got) anything. (We have nothing.)*

a **wir haben:** *we have* The verb form with **wir:** *we* is the same as with **Sie:** *you.*

b **nichts:** *nothing* This must not be confused with **nicht:** *not.*

38 **Sind Sie Deutsche?** *Are you German (Germans)?* The official is asking if they are ALL German, not just Herr Kühn. **Sie:** *you* is used when you are speaking both to one person and to several people, just like English *you.* The verb form here does not follow the usual pattern.

39 **Ja, wir sind Deutsche.** *Yes, we're German.* Notice how easy German verb forms are. **Sind** is used with **wir:** *we,* **Sie:** *you* and **sie:** *they,* just like English *are* (**L1, N29** and **38**).

40 **Aber Sie wohnen nicht in Deutschland?** *But you don't live in Germany?* As in English, the fact that this is a question is indicated partly by context and partly by intonation.
Sie wohnen Remember **-en** is the normal ending with **Sie:** *you.*

41 **Nein, wir wohnen in Brasilien.** *No, we live/are living in Brazil.* Notice the verb forms with **Sie** and **wir** are again the same.

42 **Was machen Sie hier?** *What are you doing here?* Question forms are quite simple in German. You just switch the subject (**Sie**) and the verb (**machen**). **Sie machen** is a statement. **Machen Sie?** is a question (except in sentences of the kind described in Note 29). Do not be confused by English question forms, e.g. *are you doing? do you live?*, which might make you think you need three words instead of two.

43 **Danke. In Ordnung.** *Thank you. That's fine.* **In Ordnung** means literally *in order*, and is used very frequently, not only by officials, but also quite informally in situations where we would say *all right* or simply *O.K.*

Die Begrüßung   *The welcome*

44 **da sind Sie ja alle!** *There/here you all are!*

a In such expressions, **da** can mean either *here* or *there*.

b **ja**   This word most commonly means *yes*, but Germans pepper their speech with it in sentences where it adds nothing essential to the meaning.

45 **Das ist Ihre Frau, nicht wahr?** *This is your wife, isn't it?*

a Remember **das** means *this* or *that*, as well as *the*.

b **Ihre Frau**   Like **ein** and **mein**, **Ihr**: *your* must add an **e** before any feminine noun.

46 **Wie geht es Ihnen?** *How are you?* (*How goes it with you?*) This phrase will puzzle you somewhat until you have learned more of the language, but you can learn it and use it correctly without analysing it.

47 **Vielen Dank! Sehr gut.** *Very well, thank you very much.*

a Note that Germans tend to thank the person first and then answer the question.

b **Vielen Dank!** There are many ways of expressing thanks in German, just as there are in English. While you should be able to recognize them all, you only need to use one of them yourself.

48 **Und Ihnen?** *And you?* This is a shortened form of **wie geht es Ihnen?** (L1, N46).

49 **Kommen Sie!** *Come along!* (*Come!*) This is known as the COMMAND form or IMPERATIVE of the verb and is used for ordering or requesting someone to do something.

50 **Oh, das ist schön.** *Oh, that's splendid.* **Schön** means *fine, nice, lovely* according to the context.

51 **Wir fahren sofort in Ihr Hotel.** *We'll drive to your hotel at once.*
a In situations where we say *we'll* or *I'll do something*, there is no special form in German. You use the same verb form that you use to express *we do* or *I do* (something).
b **sofort in Ihr Hotel** Note the German order – time before place.
c **in Ihr Hotel:** *to your hotel* **In** can mean *to* as well as *in.*
d **Ihr Hotel** Remember, **Ihr** is *your* before neuter nouns.

Part three

Wer sind Sie? *Who are you?*

52 **Und wie heißen Sie?** *And what is your name?*
Note the use of **wie,** *how* with this verb (N14).
e.g. **Wie heißt Ihr Kollege?** *What is your colleague's name?*

Lektion zwei   Hotel König

Lesson two   König Hotel

What happens

In this lesson we join the Kühn family at their hotel in Frankfurt.

In Part 1 the hotel reception clerk describes the hotel. Then he explains that Herr Kühn wants a car; the clerk's brother runs a car hire business. In Part 2 the Kühns register at the hotel and go to their rooms. Later Frau Kühn and Renate go to the hotel restaurant.

New words in this lesson

die the (plural, for all nouns)
ein, eine one
kein, keine no, not a
unser, unsere our
sein, seine his, its

selbst self (myself, himself, etc.)

ihn him, it
mich me
sie her, them

2

uns us

wen? whom?
wieviel? how much?

eins one
zwei two
drei three
vier four
fünf five
sechs six
sieben seven
acht eight
neun nine
zehn ten
siebzehn seventeen
sechsundzwanzig twenty-six
achtundzwanzig twenty-eight

der Ausweis identity card
der Bruder brother
der Empfangschef reception-clerk
der Führerschein driving-licence
der Hoteldiener porter
der Kaffee coffee
der Kellner waiter
der Lift lift
der Mann husband
der Meldezettel registration form
der Name name
der Personalausweis identity-card
der Platz seat
der Schlüssel key
(die Schlüssel) (keys)
der Tisch table
der Wagen car
der Zucker sugar

die Adresse address
die Autovermietung car-hire business
die Dusche shower
die Familie family
die Limonade lemonade
die Nacht night
die Nummer number
(die Nummern) (numbers)
die Reservierung reservation
die Sache thing

die Sahne cream
die Zentralheizung central heating
die Zimmerreservierung reserving a
room

das Bad bath(room)
das Doppelzimmer double room
(die Doppelzimmer) (double rooms)
das Einzelzimmer single room
(die Einzelzimmer) (single rooms)
das Eis ice-cream
das Frühstück breakfast
das Geschäft business, shop
das Glas glass
das Restaurant restaurant
das Schokoladeneis chocolate ice-cream
das Telephon telephone
das Zimmer room
(die Zimmer) (rooms)

die Herrschaften (Pl.) ladies and gentlemen, sir and madam

brauchen to need
bringen to bring, take
erwarten to expect
kaufen to buy
kosten to cost
mieten to hire
nehmen to take
rufen to call
tragen to carry
trinken to drink

möchten would like
wollen to want

anrufen to ring up, telephone
ausfüllen to fill in

frei free
groß big
kaputt out of order
preiswert cheap
zweite second

für for
mit with
ohne without

14

dann then
schon already

nach oben upstairs

extra extra, additional
gern with pleasure
hoffentlich I hope (so)
leider unfortunately
lieber rather, preferably
natürlich of course
noch still
nur only
sehr very

also so, therefore
doch oh yes!
oder or

auf Wiedersehen! good bye!
besten Dank! thanks a lot!
ein paar Sachen a few things
es ist inbegriffen it is included
im ersten Stock on the first floor
kommen Sie! come this way!
nicht weit von hier not far from here
viel Zeit much time
vier Uhr four o'clock
was möchten Sie gern? what would you like?
wie ist Ihr Name? what's your name?
wieviel kosten sie? how much do they cost?
wollen Sie Platz nehmen? would you like to take a seat?

Notes

Part one

1 **Das Hotel König ist nicht sehr groß.** *The König Hotel is not very big.*

a **das Hotel König** Names of hotels commonly appear after the word **Hotel**.

b **groß** This word describes the hotel. Words which describe the qualities or deficiencies of a thing or a person are called ADJECTIVES. It will be a relief to you to know that if an adjective comes AFTER the noun (usually after **ist**) it shows no ending to indicate the class of the noun it describes.

2 **Unser Hotel hat Einzelzimmer und Doppelzimmer.** *Our hotel has single rooms and double rooms.*

a **unser Hotel** Unser: *our* before masculine or neuter nouns behaves like **mein** and **Ihr** in that its exact form depends on the class of the following noun, i.e. whether it is a **der, die** or **das** noun. **Hotel** is neuter (**das**).

b **Einzelzimmer und Doppelzimmer:** *single rooms and double rooms* These are plural forms.

3 **Alle Zimmer haben ein Bad oder eine Dusche.** *All rooms have a bath or a shower.*

haben You remember you met this form with **Sie:** *you* and **wir:**

15

we in Lesson **1**. This form is also correct when talking ABOUT things or people, as long as there is more than one thing or person. That is, it goes with **sie**: *they,* or with anything that can be substituted for *they* – in this case **alle Zimmer.**

4 **Heute erwarte ich Familie Kühn.** *Today I'm expecting the Kühn family.*

a Note the order of the first three words in the German sentence. Remember that the verb in German cannot be moved from position 2 (**L1, N29a**).

b **erwarte** -e is the usual ending with **ich.**

c **Familie Kühn** *The* is missed out in the German expression.

5 **Herr Kühn braucht einen Wagen.** *Herr Kühn needs a car.*

a **braucht** -t is the usual ending with **er**: *he,* **sie**: *she* or **es**: *it,* or with a person's name or title (**L1, N4b**).

b **einen Wagen** **Wagen** is masculine – a **der** noun. According to **L1, N28a,** *a* before all masculine nouns is **ein (ein Kollege, ein Koffer).** This form **einen** shows that *a* before a masculine noun is NOT always **ein.** To know why it is sometimes **ein** and sometimes **einen,** it is necessary to take a closer look at the sentence **Herr Kühn braucht einen Wagen.** We have already spoken about the SUBJECT of a sentence (**L1, N4b**) and now we must speak about the OBJECT. In this sentence, **Herr Kühn** is the SUBJECT and **einen Wagen** is the OBJECT. Whether you are familiar with these terms or not, you show your awareness of subjects and objects by making correct sentences. In English, this generally means putting them in the right order: 1. subject 2. verb 3. object, e.g. *I/like/John.* But it may also mean putting a word in the correct form, e.g. *John/likes/*ME (not *I* because *I* is only used for the subject).

In German, you have to note two things:

1. The subject and object CAN move their positions, so you have to think about the ROLE of the word in the sentence and not just its position.

2. Words like **ein, mein, Ihr, der,** etc. can have different endings according to the role in the sentence of the noun they precede. This role is called a CASE, and the various possible roles or cases have names, which it will be necessary and time-saving to learn. The case for the subject of a sentence is called the NOMINATIVE case; you learnt it in Lesson **1.** The case for the OBJECT of a sentence is called the ACCUSATIVE case, and it is dealt with in

this lesson; **-en** is the accusative ending for the masculine singular.

Note: the verb *to be* does NOT take an OBJECT, hence we have in Lesson 1: **Ich bin ein Kollege von Walter Kühn** (NOT **einen**).

6 **Er möchte einen mieten.** *He would like to hire one.*

a **er möchte**   This breaks the rule of the usual **-t** ending with **er**. This is because the verb describes not something he LIKES doing, but something he WOULD like to do.

b **einen**   Here **einen** means *one*. It has an **-en** ending because it is the object and because it refers to **Wagen**, which is masculine. **-en** is the masculine ending of the accusative.

c **mieten**   This is the infinitive form (L1, N33b). It tells us what he would like to do, thus completing the verb phrase (**möchte mieten**: *would like to hire*). Since many verbs require 'completing infinitives' it is essential to remember that they go at the END of the sentence and not right after the 'finite' verb – the verb with a subject – as in English, e.g. **Er möchte in Brasilien arbeiten**: *He'd like to work in Brazil.*

7 **Mein Bruder hat eine Autovermietung.** *My brother has a car-hire business.*

eine Autovermietung   **Eine** is *a* before any feminine noun (L1, N28b). **Eine Autovermietung** is the object, therefore **eine** must be accusative. Nominative and accusative endings are the same for feminine nouns.

8 **Sein Geschäft ist nicht weit von hier.** *His business is not far from here.*

sein Geschäft   **Sein** is *his* before masculine and neuter nouns (just like **ein** and **mein**). **Geschäft** is neuter (**das**).

9 **Ich rufe ihn jetzt an.** *I shall phone him/ring him up now.*

a **ich rufe ... an**   The verb here is composed of two parts, the usual part that shows the ending **-e**, to go with **ich**, and another part, **an**. English has plenty of verbs like this: *go out, go on, come in, look over*, etc. The difference in their use is that in English we nearly always find the second part immediately after, or certainly quite close to the first part, whereas in German the second part MUST go to the end of the sentence. This kind of verb, very common in German, is called a SEPARABLE verb.

b **ihn**: *him*   In this instance, English and German are the same in that they have different words for the nominative and accusative.

2

	English	German
Nominative	*he*	**er**
Accusative	*him*	**ihn**

10 **Seine Telephonnummer ist 43 62 15.** *His phone number is 436215.*
seine Telephonnummer **Seine** is *his* before all feminine nouns.
(Compare **eine, meine, Ihre.**) **Telephonnummer** is a compound noun,
so it takes its class (**der, die** or **das**) from the second component
(**L1, N10a**). **Nummer** is feminine.

11 **Hoffentlich hat Herr Kühn seinen Führerschein hier.** *I hope*
Herr Kühn has his driving licence here.

a Note the word order – the verb (**hat**) MUST be in second position
(**L1, N29a** and **L2, N4a**) and the subject, **Herr Kühn,** follows it.

b **hoffentlich** This is a most useful word. It means *it is to be*
hoped. There is no one word equivalent in English. It will
translate *I hope, we hope, everyone is hoping.*

c **seinen Führerschein** This is the object of the sentence and
Führerschein is masculine, so **sein:** *his* must add the masculine
accusative ending **-en.** (Compare **einen Wagen L2, N5b.**)

Part two

Zimmerreservierung *Booking rooms*

12 **Guten Tag, die Herrschaften!** *Good afternoon* (*good day*) *sir and*
madam!

a English has no expression like **die Herrschaften.** Its usual meaning
is *ladies and gentlemen.*

b **Die** is *the* before any plural noun, no matter what class the
singular belongs to.

13 **Sie erwarten uns, nicht wahr?** *You are expecting us, aren't you?*
uns This is the accusative of **wir:** *we.*

14 **Ja, ich habe eine Reservierung für eine Nacht.** *Yes, I have a*
reservation for one night.

a **ich habe eine Reservierung** **Eine Reservierung** is the object, but
remember that **eine** is the form for both nominative and
accusative feminine (**L2, N7**).

b **für eine Nacht** **Eine** here means *one.*

15 **Ich habe ein Doppelzimmer und ein Einzelzimmer für Sie.** *I have*
a double room and a single room for you.
ein Doppelzimmer und ein Einzelzimmer (**L2, N2b**) You have
met these words earlier as plural forms. It is quite clear from

the presence of **ein** in front of them that these are singular forms. The plurals of some masculine and neuter words are identical with the singular forms. The meaning is indicated either by the word in front, e.g. some form of **ein**, or from the context.

Ein Doppelzimmer und **ein Einzelzimmer** are both objects. Therefore these must be accusative forms of **ein**. **Zimmer** is neuter, so you can see that the nominative and accusative forms of **ein** are identical if the noun is neuter. Since this is also true of feminine nouns, the masculine is the only one which has a different form for the accusative.

16 **Wieviel kosten sie?** *How much do they cost?* **-en** is the usual verb ending with **sie**: *they*. Note the question form in German simply switches subject (**sie**) and verb (**kosten**). English question forms are more complicated and require the use of *do* (L1, N42).

17 **Das Doppelzimmer mit Bad kostet 28 DM (achtundzwanzig Mark).** *The double room with bath costs 28 marks.*

a **28 DM (achtundzwanzig Mark)**   Prices in marks are written with the figure and the letters DM after it. DM stands for **Deutschmark** (*German marks*). Only a banker or a foreigner would say **Deutschmark** nowadays. **Mark** is enough, and although **Mark** is singular it is used for any number of marks.

b **achtundzwanzig**   It will be fairly obvious that this means *eight and twenty*. All numbers from 21 to 99 are expressed like this, with the units digit first. They are always written as one word.

18 **Und das Einzelzimmer mit Dusche kostet 17 DM (siebzehn Mark).** *And the single room with shower costs 17 marks.*

17 DM (siebzehn Mark)   The 'teens' are very easy in German, because the system is almost identical with English. German is in fact easier, since you simply join two numbers together. 3 is **drei**, 10 is **zehn**, 13 is **dreizehn**. There are only two departures from this rule, namely 16 and 17. 7 is **sieben**, 10 is **zehn**, 17 is **siebzehn**; 6 is **sechs**, 10 is **zehn**, 16 is **sechzehn**. If you try sounding an **s** between **ch** and **z** you will see why it is missed out.

19 **Ist das Frühstück extra?** *Is breakfast extra?*
In general, German uses or omits a word for *the* where English does, but there are exceptions to be noted—as here (meals require a word for *the* in German).

20 **Brauchen Sie den Personalausweis?** *Do you need my (the) identity card?*

2

a **brauchen Sie?** Remember the question form in German switches the usual subject-verb order to verb-subject. Questions break the rule about the verb remaining in second position.

b **den Personalausweis** This is the object in the sentence. **Den** is the accusative of **der.** Note that it follows the masculine accusative pattern and ends in **-en** (compare **einen**) L2, N5b.

21 **Nein, nur die Ausweisnummern.** *No, just the identity card numbers.*
die Ausweisnummern Remember **die** is *the* before any plural noun (**L2, N12b**). **Nummer** is feminine and, as you know, nearly all feminine nouns form the plural by adding **-n** or **-en** (**L1, N35b**).

22 **Nehmen Sie bitte einen Meldezettel,** *Please take a registration form,*

a **nehmen Sie** This is the command or request form of the verb and is, as you see, identical with the question form. (Compare **Brauchen Sie? L2, N20a.**) Confusion is avoided by tone of voice (in speech) or punctuation (in writing).

b **einen Meldezettel** By now you are familiar with **einen,** the masculine accusative form.
Every guest in German hotels is required to fill in a registration form, giving name, address, passport number if not German, identity-card number if German. All Germans over sixteen carry a **Personalausweis** (frequently shortened to **Ausweis**) with a photograph, name, date of birth and number.

c **bitte** **Bitte** may appear at the beginning or end of the request or immediately after the subject (**Sie**) as here.

23 **und füllen Sie ihn aus!** *and fill it in!*

a **füllen ... aus** This is another separable verb (L2, N9a). The position of *in* just happens to coincide with that of **aus** in this instance. Remember that in German the second part of the verb MUST be at the end of the sentence.

b **ihn** This is the masculine accusative again, but this time it means not *him* but *it.*

24 **Unser Name, unsere Adresse und die Ausweisnummer, nicht wahr?** *Our name, address and the identity-card number, is that right?*
unser Name, unsere Adresse Note that *our* must be repeated in German if the second noun is of a different class from the first. **Unser** is *our* before **der** or **das** nouns. **Name** is masculine. **Unsere** is *our* before **die** nouns. **Adresse** is feminine. Note that this follows the pattern of **ein, mein, sein, Ihr.**

25 **Jetzt rufe ich den Hoteldiener.** *I shall call the porter now.* Note again the inverted order of the verb **rufe** and the subject **ich** as the sentence begins with **jetzt**: *now,* and the verb MUST come second.

26 **Wen?** *Whom?* Many people would simply say *who?* but we have translated it as *whom?* to show that it is the accusative. English still retains a few traces of this system, but it is significant that it does not really matter nowadays whether you say *who?* or *whom?* in this instance, whereas in German it does matter that you say **wer?** when it is the subject and **wen?** when it is the object. Notice that this follows the **der, den** pattern.

27 **Den Hoteldiener.** *The porter.* **Den** is accusative, of course. You have to remember to use the accusative form even when the rest of the sentence is not said, but understood from what has been said before.

28 **Er bringt Ihr Gepäck in Ihre Zimmer.** *He will take your luggage to your rooms.*

a **er bringt** English speakers use *bring* only when motion towards the speaker is indicated. From this sentence you can see that the German verb can be used to indicate the opposite direction, too.

b **Ihr Gepäck** This is the object and **Gepäck** is neuter, so you can see that **Ihr** can be both nominative and accusative before neuter nouns. This follows the **ein** pattern.

c **in Ihre Zimmer** **Zimmer** is a neuter noun, so from what has just been said (**Ihr:** *your* before neuter nouns, for both subject and object) you know that **Zimmer** must be plural here, since there is an **-e** ending on **Ihr.** The plural form of *your* is **Ihre,** exactly the same as *your* before feminine singular nouns. (It is like **die,** which can also be plural or feminine singular.)

Die Hotelzimmer *The hotel rooms*

29 **Bitte, kommen Sie!** *Come this way, please!* We must add *this way* in English, though **kommen Sie!** is enough in German (L2, N22).

30 **Ich trage das Gepäck nach oben.** *I'll carry the luggage upstairs.*

a **das Gepäck** This is the object, so it is accusative. We know that **Gepäck** is neuter, and we can see that the accusative neuter is again the same as the nominative. You now have enough examples to know that ALL neuter forms are the same in the nominative and the accusative.

b **nach oben** **Oben** means *up above* or *upstairs.* **Nach oben** indicates movement upwards. You could not use **nach oben** to say something IS upstairs.

31 **Meine Reisetasche nehme ich selbst.** *I'll take my bag myself.*

2

a Here is an example showing clearly how the order of subject, verb and object can be quite different in German (see Note **5b**). The speaker chooses to put **meine Reisetasche** first, but it is quite clear both from the sense and from the form **ich** that **meine Reisetasche** must be the object and **ich** the subject. **Meine Reisetasche** is accusative feminine. **Meine,** like **eine,** serves for both nominative and accusative feminine. Note that the rule about the verb being the second item holds good here too.

b **selbst** A pleasant surprise, for a change! **Selbst** will do for *myself, himself, herself,* without any adapting.

32 **Haben Sie keinen Lift hier?** *Have you no lift here?* **keinen Lift** German has a special word for *not a, not any* or *no* before a noun, and such expressions can only be dealt with by using this word **kein.** It changes according to the class and case of the following noun in precisely the same way as **ein. Keinen** is the masculine accusative form.

33 **Doch, wir haben einen,** *Yes, we do have one,* **Doch** meaning *yes* is used only in contradiction. The question must, therefore, always be a negative one.

34 **aber leider ist er kaputt.** *but unfortunately it is out of order.* Notes **33** and **34** form one sentence in the text, but it can be divided into two completely self-contained units, each with its own verb and subject. Within each unit all the rules of word order apply, without either being affected by the other. When this is so, the two parts are joined together by a word like **aber,** which does not count as a sentence item and therefore has no effect on word order.

Leider is the item which causes the switching of subject (**er**) and verb (**ist**), so that **ist** is the second item. This follows the 'verb must be second' rule for statements.

35 **Haben wir die Schlüssel für unsere Zimmer?** *Have we got the keys for our rooms?*

a **die Schlüssel** **Schlüssel** is masculine. Like **Zimmer** its plural form is identical with the singular. Remember **die** is *the* before all plurals (**L2, N12b**). Since **die Schlüssel** is the object of the sentence, you see that **die** can be either nominative or accusative.

b **für unsere Zimmer** **Unsere** is *our* before any plural noun.

36 **Ja, ich habe unseren Schlüssel,** *Yes, I've got our key,* **unseren Schlüssel** **Unseren** is accusative masculine.

37 **und Renate hat ihren.** *and Renate has hers.*

a **und** is a word like **aber,** which joins two sentences into one.

b **ihren** This is the accusative masculine of the possessive pronoun **ihrer, -e, -es** similar in form to the possessive adjective **ihr, -e,** but not identical with it; possessive pronouns are declined as **dieser, -e, -es,** *this, that* – see Appendix 3. Remember **ihr** (small **i**) means *her*; **Ihr** (capital **I**) means *your* so **Ihrer** means *yours.*

38 **Ihre Zimmer, Nummer 7 (sieben) und 9 (neun), sind hier im ersten Stock.** *Your rooms, numbers 7 and 9, are here on the first floor.* **im ersten Stock** You will not fully understand this phrase yet, but you can take it on trust and use it without analysing it.

39 **Brauchen Sie mich noch?** *Do you need me any more?*

a **mich** This is the accusative of **ich.**

b **noch** This word has many possible translations. The basic meaning is *still, yet. more.*

Das Hotelrestaurant *The hotel restaurant*

40 **Guten Tag, die Damen!** *Good afternoon, ladies!* Only Frau Kühn and Renate are there. Note that it is necessary to say **die Damen.**

41 **Wollen Sie Platz nehmen?** *Would you like to take a seat?* (*Do you want to . . . ?*) Note that no word for *a* is used.

a **Wollen Sie,** like **möchte,** obviously requires a completing infinitive, which appears as the last item in the sentence (**L2, N6c**).

b **Platz nehmen:** *take a place* This is a rather formal way of inviting someone to sit down.

42 **Ja gern, danke!** *Yes, with pleasure, thank you!* **gern:** *gladly/with pleasure*

43 **Was möchten Sie gern?** *What would you like?*

44 **Ich möchte einen Kaffee trinken.** *I'd like (to drink) a coffee.*

a It is not essential to include **trinken** in such a sentence, but it very often is included. Note the position of **trinken** – the completing infinitive.

b **ich möchte:** *I would like* Note that **möchte** goes with both **ich** and **er** (**L2, N6a**).

45 **Möchten Sie Ihren Kaffee mit Zucker und Sahne?** *Would you like your coffee with sugar and cream?* **Ihren** This is the accusative masculine of **Ihr.** It follows the usual pattern **den, einen, ihren, unseren.**

46 **Nein, ich trinke ihn lieber ohne Zucker und Sahne.** *No, I prefer it without sugar and cream.* (*I drink it for preference...*) To say

2

you would *prefer (rather have/do)* something, you must use the appropriate verb plus **lieber,** e.g. **Ich nehme lieber ein Zimmer mit Bad:** *I prefer to take a room with a bath.*

47 **Nein, Renate, kein Eis jetzt, bitte.** *No, Renate, no ice-cream just now, please.*

kein Eis **Eis** is neuter. **Kein** follows the **ein** pattern.

48 **und wir wollen noch ein paar Sachen kaufen.** *and we still want to buy a few things.*

a Note the word order; a verb like this requires a completing infinitive (**kaufen**) at the END of the sentence.

b **Noch** here has the sense that there is STILL something to be done.

c **ein paar Sachen** As with other expressions of quantity, there is no word for *of.* **Ein paar** means *a few.*

49 **Dann bringe ich also einen Kaffee, eine Limonade und kein Eis.** *Then I am to bring one coffee, one lemonade and no ice-cream.*

a **dann:** *then, in that case* This usage is very common in speech, the word **dann** beginning the sentence and thus causing inversion of subject and verb. It is colloquial and is frequently used out of habit when it is quite unnecessary to the meaning. **Also:** *so, then, therefore* is identical in meaning here, yet the waiter feels it necessary to say both.

b **einen Kaffee, eine Limonade und kein Eis** These are all accusatives, one of each class — masculine, feminine and neuter. Seeing them all together will show you the patterns and perhaps clarify any confusion that may be depressing you.
Do not allow the unexpected and unwelcome revelations in this lesson to overwhelm you. They have been presented to you 'en masse' because an early sense of language system is a help in self-instruction courses. You are NOT expected to master all the points completely before you go on to Lesson **3.** Absorb what you can now and then allow yourself to experience the systems as you proceed, practising them and giving yourself time to let things fall into place.

Part three

Die Paßnummer *The passport number*

50 **Nein, ich habe leider keine.** *No, I'm afraid I haven't got one.*
keine This is the accusative feminine singular, because he is referring to **Reservierung. Keine** can stand alone, like **einen,** when a noun is implied but not stated (L**2,** N**6**).

24

51 **Ich nehme es.** *I'll take it.*
es   This is the accusative neuter, because it refers to **Zimmer.**
Note that **es** is also nominative neuter. You can see now that
you need only concern yourself with accusative MASCULINE forms,
since accusative feminine, neuter and plural forms are the same
as the nominative forms.

52 **Wie ist Ihr Name?** *What (how) is the (your) name?* Here is
another way of asking someone's name. This one is rather more
official than **Wie heißen Sie?**

Das Auto   *The car*

53 **Ich habe mein Auto nicht hier.** *I haven't got my car here.*
As a rule, **nicht** is placed after the verb and after the object/s
of a sentence but before any other word or phrase it negates.

54 **Möchten Sie ihr Auto?** *Would you like* HER *car?*
ihr   This is the accusative neuter (L2, N37b).

55 **keine Autoschlüssel.** *no car keys.* **Keine,** *no, not any,* is used
before a plural noun of any class. If you remember that **Schlüssel**
is masculine, **keine** will tell you that this must be plural
(otherwise it would have to be **keinen**).

56 **Ihr Mann hat sie.** *Her husband has got them.*
a   **Mann** means *husband* as well as *man.*
b   sie   In this sentence **sie** means *them,* so in this case German is
easier than English. English has two different words – *they* and
them; **sie** is both.

Lektion drei   Wiedersehen in München   **3**

Lesson three   Reunion in Munich

What happens

In this lesson the scene changes to Munich, to the home of the
Pfaffinger family. Walter Kühn's sister, Grete, is married to Max
Pfaffinger, who has a small joinery business. They have one son,
Franz, who is two or three years older than Renate.

3

In Part 1 Grete is expecting the Kühn family for lunch. In Part 2 they arrive and have lunch. Franz and Renate talk – they have not met since they were children. Max and Walter make plans for the following day.

New words in this lesson

der **Appetit** appetite
der **Automat** slot machine
der **Club** club
der **Fisch** fish
(der) **Freitag** Friday
der **Hof** yard
(der) **Hunger** hunger
(der) **Mittag** noon
der **Pullover** pullover, sweater
der **Salat** salad
der **Stadtbummel** stroll (in the town)
der **Vater** father
der **Verwandte (die Verwandten)**
  relative/s

die **Autowerkstatt** garage
die **Bekanntschaft** acquaintance
die **Bremse (die Bremsen)** brake/s
die **Kartoffel** potato
die **Mutter** mother
die **Portion (die Portionen)** helping/s
die **Schachtel** packet
die **Schwester** sister
die **Tür** door
die **Vorbereitung** preparation
die **Werkstatt** workshop

das **Bier** beer
das **Essen** meal
das **Kino** cinema
das **Männergespräch** men's talk
das **Mietauto** hired car
das **Mittagessen** lunch
das **Wiedersehen** reunion

die **Leute (Pl.)** people

du **bist (sein)** you are
können to be able, can

ich **kann,** du **kannst** I can, you can
müssen to have to, must
sollen to be to, should
wollen to want to
(ich **will)** (I want to)

dich you (acc.)

essen (ißt) to eat
fahren (fährt) to go (in vehicle)
geben to give
gehen to go
nehmen (nimmt) to take
sehen (sieht) to see, look
tragen to wear

bekommen to get
holen to fetch
rauchen to smoke
schmecken to taste
verstehen to understand

ankommen to arrive
aufmachen to open
ausgehen to go out
mitkommen to come along (with)

ein bißchen a little bit
dein, deine your
dritte third
hübsch smart
jung young
schlecht bad
viel much
wenig little
wirklich really
wunderbar wonderful
zwölf twelve

gleich nearly, any minute
heute abend this evening

26

immer always
morgen tomorrow
morgen früh tomorrow morning
nie never
noch einmal again
noch nicht not yet
oft often
selten seldom, rarely

wann? when?
wohin? where to?

genug enough
gut well
nichts mehr nothing more
selbstverständlich of course
zusammen together

danke vielmals thanks a lot
einverstanden agreed

erste Bekanntschaft first acquaintance
es gibt there is
es ist halb eins it is half past twelve
herzlich gern with pleasure
herzlich willkommen in München!
  a hearty welcome to Munich!
hoffentlich essen sie es gern I hope they
  like (eating) it
Hunger haben to be hungry
ins = in + das to the
möchtest du noch etwas? would you like
  some more?
noch ein bißchen a little more
oh je! heavens!
prost! cheers! your health!
sehr gern with great pleasure
vor in front of
wie spät ist es? what time is it?
zu Haus at home
zu Mittag for lunch

3

Notes

Part one

1 **Ich erwarte heute Familie Kühn zu Mittag.** *I'm expecting the Kühn family at noon today.*

a **heute** ... **zu Mittag** When two expressions of time occur in the same sentence in German, the general usually precedes the particular, e.g. **morgen zu Mittag**: *at noon tomorrow.*

b **Zu Mittag** means literally *at midday.* The use of **zu Mittag**, however, nearly always implies *for lunch* – as it does here.

2 **Oh je! Es ist gleich 12 (zwölf) Uhr.** *Heavens! It's nearly twelve o'clock.*

a **Oh je!** A completely inoffensive expletive indicating surprise and concern, or even alarm.

b **Gleich** means *immediately.* When it is used before a precise time, we would render it *nearly* or *coming up to.*

3 **Das Mittagessen ist noch nicht fertig.** *Lunch isn't ready yet.*

a **das Mittagessen** In German you must say **das Mittagessen** (L2, N19). **Das Essen** means *food* or *meal,* so **das Mittagessen** means *midday meal.*

b **noch nicht**: *not yet* The two words cannot be separated in this kind of sentence as they can in English.

4 **Es gibt Fisch und Kartoffelsalat.** *There is fish and potato salad.*

a **es gibt** This is an idiom meaning *there is* or *there are.* It is

27

3

followed by an object or objects in the accusative case. (This does not show here because **Fisch** and **Kartoffelsalat** have no qualifying words in front.).

b **Kartoffelsalat** Any culinary expression like *potato salad* – in which the first word describes the content – is a compound noun in German.

c **Fisch und Kartoffelsalat:** *fish and potato salad,* a common Bavarian dish

5 **Hoffentlich essen es Lore und Renate gern.** *I hope Lore and Renate like it.*

a **hoffentlich** Remember this means *it is to be hoped* (L2, N11b). Since the verb **essen** CANNOT be moved from second position, the subject (**Lore und Renate**) is placed after the verb. **Es** comes between **essen** and **Lore und Renate,** because the object – **es** – is very short and the subject – **Lore und Renate** – is long. Such considerations can sometimes upset rules of word order.

b **essen ... gern** These two words must be explained together in this very idiomatic expression. **Essen** means *eat* and **gern** means *gladly* or *with pleasure* (L2, N42). The combination of the two would be rendered in English by *like eating* or *enjoy eating.* In fact, one can dispense with *eating* and simply say *like,* since the implication is obvious. The combination of any verb with **gern** means *to like* or *enjoy* whatever activity the verb describes, e.g. **Wir wohnen gern in Rio:** *We like living in Rio* (L2, N43).

6 **Walter und wir, Familie Pfaffinger, essen es sehr gern.** *Walter and we, the Pfaffingers, like it very much.*
sehr gern: literally *very gladly* *Very much* is the meaning here. We now have: **essen ... gern:** *like (to eat),* **essen ... sehr gern:** *like (to eat) very much,* **essen ... lieber:** *prefer (to eat)* (L2, N46).

7 **Sie müssen gleich hier sein.** *They're bound to be here any minute.*

a **Sie müssen:** *they must* **Müssen** is used rather idiomatically here. It is a verb like **Sie möchten:** *you'd like to* and **Sie wollen:** *you want to,* which you met in L2, N6c, N41 and N48a. They require a completing infinitive which appears at the end of the sentence.

b **sein:** *be* This is the completing infinitive belonging with **Sie müssen.** You may be surprised to find the infinitive form **sein:** *to be* so unlike the other forms (**bin, ist, sind**) you already know. It is quite irregular; that is, there is no apparent connection between its various forms. The same is true in English of *to be* which has the forms *am, is, are, be.*

28

8 **Wann kommen unsere Verwandten?** *When are our relatives coming?*

a **kommen**   Remember, the one word **kommen** means *are coming*.

b **Unsere** is *our* before all plural nouns, whether they are nominative or accusative (L2, N35b).

9 **Sie wollen zu Mittag hier sein.** *They intend to be here for lunch.*

sie wollen . . . sein   **Wollen** normally means *want to* (L2, N41 and N48), but it can also express intention. **Sein,** the completing infinitive, appears at the end of the sentence.

10 **Kann ich meinen Pullover tragen?** *Can I wear my sweater?*

a **kann ich . . . tragen:** *can I wear.* . . . Note this new meaning of **tragen;** in Lesson 2 you met it with the meaning *carry.* **Kann** is another verb which requires an infinitive to complete the sense of the verb phrase. The infinitive here is **tragen,** placed as usual at the end of the sentence. The verbs which require this construction and which express a kind of attitude towards taking some action (*want to, would like to, must* or *have to, can* or *be able to*) are called MODAL verbs, and since they are so frequently used it is convenient to know this term.

b **meinen Pullover**   This is the object and **Pullover** is masculine. Therefore **mein** requires the masculine accusative ending **-en,** which should now be quite familiar. **Pullover** is one of many English words 'borrowed' by German. They are given a **der, die** or **das** classification and usually a German pronunciation, so although they look the same as English in writing, you may not recognize them when you hear them spoken. As with **Pullover** the meaning may not be identical with the English meaning.

11 **Natürlich kannst du ihn tragen.** *Of course you can wear it.*

a Note the word order again when the first item (**natürlich**) is not the subject. By now you will probably have become quite used to this pattern.

b **kannst du**   **Du** is a new way of saying *you* (referring to one person only) and has a new verb form to match it, ending in **-st.** (The English equivalent would be *thou canst.*) Whether one uses **du** or **Sie** when speaking to someone depends on the relationship between the two people concerned. Briefly, **du** is used wherever a certain degree of familiarity exists, that is between relatives, close friends, children up to about 15 or 16, adults and children (un-related) till the young people are about 15, and often between members of groups held together by something other than blood or close personal relationships, e.g. students, soldiers of equal rank. The golden rule for a foreigner, except when speaking to children, is to use the **Sie** form until the German person proposes the change to **du.**

c **ihn:** *it* – refers to **Pullover,** which is masculine. It is the object of the sentence, so the accusative is required.

12 **Er ist hübsch.** *It's smart.*
hübsch The basic meaning is *pretty,* but as you see, it can be applied to things we would call *nice, attractive,* or *smart* – depending on the context in which it is used.

13 **Kann ich noch eine Schachtel Zigaretten kaufen?** *Can I buy another packet of cigarettes?*
noch eine Schachtel Zigaretten **Noch eine** means *one more of the same thing, another.*

14 **Nein, du sollst nicht so viel rauchen.** *No, you're not to (shouldn't) smoke so much.* **Sollen** is another modal verb (L3, N10a). The completing infinitive is placed at the end of the sentence. Note that when the verb phrase is negative, **nicht** comes immediately after the modal verb. The **-st** ending follows the regular pattern when the subject is **du.**

15 **Jetzt ist es halb eins.** *It's half past twelve now.*
halb eins **Eins** means *one,* of course, so this way of saying twelve thirty calls for some mental adjustment. You must always think of the NEXT hour coming up, NOT the one that is past. **Halb eins** means *half on the way to one o'clock,* therefore *half past twelve.* **Halb zwei** is *one thirty. Two thirty* is **halb drei.**

16 **Hier kommen sie an.** *Here they are.* **Ankommen** means *arrive,* and its use implies that Grete actually sees the car coming to a halt. It is a separable verb, so **an** appears at the end of the sentence.

17 **Das Auto fährt gerade in den Hof.** *The car is just driving into the yard.*

a **fährt** You encountered **fahren** in Lesson 1. But you will see that it has acquired an Umlaut here, signifying a change in the pro-nunciation of the vowel **a.** Quite a large number of verbs have this feature when the subject is singular, but not *I.* The only way of knowing which ones change is by learning them. They will be referred to from now on as vowel-changing verbs.

b **in den Hof:** *into the yard*   You are already familiar with **in** meaning *to* (**in ihr Hotel**) but this is the first time it has been obvious that when **in** means *to* or *into,* it is followed by the accusative case.

18 **Soll ich die Tür aufmachen?** *Shall* (*should*) *I open the door?*
aufmachen   You will probably sense that **aufmachen** is a separable verb. However, this is the infinitive form (the form in which you would find it listed in the dictionary). Note that the two parts, which are normally split up, join together when the infinitive is required (L2, N9a, N23a and L3, N16).

19 **Nein, das mache ich selbst.** *No, I'll do that myself.* Note the word order (L2, N31a) and remember **das** can mean *that* as well as *the.*

20 **Du gehst in die Werkstatt**   *You go to the workshop*
a **du gehst** (**gehen:** *go*)   The stem is **geh-.** The **-st** ending matches **du.**
b **in die Werkstatt**   **In** meaning *to* is followed by the accusative, but remember **die** is the form for both nominative and accusative with feminine nouns.

21 **und holst deinen Vater.** *and fetch your father.*
deinen Vater   When you use **du** to a person and not **Sie,** you also use a different word for *your* – **dein.** This word follows precisely the same pattern as **ein, mein, ihr,** etc. with regard to endings indicating class (masculine, feminine, neuter) and case.

Das Mittagessen *Lunch*

22 **Möchtest du noch etwas?** *Would you like some more?*
möchtest du?   The **e** before the **-st** ending makes the pronunciation easier. Remember that the endings for this verb are a little different from the standard pattern of endings which you know, since the verb expresses what one *would* or *might like* (L2, N6a). Compare **Er wohnt in München:** *He lives in Munich.* and **Er möchte in München wohnen:** *He'd like to live in Munich.* (There is no completing infinitive in the phrase **Möchtest du noch etwas?** because **essen:** *to eat* is understood from the context.)

23 **Du ißt wirklich wenig, Lore.** *You really don't eat much, Lore.*
a **du ißt**   Since this is a form of **essen:** *to eat,* you see that it requires a vowel change from **e** to **i** when the subject is **du.** Note too that we write **essen** (with **ss**) but **ißt** (with **ß**). You may like to know why we do not use **ß** in the first case:

31

3

this symbol is never used between two vowels (here, two e's) the first of which is a SHORT sound. (Cf. **Adresse (L2)**.)

b **wirklich wenig:** lit. *really little* *Really ... not much* sounds better in English and means exactly the same.

24 **Sie ißt nie viel.** *She never eats much.*

a **sie ißt** Ißt is used with both **sie** and **du.** Do not confuse **ißt** with **ist:** *is.*

b **nie** An adverb is placed AFTER the verb, never between the subject and verb, as is often the case in English.

25 **Aber siehst du Renate!** *But do you see Renate!* This is not a real question, although the question order is used. In English *Just look at Renate!* would render the same sense better. **Siehst** comes from **sehen,** another vowel-changing verb.

26 **Ihren Appetit möchte ich haben!** *I wish I had her appetite!* (*I'd like to have her appetite!*) **Ihren Appetit** is placed in first position to give it the kind of emphasis which is achieved by voice stress in English.

27 **Sie kann nie genug bekommen.** *She can never get enough.* **kann** Note that this is the same form as is used with **ich** (L3, N10a). This is a feature of all modal verbs (**will, möchte, soll**).

28 **Du nimmst noch ein bißchen, nicht wahr?** *You'll have (take) a little more, won't you?*

a **du nimmst** **Nehmen** is another vowel-changing verb, and in this instance, not only does **e** change to **i,** but **h** disappears and an extra **m** replaces it.

b **ein bißchen:** *a little bit* The ending **-chen** (like **-lein**) is a diminutive. **Ein bißchen** is often rendered as *a bit* or *a little* in English but strictly speaking it should be rendered as *a LITTLE bit.*

29 **Franz nimmt oft zwei oder drei Portionen.** *Franz often has two or three helpings.* **nimmt** When there is a vowel change, you see that it happens both with **du** and with **er, sie, es** or anyone or anything for which **er, sie,** or **es** can be substituted – Franz in this case (L3, N17a).

30 **Junge Leute haben immer Hunger.** *Young people are always hungry.* **haben ... Hunger:** *are hungry* The German idiom is *to have hunger.* **Hunger** is therefore a noun and is written with a capital.

Erste Bekanntschaft *First acquaintance*

31 **Renate, kommst du mit?** *Renate, are you coming with me?*

There is no need for *me* in German. The use of the separable verb **mitkommen** is enough. You could say *Are you coming too?*

3

32 Wohin willst du? *Where are you going?*

a **Wohin?** must be used in German instead of **wo** when the sense is *where* TO, although *to* can be left out in English.

b **willst du?** This use of **willst** expresses intention (L3, N9). When it is clear from the context that the completing infinitive would be **gehen,** it can be omitted without risk of misunderstanding, e.g. **Ich will jetzt nach oben:** *I'm going up now.*

33 Gibt es dort Zigaretten? *Do they have cigarettes there?*
gibt es? You have met **es gibt** meaning *there is* (L3, N4a). It has essentially the same meaning here, but requires some adapting in translation.

34 Was!? Rauchst du auch? *What! Do you smoke too?* It is quite common to find both an exclamation and a question mark after **was,** indicating both astonishment and curiosity.

35 Das kann ich gut verstehen. THAT *I can well understand.*
Remember **gut** can mean both *good* and *well*. It can therefore be either an adjective or an adverb.

36 Was machst du heute abend? *What are you doing this evening?*
heute abend Heute means *today* (L3, N1), **der Abend:** *evening.* These two combined form the only way of saying *this evening* in German. In this set expression you write **abend** with a small **a.**

37 Freitagabend gehe ich immer aus. *I always go out on Friday evening.*
Freitagabend Note that this is one word. When you refer to a particular part of a certain day – *Sunday morning, Tuesday afternoon,* etc., you always join up the words.

38 Wohin gehst du? *Where do you go?*

a **wohin?** Remember you must use **wohin?** and not just **wo?** as it means *where to?*

b **gehst du?** Renate uses **gehst du?** in preference to **willst du?** (L3, N32b) because she is speaking generally about every Friday evening.

39 Ins Kino oder in unseren Club. *To the cinema or to our club.*

a **ins Kino In** meaning *to* requires the accusative case. **Kino** is neuter, so it would be **in das Kino. Ins** is short for **in das** and is nearly always used. **Ins,** then, always means *to* or *into* and the following word is always neuter.

b **oder in unseren Club** *To* THE *club* would be **in den Club** (another

3

word 'borrowed' from English). The accusative masculine ending is required on **unser.**

40 **Willst du mitkommen?** *Do you want to come along?* (L3, N31)
Mitkommen is the infinitive form, so **mit** and **kommen** are joined up (L3, N18a).

Männergespräch *Man talk*

41 **Prost, Max!** *Cheers, Max!* This is the commonest German toast for informal occasions.

42 **Und noch einmal: herzlich willkommen in München!** *And once again: a hearty welcome to Munich!*
noch einmal einmal: *one time, once,* noch einmal: *once more* (L3, N13, N22 and N28)

43 **Nicht wahr, Walter, du hast ein Mietauto?** *You've got a hired car, Walter, haven't you?*

a It is possible in colloquial language to have **nicht wahr?** at the beginning of the sentence, but it has no effect on the word order.

b **du hast** Note that the **du** form of **haben** (**hast**) is identical with the old form (*thou*) *hast* in English.

44 **Wie fährt es?** *How is it running?* (*How is it going?*)
Use **fahren** for *to go* when speaking of vehicles moving or people travelling in vehicles, and **gehen** of people going on foot.

45 **Nicht schlecht, aber ich muß es morgen in die Autowerkstatt fahren.** *Not too badly* (*not bad*), *but I must take it to the garage* (*car repair shop*) *tomorrow.*

a **nicht schlecht** Remember adjectives can be used as adverbs, so **schlecht** can mean *bad* or *badly.*

b **ich muß es ... fahren:** *I must take it* From the construction of the sentence, you will see that **muß** is a modal verb. It is the **ich** form of **müssen** (L3, N7a). Note too the use of ß in **muß** but **ss** in **müssen** (L3, N23a). *Take* is **fahren** because he is speaking of a car.

c **in die Autowerkstatt** The accusative **in** meaning *to.*

d **morgen in die Autowerkstatt** Adverbial phrases of time precede those of place, e.g. **Sie wollen zu Mittag hier sein.**: *They intend to be here at midday.* **Ich gehe Freitagabend ins Kino.**: *I go to the cinema on Friday evenings.*

46 **Wir können zusammen fahren.** *We can go* (*drive*) *together.*
wir können This is the plural form of **kann.**

47 **Fährst du viel?** *Do you drive much?* The **du** form, like the **er** form, shows a vowel change.

48 **Nein, ich fahre selten.** *No, I seldom drive.* The **ich** form, **fahre,** shows no irregularity.

49 **Bist du morgen früh frei,** *Are you free tomorrow morning,* This word order – **frei** at the end – is very German, though not obligatory.

a **Bist** is the **du** form of *are.*

b **morgen früh** Früh really means *early.*

50 **oder mußt du arbeiten?** *or must you work?* The **du** form of **müssen** just adds -**t** after the ß and not -**st** for obvious reasons.

51 **Nein, morgen bin ich zu Haus.** *No, I'll be at home tomorrow.*
Ich bin can mean *I'll be* as well as *I am.* So, **Bist du morgen frei?** (L3, N49) is also equivalent to *Will you be free tomorrow?*
compare **ich mache:** *I'll do* (L3, N19).
du nimmst: *you'll take* (L3, N28a)
As you can see, *we'll, you'll, I'll, do something* do not require anything other than the verb forms you are already familiar with.

52 **Dann sehe ich dich also?** *So I'll see you then?*

a **sehe ich** (sehen: *see*) (L3, N25 – **du siehst**) This is another vowel-changing verb; **e** changes to **ie** in the **du** form. Remember that if there is a change, it occurs in both the **du** and **er** forms. You will also realize that there is no way of predicting the sort of changes which will occur. They just have to be learnt through use.

b **Dich** is the accusative of **du.**

53 **Schön! Und dann machen wir alle zusammen einen Stadtbummel, ja?** *Fine! And then we'll all take a trip into town, shall we?* The **ja?** at the end serves the same purpose as **nicht wahr?** but is much more colloquial.

Part three

Noch einmal München *Munich again*

54 **Was machst du dort?** *What are you going to do there?* **Machst du** can even mean *are you going to do?*

Wer hat Zeit für mich? *Who has time for me?*

55 **für mich** Notice that **für** is followed by the accusative case. ↳

Er möchte sie wiedersehen *He'd like to see her again*

56 **Wiedersehen** is the completing infinitive of a separable verb, so both parts are joined together.

57 **Bist du morgen zu Haus?** *Will you be at home tomorrow?*
zu Haus Note this phrase for *at home.*

4 Lektion vier   Straßenbahnfahrt

Lesson four   A ride in a tramcar

What happens

In the main part of this lesson you 'accompany' Renate on her first solo outing in the city of Munich. Things have changed since she was last there, including the tramway system, and she has some difficulty finding out exactly what to do.

In Part 1 a tramcar ticket inspector complains about the difficulties of dealing with tourists. In Part 2 Renate takes a ride on a tram and helps a fellow passenger.

New words in this lesson

der Ausländer, die Ausländer foreigner/s
der Beruf job, profession
der Besuch visit
der Fahrgast passenger
der Fahrschein ticket
der Freund friend
der Fuß foot
der Hund, die Hunde dog/s
der Kontrolleur inspector
der Mann man
der Pfennig, die Pfennige penny/pennies
  (smallest unit of German currency)
der Platz room, space
der Schaffner conductor
der Schein (bank)note
der Tourist, die Touristen tourist/s
der Zehnmarkschein ten Mark note
der Zugführer driver (tram/train)

die Ahnung idea
die Arbeit work
die Auskunft information
die Fahrt, die Fahrten trip/s, journey/s
die Einzelfahrt single ticket
die Hälfte half
die Haltestelle (tram) stop
die Hilfe help

die Linie number
die Mark mark (German currency unit)
die Minute, die Minuten minute/s
die Mitte middle, centre
die Nähe neighbourhood
die Richtung direction
die Stadt town
die Stadtmitte town-centre
die Station, die Stationen stop/s
die Straßenbahn, die Straßenbahnen
  tram/s, tramway
die Straßenbahnfahrt tram journey
die Viertelstunde quarter of an hour

das Geld money
das Kind, die Kinder child/children
das Kleingeld change (money)
das Rathaus town-hall
das Straßenbahnsystem tram system
das Stück, die Stücke coin/s, piece/s

die Eltern (Pl.) parents

einige some
man one, you

dürfen (ich darf) to be allowed to

bleiben to remain
fragen to ask
geben (er gibt) to give (he gives)
gehören (D) to belong
kennen to know, be familiar with
lieben to love
lösen to buy (ticket)
schließen to close
sprechen (spricht) to speak
stehen to stand, to be
warten auf to wait for
wechseln to change (money)
wohnen to stay
zahlen to pay

aussteigen to get off, alight
einsteigen to get on
umsteigen to change (bus etc.)
vorstellen to introduce

alle every
automatisch automatically
fremd strange, foreign
freundlich friendly
fünfzehn fifteen
gewöhnlich usually
höflich polite
Münchner of Munich
nett nice
schwer hard
schwierig difficult
vierte fourth

direkt directly
endlich at last

hinten at the back
in der Nähe around here
manchmal sometimes
vorn in front, at the front
zurück back

am besten best, the best way
bestimmt definitely
denn then
fast almost
so so
ziemlich rather, fairly, quite

an at
bei with, at, from
beim = bei + dem
entlang along
im = in + dem on the
mit by
nach after
zu to
zum = zu + dem to the
zur = zu + der to the

ach so! I see!
das schon I can, that is possible
doch yes
entschuldigen Sie! excuse me!
es dauert so lange it takes such a long
  time
es macht Spaß I enjoy it
na well
nichts zu danken! that's all right.
  it's a pleasure
von Beruf by profession
Vorsicht! look out! be careful!
zu Fuß on foot
zu Besuch on a visit

Notes

Part one

1 **Darf ich mich vorstellen?** *May I introduce myself?*

a **darf ich?** This is another modal verb, **dürfen** meaning *be allowed to* and requires a completing infinitive.

b **Mich** can mean *myself* as well as *me* in such expressions as *introduce myself,* when the speaker is both object and subject.

c **vorstellen** This is a separable verb, so unless the infinitive is required, as it is here, **vor** would be detached and would be placed at the end, e.g. **Ich stelle Sie vor:** *I'll introduce you.*

4

2 Ich bin Kontrolleur von Beruf, *I'm an inspector by profession,*
von Beruf: *by trade/profession*

3 Kontrolleur bei der Münchner Straßenbahn. *Inspector with the City of Munich tramway.*

a Münchner is the adjective formed from **München** and does not change in form no matter what follows. Adding **-er** to the name of a city is the normal way of forming the adjective describing something belonging to the city, e.g. **Berliner, Frankfurter, Hamburger.** In the case of **Münchner** the final **e** before the ending disappears.

b bei der Münchner Straßenbahn Straßenbahn is feminine – **die Straßenbahn** – and the feminine accusative is the same as the feminine nominative – **die.** Yet here is **der** before a **die** word. It is, in fact, another 'case', which just happens to be identical in form with masculine nominative **der.** The case is called the DATIVE and has several uses, which we shall deal with as they arise. The reason for its use here is the word **bei,** which must always be followed by the dative case.

4 Ich bin immer höflich und nett zu den Leuten. *I'm always polite and nice to people.*

zu den Leuten Remember **junge Leute:** *young people* (L3, N30). There must be a reason for the extra **-n** on **Leuten**; and since **Leute** can in no circumstances be singular, **den** cannot be masculine accusative. This is the DATIVE PLURAL. **Den** happens to have the same form as the masculine accusative, but note that there is a change in the noun itself here (the added **-n**) which is unusual and helps to dispel any possible confusion. All dative plural nouns require **-n** added to the nominative plural (unless there is one there already as is the case with feminine plurals). A few nouns borrowed from other languages, e.g. **Auto, Hotel,** do not require **-n** in the dative plural. The reason for the dative here is **zu,** which, like **bei,** must always be followed by the dative case.

5 Aber manchmal ist es schwer, freundlich zu bleiben. *But sometimes it is difficult to remain friendly.* Remember **etwas zu verzollen:** *something to declare* (L1, N33b). You have since met the infinitive forms of verbs frequently, but always completing modal verbs, which do not require **zu:** *to* before the infinitive, e.g. **Sie wollen zu Mittag hier sein:** *They want to be here at midday.* **Kann ich meinen Pullover tragen?:** *Can I wear my sweater?* **Müssen Sie**

morgen arbeiten?: *Do you have to work tomorrow?* **Zu** is always required in such phrases as IT *is hard* TO DO SOMETHING, where the infinitive phrase could be substituted for IT: *To do something is hard.* Note that in writing, it is necessary to separate the infinitive phrase from the rest of the sentence by a comma.

6 **Nach München kommen viele Touristen: Deutsche und Ausländer.** *Many tourists come to Munich: Germans and foreigners.*

a **Deutsche** This is the plural form, *Germans,* used by itself (without a word for *the*).

b **Ausländer** This is identical with the singular (like **Zimmer**).

7 **Einige Ausländer sprechen ziemlich gut Deutsch und verstehen fast alles.** *Some foreigners speak German fairly well (speak fairly good German) and understand nearly everything.*
einige This is an adjective meaning *some* – not to be confused with **eine**: *a, an, one.* It is used when comparing one group of people with another (as here), or when singling out one group from the majority.

8 **Aber einige wollen nicht lernen und verstehen nichts.** *But some don't want to learn and understand nothing.*
lernen This is the completing infinitive of **wollen** and comes at the end of that statement, so it is keeping the rules of word order. What follows **und** can be regarded as another statement about the same people. **Verstehen** is a new verb with the same subject as **wollen (einige)**, and is not an infinitive, though it has the same form.

9 **Dann macht meine Arbeit keinen Spaß.** *Then my work is no pleasure.*
macht ... keinen Spaß **Spaß machen** is very idiomatic, meaning *to be a pleasure,* or *to give pleasure, to be good fun.*

Part two

An der Haltestelle *At the tram-stop*

10 **Haltestelle** is feminine – **die Haltestelle** – so **der** in the title must be the dative. Once again, the reason for it is the little word **an**: *at* which requires the dative case when it means *at.*

11 **Warten Sie auch auf die Straßenbahn?** *Are you waiting for the · tram too?*
warten ... auf die Straßenbahn **Warten auf** means *to wait for* (a

4

person or thing). When it is used together with **warten, auf** is always followed by the accusative.

12 Ja, ich warte schon eine Viertelstunde, aber es kommt keine.
Yes, I've been waiting for a quarter of an hour already, but none has come.

a ich warte schon Note that this is the same tense of the verb that you have been familiar with since Lesson **1**, the Present tense, although the English – *I've been waiting* – is a Past tense form. Since the action – *waiting* – is still continuing at the time of speaking, the use of the Present tense is really quite logical. **Schon:** *already* nearly always follows the verb when the sense is HAVE BEEN *doing something.*

b eine Viertelstunde vier: *four;* **Viertel:** *quarter;* **die Stunde:** *hour;* **eine Viertelstunde:** *a quarter of an hour.* There is no need to translate *for* when talking of a period of time.

c aber es kommt keine: lit. *but there comes not one* Again, English would favour a past tense form – *none has come.*

13 Sind Sie fremd hier? *Are you a stranger here?*
fremd This is an adjective meaning *strange* or *foreign.* It is always used in preference to the noun for *stranger* or *foreigner* in such expressions as **Sind Sie fremd hier? Ich bin fremd hier.**

14 Spricht man dort so gut Deutsch? *Do they speak German so well there?*
spricht man Man is the German for *one* when it means *people, you, they.* It is considered singular and the **er** form of the verb is used with it. **Man spricht:** *one speaks.* In Part 1 you encountered **sprechen,** so you can see that this is a vowel - changing verb. The **du** and **er** forms have **i** instead of **e.**

15 Oh nein, ich bin Deutsche. *Oh, no, I'm German.* **Deutsche** is feminine and is really an adjective used as a noun. **Deutsche** can also be plural.

16 Ach so! Wohnen Sie hier in der Nähe? *Oh I see! Are you staying around here?*
hier in der Nähe: lit. *here in the neighbourhood* **Nähe** is feminine, so this is dative. A dative is used after **in,** when it means *in (a place)* and not *to* or *into.* This question of **in** sometimes requiring the accusative – **ins Kino, in den Club** – and sometimes dative may seem complicated now, but it becomes clearer with practice. It is very important to grasp that, in general, the accusative indicates motion towards a place, the dative indicates location.

40

17 Ja, ich wohne mit meinen Eltern bei Verwandten. *Yes, I'm staying with my parents with (at the house of) relatives.*

a mit meinen Eltern   This is the dative plural after **mit,** which is always followed by the dative.

b bei Verwandten   **Bei** can have various meanings, but it always takes the dative. One of the commonest meanings is *at the house of.* **Bei Pfaffingers:** *at the Pfaffingers' (house)*

18 Bestimmt kennen Sie unser Münchner Straßenbahnsystem noch nicht, oder? *You certainly won't be familiar with our Munich tram system yet, or are you?*

oder? *or (are you)?* This is a more colloquial way of seeking confirmation than **nicht wahr?** It is preferred when the preceding statement is negative as here. This expression is particularly favoured in Southern Germany, Austria and German-speaking Switzerland.

19 Am besten fragen Sie den Schaffner dort. *You'd do best to ask the conductor there.*

a am besten   This is an adverbial phrase meaning *in the best way* and it is frequently combined with an instruction – like **fragen Sie:** *ask!* – to mean *The best way is to (ask).* E.g. **Am besten lernen Sie Deutsch:** *The best way is to learn German.* **Am besten warten wir hier:** *We'd do best to wait here.*

b den Schaffner   This is the accusative. **Fragen,** when it means *ask* A PERSON, takes the accusative.

Der Schaffner gibt Auskunft   *The conductor gives some information*

20 Auskunft (feminine) requires no word for *some* before it. You will often notice that we use the word *some* in English where no equivalent word is used in German.

21 Entschuldigen Sie, bitte! *Excuse me, please!* This is the correct approach to a stranger from whom you are requesting information, e.g. in the street. Note there is no need to say *me* in the German phrase.

22 Wie komme ich zum Rathaus? *How do I get to the Town Hall?*

a wie komme ich (zu)   This is the best phrase for asking the way to somewhere.

b zum Rathaus   **Zum** is short for **zu + dem,** and since you know **zu** is always followed by the dative, **dem** must be the masculine or neuter dative of **der.** In fact it is both, so you only have one new form to learn here. **Haus** is neuter. These little words like

41

4

zu, in, bei, an are often combined with the forms of der, die, das which follow, e.g. ins = in + das (L3, N39a); im = in + dem; zum = zu + dem; zur = zu + der; am = an + dem; beim = bei + dem.

23 Sie steigen hier in die Linie 6 (sechs) ein. *You get on a number six tram here.*

a Einsteigen means *to board (a vehicle)* but you can see that the verb alone is not enough; you must follow the main part of the verb by in + the accusative if the vehicle is mentioned.

b Linie means the route followed by a certain tram, distinguished from others by its number; the best English rendering is *number*.

24 Nein, nach 4 (vier) Stationen steigen Sie aus. *No, after four stops you get off.*
nach vier Stationen Die Station means a stopping point on a route followed by a vehicle. The plural is Stationen; nach is always followed by the dative, so this is the dative plural.

25 Dann gehen Sie zu Fuß die Theatinerstraße entlang *Then you walk (go on foot) along the Theatinerstraße*
die Theatinerstraße entlang Entlang: *along* follows its complement – die Theatinerstraße – instead of preceding it. It takes the accusative case.

26 Hier steht ein Fahrscheinautomat. *Here is (stands) a ticket-dispensing machine.* The most modern tramway systems have ticket machines at fare stages.
ein Automat Der Automat is unusual in that the noun itself has an -en ending in every case except the nominative singular.

27 Mit einem Zweimarkstück bekommen Sie einen Fahrschein für drei Fahrten. *For a two mark piece you get a ticket (valid) for three journeys.*

a Fahrten Eine Fahrt is a ride by tram or bus, a train journey or a passage by boat.

b mit einem Zweimarkstück Mit is always followed by the dative. Stück is neuter, so ein must have -em added (L4, N22b – dem).

28 Danke für Ihre Hilfe! *Thank you for your help!* This is a phrase to learn by heart. Remember that für is always followed by the accusative.

In der Straßenbahn *In the tramcar*

29 Bleiben Sie nicht hier vorn! *Don't stand (stay) at the front here!* Note how you say DON'T do something in German.

30 In der Mitte und hinten ist noch viel Platz. *In the middle and at*

42

the back there's still plenty of room.

a **in der Mitte** Remember that **in** is followed by the dative, when it describes a location, i.e. not *to* or *into*.

b **ist** In English we have to say THERE *is*. This is not necessary in German when the sentence starts by stating the location.

31 **Vorsicht! Die Türen schließen automatisch.** *Careful! The doors shut automatically.*

automatisch In German -**isch** as an adjectival or adverbial ending is often equivalent to English *-ic* or *-ically.*

32 **Wem gehört der Hund hier?** *Whose dog is this? (To whom does the dog here belong?)*

wem gehört? This -**em** ending is becoming familiar to you as a dative ending (**dem, einem**). **Wer?:** *who?* follows the **der** pattern and **wem** is the dative of **wer?** The reason why the dative is necessary here shows you more clearly why there is a dative case at all. Remember the phrase **Der Schaffner gibt Auskunft.** The conductor gives – what? Answer: *information. Information* (**Auskunft**) is the object and is accusative. If we say **Der Schaffner gibt Renate Auskunft,** Renate is also a kind of object of **gibt,** but answering the question TO *whom?* The conductor gives information – to whom? Answer: *(to) Renate.* **Auskunft** is called the DIRECT OBJECT, for which we have the accusative case; Renate – who received it – is called the INDIRECT OBJECT. We need some way of distinguishing the indirect object from the direct object in a sentence. In the kind of system German uses, the obvious answer is another case with different endings. Some verbs, because of their meaning, require a dative object. Things *belong* TO people. **Gehören** is such a verb. These verbs are shown in the vocabularies by a (**D**). **Wem gehört?** is the best way of asking *whose is?*

33 **Für Kinder, Hunde und Gepäck zahlen Sie die Hälfte.** *For children, dogs and luggage you pay half-fare (the half).*

a **Kinder** The singular is **das Kind.** A number of nouns form the plural by adding -**er** to the singular. (See Appendix **8.**)

b **Hunde** The singular is **der Hund.** A large number of nouns, mainly masculine, form the plural by adding -**e** to the singular.

34 **Wo ist denn mein Geld?** *Where is my money (then)?/Where's my money got to?* **Denn** is very commonly used in German questions and exclamations for emphasis, as here; English might use *then,* but does not always need a corresponding expression. Used in this way, **denn** cannot appear at the beginning of the sentence.

4

35 **Doch, das schon, aber es dauert immer so lange.** *Yes, I can, but it always takes so long.*

a **doch** This means *yes* when it is contradicting something and is generally in answer to a negative question, like *Can't you?*, *Isn't it?* etc. E.g. **Haben Sie keinen Lift hier?:** *Have you no lift here?* **Doch, aber leider ist er kaputt:** *Yes, there is, but unfortunately it has broken down.* **Gehen Sie nicht in den Club?:** *Aren't you going to the club?* **Doch, aber noch nicht:** *Yes, I am, but not yet* (L2, N33).

b **Das schon** is impossible to explain by any attempt at an English rendering. Here it has the sense of *that is possible, but . . .*

36 **ich bekomme 15 (fünfzehn) Pfennig zurück.** *I get fifteen pfennigs back.* 1 **DM** = 100 **Pfennig. Pfennige** is the grammatical plural of **Pfennig,** but is, in fact, rarely used. One just says **15 Pfennig.**

Part three

Keine Zeit *No time*

37 **keine Zeit mehr** *no time* **Mehr:** *more* is often added in German, though it is unnecessary in English.

38 **Mit der Straßenbahn sind wir in einer Viertelstunde dort.** *By tram we'll be there in a quarter of an hour.* In German **mit** is used with vehicles where *by* is used in English.

Auskunft *Information*

39 **Ja, das kann man.** *Yes, one can.* **Man kann** alone is just not German. The complete sentence understood is **Ja, man kann** *mit dem Fahrschein umsteigen,* so **das** stands for the whole phrase in italics.

Ein Schaffner fragt *A conductor enquires*

40 **bei seinem Freund** *at his friend's* **Bei** can mean *at* one's place of work, as well as one's home. Here, it means he works in his friend's garage.

41 **am Frankfurter Platz Nummer 16 (sechzehn)?** *at number sixteen, Frankfurt Square?* Numbers are given AFTER the name of the street, avenue, square (**Platz**), etc.

Lektion fünf   In der Stadt

Lesson five   In the town

What happens

In this lesson Herr and Frau Kühn are in town on different errands.
In Part 1 a post office clerk gives details of his job. In Part 2
Herr Kühn buys stamps and sends an airmail letter and a telegram.
Lore and a policeman help a stranger to the city and Lore meets
Grete Pfaffinger for tea or coffee and cakes.

New words in this lesson

der **Apfel** apple
der **Bahnhof** station
der **Besucher, die Besucher** visitor/s
der **Brief, die Briefe** letter/s
der **Dienst** work (hours on duty)
der **Kuchen** cake
der **Nachmittag** afternoon
der **Onkel** uncle
der **Park** park
der **Polizist** policeman
der **Postbeamte** post office clerk
der **Schalter** counter
der **Schwager** brother-in-law
der **Tee** tea
der **Vormittag** morning
der **Weg** way

die **Arbeitszeit, die Arbeitszeiten**
  working hours
die **Bank, die Banken** bank/s
die **Briefmarke, die Briefmarken** stamp/s
die **Frage** question
die **Gesundheit** health
die **Postkarte** postcard
die **Tasse** cup
die **Uhr, die Uhren** watch/es, clock/s
die **Zitrone** lemon

das **Café** café
das **Formular, die Formulare** form/s

das **Mädchen** girl
das **Postamt** post office
das **Hauptpostamt** main post office
das **Telegramm** telegram
das **Uhrengeschäft** watchmaker's
das **Vergnügen** delight, pleasure
das **Viertel** quarter

(der) **Montag** Monday
(der) **Dienstag** Tuesday
(der) **Mittwoch** Wednesday
(der) **Donnerstag** Thursday
(der) **Freitag** Friday
(der) **Samstag** Saturday
(der) **Sonntag** Sunday

ihr, ihre their

helfen (D) (er hilft) to help
wissen (ich weiß) to know (a fact)

beantworten to answer
beginnen to begin
bestellen to order
dauern to last
erklären to explain
finden to find
öffnen to open
schaden (D) to harm
schicken to send

45

5

wiegen to weigh
zeigen to show

aufgeben to send
aufhören to finish

früh early, in the morning
heute nachmittag this afternoon
lange long
zuerst first

geradeaus straight ahead
rechts on the right

erst only, just
etwa about, approximately
genau exactly
regelmäßig regularly

sondern but
wie like

am at the
auf at
beim by the, near the
bis until

im in the

achtzehn eighteen
dreizehn thirteen
elf eleven
sechzig sixty
zwanzig twenty

Entschuldigung! excuse me! I beg your
   pardon
es tut mir leid I am sorry
ganz leicht quite easy
gern trinken to like (drinking)
Herr Ober! waiter!
leider I'm afraid, unfortunately
mit Luftpost by airmail
nach rechts to the right
um...Uhr at...o'clock
um wieviel Uhr? what time?
Viertel vor acht quarter to eight
Viertel nach fünf quarter past five
wie lange? how long?
wie viele? how many?

ihm him (dat.)
ihnen them (dat.)
mir me (dat.)

Notes

Part one

1   Ich bin ein Postbeamter wie mein Onkel, Peter Lenz, und mein
    Schwager, Christian Riemer. *I'm a post office clerk, like my uncle,*
    Peter Lenz, and my brother-in-law, Christian Riemer.
    ein Postbeamter (L1, N10 – der Paßbeamte) To understand why
    Beamte requires an -r when it is used with ein and not when it is
    used with der, it is necessary to realize that Beamte is really a
    kind of adjective being used as a noun, and is treated like an
    adjective used before a noun. You will be able to understand this
    better when you have learnt how adjectives behave in this posi-
    tion. Meantime, it is enough if you understand that when der (or
    any word giving the same kind of information as der) is not in
    the phrase, the all-important -r of der is transferred to Beamte.
2   Sie arbeiten aber nicht mit mir zusammen, *However they don't*
    work along (together) with me,
    mit mir   Mit, as you know, is always followed by the dative

case. **Mir** is the dative case of **ich**: nominative **ich**: *I;* accusative **mich**: *me;* dative **mir**: *me, to me* (L4, N32).

3 **sondern im Hauptpostamt beim Bahnhof.** *but in the main post office by the railway station.*

a **sondern** We have met **aber** meaning *but, however;* now here is **sondern** meaning *but*. Sondern is used only after a negative, in constructions of the kind: NOT *so and so,* BUT (instead) *so and so.*

b **im Hauptpostamt** **im = in + dem.** In must be followed by the dative here, as it does not mean *to* or *into*. **Hauptpostamt**: *main post office.* You will meet many words of which **Haupt-** is the first component, indicating *main* or *chief.*

4 **Montag und Mittwoch beginnt mein Dienst um Viertel vor acht (7.45 Uhr) und dauert bis Viertel nach fünf (17.15 Uhr).** (*On*) *Mondays and Wednesdays my work begins at a quarter to eight and lasts till a quarter past five.*

a **Montag und Mittwoch** Notice that it is possible to use **Montag** – or any day of the week – to mean ON that day, without necessarily adding a word for *on*. Notice also that it can mean EVERY *Monday* (or *Mondays*).

b **mein Dienst** This expression, which literally means *service,* is always used when referring to one's shift or hours of work.

c **um Viertel vor acht** *At* before a precise time on the clock is always **um**. **Viertel** comes from **vier**: *four.* Any time between the half-hour and the next hour coming up is expressed by **vor,** the equivalent of English *to* in expressions of clock time.

d **bis Viertel nach fünf** **Bis** means *till/until*. **Nach** you have met before, but not with this meaning. Any time between the hour and the next half-hour is expressed by **nach,** the equivalent of English *past* in expressions of clock time.

5 **Dienstag, Donnerstag und Freitag beginne ich schon früh um halb sieben (6.30 Uhr) und höre um drei (3 Uhr) mit der Arbeit auf.** (*On*) *Tuesdays, Thursdays and Fridays, I begin early at half past six and stop work at three.* Remember the verb stands in second position. The three days mentioned at the beginning of the sentence are taken together and considered as item one.
Aufhören mit + dative means *to stop* (an activity).

6 **Samstagvormittag muß ich auch zur Arbeit,** (*On*) *Saturday mornings, too, I have to go to work,*
Samstagvormittag **Vormittag** means *morning* or *forenoon*. When coupled with the name of a day, it is all written as one word.

7 **aber am Sonntag habe ich immer frei.** *but on Sunday(s) I'm always off duty.*

a **am Sonntag** ON a day – if a word for *on* is included - is always am (compare **L5, N4a**).

b **habe ich frei** The use of **habe** will surprise you here, but this idiom is always used to mean *off duty* as opposed to *being free*, i.e. having no engagements.

Part two

Auf dem Postamt   *In the Post Office*

8 **Auf dem Postamt** It is one of the difficulties of the German language that there are several words for *in, at* and *to*. **Auf** is occasionally used to mean *in*.

9 **Bitte schön?** This phrase is used by people offering a service (shop assistants, waiters, post office and bank clerks) in situations where we would use *Can I help you?/What would you like?* This is the meaning when it has a question mark.

10 **Wie viele brauchen Sie?** *How many do you need?* **Wie viele?** has an **-e** when it refers to things that can be counted. Without an **-e** (**wieviel?**) it means *how much?* e.g. **Wieviel kostet das Zimmer?**: *How much does the room cost?*

11 **Den Brief nach Brasilien möchte ich mit Luftpost schicken.** *I want to send the letter to Brazil by air mail.* Note the word order. **Den Brief nach Brasilien** is counted as item one.

12 **Geben Sie ihn mir, bitte!** *Give it to me, please!* **ihn mir** Here is a very clear demonstration of the use of both accusative and dative cases. **Ihn**: *it* refers to **den Brief** and is the direct object, i.e. the thing being given. **Mir**: *to me* is the indirect object, i.e. the person the letter is being given to. Note also the order – **ihn** precedes **mir**. In English, one could say *give it to me, give it me,* or *give me it.* In German, there is no choice. The **ihn mir** order is obligatory.

13 **Ich muß ihn zuerst wiegen.** *I must weigh it first.* Note that **ihn** (direct object) comes right after the first verb.

14 **Jetzt möchte ich ein Telegramm aufgeben.** *Now I'd like to send a telegram.* **aufgeben** This is the infinitive after **möchte**. **Aufgeben** only means *send* when something is handed over for dispatch. The usual

meaning is *hand in* or *give up* – here referring to the telegram form filled in by the customer.

15 **Telegrammformulare bekommen Sie am Schalter 11 (elf).** *Telegram forms are available at counter eleven.*

a **bekommen Sie:** *you get,* meaning *you will be given* In official language we would use *is/are available* in English.

b **am Schalter elf** (**am** = **an** + **dem**) **Schalter** means *counter* or *window* – for example in a post office or bank – where the service area is divided into compartments for different services and there is always a glass partition between the public and the clerk.

16 **Ich danke Ihnen!** *I thank you.* **Ihnen** is the dative of **Sie.** The dative is always required when **danke** is used in a verb phrase. This makes sense if you think of **danken** as *to give thanks.* You must give thanks TO someone, therefore the dative is required.

Ein Polizist hilft *A policeman helps*

17 **Entschuldigung! Können Sie uns bitte helfen?** *Excuse me! Can you help us, please?*
helfen This is the completing infinitive after **können Sie...?** Compare **helfen** with **hilft** and you will see that **helfen** is another vowel-changing verb. Like **gehören** and **danken** it must be followed by the dative case. Think of it as *to give help to* – compare **danken** (L5, N16). **Uns** is dative as well as accusative.

18 **Wir möchten dem Mädchen hier den Weg zum Luitpold Park zeigen.** *We'd like to show the young lady here the way to the Luitpold Park.*

a **dem Mädchen** This is the dative of **das Mädchen:** *girl, young lady.* This word is neuter because **-chen** is a diminutive ending.

b **dem Mädchen den Weg ... zeigen** **Dem Mädchen** (dative) and **den Weg** (accusative) are both objects of **zeigen:** *show,* which, like **geben:** *give,* frequently has two objects – the thing being shown and the person(s) to whom it is being shown. Again, the order of the two objects is not optional; but the order here is different from the order in (L5, N12). Compare **ihn mir** (direct object first) (L5, N12) and **dem Mädchen den Weg** (indirect object first). In the first pair, both are pronouns. In the second pair, both are nouns.

19 **Ich erkläre Ihnen den Weg.** *I'll explain the way to you.*
Ihnen den Weg Note the order here – dative first, then accusative; or indirect object before direct object. At this stage,

it must seem that there is little sense or consistency in the order of direct and indirect objects. Thus far, you have two clear rules: if both are pronouns, direct object first; if both are nouns, indirect object first. Here we have one noun and one pronoun, and the indirect object, **Ihnen,** comes first. As you will see in the course of this lesson, whenever there is a noun and a pronoun, the pronoun precedes the noun, irrespective of case.

20 **Sie gehen etwa 5 (fünf) Minuten geradeaus und dann nach rechts.**
Walk straight ahead for about five minutes and then turn right.
nach rechts **Nach** here means *to* or *towards*. Remember it also means *to* with towns and most countries.

21 **Um wieviel Uhr öffnen die Banken heute nachmittag?** *What time do the banks open this afternoon?*

a **um wieviel Uhr? Um:** *at* cannot be omitted in German.

b **heute nachmittag** Cf. **heute abend** (L3, N36). **Heute nachmittag** is the only way of saying *this afternoon* in German.

22 **Das weiß ich leider nicht genau.** *I'm afraid I don't know exactly.*
I'm afraid, when used superficially like this, can be rendered by **leider:** *unfortunately.*
weiß ich From this form, which goes with **ich,** you will realize that the verb does not follow the usual pattern and must be specially learned.
You have now met two verbs meaning *to know* – **wissen:** *to know a fact ;* **kennen:** *to know/be acquainted with a place* or *a person.*

23 **Es ist mir ein Vergnügen, unseren Besuchern zu helfen** *It's a pleasure for me to help our visitors* (There is a similar construction in L4, N5.)

a **mir** The dative case is used here, indicating pleasure *to* or *for* the speaker.

b **unseren Besuchern zu helfen** **Helfen** requires the use of the dative case for its object; **unseren Besuchern** is dative plural.

24 **und ihnen ihre Fragen zu beantworten.** *and to answer their questions for them.*
ihnen ihre Fragen **Ihnen** is the dative of **sie:** *they,* as it means *for them.* **Ihre Fragen** is the direct object and is a noun. When there is one pronoun object and one noun object, the pronoun always comes first (L5, N19).

Im Café *In the café*

25 **Ich bin erst 10 (zehn) Minuten hier.** *I've only been here for ten minutes.* **Ich bin** can be used, since the speaker is still there.

erst zehn Minuten **Erst** is normally used for *only* or *just* before a period of time.

26 **Wollen wir ein Stück Kuchen essen?** *Shall we have (eat) a piece of cake?*

a **wollen wir . . . ?** Although **wollen** means *want to,* it is here used in making a suggestion which includes the speaker. It is rendered in English by *shall we?* whenever it is used in this sense.

b **ein Stück Kuchen essen** In English we often use *have* when speaking of something to eat or drink. In German **haben** can never be used in this sense; use **essen** or **trinken,** as appropriate, or **nehmen.**

27 **Trinkst du gern Kaffee?** In a GENERAL context this would mean *Do you like coffee?* Here, Lore is asking about Grete's liking for coffee on this occasion, so it implies *Will you have coffee?*

28 **Kaffee schadet meiner Gesundheit.** *Coffee is bad for my health.* (*Coffee harms my health.*) From the **-er** ending on **mein,** you can see that this is the dative case, feminine. **Schaden,** like **helfen** and **danken** requires its object to be in the dative case. If you think of it as *do harm* TO, it is easier to understand.

29 **Herr Ober!** *Waiter!* This is the correct way to summon any waiter in German.

30 **Was kann ich den Herrschaften bringen?** *What can I bring the ladies and gentleman?* **Herrschaften** can mean any mixture of ladies and gentlemen. The waiter thinks the man sitting at the same table must be with Lore and Grete, otherwise he would say **den Damen** not **den Herrschaften** (L2, N12).
den Herrschaften This is the dative plural, of course, since it is the indirect object of **bringen.**

31 **Und bringen Sie uns auch zwei Stück Apfelkuchen mit Sahne!** *And bring us also two pieces of apple cake with cream!* **zwei Stück:** *two pieces (of)* **Stück** is used in the singular to express a quantity of something and there is no word for *of.* Compare **zwei Glas Bier:** *two glasses of beer.* Only feminine nouns go into the plural – **zwei Tassen Kaffee:** *two cups of coffee.*

32 **Kann ich dem Herrn auch etwas bringen?** *Can I bring the gentleman something, too?* **dem Herrn** This is the dative case again, as it is the indirect object of **bringen.** Note the **-n** on **Herrn.** While it is exceptional to find any change in the noun itself, there are a few nouns which acquire an **-n** in the accusative and dative cases. **Herr** is the most common of these.

33 **Der Herr gehört nicht zu uns.** *The gentleman is not with us.*
Note that **gehört** requires **zu** when the sense is *belong* WITH
rather than *belong* TO.

34 **Oh, Entschuldigung!** *Oh, I beg your pardon!* This is the easiest way
to apologize when you have made a mistake or caused offence.

35 **Ich bekomme von Ihnen 4,20 DM (vier Mark zwanzig), bitte.** *That's*
4.20 marks you owe me, please. (I get 4.20 marks from you, please.)
von Ihnen Von is always followed by the dative case.

Part three

Geht es Ihnen gut? *Are you keeping well?*

36 **Und wie geht es Ihrer Tochter und Ihrem Sohn?** *And how are*
your daughter and son? In German *your* has to be repeated before
son, because of the different endings required.
Ihrer Tochter und Ihrem Sohn Note the dative endings on **Ihr**:
Ihrer (compare **der**) and **Ihrem** (compare **dem**).

37 **Unserer Tochter geht es auch gut,** *Our daughter is fine, too,*
Note **unserer** the dative feminine singular. The first **-er** is not an
ending, but part of the word for *our:* **unser.**

38 **Sein Autogeschäft macht ihm keinen Spaß,** *His car business gives*
(*makes*) *him no pleasure,*
ihm This is the dative of **er**:
NOMINATIVE **er**: *he*   ACCUSATIVE **ihn**: *him*   DATIVE **ihm**: *to him*

Uhrzeit und Tage *The time and the days*

39 **Morgen mittag** *Tomorrow afternoon* Sometimes **mittag** is used
instead of **nachmittag,** especially if the time referred to is not
long after twelve noon (**L5, N21b**).

40 **Nur einen Tag.** *Just one day.* A period of time in answer to a
wie lange?: *how long?* question is always expressed in the
accusative case.

Im Uhrengeschäft *In the watchmaker's shop*

41 **Zeigen Sie sie dem Kollegen hier!** *Show it to my (the) colleague*
here!
dem Kollegen Der Kollege is another of the few nouns which
acquire an **-n** or **-en** in all cases other than the nominative singular.
Automat and **Polizist** are also in this category. Compare **Herr**
(**L5, N32**).

Lektion sechs Wohnungssuche

6

Lesson six Flat hunting

What happens

In this lesson Herr and Frau Kühn go looking for a flat to rent during their stay in Munich.

In Part 1 a house agent describes his job. In Part 2 he gives the Kühns two addresses and they go to see a flat in the town and a house in the country. They decide to take the flat.

Method of indicating plural forms in vocabularies

From this lesson onwards, plurals of new nouns will be indicated in the vocabularies by showing in brackets what addition is necessary to make the noun plural. To ensure that you understand precisely what is meant, we shall give here an example of every kind of plural form, showing the bracketed addition, the plural written out in full, and a description of the change from singular to plural. Remember that the plural of **der, die** and **das** is **die.**

1 *Feminine nouns*

die Zigarette(-n)	**die Zigaretten**	(add **n** to the singular)
die Wohnung(-en)	**die Wohnungen**	(add **en** to the singular)
die Studentin(-nen)	**die Studentinnen**	(add **nen** to the singular)

2 *Masculine and neuter nouns*

der Tourist(-en)	**die Touristen**	(add **en** to the singular)
der Kunde(-n)	**die Kunden**	(add **n** to the singular)
der Herr(-en)	**die Herren**	(add **en** to the singular)
der Schlüssel(-)	**die Schlüssel**	(no change)
das Fenster(-)	**die Fenster**	(no change)
der Brief(-e)	**die Briefe**	(add **e** to the singular)
das Formular(-e)	**die Formulare**	(add **e** to the singular)
der Vater(∺)	**die Väter**	(add Umlaut to stressed vowel)
der Apfel(∺)	**die Äpfel**	(add Umlaut to stressed vowel)

6

der Gast(¨e)	die Gäste	(add Umlaut plus **e**)
der Platz(¨e)	die Plätze	(add Umlaut plus **e**)
das Kind(-er)	die Kinder	(add **er** to singular)
das Haus(¨er)	die Häuser*	(add Umlaut plus **er**)
der Mann(¨er)	die Männer	(add Umlaut plus **er**)
das Büro(-s)	die Büros	(add **s** to singular)
das Auto(-s)	die Autos	(add **s** to singular)

* N.B. Umlaut on first vowel where two occur together.

In instances where forming the plural is too complex to show in this way, the whole form is written out in full: e.g. **das Zentrum (Zentren)**.

New words in this lesson

der **Augenblick**(-e) moment
der **Dezember** December
der **Elektroherd**(-e) electric cooker
der **Kunde**(-n) customer
der **Mieter**(–) tenant
der **Monat**(-e) month
der **Strom** electricity
der **Vermieter**(–) landlord
der **Wohnungsvermittler**(–) house agent
der **Zettel**(–) note, slip of paper

die **Anzeige**(-n) advertisement
die **Besichtigung** viewing
die **Couch** couch
die **Eßecke**(-n) dining area
die **Etage**(-n) storey, floor
die **Küche**(-n) kitchen
die **Lage** situation, site
die **Lokalzeitung**(-en) local paper
die **Miete**(-n) rent
die **Sitzbank** bench-type seat
die **Stunde**(-n) hour
die **Toilette**(-n) W.C.
die **Wohnung**(-en) flat, apartment
die **Wohnungssuche** flat (house) hunting
die **Wohnungsvermittlung** house agency
die **Zeitung**(-en) newspaper

das **Angebot**(-e) offer

das **Badezimmer**(–) bathroom
das **Büro**(-s) office
das **Fenster**(–) window
das **Gesuch**(-e) request
das **Haus**(¨er) house
das **Land** country
das **Mietgesuch** accommodation wanted
das **Schlafzimmer**(–) bedroom
das **Wohnzimmer**(–) living room
das **Zentrum (Zentren)** centre

bleiben to stay
fliegen to fly
gefallen (es gefällt mir) to please (I like it)
klingen to sound
lesen (liest) to read
liegen to be (situated), to lie
schlafen (schläft) to sleep
schreiben to write
(sein) ihr seid (to be) you are (pl. form)
stehen to be (standing, situated)

besichtigen to view
danken(D) to thank
führen to lead
glauben to think, believe
hören to hear
passen (D) to suit

sagen to say
setzen to put, place
suchen to look for
vermieten to let

anbieten to offer
hereinkommen to enter

besser better
billig cheap
hoch high
klein small, little
möbliert furnished
möglich possible
neu new
ruhig quiet
schlimm bad
sonnig sunny
täglich daily
teuer expensive
unmöbliert unfurnished
viele many
vierhundert four-hundred
zufrieden content

bald soon
gleich at once
übermorgen the day after tomorrow

ganz completely
links on the left
noch mehr even more
vielleicht perhaps
weg gone
zu too

ab from

gegenüber opposite
hinter behind
neben next to
unter under
vor ago

alles everything
beide both
dir you (dat.)
ihr you (pl. fam.), her (dat.)

auch too, also
denn as, because
entweder...oder either...or
teils, teils fairly good, so-so
wenn when, if

was für? what sort of?
wie? how?

auf dem Land in the country
auf jeden Fall in any event
bei Jäger apply to Jäger
bei mir here (at my house)
das freut mich I'm glad
das ist sehr schade it is a great pity
die Wohnung gefällt mir I like the flat
guten Abend good evening
guten Morgen good morning
ich glaube ja yes, I think so
im Augenblick at the moment
im Monat per month
nach Haus home(ward)
sagen Sie mir Bescheid let me know
Sie kommen zu spät you're too late
vor einer Stunde an hour ago
zum Beispiel for example

6

Notes

Part one

1 **Ich bin von Beruf Wohnungsvermittler.** *I'm a house agent by profession.*
   Wohnungsvermittler   The meaning of this word is not precisely the same as house agent in English, since he deals with the renting of flats and houses and not with sales.

6

2 **Mein Büro liegt im Zentrum von München.** *My office is in the centre of Munich.*
liegt: *lies* **Liegen** is used instead of **sein** when the meaning is *to be situated.*

3 **Entweder bieten sie eine Wohnung an, oder sie suchen eine.**
They either have a flat to let (are offering a flat) or they are looking for one.
entweder...oder: *either...or* The two words must precede the elements which are being contrasted, in this case, the VERBS. Compare **Sie bieten entweder eine Wohnung oder ein Haus an** (the OBJECTS are contrasted) and **Entweder er oder sein Bruder ist Lehrer** (SUBJECTS contrasted). Except in the last case (contrast of SUBJECTS), if **entweder** begins the sentence, it normally causes subject-verb inversion, but **oder** like **und** and **aber** does not: **Entweder kommt er, oder er ruft an.**

4 **Wenn sie zum Beispiel ihre Wohnung vermieten wollen,** *if, for example, they want to let their flat,*
wenn **Wenn** means *if, when* (referring to a future possibility) or *whenever.* It is one of a number of words which, as you see, have an outstanding effect on word order! The verb (**wollen**) appears at the end of this part of the sentence, which, although it has a subject (**sie**) and a verb (**wollen**), does not make sense without the other part of the sentence and cannot stand alone. It is said to be dependent on the other part of the sentence, the main part, which is recognizable by the fact that it CAN stand alone. Such sentence segments, each containing a subject and verb of its own, are called CLAUSES. So far, we have dealt with sentences of one clause only, or of two completely independent clauses joined by a word such as **und** or **aber**. Sentences containing a main clause (which makes sense by itself) and one or more so-called dependent clauses (which do not) will occur quite frequently from now on, and you will find that the dependent clauses always have their verbs at the end. One of the commonest types of dependent clause is the *if* or **wenn** clause, e.g. **Wenn Sie Deutsch sprechen,:** *If you speak German,;* **Wenn ich mit dem Auto fahre,:** *If I go by car.* Note that clauses are separated from each other by commas.

5 **setze ich eine Anzeige in die Zeitung.** *I put an advertisement in the newspaper.*

a This is the main clause completing the sentence beginning **Wenn sie ihre Wohnung vermieten wollen.** Verb and subject are reversed here because the whole **wenn** clause is regarded as item one of the complete sentence, and the 'verb comes second' rule applies. There is, however, no compulsion to begin the sentence with the **wenn** clause; if the main clause comes first, there is no inversion of subject and verb: **Ich setze eine Anzeige in die Zeitung, wenn sie ihre Wohnung vermieten wollen.**

b **in die Zeitung** This is accusative case because the sense is INTO.

6 **Ich lese täglich die Lokalzeitungen.** *I read the local papers daily.* In German, an adverb (**täglich**) very often comes between the verb (**lese**) and its object (**Lokalzeitungen**) although there is no strict rule about this arrangement.

7 **Unter den Wohnungsanzeigen stehen viele Wohnungsangebote aber noch mehr Wohnungsgesuche.** *Among the Accommodation advertisements, there are many 'Flats to let' but even more 'Flats wanted'.*

a **unter den Wohnungsanzeigen** This is dative plural. **Unter** can be followed by either accusative or dative, according to whether any movement is involved or not.

b **stehen:** lit. *stand* Compare L6, N2, where *is* is rendered by **liegt.** As you can see you cannot always use a part of **sein** to translate *is, are,* etc. **Stehen** is always used when referring to something in print, e.g. **Es steht in der Zeitung:** *It's in the newspaper.*

c **noch mehr** Noch means, basically, *still, yet.* When it is used as an intensifier with expressions of quantity or comparatives (**noch viele, noch zwei, noch ein Bier, noch besser**) you have to think of the appropriate word in English – *even, more, another.*

8 **Es freut mich, wenn Mieter und Vermieter zufrieden sind.** *I'm glad if/when tenant and owner (landlord) are satisfied.*

a This sentence has two clauses, and this time the main clause comes first.

b **es freut mich:** lit. *it rejoices me* This is probably the most usual way of saying *I'm glad* and is an idiom worth learning by heart. Some phrases are more useful than others. This kind of phrase, beginning with **es,** is called an impersonal expression and you will encounter many such expressions.

c **wenn Mieter und Vermieter zufrieden sind.** Remember the verb (**sind**) goes to the end in a **wenn** clause.

57

Part two

Beim Wohnungsvermittler   *At the house agent's (house agency)*

9   **Wohnungsvermittler** is a PERSON, but when it is preceded by **bei**, the whole phrase means at his place of work, office. It is therefore permissible to use the term (in English) for the place as well as the person. Remember **beim = bei + dem.**

10   **Wir suchen eine Wohnung.** *We're looking for a flat.*
eine Wohnung   English has no equally useful equivalent. **Wohnung** just means a place to live, so it can mean a house as well as a flat in certain contexts.

11   **Was für eine Wohnung möchten Sie?** *What sort of dwelling would you like?*
was für?: *what kind of? what sort of?* This phrase needs some mental application before you use it automatically. Because of its sound other associations are a possible danger for the English learner! Another pitfall is the fact that **für** alone takes the accusative, but this has no bearing on this whole phrase. The case of the following word depends on its function in the sentence:
Was für ein Wagen ist das?: *What kind of car is that?* (nominative)
Was für einen Wagen haben Sie?: *What kind of car have you got?* (accusative)

12   **Ein Haus oder eine Etagenwohnung, möbliert oder unmöbliert?**
A house or a flat (in a block), furnished or unfurnished?

a   **Etagenwohnung**   This is the more precise word for *flat,* as long as you mean one in a block, and not just part of someone's house.

b   **unmöbliert**   It will be reassuring to find such similarities in system between German and English from time to time! The prefix **un,** in German as in English, often forms the opposite adjective or adverb.

13   **Ich weiß nicht. Lore, was gefällt dir besser?** *I don't know. Lore, what would you prefer (pleases you better)?*

a   **gefällt dir**   **Gefallen** means *to please.* Here is another way of expressing likes and preferences (**gern** and **lieber** won't serve on every occasion). Note: a) it is a vowel-changing verb; b) it is followed by the dative case (**dir** is the dative form of **du**); the person who *likes* is in the dative, i.e. is an object in the German phrase; and whatever or whoever is being liked or disliked (object in the English phrase) becomes the subject in the German phrase, e.g. **Er gefällt mir:** *I like* HIM (*he pleases me*).*;* **Ich gefalle ihm:** HE *likes* ME (*I please him*).

b **besser**   Here is another similarity between English and German: *good:* **gut,** *better:* **besser,** *best:* **best.**

14 **Können Sie uns vielleicht ein paar Adressen geben?** *Can you (could you) perhaps give us a few addresses?*

a **vielleicht**   Note that, as a rule, an adverb is as close to the verb as other rules of word order will permit.

b **ein paar:** *a few*   This phrase you already know from **ein paar Sachen:** *a few things* in Lesson 2. It remains as it is no matter what the class or case of the following noun.

15 **Ich habe im Augenblick nur eine Adresse von einer Wohnung in der Stadt und eine von einem Haus auf dem Land.** *At the moment I have only one address of a flat in town and one of a house in the country.*

a **Im Augenblick** is an idiom meaning *at present, just at the moment.* **Im** = **in** + **dem.** Note that it immediately follows the verb (**habe**) bearing out what was said in N6 of this lesson.

b **von einer Wohnung ... von einem Haus**   **Von** has various meanings. (You have already met *from.*) Here it is doing service as a possessive (address *of* a flat, *of* a house). Remember it is ALWAYS followed by the dative case. **Einer** is the dative of **eine** (feminine singular) and follows the **-er** pattern of the dative feminine singular (**der, meiner, Ihrer** – Lesson 5).

16 **Dann fahren wir zu den beiden und besichtigen sie gleich.** *Then let's go to both and take a look at (view) them right away.*

a **fahren wir**   *Let's* do something is rendered by the **wir** form.

b **zu den beiden**   This is dative plural after **zu.** **Beide:** *both* is often preceded by some part of **die** (*the* in plural).

17 **Ich schreibe Ihnen die Adressen auf einen Zettel.** *I'll write (down) the addresses on a bit of paper for you.*

a **Ihnen**   This is dative, of course, meaning *for you* in this instance. This rather friendly use of **Ihnen** is very common.

b **auf einen Zettel**   **Auf** is generally used to translate *on* or *on to.* It must be followed by the accusative here, since the writing is being put *on to* the paper.

18 **Wenn möglich, sagen Sie mir bald Bescheid.** *If possible, let me know (your decision) soon.*
sagen Sie mir Bescheid   **Bescheid** really means *decision, information, answer,* but it is sufficient to say *let me know* in

6

English. It is an idiom used on occasions when one party has to await a decision or some information from another.

Erste Besichtigung *First visit*

19 **Erste**: *first* is an ordinal number (1st, 2nd, 3rd etc.) and bears as little similarity to **eins** as *first* does to *one*. These ordinal numbers are adjectives, of course, and must have endings appropriate to the case and class of the following noun. You may have noticed from the lesson headings that the ending (**erste, zweite, vierte**) is always **-e** before a feminine noun (like **Lektion**). **Besichtigung** is also feminine. Forming ordinal from cardinal numbers is even easier in German than in English – one simply adds **-te** to the cardinal number, except for **erste**: *first* and **dritte**: *third*. Hence **vier** (*4*), **vierte** (*4th*); **fünf** (*5*), **fünfte** (*5th*).

20 **Kommen Sie bitte herein!** *Won't you come in, please!*
Kommen Sie herein! is the request or command form of the verb. **Hereinkommen** is a separable verb and **herein,** as the separable prefix, goes to the end.

21 **Ich zeige sie Ihnen.** *I'll show it to you.*
sie Ihnen   Here we have two pronoun objects, one accusative (**sie**) and one dative (**Ihnen**). When both objects are pronouns, remember, the accusative comes first (L5, N12).

22 **Und ab wann?** *And (starting) from when?*
ab wann? Ab is used in German when you are referring to a date or time of the commencement of a state of affairs which is going to last for some time, e.g. **Ab sieben Uhr bin ich frei**: *I'm free from seven o'clock onwards.*

23 **Ab dem 15. Dezember, wenn möglich.** *From the 15th of December, if possible.*
Ab is followed by the dative. **Fünfzehnte** is *fifteenth*. There is an **-n** on the ordinal number here, partly because it is dative case and partly because **dem** appears in the phrase. This expression is a stock type and you can use it with any date. You will learn more about this later.

24 **Das paßt mir gut, denn im Dezember fliege ich zu meiner Tochter nach New York.** *That suits me fine, as in December I'm flying out to (see) my daughter in New York.*

a **das paßt mir gut   Passen**: *to suit*, takes the dative case.

60

b **Denn** meaning *because, for, as,* does not have any effect on normal word order. **Im Dezember** causes inversion of **ich fliege.**

c **im Dezember** *In* any month (months are masculine) is always **im** (dative).

d **zu meiner Tochter nach New York** Both phrases imply motion in the mind of the speaker; although you might translate it *'to my daughter in New York, in New York* must be **nach New York** in German, because Frau Riemer is associating it with **ich fliege,** i.e. she thinks of New York as HER destination.

25 **Ich will drei bis vier Monate bei ihr bleiben.** *I intend to stay three to four months with her.*

a **drei bis vier Monate** This is a LENGTH of time; it answers the question *how long?* Such expressions of time are given in the accusative, e.g. **Ich bleibe einen Monat/eine Woche/einen Tag:** *I'm staying (for) a month/week/day.*

b **bei ihr:** *with her* or *at her home* **Bei** takes the dative. **Ihr** is the dative of **sie:**

	German	English
NOMINATIVE	**sie**	*she*
ACCUSATIVE	**sie**	*her*
DATIVE	**ihr**	*her*

Note once again that the two adverbial phrases – **drei bis vier Monate** and **bei ihr** - are arranged according to the time before place rule.

26 **Die Tür rechts führt ins Wohnzimmer.** *The door on the right leads into the living-room.*
ins Wohnzimmer Although no real movement is involved, the accusative is nevertheless used, because **in** meaning *into* as opposed to *in* is ALWAYS followed by the accusative.

27 **Hinter dem Wohnzimmer liegt das Schlafzimmer.** *Behind (beyond) the living-room is the bedroom.*
hinter dem Wohnzimmer Hinter (like **in, auf, an**) can be followed by either accusative or dative, and for the same reason. The dative is used here because a location is referred to (**L4, N16**).

28 **Ist die Küche hier links neben dem Wohnzimmer?** *Is the kitchen here on the left next to the living-room?*
neben dem Wohnzimmer Neben also belongs to the group which can be followed by either accusative or dative.

29 **400 (vierhundert) DM im Monat.** *400 marks a month.*

6

im **Monat**: *in the month* or *per month*, in **der Woche**: *per week, a week*, im **Jahr**: *per year, a year*.

30 **Das ist nicht zu teuer.** *That's not too dear.*
zu This is truly a multi-purpose little word. As well as translating many of the possible meanings of *to*, it also translates *too* before any adjective or adverb, e.g. **zu viel**: *too much*, **zu klein**: *too small*.

31 **Mir auch.** *So do I.* The exact translation of *so do I* will, of course, depend on the previous remark. Here it is **mir auch,** because of **gefallen.** Compare this with **Ich trinke gern Bier**: *I like beer*. **Ich auch**: *So do I*.

32 **Das freut mich.** *I'm glad (about that).* (L6, N8b) **Es freut mich** is used when there is more to follow – *I'm glad when, I'm glad that...* **Das freut mich** is used when that is all one has to say.

Zweite Besichtigung *Second visit (viewing)*

33 **Wollen Sie das Haus noch besichtigen?** *Did you want to see over the house?* The **noch** is very difficult to render in English, except by using *did* instead of *do*; Herr Pichlbauer is thinking that the house is already taken and they still want to see it.

34 **Ja, wenn Sie Zeit haben, gern.** *Yes, we'd like to, if you have time.*
wenn Sie Zeit haben Verbs in **wenn** clauses go to the end of the clause (L6, N5a). It may appear that this **wenn** clause is standing alone, but it does not make sense apart from the question to which it is the answer. Dependent clauses can stand alone only in answer to a question.

35 **Es tut mir leid, aber Sie kommen zu spät.** *I'm sorry, but you('ve) come too late.*
Sie kommen zu spät This has to be translated into English either by using the past tense or by *you* ARE *too late*. You can't use **sein**: *to be* in this phrase in German. **Kommen** is usually the appropriate verb, but not always.

36 **Vor einer Stunde war ein Herr bei mir.** *An hour ago a gentleman was here (at my house).*
a **vor einer Stunde** **Vor** means *ago* here and when used in this sense it is ALWAYS followed by the dative.
b **war** This is the past tense of **ist**.

37 **Oh, das ist aber sehr schade!** *Oh, that's a great pity.*
This is an idiom to be learnt without analysis. **Aber** is quite gratuitous here but adds flavour if nothing else (like **doch, ja,** and a few other little words).

62

38 Haben Sie vielen Dank, Herr Pichlbauer! *Thank you, Herr Pichlbauer!* This phrase is more formal than our English rendering, but not so stilted as, for instance, *Our thanks to you!*

39 Dann fahren wir jetzt nach Haus. *We'll just go home now.*

a **dann** It must on no account be assumed that **dann** means *just*. *Just* happens to suit the context here. It normally means *then, in that case.*

b **Nach Haus** means *home* as long as motion is implied (like **nach** before a town or country, **nach oben, nach rechts**). Compare with **zu Haus**: *at home.*

Welche Wohnung?   *Which flat?*

40 Welche? is the interrogative (question asking) adjective *which?* It has an **-e** (like **erste, zweite**) because **Wohnung** is feminine.

41 Ah, da seid ihr ja! *Ah, so there you are!*

seid ihr This is yet another version of *you are.* You've already learned **Sie sind** and **du bist. Ihr seid** could be described as the plural of **du bist,** which (unlike **Sie sind**) can only be used to ONE person. **Sie sind** is considered too formal to address several people with whom one is on intimate terms, so another form (the **ihr** form) is used on such occasions. It is the equivalent of the old *ye* forms in English. It is interesting that when the people addressed include some to whom the speaker would use **Sie** individually, familiarity prevails over formality, and the **ihr** form is used. **Seid** happens to be irregular: **Ihr** forms normally conform to a fixed pattern, as you will see from what follows.

42 Ihr kommt spät. *You're late.* (L6, N35)

ihr kommt This is the **ihr** form of **kommen.** One simply adds **-t** to the stem (**komm-**) of the verb.

43 Von den zwei Angeboten war das Haus schon weg. *Of the two (offers) to let, the house was already taken.*

weg This word really means *away, gone* – so in this context, *no longer available* or *taken.*

44 Renate kann auf der Couch im Wohnzimmer schlafen. *Renate can sleep on the couch (sofa) in the living-room.*

auf der Couch **Auf** requires the dative case here, since there is no movement involved.

45 Die Fenster sind groß, und die Lage ist ruhig und sonnig. *The windows are large, its (the) situation is quiet and it gets the sun.*

die Lage ist ruhig und sonnig The English version has to be

6

adapted since a straight translation would sound as if the district would be sunny while districts very near were not.

46 Die Eßecke in der Küche hat eine Sitzbank. *The dining (eating) area in the kitchen has a bench type seat.*
Eßecke: lit. *eating corner* German kitchens often have an eating area in a corner with built-in bench seating along two walls.

47 Nehmt ihr die Wohnung also? *Are you going to take the flat then?*
nehmt ihr This is the **ihr** (or familiar plural) form of **nehmen** and conforms to the rule – add **-t** to the stem (**nehm-**).

48 Ich glaube, ja. *Yes, I think so.*
A useful idiom to learn by heart. You will also hear people say just **ich glaube** without the **ja,** meaning *I think so.*

7

Lektion sieben   Im Reisebüro

Lesson seven   In the travel agency

What happens

In this lesson, plans are made for a visit to Berlin. Herbert Kühn, the son of the family, is studying in Berlin, and since he is about to become engaged, the other members of the family are particularly eager to see him and attend the engagement celebration.

In Part 1 the clerk in the travel agency talks about working there. In Part 2 the Kühns and the Pfaffingers discuss the best way to get in touch with Herbert; Herr Kühn books seats on the coach and telephones Herbert in Berlin.

New words in this lesson

der **Anruf**(-e) call (telephone)
der **Betrieb**(-e) firm, business
der **Bus**(-se) bus, coach
der **Gang**(¨e) aisle, gangway
der **Herbst** autumn
der **Junge**(-n) boy, son
der **Liegesitz**(-e) tip-back seat

der **November** November
der **Sohn**(¨e) son
der **Sommer** summer
der **Tag**(-e) day
der **Winter** winter
der **Zug**(¨e) train

die Angestellte(-n) employee, (female)
die Fahrkarte(-n) ticket
die Jahreszeit(-en) season
die Person(-en) person
die Reise(-n) journey
die Ruhepause(-n) break, pause
die Saison(-s) season
die Stewardeß(-ssen) hostess
die Tageszeit(-en) time of day
die Verlobung(-en) engagement
die Vermittlung(-en) operator
die Woche(-n) week

das Ende(-n) end
das Fernamt long distance telephone exchange
das Ferngespräch(-e) long-distance call
das Frühjahr spring
das Gespräch(-e) conversation telephone call
das Jahr(-e) year
das Reisebüro(-s) travel agency
das Schiff(-e) boat
das Skilaufen skiing
das Studentenheim(-e) students' hostel, hall of residence
das Wetter weather

empfehlen to recommend
(haben) hätten Sie gern? (to have) would you like?
(müssen) ihr müßt (to have to) you have to
(sein) wäre es? (to be) would it be?
sitzen to sit
stattfinden to take place
verlassen to leave
werden (er wird) to get, to become

besuchen to visit
buchen to book
grüßen to greet, give regards to
machen to have, take
reisen to travel
telephonieren(D) to telephone
versorgen to look after

abholen to collect
anfangen to begin, start

anmelden to place, book

sich freuen auf to look forward to

euch you (acc. and dat.)

beliebt popular
bequem comfortable
einfach easy, simple
euer, eure your
frei vacant
nächst next
schwer difficult
siebte seventh

abends in the evening
heutzutage nowadays
morgens in the morning
nachts by night
nun now
tagsüber during the day

doch surely
ganz genau exactly
kaum hardly
nämlich namely, because, you see
riesig immensely
schnell soon, quickly
schon certainly
wieder again
zweimal twice

warum? why?
welcher? which?

an on
auf in
beim with the
in at
mit by, in
seit for, since
über about
zu at

als as
daß that
soviel as far as

65

7

auf welchen Namen? in what name?
bis bald! see you soon
dieser this, that
es wird meiner Frau schlecht my wife gets ill

in diesem Sommer this summer
nicht ganz einfach not so easy
wie as
wir dürfen nicht we cannot
zu Ende over

Notes
Part one

1 **Ich arbeite jetzt seit zwei Jahren als Angestellte in einem Reisebüro.** *I've been working for two years now as a clerk in a travel agency.*

a **seit zwei Jahren** Seit means *since* and always requires the dative. This is the dative plural, which nearly always adds -n. In *have been doing something* expressions followed by a period of time, **seit** with the dative or **schon** with the accusative are normal, e.g. **Ich warte schon eine Viertelstunde:** *I've been waiting now for a quarter of an hour.* **Wir wohnen seit vier Monaten hier:** *We've been living here for four months now.*

b **als Angestellte** Als has other meanings, but it is always used for *in the capacity* or *role of*. **Angestellte** means someone who is *employed*, so it is really an adjective and can be either masculine or feminine. This is the feminine version. **Angestellte** has come to mean a clerk/clerical worker as opposed to someone on the shop floor or an executive.

2 **Dieses Reisebüro gibt Auskunft über Reisen mit dem Zug, dem Schiff und dem Flugzeug.** *This travel agency gives information about journeys by train, ship and aeroplane.*

a **dieses Reisebüro** Dies- plus the appropriate ending is the word for *this* or *that*. It follows the **der/die/das** pattern of endings precisely – **dieser/diese/dieses.** Büro is neuter.

b **Auskunft über Reisen** *About* is **über** plus accusative case. **Eine Reise** is a longer trip away from home, usually including a stay somewhere. Compare L4, N27a.

3 **Auch Busreisen sind zu allen Jahreszeiten sehr beliebt.** *Coach trips are also very popular in all seasons.*
zu allen Jahreszeiten: lit. *at all times of year* **Alle:** *all* follows the **die** (plural) pattern – hence the dative plural -n (after **zu**).

4 **Die Herbstsaison ist nun zu Ende,** *The autumn season is now over,*
die Herbstsaison Der Herbst (*harvest*) means *autumn*, but **Saison** is added when the meaning is the business or trade carried out in that season.

66

5 aber eine Ruhepause gibt es in unserem Betrieb kaum. *but in our business there's hardly any (a) slack season (break).*

a **Es gibt** has an object **eine Ruhepause**, accusative. See L3, N4a.

b **Kaum:** *scarcely, hardly,* is often used to make a negative less absolute, so the translation must be adapted accordingly. *Not really* will serve in most instances, e.g. **Haben Sie Zeit? Kaum:** *Have you time? Not really.*

6 Jetzt im November fängt die Wintersaison an. *Now, in November, the winter season begins.*

fängt die Wintersaison an **Anfangen** means *begin.* Separable verbs follow the general rule about the verb standing second. Note that **anfangen** is a vowel-changing verb, acquiring an Umlaut in the **du** and **er** forms.

7 Wie fast alle Leute heutzutage mache auch ich zweimal im Jahr Urlaub. *Like nearly everyone nowadays, I too take a holiday (go on holiday) twice a year.*

a **wie** Till now you have met **wie** in questions, meaning *how?* It also means *like* or *as.*

b **mache auch ich zweimal im Jahr Urlaub** **Urlaub machen:** *to go on holiday* is treated almost like a separable verb, though it is two words. **Urlaub** goes to the end of the sentence.

c **zweimal im Jahr** You already know **einmal:** *one time, once.* Any *number of times* is easy to translate: one simply adds **-mal** to the number, e.g. **viermal:** *four times,* **zehnmal:** *ten times.*

8 In diesem Sommer war ich in Italien; *I was in Italy this summer;*

a **in diesem Sommer** She means *last summer,* of course. Time WHEN can be rendered by either dative or accusative and the correct choice can be rather subtle. Take it as a general rule that if **in** is used it must be followed by the dative. There are certain phrases that are always accusative, e.g. **jeden Tag:** *every day;* **voriges Jahr:** *last year;* **vorige Woche:** *last week.*

b **war ich** In Lesson 6 (N36) you met **war ein Herr bei mir.** You can see that the **ich** form is the same.

9 und im Frühjahr werde ich wieder zum Skilaufen nach Österreich fahren. *and in the spring I shall be going to Austria again for the skiing.*

a **werde ich ... fahren** This is, in fact, the future tense, which is rarely required. She could have said **fahre ich** without being misunderstood. However, you must be acquainted with it, and it presents no difficulty at all. As you see, it is in two parts (as in

English): an auxiliary verb (**werden**) plus the infinitive. The word order is exactly the same as you would use with **müssen** or **wollen** + infinitive. **Werden** is a verb in its own right, meaning *become,* but when used with a completing infinitive it means *shall* or *will.* As it happens, it is a vowel-changing verb with an irregularity in the **du** form: **ich werde, du wirst, er wird.**

  b **zum Skilaufen nach Österreich** Adverbial phrases of PLACE are always last.

  c **zum Skilaufen** **Skilaufen** is the verb *to ski.* Any infinitive can be used as a noun simply by giving it a capital letter and a **das** classification (like English – *ing: hunting, fishing,* etc.).

10 **Ich freue mich schon darauf.** *I'm already looking forward to it.*

  a **ich freue mich** This is called a REFLEXIVE verb, and **mich** is here a REFLEXIVE pronoun. Reflexive pronouns are used where the subject (**ich**) and the object (**mich**) are the same person or thing. You are familiar with reflexive verbs in English (*I wash* MYSELF) where the reflexive pronouns end in *-self/selves.* Unfortunately there are many verbs which are reflexive in German but not in English, so they just have to be learnt. **Ich freue mich auf** + accusative always means *I'm looking forward to* something or *I'm happy about* something.

  b **darauf** **Auf** is part of the verb phrase in the previous note, and when the object is IT instead of a noun (i.e. the holiday in Austria), you can combine **auf** with **da** (standing for IT). To avoid the awkward pronunciation **da auf** an **r** is inserted. **Da** can be combined with **in, an, zu, über** and several other words in the same way.

Part two

Gespräch über den Sohn *Conversation about the son*

11 **wann wollt ihr deinen Bruder in Berlin besuchen?** *when do you intend visiting (to visit) your brother in Berlin?*
    wollt ihr The familiar plural (**ihr** form) of modal verbs follows the usual pattern. The **ihr** refers to Renate and her parents.

12 **Soviel ich weiß, findet die Verlobung am 6. Dezember statt.** *As far as I know, the engagement takes place (is) on the 6th December.*

  a **soviel ich weiß** This phrase is so like the English it will present no difficulty. It is, of course, a dependent clause, since it has a verb and subject and as it begins the sentence, the next word will be the verb in the main clause. **Soviel** means literally *so/as much.*

b **findet die Verlobung am 6. Dezember statt**   **Stattfinden** is a separable verb. Verb and subject are reversed because the dependent clause is the first item in the sentence.

c **am 6. (sechsten) Dezember** *On* any date is **am +** the number (6 = **sechs**) with **-ten** added (**sechsten, vierten, zweiten**) (L6, N23). One need only WRITE the figure and a full stop, however (**6.**).

13 Warum telephoniert ihr ihm denn nicht? *Why don't you phone him then?*

ihm   **Telephonieren** takes the dative.

14 Es ist schwer, ihn anzurufen. *It is difficult to telephone him.* (L4, N5). **Es ist +** an adjective plus a verb requires **zu** followed by the infinitive, when the verb phrase could be substituted for IT. (*To telephone him is hard.*)

anzurufen   When the verb happens to be separable, notice that **zu** is sandwiched between the separable prefix and the main part of the verb.

15 Ihr wißt doch, daß er in einem Studentenheim wohnt. *You know that he lives in a students' hostel.*

a **ihr wißt**   The infinitive is **wissen,** so you can see that the **ihr** form is regular. It requires the ß because it is a short syllable before a **t.** Remember you don't have to use the ß but you must be able to recognize it. Note **ss** in **wissen** (not ß) because **i** is a short sound, and another vowel, **e,** follows (L3, N23a).

b **daß er in einem Studentenheim wohnt** (L6, N4)   **Daß** and **wenn** are probably the two most common words beginning dependent clauses. **Daß** also sends the verb (**wohnt**) to the end of the clause. Do not confuse **daß** (meaning *that*) followed by a whole statement of fact and **dies-** or **das** (also meaning *that*) followed by a noun:

Dieses Reisebüro ist sehr gut.

Das ist unser Reisebüro.

Ich weiß, daß das Reisebüro sehr gut ist.

16 An welchen Tagen ist er immer zu Haus? *On which days is he always at home?*

an welchen Tagen? (L6, N40)   The basis is **welch-** and it follows the **der** pattern (like **dies-:** *this/that*) as regards endings.

Welchen is the dative plural, following the rule with **an** meaning *on* a date.

17 Tagsüber ist er selten zu Haus, und auch abends ist es nicht ganz einfach. *During the day he is rarely at home and in the evenings it isn't quite simple either.*

auch ... nicht: lit. *also not* Taken together, the English translation is usually *either* or *neither.*

18 Dann müßt ihr euer Gespräch beim Fernamt anmelden. *Then you must give notice of your call at the long-distance Exchange.*

euer This is the word for *your* when you are addressing people in the familiar plural – **ihr.** It has precisely the same endings as all the other possessives **(mein, sein, Ihr,** etc.), e.g:

euer Bruder: *your brother* **eure Schwester:** *your sister*
euer Haus: *your house* **eure Kinder:** *your children.*

Note that the second **e** present in the nominative singular masculine and neuter drops out when it acquires any ending.

19 Wir dürfen nicht mehr lange warten, *We can't (mustn't) wait (delay) any longer,*

a wir dürfen nicht Remember, **dürfen** is another modal verb (like **wollen, müssen, können, sollen**) meaning *to be allowed to* or *to be permitted to do something.* It is often rendered in English by *can.* This is quite correct, so long as it is not confused with **können:** *to be able to.* It is very important for English learners of German to beware of the translation of I MUSTN'T into German: **Ich darf nicht warten:** *I mustn't wait.*
Ich muß nicht warten: *I don't have to wait.*

b nicht mehr lange Strictly speaking, the meaning of this idiomatic phrase is *not long now,* e.g. **Es dauert nicht mehr lange:** *It won't be long now.*

20 denn nächste Woche wollen wir schon reisen. *for we want to travel no later than next week.*

a nächste Woche (L7, N8a) This is a 'time when' expression in the accusative.
nächstes Jahr: *next year* **nächsten Monat:** *next month*

b schon It is sometimes difficult to get just the right meaning of **schon** in English. *No later than* is the nearest equivalent here.

Busplätze buchen *Booking coach seats*

21 Ich empfehle Ihnen eine Fahrt mit dem Bus. *I recommend (to you) a trip by coach.*

ich empfehle Ihnen **Empfehlen** (like **danken** and **helfen**) always takes the dative.

22 **Für wann hätten Sie die Plätze gern?** *For when would you like the seats?*

hätten gern This is a form of **haben** called the subjunctive, which is frequently used coupled with **gern** in this kind of courtesy phrase instead of **möchten** (which is, in fact, also subjunctive).

23 **Wäre es möglich, am 26. November zu fahren?** *Would it be possible to travel on the 26th November?*

This is the same kind of contruction as in L4, N5 and L7, N14.

wäre Wäre is the subjunctive of **sein**. Instead of just saying **ist es möglich,** Herr Kühn uses the more courteous form **wäre.** You will meet the subjunctive in many courtesy phrases.

24 **Für drei. Zu welcher Tageszeit fahren die Busse?** *For three. At what time of day do the buses go?*

zu welcher Tageszeit Welcher is dative singular feminine as **zu** requires the dative and **Zeit** is feminine singular.

25 **und kommen morgens um 9 Uhr in Berlin an.** *and arrive in Berlin at 9 a.m.*

morgens This is analogous to **abends** and therefore means *in the mornings* (i.e. *every morning*).

26 **Wir fahren also nachts?** *We travel by night then?*

nachts This word usually means *at night,* implying EVERY *night.* Here it simply means *by night.*

27 **Und eine Stewardeß versorgt Sie auf der Fahrt.** *And a stewardess looks after you on the journey.*

auf der Fahrt This is the dative case since no movement is implied.

28 **Dann hätte ich gern diesen Fensterplatz.** *Then I'd like that window-seat.*

a **hätte ... gern** (L7, N22)

b **diesen Fensterplatz** Platz is masculine singular and the accusative is required, so **-en** is added to **dies-.**

29 **Es wird meiner Frau nämlich schnell schlecht.** *You see, my wife soon (quickly) gets ill.*

es wird meiner Frau schlecht This is very idiomatic German. **Schlecht** really means *bad,* but in this phrase, *sick* or *ill.* **Wird** is used here in its basic meaning (*to become*) and **meiner Frau** is dative case. Very often you will meet this kind of phrase without the **es** as subject, e.g. **Mir wird schlecht:** *I get sick;* **Mir ist schlecht:** *I am sick/ill.*

30 **Und der Platz neben ihr ist auch noch frei.** *And the seat beside her is also still vacant.*

neben ihr **Neben:** *beside, near, next to* belongs to the group of words (**an, auf, hinter, in**) which can be followed by either accusative or dative, depending on whether movement is implied or not. Since none is implied here, the dative is used.

31 **Auf welchen Namen kann ich buchen?** *In what name can I make the reservation?*

auf welchen Namen This is the stock phrase on such occasions and is in the accusative case. **Der Name** (nominative) is one of the small group of nouns which acquires an **-n** in all cases in the singular except the nominative (like **Herr, Automat,** etc.).

32 **Ich möchte die Karten morgen abholen.** *I'd like to collect the tickets tomorrow.*

abholen You have already met **holen** *to fetch* in Lesson 3. **Abholen** is used when the meaning is rather *to collect/pick up/meet* (by arrangement), e.g. **Ich hole Sie vom Flughafen ab:** *I'll meet you at the airport.*

Ferngespräch *Trunk call*

33 **Hallo, hören Sie?** *Hello, can you hear (me)?*
hören Sie We would say 'CAN *you hear?*' German (more logically) uses the present tense (*do you hear?* or *are you hearing?*).

34 **Herbert, bist du es?** *Herbert, is that you?* (*are you it?*)
Remember **Das bin ich:** *that's me* (L1, N21). The verb form matches the person being identified (**du**) in such phrases, and **das** or **es** is the complement.

35 **Ich glaube schon.** *I believe so.* Herbert is being funny, even slightly sarcastic here. This is the force of **schon** in this instance.

36 **Junge, wie geht's dir?** *How are you, my boy?*
  a **Junge** To say **mein Junge** would be either too formal or somewhat peremptory in German.
  b **wie geht's dir?** This is an abbreviation of **Wie geht es dir?** and is very commonly used.

37 **Wir werden dich bald besuchen, dich und Eva.** *We shall be visiting you soon, you and Eva.*
werden ... besuchen This is the future tense (L7, N9a) compound of **werden** plus the infinitive of the verb (**besuchen**).

The infinitive is placed at the end of the sentence or clause, as usual – **dich und Eva** really comes as an afterthought.

38 **Am 27. November kommen wir zu euch.** *We're coming to you on the 27th November.*

zu euch Euch is the dative of **ihr**: *you* (familiar plural).

39 **Wir schreiben euch alles ganz genau.** *We'll write to you with all the details.*

a **Euch** is the dative of **ihr**: *you*. Herr Kühn is including Eva, Herbert's fiancée.

b **alles ganz genau**: lit. *'everything quite precisely'* **Ganz genau** is a very common idiom for *exactly* or *precisely*.

40 **Also, bis bald!** *Well, see you soon.*

Bis is used in such expressions where English uses *see you*, e.g. **Bis heute abend**: *See you this evening.* Remember, however, that **bis** really means *till* or *until*.

41 **Wir freuen uns schon riesig auf euch.** *We're looking forward tremendously to seeing you.*

a **wir freuen uns** ... **auf euch** (L7, N10a) Uns is really a reflexive pronoun here. **Auf** is part of the verb phrase (but NOT a separable prefix) and takes the accusative in this idiom. **Euch** is the accusative as well as the dative of **ihr**: *you*. Note that this phrase is adequate in German, whereas English has to add *seeing*.

b **riesig** This word denotes great enthusiasm and adds a touch of colour to the utterance. Use it sparingly, however.

42 **Wir auch. Grüßt alle in München!** *So are we. Regards to everyone in Munich!*

a **wir auch**: *we too* – implying *we are looking forward to seeing you too.*

b **grüßt** This is, in fact, the request form of the familiar plural, and as you see, identical with the statement form **ihr grüßt**. One simply drops the **ihr**.

Part three

Was für ein Haus? *What kind of house?*

43 **gegenüber dem Stadtpark.** *opposite the city park.* **Gegenüber** is always followed by the dative case (like **bei, mit, zu, von, seit, nach**).

7 Welcher Zug? *Which train?*

44 Hier an diesem vor uns. *Here at this one in front of us.*
vor uns Vor here means *in front of.* You have encountered it
meaning *ago* (**L6, 36a**), so it can refer to time and place. When it
refers to place, it can be followed by either dative, or accusative.
When it refers to time, it is always followed by the dative.

8 **Lektion acht   Im Kaufhaus**

Lesson eight   In the department store

What happens

The Kühns are shopping for presents for Herbert and Eva, and for
the Pfaffingers.
   In Part 1 the girl at the shop's information desk complains about
the range of questions she is expected to answer. In Part 2 Frau
Kühn and Renate buy a present for Herbert's fiancée, Eva, and Herr
Kühn buys a belt and a briefcase. They also buy a set of tumblers
for Grete Pfaffinger.

New words in this lesson·

der **Arbeitsplatz**(¨e) place of work
der **Geschmack** taste
der **Gürtel**(–) belt
der **Informationsstand**(¨e) enquiry desk
der **Kunststoff**(-e) synthetics, plastics
der **Preis**(-e) price
der **Saft**(¨e) juice
der **Stand**(¨e) stall, stand
der **Stuhl**(¨e) chair
der **Unterschied**(-e) difference

die **Abteilung**(-en) department
die **Auswahl** selection
die **Bedienung** service
die **Blume**(-n) flower
die **Figur** figure

die **Fremdsprache**(-n) foreign language
die **Haut** skin
die **Idee**(-n) idea
die **Kasse**(-n) cash desk
die **Kollegmappe**(-n) briefcase
die **Lederware**(-n) leather article
die **Locke**(-n) curl
die **Rechnung**(-en) bill, invoice
die **Seide**(-n) silk
die **Tasche**(-n) bag
die **Textilabteilung**(-en) textiles dept.
die **Verkäuferin**(-nen) sales girl

das **Alter** age
das **Auge**(-n) eye
das **Ehepaar**(-e) married couple
das **Erdgeschoß**(-sse) ground floor

74

das Geschenk(-e) gift, present
das Haar(-e) hair
das Haushaltsgerät(-e) household utensils
das Kaufhaus("er) department store
das Krokodilleder crocodile skin
das Leder leather
das Porzellan china, porcelain
das Saftservice set of tumblers
das Seidentuch("er) silk scarf
das Service set
das Tuch("er) scarf
(das) Weihnachten Christmas

behalten to keep
denken an to think of
(sollen) ich soll (shall, should) I should

bedienen to serve
bezahlen to pay
parken to park
passen zu (D) to go with, match
wählen to choose

einpacken to wrap up

sich befinden to be (situated)
sich beschweren to complain
sich entschließen to make up one's mind
sich erkundigen nach (D) to enquire after
sich wundern to be surprised

achte eighth
alt old
andere other
dunkel dark
echt pure
hart hard
Hundert(e) hundred(s)
jeder every, each

lockig wavy
mehrere several
modern modern
rund round
schlank slim
seiden of silk
todmüde dead-tired
verschieden various

blau blue
bunt multi-coloured
einfarbig of one colour
grün green
rot red

aus of, made of
in at
nach according to, in keeping with
oben upstairs
unten downstairs
zwischen between

besonders especially
bloß I wonder
ganz entirely
mehr more
sicher certainly

dafür in return for that
das stimmt that's true
dazu in addition
dort drüben over there
eine so such a
gar nicht not at all
und so weiter (usw.) et cetera (etc.)
wenn if
wessen? whose?
wie macht man es bloß? just how does one do it?
zu Weihnachten for Christmas

Notes

Part one

1 **Sie befinden sich am Informationsstand eines großen Münchner**

8

Kaufhauses. *You are at the enquiry desk of a large Munich department store.*

a Sie befinden sich: lit. *you find yourself* This is a reflexive verb and **sich** is the reflexive pronoun for *you*. Reflexive pronouns are easy, because **sich** is the only new one you have to learn. It is used also with **er, sie** and **es**. The others are all the same as the personal pronouns in the accusative case: **mich, dich, uns, euch.**

b eines großen Münchner Kaufhauses Here is the LAST case you have to learn! It is called the genitive and is, in fact, what we call the POSSESSIVE case in English. Its forms and uses are so similar to English that it should cause you little trouble. Think of a phrase like *the man's hat* or *Mary's scarf* and you see immediately why it is called the possessive case. And even the **s** is also the German way of showing possession, at least in the masculine and neuter (though without the apostrophe). Sometimes, however, the method of adding *'s* is clumsy. In English one would not say *the department store's enquiry desk,* but *the enquiry desk of the department store.* So *of* as well as *'s* can be a signal of the genitive. Like the other cases, it has distinctive endings on **ein, der,** and other words which follow the same patterns: in the masculine and neuter this ending is **-s** or **-es** (**des, eines, dieses, unseres,** etc.). You will have noticed, however, that there is a similar ending on the noun itself – **Kaufhause*s*.** If there is an adjective as well as **eines** or some similar word, it ends in **-en (großen).** Adjectives formed from names of towns (**Münchner, Frankfurter**) never change.

2 Dieser runde Stand im Erdgeschoß ist mein täglicher Arbeitsplatz. *This circular stand on the ground floor is my daily place of work.*

a dieser runde Stand Dies- requires the nominative masculine singular ending, showing that **Stand** has a **der** classification and is the subject of the sentence, hence **dies*er*.** The adjective *round* is **rund,** and if it is placed BEFORE the thing it describes, it must conform to a certain pattern as regards endings. There are two different sets of endings for adjectives, depending on whether the adjective stands alone before the noun, or there is a **der** word (**der/die/das/dieser/welcher/jeder**) or an **ein** word (**ein/klein/ mein/dein/unser** etc.) before it. (See Appendix 1.) If the phrase containing the adjective is nominative and a **der** word is there in front of it, the ending is always **-e**, as it is here.

b ist mein täglicher Arbeitsplatz Here, the phrase containing the

76

adjective is nominative, but there is an **ein** word in front, namely **mein,** and you see that the ending is -er, because **Arbeits-platz** is masculine. You have become familiar with -er as a nominative masculine 'signal', and when there is an **ein** word before the adjective, the -er is put on to the adjective. Compare:

dieser **runde Stand; d**er **tägliche Arbeitsplatz** with
ein runder **Stand; mein täglich**er **Arbeitsplatz**

3 **Jeden Tag sitze ich viele Stunden auf diesem harten Stuhl hier**
Every day I sit for many hours on this hard chair here

a **jeden Tag**   This is a 'time when' phrase always given in the accusative. **Jeder, jede, jedes:** *each* or *every,* is a **der** word.

b **auf diesem harten Stuhl**   This is the dative after **auf** (no movement involved). There is a **der** word (**diesem**) before the adjective, but it is not nominative as in N2a above. This form of the adjective ending in -en is the only other ending possible (besides -e) when a **der** word appears before the adjective. This, then, completes the set of possible adjective endings after a **der** word. There are five instances where the ending is -e: the three singular nominatives (**der, die, das**) and the accusative singular, feminine and neuter (which are always the same as the nominative). Otherwise, the ending after a **der** word is ALWAYS -en.

4 **und beantworte Hunderte von Fragen, zum Beispiel:** *and answer hundreds of questions, for example:*

a **Hunderte**   This has a capital H because it is a noun.

b **zum Beispiel**   As in English, this phrase is so commonly used that it has an abbreviated form, **z. B.**

5 **Wo kann man hier parken? oder Wo befinden sich Haushalts-geräte und so weiter?** *Where can one park here? or Where are (located) household utensils and so on?*
und so weiter   This is the German equivalent of *et cetera* (*etc.*) and also has an abbreviated form, **usw.**

6 **Die eine erkundigt sich nach den verschiedenen Abteilungen, die andere sucht ihre Kinder,** *One enquires about the various departments, the other is looking for her children,*

a **die eine ... die andere**   These are given **die** classifications here, but the same words could be used with **der,** — **eine** and **andere** being adjectives (though used as nouns) and having the -e ending.

b **erkundigt sich nach:** lit. *informs herself about*   **Sich** is the reflexive pronoun used with **sie:** *she* (L8, N1a).

c **nach den verschiedenen Abteilungen** This is dative plural after **nach. Verschieden** is the adjective *various.* **-en** is added according to the rule in **L8, N3b.**

7 **und der dritte beschwert sich über schlechte Bedienung.** *and the third complains about bad service.*

a **beschwert sich** Remember that many verbs are reflexive in German which are not so in English. **Sich** is the reflexive pronoun used with **er** (**L8, N1a** and **N6b**).

b **über schlechte Bedienung** This is the accusative feminine, and this time the adjective stands alone (no **der** or **ein** word preceding). When this happens, you may take it as a rule with two exceptions (See Appendix **1c.**) that the adjective has the SAME ENDING as a **der** word would have if it were there:
e.g. **über dies*e* Bedienung über schlecht*e* Bedienung**

8 **Dazu muß ich mehrere Fremdsprachen sprechen.** *In addition, I have to speak several foreign languages.*
mehrere This is accusative plural, therefore the ending is **-e** (**L8, N7b**).

9 **Und Sie können mir glauben, daß ich jeden Abend immer todmüde bin.** *And I can assure you that every night I'm always dead tired.*
Und Sie können mir glauben: lit. *and you can believe me*
Glauben takes the dative of the person to be believed. *Believe me!:* **Glauben Sie *mir*!** *I don't believe you:* **Ich glaube *Ihnen* nicht.**

Part two

In der Textilabteilung *In the drapery department*

10 **Können Sie uns ein hübsches Seidentuch zeigen?** *Can you show us a nice silk scarf?*
ein hübsches Seidentuch Seidentuch is neuter and this is the accusative (object of the sentence). As with **mein täglich*er* Arbeitsplatz** (**L8, N2b**), the ending which would appear on **der/das** is TRANSFERRED to the adjective:
da*s* hübsche Seidentuch de*r* tägliche Arbeitsplatz
ein hübsch*es* Seidentuch mein täglich*er* Arbeitsplatz.

11 **Ja sicher. Wir haben eine große Auswahl an seidenen Tüchern.** *Yes, certainly. We have a large selection of silk scarves.*

a **eine große Auswahl** This is uncomplicated. Since the ending on **die** is the same as on **eine,** the adjective will be the same with both.

b **Auswahl an seidenen**   **Auswahl an** + dative is how one says *choice of* or *selection of.* **Seiden** is the basic adjective *silk.* It stands alone, so it must show the same ending as dative plural of **der,** that is **-en,** hence **seidenen** (L8, N7b).

12 **An was für ein Tuch denken Sie, ein einfarbiges oder ein buntes?** *What kind of scarf have you in mind, a plain (one-coloured) one or a multi-coloured one?* **ein einfarbiges oder ein buntes**   The word **Tuch** is omitted from both phrases, but nevertheless understood, so the adjectives behave exactly as if **Tuch** were there. The **-s** of **das** (which is not there) must appear on the adjectives, exactly as in **N10** above.

13 **Dieses rote mit grünen und blauen Blumen paßt zu vielen Sachen.** *This red one with green and blue flowers goes with lots of things.*

a **dieses rote**   Again, **Tuch** is omitted, but it makes no difference. **Dieses** is a **der** word, and shows the **-s** ending of **das,** so the adjective requires an **-e** only (L8, N3b).

b **mit grünen und blauen Blumen**   Dative is required after **mit,** and so adjectives must show dative plural ending **-en,** (L8, N11b).

c **paßt zu vielen Sachen**   **Passen zu** + dative means *to go with, match.* **Viele:** *many,* requires the dative plural ending **-n.**

14 **Renate, ich sehe, du hast guten Geschmack.** *Renate, I see you have good taste.* A comma is required after **ich sehe,** because what follows is another clause. It is really a **daß** clause without the **daß,** therefore the verb is in its usual place. In speech particularly one tends to avoid using **daß.** **Guten Geschmack** is accusative masculine (**den**) – therefore **gut** requires the **-en** ending, (L8, N7b).

15 **Dafür ist es aber auch echte Seide aus Indien.** *But for that (price) one is after all getting (it is after all) pure silk from India.* **echte Seide**   **Seide** is feminine, therefore **echt** requires an **-e** (L8, N7b).

16 **Ich glaube, das wird Eva auch gefallen.** *I think Eva will like it (that) too.* (Another avoidance of a **daß** clause; note the comma after **glaube.**) **das wird Eva auch gefallen:** *that will please Eva too.* This is the future tense construction with **wird** plus the infinitive at the end. Remember **gefallen** takes the dative (here **Eva**), but this rarely shows with proper names.

17   **Lederwaren**   **Das Leder:** *leather;* **die Waren:** *goods* (*wares*)
Waren very often forms the second part of such compound nouns. The first part of it is the name of the material from which the goods are made.

18   **Ich kann mich nicht entschließen.** *I can't make up my mind* (*decide*). **Sich entschließen** is another verb which is reflexive in German but not in English. **Mich** here, is a reflexive pronoun. Notice the word order here. Normally, the reflexive pronoun appears directly after the verb:
Sie befinden *sich.*   **Die eine erkundigt** *sich.*   **Ich freue** *mich.*
but with a modal verb construction it comes after the modal verb:
Ich kann *mich* **nicht entschließen.**
Sie müssen *sich* **nach dem Preis erkundigen.**
Man darf *sich* **nicht beschweren.**

19   **Soll ich den Gürtel aus Krokodilleder kaufen oder diese braune Kollegmappe?** *Shall I* (*should I*) *buy the crocodile leather belt or this brown briefcase?*

a   **aus Krokodilleder**   *Made of* is **aus:**
    aus Leder: *leather*   **aus Seide:** *silk*   **aus Glas:** *glass*

b   **diese braune Kollegmappe**   (accusative feminine). **Diese** shows the **die** ending, so **braun** only requires an **-e** (L8, N3b).

c   **Kollegmappe**   This word needs a little explanation. It means literally, *college folder,* and is applied more to the type of zip fastening case one carries under the arm than to the more elaborate **Aktentasche** which is much larger and is carried by a handle.

20   **Im Preis ist kein großer Unterschied zwischen den beiden.**
There is no great difference in (*the*) *price between the two.*

a   **kein großer Unterschied**   This is nominative masculine. **Kein** does NOT show the **-er** ending of **der,** so the **-er** is added to **groß** (L8, N2b).

b   **zwischen den beiden**   **Beide:** *both* is often used when in English we would use *two.* If THE (i.e. any form of **die**) is there, use **beide** rather than **zwei,** e.g. **die beiden Herren:** *the two gentlemen.*
    Zwischen: *between* can be followed by either the dative or accusative. No movement is involved here, so it is dative (plural).

21   **Das stimmt. Wissen Sie was? Ich nehme beides.** *That's true. Do you know what? I'll take both.*

beides This is a neuter singular ending, and when this is used in preference to the plural **beide,** the collective unity of the two things is being stressed. This is a subtlety, however, and you should not concern yourself too much with subtleties at present.

22 **Dann kann Ihr Sohn wählen, welches ihm besser gefällt.** *Then your son can choose whichever (thing) he prefers (likes better).*

a **welches** The neuter form **welches** is used because **Gürtel** is masculine and **Mappe** is feminine.

b **welches ihm besser gefällt** The verb goes to the end because this is a dependent clause – an indirect question, in fact. One must distinguish in German between
Welches gefällt ihm besser?: *Which* DOES *he like better?* and **welches ihm besser gefällt:** *which he likes better.*

23 **Wenn ihm dieser Gürtel nicht gefällt, behalte ich ihn.** *If he doesn't like this belt, I'll keep it.*
behalte ich ihn The verb is the first word in the main clause, because the other clause comes first and counts as item one of the whole sentence (**L6, N5a**).

24 **Und wenn seine alte Kollegmappe noch gut genug ist, bekommt meine Tochter die neue zu Weihnachten.** *And if his old briefcase is still in good enough condition, my daughter will get the new one for Christmas.*

a **die neue** **Kollegmappe** is omitted, but the adjective agrees with it. **Die** shows the accusative feminine ending, but the adjective requires an **-e** anyway (**L8, N3b**).

b **zu Weihnachten** This is idiomatic, meaning *on the occasion of Christmas.*

25 **Dann kann ich Ihnen also die beiden Sachen einpacken?** *So I can wrap the two things up for you then?*
beiden **-en** is the usual ending after a **der** word, except for the five instances where it is **-e** (**L8, N3b**).

26 **Hier ist Ihre Rechnung. Bezahlen Sie bitte an der Kasse dort drüben!** *Here is your bill. Please pay at the cash desk over there!*

In der Geschenkabteilung unten *Downstairs in the gift department*

27 **erste Verkäuferin** *first sales assistant,* or *sales* GIRL since this is feminine. The masculine form is **Verkäufer.** When both forms exist, the feminine is frequently the masculine form with **-in**

8

added: **der Verkäufer**   **die Verkäuferin**
    der Student   **die Studentin**

28 **War das nicht ein nettes Ehepaar?** *Wasn't that a nice (married)*
couple?

ein nettes Ehepaar **die Ehe:** *marriage,* **das Paar:** *pair, couple*
Nett requires an -es ending because there is no **das** or word like
das preceding it (L8, N10):
das nette Ehepaar **ein nettes Ehepaar.**

29 **Er hatte schöne schwarze Augen und dunkles lockiges Haar,**
nicht wahr? *He had lovely black eyes and dark curly hair,*
hadn't he?

a **er hatte** This is a past tense form of **haben:**
er hat: *he has* **er hatte:** *he had.*

b **schöne schwarze Augen** This is accusative plural, so the
adjective (standing alone) must show the -e ending of **die.** Note
that each 'independent' adjective (i.e. not a **der** or an **ein** word)
has the SAME ending, (L8, N7b).

c **dunkles lockiges Haar** The adjectives show the -s of **das**
because **Haar** is neuter – **das Haar. Dunk***el*: *dark* – note that the
e drops out when one puts an ending on to it (**dunk***les*).

30 **Ich wundere mich mehr über die schlanke Figur seiner Frau.**
I am more impressed (surprised) by his wife's slim figure.

a **Ich wundere mich** ... **über** + accusative: *I am surprised at* is
another reflexive verb.

b **die schlanke Figur** This is accusative (after **über**) singular
feminine and **die** is there, so the ending is -**e.** Remember from
N3b that when a **der** word is there, the adjective ends either
in -**e** or -**en** and there are only five instances when it can be -**e.**
This is one of the five.

c **seiner Frau:** *of his wife* or *his wife's* This is the genitive of the
feminine. (See L8, N1b for masculine and neuter.) The ending
is -**er,** which is the same as the dative ending for the feminine.
So, apart from this fact, you have nothing new to learn for the
genitive feminine.

31 **Wie macht man es bloß, daß man in ihrem Alter noch eine so**
schöne Haut hat? *Just how is it done, that she (one) still has such*
a lovely skin at her age?

a **In ihrem Alter:** *at an age* is always **in** + dative, e.g.
in meinem Alter: *at my age* **in diesem Alter:** *at that age.*

b **eine so schöne Haut** *Such,* when it means *to that degree* (and not of that type), i.e. when it precedes an adjective, is just **so.** Note the word order – **eine so schöne Haut:** *such a lovely skin.*

32 **Auch das Saftservice für ihre Verwandten war ganz nach meinem Geschmack.** *The set of tumblers for her relatives was just my taste as well.*
nach meinem Geschmack **Nach** here means *according to, in keeping with.*

33 **Nein, ich liebe diese modernen Kunststoffe gar nicht.** *No, I don't care for these modern synthetic materials at all.*

a **diese modernen Kunststoffe** **Diese** is a **der** word, so the adjective ending will be **-e** or **-en.** Here it is plural, so the ending can only be **-en** (L8, N3b).

b **Kunststoff** **Der Stoff** is *material.* **Kunststoff** is ANY artificial or synthetic material, but refers usually to plastic.

c **gar nicht:** *not at all* These two words cannot be separated.

34 **Etwas Hübsches aus Glas oder Porzellan gefällt mir viel besser.** *I much prefer something attractive in glass or china.*
etwas Hübsches Any adjective after **etwas** has a capital letter (it is felt to have a noun function) and the ending **-es** (i.e. of a neuter adjective standing alone). E.g. **etwas Gutes:** *something good,* **etwas Modernes:** *something modern.*

Part three

An der Kasse *At the cash desk*

35 **Wessen Kassenzettel ist das?** *Whose sales chit is that?*
Wessen? is the genitive of **wer?:** *who?*

36 **des Fräuleins** *of the young lady/the young lady's.* **-es,** remember, is the genitive ending on **der** and **ein** words if the following noun is masculine or neuter. The noun has an ending too (**Fräuleins**) if it is masculine or neuter (L8, N1b).
Compare **eines Kaufhauses** with **des Fräuleins.**
The ending on the noun is usually **-es** if there is only one syllable (**Mannes**) or, of course, if it ends in **-s** already (**Hauses**); otherwise, it is **s** (**Fräuleins**) in normal circumstances.

37 **es ist das Service der Dame und des Herrn neben ihr.** *it's the set of the lady and (of the) gentleman beside her.*

a **der Dame** This is the genitive singular feminine, so **-er** is the ending on the word before the noun (L8, N30c); feminine nouns have no genitive ending.

8

b des Herrn This is the genitive singular masculine. **Herrn** is an exception to the rule, as it has **-n** in every case except the nominative.

Am Informationsstand *At the enquiry desk*

38 meine kleine Tochter *my small daughter* You have now seen enough examples to realize that feminine adjectives in the singular (nominative or accusative) ALWAYS end in **-e**.

9

Lektion neun   Besichtigungen

Lesson nine   Sight-seeing

What happens

In this lesson, the members of the Kühn family are pursuing their own interests in the city. Walter and Lore go on a sight-seeing tour and Renate visits the 'Haus der Kunst', one of the art galleries.

In Part 1 a tour guide describes his plans for the day. In Part 2 Renate tells her parents about the exhibition of modern art. She asks permission to go to a discothèque with a friend of Franz's and Herr Kühn shows her how to phone from a call box. Lore goes to pack for the trip to Berlin.

New words in this lesson

der **Apparat**(-e) telephone
der **Bekannte**(-n) acquaintance, friend
der **Garten**(¨) garden
der **Hörer**(–) receiver
der **Januar** January
der **Oktober** October
der **Reiseführer**(–) guide
der **Spaziergang**(¨e) walk

die **Abfahrt**(-en) departure

die **Ausstellung**(-en) exhibition
die **Besichtigung** sight-seeing
die **Diskothek**(-en) discothèque
die **Fernsprechzelle**(-n) call-box
die **Führung**(-en) conducted tour
die **Geduld** patience
die **Kunst** art
die **Rundfahrt**(-en) round trip, tour
die **Sehenswürdigkeit**(-en) sight
die **Tante**(-n) aunt
die **Verabredung**(-en) appointment

das **Bild**(-er) picture, painting
das **Museum** (die **Museen**) museum
das **Ortsgespräch**(-e) local call
das **Taxi**(-s) taxi
das **Telephonbuch**(¨er) telephone
  directory
das **Theater**(–) theatre
das **Tonsignal**(-e) pip

jeder everyone, each person
jemand someone, somebody
niemand no one, nobody

(**können**) **wir konnten** (to be able to)
  we could
lassen (**läßt**) to leave
(**sein**) **wir waren** (to be) we were
vergessen (**vergißt**) to forget
(**wollen**) **ich wollte** (to want to) I wanted

begrüßen to welcome
machen to make, go
packen to pack
wählen to dial

abfahren to leave
abnehmen to pick up, take off
einladen to invite
einwerfen to put in, insert

sich melden to answer

anderthalb one and a half
berühmt well-known, famous
besetzt engaged
deutsch German
historisch historical
kurz short
zweistündig lasting two hours

aber however
danach afterwards
noch lange nicht far from
noch vor before
spätestens at the latest
vorher before

woher? where from?

dagegen against it
eben just
eigentlich actually, really
überhaupt nicht not at all
zurück back

aus out of
bei at
durch across, through
gegen towards, about
statt instead of
über across, through, about
vor before
während in the course of, during
wegen because of

alles, was schwierig ist anything difficult
Bescheid wissen to know how, understand
bis ... Uhr by ... o'clock
das heißt that is, i.e.
das macht nichts never mind
eine Führung machen to go for a tour
einen Spaziergang machen to go for a
  walk
viel Neues much that was (is) new
wenn es euch recht ist if it's all right
  with you
wenn Sie nichts dagegen haben if you
  don't mind

Notes

Part one

1 **Ich begrüße Sie zu unserer zweistündigen Rundfahrt durch München.** *I welcome you to our two-hour tour of Munich.*
a **zu unserer zweistündigen Rundfahrt** Zu is followed by the

dative, and **unserer** shows the dative singular feminine ending (**-er**). There is therefore no need to show it in the adjective (**zweistündig**) so this just ends in **-en.** **-e** and **-en** are the so-called WEAK adjective endings, used when another word shows by ITS ending the class and case of the following noun. Remember that there are only five instances in which the weak ending can be **-e** – the three singular nominatives, and the feminine and neuter accusative singular (**L8**).

b **zweistündig**   This is an adjective constructed from **zwei** and **Stunde.** Any number can be substituted for **zwei,** e.g. **eine vier-stündige Reise:** *a four hour journey.*

2 **Während der Fahrt werde ich Ihnen einige Sehenswürdigkeiten unserer Stadt zeigen.** *During the drive I shall be showing you some of the sights of our city.*

während der Fahrt   **Während** is one of the few words which must be followed by the genitive case. You remember that the genitive feminine endings (**der, einer,** etc.) are the same as the dative.

3 **Zuerst werden wir über den Karlsplatz zur Residenz und zu Münchens berühmtem Nationaltheater fahren.**
First we shall go across the Karlsplatz to the (royal) Residence and to Munich's famous National Theatre.

a **über den Karlsplatz zur**   **Über** meaning *across* is followed by the accusative.

b **zu Münchens berühmtem**   **Münchens** is genitive. The adjective **berühmtem** must show the dative singular neuter ending (**-em**), since no **der** or **ein** word precedes it. When the adjective shows the class and case of the following noun, it is said to have a STRONG ending – i.e. the ending a **der** word would have if it were there.

4 **Danach wollte ich eigentlich mit Ihnen in den Englischen Garten gehen.** *After that I really intended going with you to the Englischer Garten (English Garden).*

a **danach**   **Da-** can be combined with **in, auf, zu, an,** etc. with the meaning *it* or *that.*

b **wollte ich ... gehen**   **Wollen:** *want to,* can also mean *intend.* This is a past tense form, which is called the IMPERFECT tense. You already know **war:** *was* and **hatte:** *had,* which are also imperfect tense.

c **in den Englischen Garten**   **Englisch** is an adjective, and only has a capital **E** here because it is a proper name. It has the weak **-en** ending since **den** precedes it.

5 **Wegen des schlechten Wetters können wir aber nicht aus dem Bus.** *On account of the bad weather, however, we can't go out of the coach.*

a **wegen des schlechten Wetters Wegen:** *on account of, because of,* must be followed by the genitive case, recognizable by **des** (genitive of **das**) and by the **-s** on **Wetters**. **Schlechten** has the weak adjective ending **-en** (L9, N1a).

b **können wir nicht aus dem Bus Gehen** is so obviously implied, that it is not necessary to say it. It is possible to omit **gehen** as a completing infinitive after **wollen** and **können** if the meaning is quite clear. **Aus** must ALWAYS be followed by the dative case.

c **aber** When placed after the verb, **aber** means *however.*

6 **Wenn Sie nichts dagegen haben, machen wir statt des kleinen Spaziergangs eine kurze Führung durch einige der historischen Abteilungen des Deutschen Museums.** *If you are agreeable (if you have no objection) instead of the little walk, we'll take a brief look round some of the historical sections of the Deutsches Museum.*

a **wenn Sie nichts dagegen haben,** This is a useful courtesy phrase to learn by heart. It is a **wenn** clause (verb at the end – **haben**) and means literally, *if you have nothing against it.* **Dagegen** is a combination of **da** + **gegen**: *against.* See **danach,** (L9, N4a).

b **statt des kleinen Spaziergangs** Here, you will recognize the genitive of **der kleine Spaziergang**. **Statt**: *instead of,* must be followed by the genitive (like **während** and **wegen**).

c **eine kurze Führung Führung** really means a *conducted tour.* **Kurze -e** is ALWAYS the ending on an adjective before a nominative or accusative feminine noun.

d **des Deutschen Museums** Though **Deutsch** is an adjective here, it has a capital **D** because it is part of a title (L9, N4c). This phrase is the genitive of **das Deutsche Museum**. **Deutschen** has the weak adjective ending.

e **durch einige Durch:** *through,* is followed by the accusative case.

7 **Gegen drei Uhr werden wir wieder zurück sein.** *We shall be back again towards three o'clock.*

wieder zurück These two words, often occurring together, are always arranged the other way round from English because of the time before place rule for adverbs.

9

Part two
Eine Ausstellung   *An exhibition*

8 **Na, Renate, woher kommst du?** *Well, Renate, where have you been? (. . . where are you coming from?)*

a **na** This word belongs exclusively to spoken German. It is just a meaningless 'starter' to a remark.

b **woher kommst du? Woher?** means *where from (whence)?* We only require the word *where?* in English whereas German, as you now know, has three – **wo?:** *where?*, **wohin?:** *where to?*, **woher?:** *where from?*

9 **Ich komme gerade aus dem Haus der Kunst.** *I've just come from the Haus der Kunst.*

Haus der Kunst: lit. *House of Art.* **Der Kunst** is the genitive singular of **die Kunst:** *art* (of any kind). This is one instance where German requires *the* and English does not – i.e. in talking of abstractions or generalities.

10 **Schade, daß wir nicht mit dir gehen konnten.** *Pity (that) we couldn't go with you.*

daß wir nicht mit dir gehen konnten Clauses introduced by **daß** are not main clauses, therefore the verb is placed at the end. Notice that if the verb phrase is composed of a MODAL verb (**wollen, müssen, können, dürfen, sollen**) plus a completing infinitive, the modal (**konnten**) is placed last and the infinitive (**gehen**) immediately precedes it.

Konnten is the imperfect tense of **können.** The placing of **nicht** can be tricky in dependent clauses, but it usually appears before any adverbial phrase (here, **mit dir**).

11 **Wir waren während der Zeit auf einer Rundfahrt.** *We were on a tour during that time.*

a **wir waren** This is the imperfect of **sein:** *to be.* You already know **ich/er war:** *I/he was.* One simply adds **-en** for the forms which go with **wir, Sie** and **sie** (*they*).

b **während der Zeit** **Während** is followed by the genitive (L9, N2). There would be a slight emphasis on **der** here (rendered by *that* in English) meaning the time she has just been talking about.

c **auf einer Rundfahrt** **Auf** is followed by the dative here as he says they were ON the tour already. In instances where you have to decide between the accusative and the dative, it will help you to know that you cannot have the accusative if the verb is any form of the verb *be* (*is, am, are, was, were*).

12 Viele der Bilder konnte ich überhaupt nicht verstehen. *Many of the pictures I couldn't understand at all.*

a viele der Bilder **Der Bilder** is the genitive plural, as Renate wishes to specify these particular pictures. There is the same distinction between *many* and *many of* in English.

b konnte ich This is the imperfect tense of **können** (L9, N10).
ich/er/sie konnte wir/sie/Sie konnten

c überhaupt nicht: *not at all* This is an alternative to **gar nicht** and is, if anything, more emphatic.

13 Ich mußte zuerst auch viel Neues über moderne Kunst lesen...
I had first to read much that was new to me about modern art...

a ich mußte: *I had to* This is the imperfect tense of **müssen,** and is as easy to handle and remember as **ich wollte** and **ich konnte.**

b viel Neues Remember **etwas Hübsches** (*something attractive*) in Lesson **8**? This is a similar phrase. **Neues** is given a neuter ending (*new thing*) and a capital **N,** as it is felt to be a kind of noun.

c über moderne Kunst **Über** + accusative means *about, on the subject of.* **Moderne** has an **-e** ending, like all feminine adjectives in the nominative or accusative (L9, N6c).

14 ... und dann versteht man noch lange nicht alles. *... and even then one is far from understanding everything.*
This is so idiomatic that it would be merely confusing to analyse it word for word. **Noch lange nicht** is similar in meaning to the English *not by a long chalk.*

15 Man braucht eben für alles, was schwierig ist, viel Geduld. *One just needs a lot of patience for everything (anything) that's difficult (not straightforward).*
alles, was schwierig ist *Everything that (all that) is* is **alles, was;** **was** introduces another clause with a verb of its own, which appears at the end of the clause, e.g. *all that is important:* **alles, was wichtig ist.**

Renates Verabredung *Renate's date*

16 Wolltet ihr nicht mit Onkel Max und Tante Grete ausgehen?
Weren't you intending to go out with Uncle Max and Aunt Grete?
wolltet ihr nicht? This is the **ihr** form (familiar plural) of the imperfect tense (L9, N4b). From the few examples of the imperfect tense which have already occurred, you can see that at least you have no new endings to learn.

9

ich			wir	
er	wollte	ihr wolltet	Sie	wollten (L9, N12b)
sie			sie	

17 **Ja, wir wollten sie noch vor unserer Abfahrt in ein Restaurant einladen.** *Yes, we wanted to invite them out to a restaurant before we leave (before our departure).*

vor unserer Abfahrt **Vor** means *before* here and is followed by the dative case. You now know all three meanings of **vor,** namely, *in front of, ago, before.* When it has either of the last two meanings, it is ALWAYS followed by the dative. With the first meaning, it can be followed by either dative or accusative. Note that this has been rendered in English *before we leave.* Germans tend to use a noun phrase like **vor unserer Abfahrt** or **vor unserer Ankunft** (*arrival*), when possible, whereas in English we prefer *before we leave, before we arrive.*

18 **Wenn es euch recht ist, gehe ich in der Zeit mit ein paar Bekannten in eine Diskothek.** *If it's all right with you, while you're there, I'll go to a discothèque with a few friends.*

a **wenn es euch recht ist** (L9, N6a) Here is another way of ensuring others' consent to something you propose doing. If you are not addressing people (a person) you know very well, then **Ihnen** must replace **euch,** of course.

b **in der Zeit** (L9, N11b) **Der** would have to be stressed here, too, meaning *in that time you've been talking about.*

19 **Da hast du noch anderthalb Stunden Zeit.** *Then you've still got another hour and a half.*

a **da** This is colloquial, (only used in the spoken language) and means the same as **dann:** *then, in that case.*

b **anderthalb Stunden Zeit:** lit. *one and a half hours' time* **Anderthalb** can be used with any unit of time, e.g.: **anderthalb Tage:** *a day and a half* **anderthalb Jahre:** *eighteen months.*

20 **Ich soll vorher bei ihm anrufen.** *I'm supposed to phone him first.*

a **ich soll:** *I am to, I'm supposed to* (an obligation imposed by a previous arrangement or promise). There is more than one meaning of **sollen.**

b **bei ihm** Why not just **ihn?** This would not be wrong, but Renate is thinking of his home, the place where he is, rather than just a person.

90

21 Wie telephoniert man in einer deutschen Fernsprechzelle? **9**

How does one make a call in a German telephone box?

a **in einer deutschen Fernsprechzelle** In + dative feminine. The ending showing class and case appears on **einer,** so **deutschen** has the weak adjective ending. Note that adjectives of nationality have initial capital letters only if they are part of the title of something – **Englischer Garten, Deutsches Museum;** or if they are used as nouns to describe persons – **Renate ist Deutsche.**

b **Fernsprechzelle** This word requires some explanation. **Telephonzelle** exists also, nowadays, but **Fernsprechzelle** was the original word. When resistance to foreign words (even for new inventions) was stronger than it is now, a telephone was called **ein Fernsprecher:** *a farspeaker.* Both words (**Telephon** and **Fernsprecher**) are in current use, but **Telephon** (sometimes spelt **Telefon**) is probably more common.

Ortsgespräch *Local call*

22 **Also, Renate, du siehst hier in der Fernsprechzelle das Telephon- oder Fernsprechbuch.** *Well, now, Renate, you see the telephone directory here in the callbox.*

Telephon- oder Fernsprechbuch There is no way of putting this into English, as English has no alternative to *telephone.* Note, however, that when two compound nouns with the SAME second component (**-buch**) are linked by **und** or **oder,** a hyphen replaces the second component in the first word, e.g.: **Bus- und Autofahrten Reise- und Auskunftsbüro.**

23 **Ich habe Pauls Nummer auf dem Zettel hier: 22 00 24.** *I have Paul's number on this slip of paper: 22 00 24.*

German phone numbers (local) are usually written in pairs and can be said either in pairs or individually.

24 **Dann wirfst du nur zwei Zehnpfennigstücke ein, nimmst den Hörer ab und wählst die Nummer.** *Then you just insert two 10 Pf. coins, lift the receiver and dial the number.*

wählst die Nummer In Lesson **8,** you learned **wählen:** *choose.* In telephone jargon, it means *dial.*

25 **Wenn jemand sich am Apparat meldet, ist es einfach.** *If someone answers the phone, it's simple.*

sich am Apparat meldet Apparat means *telephone* in this context. **Sich melden** is one of those expressions which in trans-

9

lation require adapting to the context, but the essential meaning is *to make one's presence known.*

26 Wenn niemand zu Haus ist, hörst du das lange Tonsignal tüüüt. *If no one's at home, you'll hear the long (uninterrupted) tone.*
niemand: *no one* **Jemand** and **niemand** are pronouns which have **der** type endings (accusative **-en,** dative **-em**), although they are not always strictly observed in the spoken language.

27 Und wenn gerade besetzt ist? *And if it's engaged just then?*
Note that one has to 'invent' a subject in English (*it*) since this kind of sentence without a subject is not possible in English.

Koffer packen   *Packing*

28 Ich fahre jetzt mit einem Taxi zu Pfaffingers nach Haus und packe unsere Koffer. *I'll take a taxi home to the Pfaffingers now and pack our cases.* Note the order of the adverbial phrases – time, manner, place.

29 Wir nehmen aber nur deinen braunen und Renates kleinen. *Now we're just taking your brown one and Renate's little one.*

a deinen braunen Deinen shows the accusative masculine singular ending, so **braunen** has the weak **-en** ending, although it happens to be the same as the strong ending here.

b Renates Note that there is never an apostrophe with the genitive in German.

30 Die anderen beiden lassen wir hier. *The other two we'll leave here.*
die anderen beiden German favours the use of **beide:** *both* where in English we have to use *two* because of the presence of *the.* Note the weak adjective ending, since **die** is there.

31 Wir dürfen aber nicht vergessen, alle bis spätestens acht Uhr zu Haus zu sein. *But we mustn't forget all to be home by eight o'clock at the latest.*

a wir dürfen nicht This is the only way we can translate *we mustn't* meaning it is *not permitted.* **Dürfen** must always be used in such instances, never **müssen.**

b vergessen, ... zu sein This is an infinitive phrase following the comma. It is essentially the same kind of construction as **Es ist schwer, immer höflich zu bleiben (L4).** and **Es ist mir ein Vergnügen, ihre Fragen zu beantworten (L5).**

c bis spätestens acht Uhr BY a certain time is **bis.** **Spätestens** sounds better before **acht Uhr** than after it, as in English.

32 Ich weiß, der Bus fährt um 9 ab. *I know the bus leaves at nine.*

A comma is essential here because there is a quite separate clause following (a clause which alternatively could be expressed with **daß** and the verb at the end).

33 **Um 8.40 Uhr (acht Uhr vierzig) – das heißt 10 Minuten nach halb neun – muß jeder an der Bushaltestelle sein.** *At eight forty – that is ten minutes after half past (eight) – everyone must be at the bus stop.*

a **Das heißt:** *that is* or *that means* is a phrase so common, that, as in English (*i.e.*) it has an abbreviated form, **d.h.**

b **jeder** This means *each* or *every* and is often used in preference to **alle** for *everyone*. It is a **der** word.

Lektion zehn Ankunft in Berlin

10

Lesson ten Arrival in Berlin

What happens

Herr and Frau Kühn and Renate arrive in Berlin and are met by Herbert and his fiancée, Eva.

In Part 1 Herbert talks about his studies and forthcoming engagement. In Part 2 Herbert and Eva meet the family at the bus stop. They arrange for a celebration dinner that evening and drive to the guest house where Herr and Frau Kühn and Renate are to stay.

New words in this lesson

der Nachtzug(ॱe) night train
der Student(-en) student

die Ankunft(ॱe) arrival
die Einladung(-en) invitation
die Pädagogik education
die Pension(-en) guest house
die Psychologie psychology
die Soziologie sociology
die Universität(-en) university
die Vorstellung introduction

das Foto(-s) photograph
das Semester (–) term

(dürfen) dürfen wir? (to be allowed to) may (can) we?
schlafen (schläft) to sleep
(sein) sie war (to be) she was

feiern to celebrate

10 studieren to study

abholen to go to meet
aussehen (du siehst aus) to look (you look)
kennenlernen to meet, get to know
wiedersehen to meet again

sich verloben to become engaged
sich gut verstehen to get on well

lieb dear
pünktlich on time
schnell fast
übernächst the next but one

gleich straight away
immer noch still
mal sometime

allein alone
bestimmt surely
ganz allein all alone
ja after all
sehr very much
vielmals very much

am (= an + dem) in the
mit to
vom (= von + dem) off the
zu with

das alte (Auto) the old one (car)
das macht gar nichts! that doesn't matter at all!
jeden Augenblick any moment
noch etwas something else

Notes

Part one

1 **Ich studiere Pädagogik, Psychologie und Soziologie im neunten Semester.** *I'm studying education, psychology and sociology. This is my ninth term.*
im neunten Semester The academic (university) year has two terms in Germany. Herbert is therefore in his fifth year.

2 **Übernächste Woche will ich mich mit Eva verloben.** *The week after next, I intend to become engaged to Eva.*
will ich mich ... verloben Note that when the completing infinitive is reflexive (**mich verloben**), the reflexive pronoun is placed as close to the modal verb (**will**) as is possible without breaking other rules. The subject (**ich**) and verb (**will**) are inverted here because **übernächste Woche** begins the sentence; but **mich** comes immediately after **ich**.

3 **Dann fahren wir zusammen zur Haltestelle und holen unsere Münchner vom Bus ab.** *Then we'll drive together to the bus stop and meet our Munich relatives off the bus.*

a **zusammen zur Haltestelle** The adverb of MANNER (*together*) comes before the adverb of place.

94

b **und holen unsere Münchner vom Bus ab** **Abholen von** means *to meet* or *pick up* at a certain place in order to proceed elsewhere. That is why **von** is used in German where in English we often use *at*, e.g. **Ich hole Sie vom Flughafen ab**: *I'll meet you at the airport.*

Part two

Die Begrüßung   *The welcome*

4 **Seid alle herzlich willkommen in Berlin!** *You're all most welcome to Berlin.*
seid willkommen!: lit. *be welcome!* This is the request form for the familiar plural, which, as you see, is exactly the same as the statement form (**ihr seid**) without the pronoun **ihr**.

5 **Du siehst gut aus!** *You look fine!*
Aussehen means *to look* or *appear* (to other people).

6 **Doch, lieber Bruder. Wunderst du dich?** *Oh but it is, dear brother. Are you surprised?*

a Remember **doch** also serves to contradict a negative statement.

b **wunderst du dich?** Note the position of the reflexive pronoun (**dich**) in questions – after the subject if it is a pronoun, as here.

7 **Mädchen, bist du groß und schlank!** *Goodness, girl, how tall and slender you are!* The German idiom is shorter and simpler here than English. Note that the question form (**bist du**) is used in exclamations like this, but with a completely different intonation.

8 **Und wie ich sehe, hast du auch keine schlechte Figur.** *And from what I see, you haven't a bad figure either.*

a **wie ich sehe**: lit. *as I see* This has a verb and subject, so it is a dependent clause. The verb and subject (**hast du**) in the main clause, therefore, appear in that order.

b **auch keine...** Just as **auch nicht** means *not ... either*, **auch kein** means *not a (any) ... either*

Die Vorstellung   *Introductions*

9 **Entschuldigt mich, ich muß sie euch natürlich vorstellen.** *Excuse me, I must introduce her to you, of course.*
entschuldigt This is the request form of the familiar plural.

10 **Das ist Eva Schultze und das, Eva, sind meine Eltern.** *This is Eva Schultze and Eva, my parents.*
das sind *These are my parents* sounds rather awkward in English,

so it is better omitted. But note that the plural of **das ist** is **das sind**: *these are.*

11 **Ich kann es immer noch nicht glauben.** *I* STILL *can't believe it.*
immer noch nicht **Immer** intensifies **noch.**

12 **Ich freue mich, Sie kennenzulernen.** *I'm happy to meet you.*
Sie kennenzulernen **Ich freue mich:** *I'm glad* can be followed by either a **daß** clause or an infinitive phrase with **zu,** as here. **Kennenlernen:** *to get (learn) to know* is really two verbs joined together, the first one **(kennen)** being treated as a separable prefix – **ich möchte sie kennenlernen:** *I'd like to meet her.* When **zu** is required, it is therefore sandwiched between the two parts, as is normal with **zu** + separable verb.

13 **Ich kenne Sie schon ein bißchen aus Herberts Briefen und von einigen Fotos.** *I know you a little already from Herbert's letters and from some photos.*
von einigen Fotos **Von** requires the dative, remember; **einigen** has the strong adjective ending (dative plural **-en**) and **Foto** is a borrowed foreign word which forms its plural by adding **-s.** Nouns which form their plurals by adding **-s** have no **-n** in the dative plural. Note that there are two different words here for *from,* **aus** and **von; aus** really means *(from) out of.*

14 **Wir werden uns sicher gut verstehen.** *We'll get on well with each other, I'm sure.*
uns verstehen **Sich verstehen** means *to get on well* WITH EACH OTHER. **Sich** and **uns** in such instances, though identical in FORM with reflexive pronouns are really RECIPROCAL pronouns, indicating that the action is mutual.

15 **Wir können dann Wiedersehen feiern.** *Then we can celebrate our reunion.*
Wiedersehen This is used as a noun here and is written with a capital, as in **auf Wiedersehen.**

Zur Pension *To the guest house*

16 **Die Stewardeß war zu jedem freundlich und nett, aber ich konnte kaum schlafen.** *The stewardess was pleasant and nice to everyone, but I couldn't really sleep.*
a **zu jedem freundlich** *Friendly to* is **freundlich zu** + dative. Adjectives describing positive feelings or attitudes towards others are usually followed by **zu.**
b **ich konnte kaum schlafen** **Kaum** means *hardly, with difficulty,*

but **konnte kaum** + an infinitive is often best translated as *couldn't really*.

17 **Es ist das alte von meinem Vater.** *It's my father's old one.*
von meinem Vater   Von + dative is becoming increasingly common in speech as an alternative to the more formal genitive.

18 **Das macht gar nichts. Wir haben ja genug Zeit.** *That doesn't matter at all. We've got plenty of time.* **Genug** means *enough*, but is frequently used as *more than enough*, therefore *plenty*.

Part three

Mit dem Auto nach Berlin   *To Berlin by car*

19 **Übermorgen, am frühen Vormittag.** *The day after tomorrow, early in the morning.*
am frühen Vormittag   In the + part of the day is **am**. The adverb **früh** is used as an adjective with a weak **-en** ending, since the **-m** of **am** shows the dative masculine ending.

Mit dem Nachtzug nach Berlin   *By night train to Berlin*

20 **Dann also auf Wiedersehen, Ute, vielleicht in Berlin.** *Well then, good-bye, Ute, till we meet again, perhaps in Berlin*
auf Wiedersehen   If you translate this *till we see each other again* or *till we meet again* the rest makes sense.

Busbekanntschaft   *Coach acquaintanceship*

21 **Haben Sie wirklich noch keine Adresse in Berlin?** *Haven't you really any address in Berlin yet?*
noch keine: *still no* (*address*)   Be careful when you put this kind of phrase into German: *not any* + noun + *yet* is **noch kein** + noun.

Lektion elf   In der Pension „Grunewald"

Lesson eleven In the 'Grunewald' guest house

What happens

The scene changes to the 'Grunewald' guest house.
    In Part 1 Frau Raffke, the landlady, explains that she has earned her living by running a guest house since her husband died. In Part 2

11 Anne Green, who is having breakfast in the dining-room, meets the Kühns. Herbert and Eva arrive and Herbert recognizes Anne as someone he knew in England.

New words in this lesson

der Aufenthalt(-e) stay
der Dialekt(-e) dialect
der Fahrer(–) driver
der Gast(ːe) guest
der Grund(ːe) reason
der Krieg(-e) war
der Mensch(-en) human being, individual, soul
der Moment(-e) moment
der Münchner(–) person from Munich
der Neffe(-n) nephew
der Toast(-s) toast
der Toaster(–) toaster
der Topf(ːe) pot
der Vetter(-n) cousin (male)

die Butter butter
die Inhaberin(-nen) owner (female)
die Marmelade(-n) jam
die Nachbarin(-nen) neighbour (female)
die Nase(-n) nose
die Scheibe(-n) slice, piece
die Schokolade(-n) chocolate
die Schwägerin(-nen) sister-in-law
die Sprachlehrerin(-nen) language teacher (female)
die Überraschung(-en) surprise

das Brötchen(–) roll
das Ei(-er) egg
das Eßzimmer(–) dining-room
das Gesicht(-er) face
das Krankenhaus(ːer) hospital
das Mal(-e) time
das Ohr(-en) ear

gehen to work (watches, clocks, toaster etc.)
(haben) er hatte (to have) he had
tätig sein to work

treffen (trifft) to meet
(wollen) ich habe gewollt (to want) I wanted

decken to lay, set
frühstücken to have breakfast
heizen to heat
kochen to cook, boil, make
kriegen to get (colloquial)
leben to live
versorgen to provide
wünschen to wish

nachgehen to go slow (watch, clock etc.)
vorgehen to go fast (watch, clock etc.)

sich gedulden to have patience, wait
sich kennen to know each other
sich lohnen to be worth it
sich setzen to sit down
sich treffen to meet each other
sich unterhalten to talk, converse
sich verabschieden to say good-bye, take one's leave

abstehend protruding
bayerisch Bavarian
gekocht boiled
häßlich ugly
heiß hot
herrlich delicious, glorious
krumm crooked
lang tall, long
leer empty
nötig necessary
seelengut kind-hearted
tot dead
unerwartet unexpected
verheiratet married
vorig last
warm warm

98

damals at that time
früher formerly
niemals never
seither since then

drinnen inside
hierher here
irgendwo somewhere

anders differently
dabei through it
darum for that reason
dazu in addition to that, as well
deshalb therefore, for that reason
eben just
mal just
nicht mehr no longer
richtig properly
sonst in other respects, otherwise
übrigens by the way
zwar it is true

aus for
außer apart from

bei from
seit since
vor before, ago

sobald as soon as
so viel wie as much as
weil because

es fehlt mir an nichts I want for nothing
es macht Ihnen nichts aus it makes no
  difference to you, doesn't matter
es soll mir recht sein I should be pleased
jetzt gehen Sie mal do go
lieber had better
nanu well, well!
schon gut that's fine
schön warm really warm, nice and warm
sich richtig unterhalten to have a good
  talk
was für ein... what a...
zu Besuch on a visit
zum ersten Mal for the first time

Notes
Part one

1 **Früher, vor dem Krieg, war ich in einem Krankenhaus tätig.**
Formerly, before the war, I worked in a hospital.
früher: lit. *earlier* The German system of forming comparatives
(*lat*ER, *nic*ER, *earli*ER) is exactly the same as the English system –
add **-er.** There are a few irregularities, and there are many
adjectives which acquire an Umlaut in the comparative, but
basically, the two systems are the same.

2 **Damals war ich noch mit dem langen Otto verheiratet.** *At that
time I was still married to lanky (tall) Otto.*
mit dem langen Otto In colloquial language, Germans often put
der/die before the name of a person well-known to them. Note
verheiratet *mit*: married TO.

3 **Er hatte zwar ein haßliches Gesicht . . . , war aber sonst ein
seelenguter Mensch.** *It is true, he had an ugly face . . . , but was
in other respects a kind-hearted soul.*
a **hatte:** *had* ich/er hatte is the imperfect tense (Appendix 12).
b **zwar . . . aber:** *it is true . . . but* **Zwar** is generally followed up
by **aber.** The **aber** clause qualifies the statement in the **zwar**
clause.

   c   **Mensch** This means a *human being* and is often used in place of **Mann** or **Frau** for stylistic purposes, as it is here. It is also one of the group of nouns which have **-en** added in every case except the nominative singular.

4   **Seit er tot ist, lebe ich allein.** *Since his death (he has been dead), I've been living alone.*

   seit er tot ist Seit: *since,* introduces a dependent clause, so the verb is at the end of the clause.

5   **Mein Neffe, Ewald, der Taxifahrer, und seine Freunde versorgen mich seither mit den nötigen Gästen.** *My nephew Ewald, the taxi driver, and his friends have since then provided me with the necessary guests.*

   a   **mein Neffe** Neffe belongs in the same group as **Mensch** (L11, N3), i.e. it ends in -n in all cases except nominative sing.

   b   **seither** This is an adverb meaning *since then, until now;* it makes it possible to use **versorgen** in the present tense.

   c   **mit den nötigen Gästen** Nötigen has the weak adjective ending after **den.** Remember that any adjective before a plural noun preceded by a **der** word ends in -en in every case.

6   **Darum ist mein Haus niemals leer, und es fehlt mir an nichts.** *Therefore my house is never empty, and I want for (lack) nothing.*

   es fehlt mir an nichts This is an IMPERSONAL construction. The subject in German is always **es:** *it,* and the English subject (*I,* in this instance) is put in the dative case.

Part two

Vorm Frühstück *Before breakfast*

7   **Vorm Frühstück** Vorm is short for **vor dem.**

8   **Sie können jetzt frühstücken,** *You can have breakfast now,* **frühstücken:** *to breakfast* or *have breakfast* It is NOT a separable verb **Ich frühstücke immer um 8 Uhr.**

9   **Ich habe drinnen im Eßzimmer den Tisch gedeckt:** *I have set the table inside (in there) in the dining-room:*

You can see at a glance that the word which completes the verb phrase – **gedeckt** – is placed at the end of the sentence. This type of verb phrase – *has/have done something* is called the PERFECT tense, and it is by far the most frequently used PAST tense in spoken German. As its name suggests, it is used when an action has been completed. As in English, the verb phrase consists of an auxiliary verb (**haben**) and another part, called the past participle (**gedeckt**). At this stage, the only difficulty is to remember to put the past participle at the end of the sentence. ENGLISH: *I have* SET *the table.* GERMAN: **Ich habe den Tisch** *gedeckt.*

As to the forming of the past participle with the category of verbs we shall be dealing with first, it could scarcely be more simple. Find the stem (the infinitive minus **-en**) – **deck** –; put a **ge-** prefix in front of it – *gedeck* – and a **-t** on the end of it – *gedeckt* – e.g.

INFINITIVE	PAST PARTICIPLE
wohnen	**gewohnt**
machen	**gemacht**
kaufen	**gekauft**

N.B. This perfect tense in German can be used even if a different form of past tense is used in English:

I bought
I have bought } *a scarf:* **Ich habe ein Tuch gekauft.**
I did buy

He lived
He has lived } *in Berlin:* **Er hat in Berlin gewohnt.**
He did live
(See Appendix **13**.)

10 **Brötchen mit Butter und Marmelade und ein gekochtes Ei.** *rolls with butter and jam and a boiled egg.*
ein gekochtes Ei Gekochtes is a past participle (**kochen:** *to boil* or *cook*) used as an adjective, just like *boiled,* in fact.

11 **Dazu habe ich einen großen Topf Kaffee gekocht.** *I've made a large pot of coffee as well.*

a **habe ich** The subject-verb inversion rule holds in any sentence where an item other than the subject is in first position. In perfect tense verb phrases, it is the auxiliary verb (**haben**) and its subject which show the inversion.

b **Kaffee gekocht** Kochen means *to boil, cook* or *make.* This verb is generally used for MAKING *coffee.*

12 **Trinken Sie so viel, wie Sie wollen!** *Drink as much as you like!*
so viel wie So ... wie translates *as ... as,* and the middle 'slot' can be filled by an adjective (**so schön wie**), adverb (**so schnell wie**), or pronoun (**so viel wie**).

13 **Ich hoffe, es macht Ihnen nichts aus,** *I hope it won't (doesn't)*
matter,
Es macht Ihnen nichts aus: *it won't make any difference to you,*
or *it won't matter to you* is a phrase used by a speaker (prefaced
by **ich hoffe** or **hoffentlich**) to forestall objections or prepare the
listener for what is coming.

14 **Aber ich habe eigentlich eine Scheibe Toast gewollt.** *But I really*
wanted a slice of toast.
gewollt This is the past participle of **wollen,** but is only used if
translating *wanted something* and not *wanted* TO DO *something.*
This will be made clearer later.

15 **Dann müssen Sie sich noch einen Moment gedulden.** *Then you*
must have patience (wait patiently) for a little longer.
sich gedulden This is the completing infinitive, so **sich** appears
as close to the modal (**müssen**) as possible. This verb is almost
always used when the meaning is *to* WAIT *patiently.*

16 **Ich habe schon einen Toaster bei meiner Nachbarin geholt,**
I did fetch a toaster from my neighbour,
bei meiner Nachbarin: *at my neighbour's house* This seems
an odd way to put it. One must think of where one is at the
time of fetching or borrowing from a person.

17 **weil mein alter nicht mehr richtig geht.** *because my old one is not*
working properly any more.
a **weil** This always introduces a dependent clause; in a **weil**
clause the verb (here **geht**) is always at the end of the clause.
b **nicht mehr richtig geht** **Gehen** is commonly used in the sense
of *working, functioning* when speaking of gadgets, machinery.

18 **Sie hat herrlich geschmeckt.** *It was (tasted) marvellous.*
geschmeckt When speaking of food, you must use **schmecken**
where in English you use some form of *to be* (L3 – **dein Essen**
schmeckt wunderbar).

19 **Und das Zimmer haben Sie schön warm geheizt.** *And you made*
(heated) the room nice and warm.
a **schön warm** This is rather colloquial for **sehr warm.**
b **Geheizt** is the past participle of **heizen:** *to heat.*

20 **Schon gut. Jetzt gehen Sie mal zum Frühstück!** *That's fine.*
Now go and have your breakfast!
mal This is actually an abbreviation of **einmal,** but it is used
liberally in speech (after verbs) without any necessary connection

with **einmal.** It can sometimes be rendered in English as *just,* but very often, there is no need to translate it at all.

21 **Drinnen sitzen übrigens noch andere Gäste, auch aus München wie Sie.** *By the way, there are some other guests sitting in there, also from Munich, like you.*

sitzen noch andere Gäste We often use *there* in English where German does not: *there are other guests sitting,* or even *there are other guests.* Where we may say *there is/are* German is often more precise and uses the verb **sitzen, liegen, stehen,** etc., as appropriate.

Bei Tisch *At table*

22 **Guten Morgen! Kann ich mich zu Ihnen setzen?** *Good morning! May I join you?*

Mich zu Ihnen setzen means more precisely *sit down beside you.*

23 **Setzen Sie sich zu uns an den Tisch!** *Sit down at the table beside us!*

a **setzen Sie sich** This is the request form of **sich setzen.** Note where the reflexive pronoun (**sich**) is placed.

b **zu uns an den Tisch** Both of these adverbial phrases are really describing place. Their arrangement is largely a matter of style. To place them in reverse order might suggest a possible connection between **Tisch** and **uns,** which is non-existent.

24 **Frau Raffke hat mir eben gesagt, daß Sie aus München kommen.** *Frau Raffke has just told me (that) you come from Munich.*

hat mir eben gesagt *Has just done* (something) is rendered in German quite simply by placing the word **eben** before the past participle (**gesagt:** *said, told*).

25 **Ja, vorige Woche haben wir auch in München gewohnt ...** *Yes, last week we* DID *stay in Munich ...*

a **vorige Woche:** *last week* (time when).

b **Auch** serves to add the emphasis expressed by DID in English.

26 **... zu Besuch bei meinem Schwager und meiner Schwägerin, der Schwester meines Mannes.** *... on a visit to my brother-in-law and sister-in-law, my husband's sister.*

a **zu Besuch bei** Bei indicates *staying at the house of.*

b **meiner Schwägerin, der Schwester meines Mannes** Meiner **Schwägerin** is dative (after **bei**), so **der Schwester** must be dative too. **Meiner Schwägerin** and **der Schwester** are said to be in apposition, i.e. grammatically parallel. This is easy to understand, but hard to remember, when it is necessary to put the second item into any case other than the nominative.

27 **Mein Vetter Franz und Onkel Max sprechen so bayerisch, daß ich zuerst kein Wort verstehen konnte.** *My cousin Franz and Uncle Max's speech is so Bavarian that I couldn't understand a word at first.*

sprechen so bayerisch: lit. *speak so Bavarian,* i.e. *in dialect*

28 **Deshalb hat sich auch die Busreise hierher für mich gelohnt.** *That's why the coach journey here was for me well worth while.*

a **hat sich gelohnt** **Sich lohnen** means something like *to be its own reward,* so **hat sich gelohnt** means *it was worth while.* Note where the reflexive pronoun **(sich)** is placed in a perfect tense construction – right after the auxiliary verb **(hat)** if the subject is a noun.

b **hierher** **-her** attached to anything indicates motion towards the speaker, hence TO this place as opposed to IN this place **(hier).**

29 **Ich habe zum ersten Mal viele verschiedene Dialekte gehört.** *For the first time I heard many different dialects.*

a **zum ersten Mal** Notice how often an adverbial phrase like this one precedes the direct object.

b **viele verschiedene Dialekte** If **viele** is followed by another adjective, that adjective has a STRONG ending (i.e. the same ending as on **viele**).

30 **Für uns hat sie sich aus einem anderen Grund gelohnt.** *For us it was worth it for a different reason.*

hat sie sich If there is subject verb inversion and the subject is a pronoun, the reflexive pronoun follows the subject **(sie)** – compare L11, N28a. It is really a question of LENGTH of subject.

31 **... aber außer einer Tasse schwarzen Kaffee hat man nichts gekriegt.** *... but apart from a cup of black coffee we (one) got nothing (to eat or drink).*

a **außer einer Tasse schwarzen Kaffee** When an expression of quantity or measurement (e.g. cup, bottle, glass) is followed by an adjective and noun, the latter are generally put in the same case as the former – dative in our example because **außer** always takes the dative. Here, Renate has used the weak adjective ending **-en** (almost as if the phrase were **außer ein***em* **schwarzen Kaffee**), rather than the strong dative **schwarz***em* which is to be found more in written German.

b **gekriegt** **Kriegen** is a colloquial substitute for **bekommen:** *to get.*

32 **Wir wollen euch zum Museum abholen.** *We've come to take you to the museum.*
    wir wollen Sometimes a phrase used in a certain situation is expressed quite differently in another language. This is the case with this whole sentence.

33 **was für eine Überraschung!** *what a surprise!*
    Was für has this second meaning (as well as *what sort of*) of *what!* in exclamations.

34 **Woher kennt ihr euch denn?** *How do you come to know each other then?*
    kennt ihr euch Euch is not a reflexive pronoun here, but a reciprocal pronoun (*each other*).

35 **Du weißt doch, Eva:** *You remember, Eva:* (implying she knows all about it!)
    Du weißt really means *you know,* of course.

36 **Ich habe vor zwei Jahren als Sprachlehrerin in Bournemouth gearbeitet.** *Two years ago I worked as a language teacher in Bournemouth.*
    gearbeitet This is the past participle of **arbeiten:** *to work.* Note that once again (L1, N5) when a **-t** is to be added to the stem – arbeit- – an **e** must be inserted between the two **t**'s. The **e** of **ge-** and the **a** of **arbeitet** in **gearbeitet** must not be run together.

37 **Wenn Herbert etwas dabei gelernt hat, soll es mir recht sein.**
    If Herbert learned something from it, I suppose it's all right with me.

 a **gelernt hat** This shows you how to arrange the verb phrase within a **wenn** clause when it happens to be a perfect tense. The auxiliary verb **hat** is placed last, and the past participle **gelernt** immediately before it. This is, in fact, what happens with a perfect tense construction in most dependent clauses.

 b **dabei** The English word *thereby* is very close in meaning to that of **dabei** here. It means *in the doing of it.*

 c **soll es mir recht sein:** lit. *it should be all right with me* Eva, in her present mood, does not feel generous enough to say simply **es ist mir recht.**

38 **Ich glaube, wir verabschieden uns jetzt lieber.** *I think we'd better be going now.*
    wir verabschieden uns lieber: lit. *we would rather take our leave*

11

now A too literal translation would sound more discourteous than what Eva says.

39 Ja, wir müssen leider weg. *Yes, I'm afraid we must.*

weg This is not part of a verb here; it can be compared with *away* in *we must away.*

40 Sobald ich kann, müssen wir uns alle irgendwo treffen und uns richtig unterhalten. *As soon as I can manage it we must all meet somewhere and have a proper chat.*

a **uns ... treffen** Whenever one can sensibly insert *each other* after *meet*, **treffen** must have the appropriate reflexive pronoun with it – *I'm meeting them this evening:* **Ich treffe sie heute abend.** *They're meeting this evening:* **Sie treffen** *sich* **heute abend.**

b **uns ... unterhalten** This is a SECOND completing infinitive after **müssen,** the first being **uns treffen.**

12 Lektion zwölf   Ein ereignisreicher Tag

Lesson twelve   An eventful day

What happens

The Kühns are enjoying their stay in Berlin. Walter and Lore are each off on business of their own today and Renate and Anne, who have become friends, have an outing together.

In Part 1 Renate tells us that Eva and Herbert have quarrelled about Anne Green. In Part 2 she describes her day with Anne, Herr Kühn has a suit cleaned and Frau Kühn buys a wig.

New words in this lesson

der Anzug(ˉe) suit
der Friseur(-e) hairdresser
der Irrtum(ˉer) error, mistake
der Schuljunge(-n) school-boy

die Ecke(-n) corner

die Galerie(-n) gallery
die Kochkunst art of cooking, cookery
die Liebe love
die Maschine(-n) machine
die Perücke(-n) wig

106

die **Reinigung**(-en) cleaner's, cleaning
die **Riesenportion**(-en) giant helping

das **Eisbein** pig's knuckle
das **Essen** food, meal
das **Jahrhundert**(-e) century
das **Problem**(-e) problem
das **Sauerkraut** sauerkraut, pickled
  cabbage
das **Schwesterchen** little sister
das **Trinkgeld**(-er) tip

drankommen to have one's turn

gespannt sein to wonder, be anxious to
  know
(**haben**) **ich habe gehabt** (to have) I've
  had
lassen to have (something done)

drehen to curl
erzählen to tell
färben to dye
passieren to happen
reinigen to clean
schenken to give (as a present)
stecken to put
stellen to stand
versuchen to try

sich ärgern to be annoyed, angry
sich etwas ausziehen to take something
  off (i.e. a garment)
sich entschuldigen bei to apologize (to)
sich erinnern to remember·
sich interessieren für to be interested in
sich schämen to feel ashamed

sich verrechnen to miscalculate
sich versöhnen to patch up a quarrel
sich (**D**) **vorstellen** to imagine
sich zanken to quarrel

dumm stupid
ereignisreich eventful
fertig ready
ganz whole, all
glatt straight, smooth
klar clear
schmutzig dirty
schrecklich terribly
solcher, solche, solches such
typisch typical
weich soft
zukünftig future

anschließend afterwards
nachher afterwards

bloß only, merely
etwas somewhat
gestern yesterday
wahrscheinlich probably

bei to
um by (the amount of), to the extent of
ob whether, if

da läßt sich nichts machen there's
  nothing to be done about it
halb sechs half past five
nun well
pfui! shame!
um Himmels willen! good heavens!
was war los? what happened?, what was
  wrong?

12

Notes

Part one

1 **Jetzt komme ich endlich dran.** *Now, at last, it's my turn.*
   komme ich dran. Ich komme an die Reihe means *I have my turn.*
   This is colloquially abbreviated to **ich komme daran.** In speech,
   daran becomes **dran.**

12

2 Ich bin gespannt, ob die beiden sich bis morgen versöhnen werden. *I'm anxious to know whether the pair of them will patch it up by tomorrow.*

a ich bin gespannt, ob . . . **Gespannt** implies a state of suspense about the outcome of a situation. In English, it is necessary to add *to know* or *to see* before one says what the suspense is.

b ob die beiden sich bis morgen versöhnen werden **Ob:** *whether (if)* is another word which introduces a dependent clause, and therefore sends the verb to the end of the clause. This clause is in the future tense (composed of **werden** and an infinitive), so **werden** is placed last, and the infinitive immediately before it. The reflexive pronoun **(sich)** follows the subject.

3 Ich habe vorher schon so eine dunkle Ahnung gehabt. *Even before (it happened), I had a sort of gloomy premonition.*
ich habe . . . gehabt The past participle of **haben (gehabt)** is quite regular, but the **b** is pronounced like a **p.**

4 Eva hat sich schrecklich über Herbert geärgert. *Eva was terribly angry with Herbert.*
über **sich ärgern über:** *to be (get) angry* WITH

5 und nachher hat er sich bei ihr entschuldigt. *and afterwards he apologized to her.*
entschuldigt From its position in the sentence (last) and the presence of **hat,** it is clear that this must be a past participle. It ends in **-t,** but there is no **ge-.** This is explained by the fact that **ent-** is an inseparable prefix (unlike **auf-, an-, ein-, aus-,** etc.) and is NEVER separated from the rest of the verb. All inseparable prefixes (like **ent-**) are UNstressed, while all separable prefixes are stressed – **ent***schuld***igen** but **an***kommen,* **aus***steigen.* If you repeat to yourself some of the past participles you have already learned, you will notice that **ge-** is always unstressed and the syllable following it is always stressed – **gedeckt, geholt, ge-kocht, geschmeckt, gehabt.** If one attempted to attach a **ge-** to **entschuldigt,** it would not conform to this essential stress pattern, as **ent-** cannot be stressed, so the **ge-** is simply dropped. This applies to all verbs with inseparable prefixes.

6 Aber es ist klar, daß Herberts Wiedersehen mit Anne ihrer Liebe nicht geschadet hat. *It is clear, however, that Herbert's reunion with Anne hasn't done their relationship (love) any real harm.*
ihrer Liebe nicht geschadet hat **Schaden:** *to damage, harm* takes the dative case **(ihrer Liebe).**

108

Der Irrtum *The mistake*

7 **Na, Schwesterchen, jetzt erzähl mal, was du den ganzen Tag gemacht hast!** *Well now, little sister, tell me what you have been doing all day.*

a **erzähl** *tell.* This is the familiar singular imperative, which is formed by simply dropping the -st ending of the **du** form, e.g.
du kommst: *you're coming;* **komm!:** *come!;*
du nimmst: *you're taking;* **nimm!:** *take!*
This holds good for any except highly irregular verbs such as **sein:** *to be,* for instance. These must be specially learned. Sometimes you will find an -e added. Both forms are deliberately included in the course, as both are equally acceptable.

b **was du den ganzen Tag gemacht hast** From the word order (verb last) you see this is a dependent clause. It is the kind of dependent clause known as an indirect question. To illustrate exactly what this means, compare the following utterances:
Was hast du gemacht?: *What have you been doing?* **Erzähl mir, was du gemacht hast!:** *Tell me what you have been doing!*
The first is a direct question, the second an indirect question.

8 **Vormittags habe ich mit Anne die Galerie des 20. (Zwanzigsten) Jahrhunderts besichtigt.** *In the morning I visited the Twentieth Century Gallery with Anne.*

a **des 20. (Zwanzigsten) Jahrhunderts** *of the Twentieth Century* Here is the genitive case. **Zwanzigsten** (an adjective) has a capital letter only because it is part of a title.

b **besichtigt** This is another past participle without a **ge-**; **be-** is another INseparable prefix, therefore UNstressed, so it cannot come after a **ge-**. (See Appendix 13.)

9 **Anschließend haben wir uns ein typisches Berliner Essen bestellt.** *Afterwards we ordered ourselves a typical Berlin meal.*
bestellt This is the past participle of **bestellen:** *to order.* **Be-** is inseparable and therefore unstressed, so **ge-** is dropped from the past participle (L12, N5 and 8b).

10 **Ich kann mich nicht erinnern, daß du dich früher besonders für Essen interessiert hast.** *I don't recall that you were formerly particularly interested in food.*

a **daß du dich ... für Essen interessiert hast** One often puts it like this in English: (*I don't remember*) *you* BEING *specially interested* *in food.* One must make a **daß** clause in German in such expressions. **Sich interessieren für** means *to take an interest* IN.

b **interessiert** This is clearly the past participle – once again without **ge-**. Briefly, any verb whose infinitive ends in **-ieren** (**studieren, reservieren, telephonieren**) has no **ge-** in its past participle.

11 **Und bezahlt haben wir für alles zusammen nur** *And for the whole lot we only paid*

a This word order is really unusual, and is used here because Renate wishes to stress the PAID. One way of giving really unusual stress to an item is to place it at the beginning. Hence we find **bezahlt,** the past participle, which normally goes at the end, right out of its usual place here.

b **bezahlt** There is no **ge-** since **be-** is inseparable and unstressed.

12 **Wie ist denn das passiert?** *How did that happen?*
   ist Sometimes in a perfect tense construction, the auxiliary verb used is not **haben** but **sein** (*to be*). This is dealt with in detail in later lessons.

13 **Stell dir vor, der Kellner hat sich um zehn Mark verrechnet!** *Just imagine, the waiter miscalculated by ten marks.*

a **stell dir vor** This is the familiar request form of **sich vorstellen. Dir** is a reflexive pronoun, but a dative one (*picture* TO *yourself*). Some reflexive verbs then require their reflexive pronouns to be dative, but this is not difficult, since all except the **sich** ones are the same as the personal pronouns in the dative (**mir, dir, uns, euch**). **Sich** can be accusative or dative.

b **um zehn Mark verrechnet** Um is the equivalent of *by* – to miscalculate *by* so much. **Verrechnet** has the prefix **ver-,** which is inseparable, so there is no **ge-** in the past participle.

Schnellreinigung *Express cleaning*

14 **wie ich sehe, hast du deinen Anzug reinigen lassen.** *I see you've had your suit cleaned.*

a The use of **wie ich sehe,** followed by a main clause in the perfect tense, is a useful way of avoiding a **daß** clause (**ich sehe, daß**).

b **hast du deinen Anzug reinigen lassen** Lassen means *to have* (*or get*) (*something done*). **Ich lasse meinen Anzug reinigen:** *I'm having my suit* CLEANED. Note that **reinigen** (the infinitive) is used for CLEANED (a past participle in English). **Lassen** can mean other things, so it is treated specially when it has this particular meaning. One feature of this different treatment is that, in a perfect tense construction, the infinitive of **lassen** is used instead of the past participle – **Ich habe meinen Anzug reinigen lassen**: *I have* HAD *my suit* CLEANED. In this kind of sentence, we have two infinitives at the end, and **lassen** must be placed last.

15 **Was war los?** *What was wrong?* This is a very idiomatic German phrase meaning *what was wrong? what went on? what happened?*

16 **Hat man versucht, dich mit deinem Anzug zusammen in die Maschine zu stecken?** *Did they try to put you and your suit into the machine together?*
hat man versucht **Versuchen** has an inseparable prefix, so there is no **ge-**. In sentences like *did they try to do something,* one completes the perfect tense phrase first (**hat man versucht**) then adds a comma, and completes the sentence with **zu** and an infinitive. (Just as one does in the present tense with a sentence like **Es ist schwer, ihn anzurufen:** *It is difficult to telephone him.*)

17 **so schmutzig war ich nicht.** *I wasn't that dirty.* This word order is to give emphasis to **nicht**.

18 **Die Frau in der Reinigung hat mich wie einen Schuljungen in die Ecke gestellt.** *The woman in the cleaner's stood (put) me in a corner like a schoolboy.*
wie einen Schuljungen **Einen** must be accusative, because it is an object of **hat gestellt** just like **mich**.

19 **Dann habe ich mir den Anzug ausziehen müssen** *Then I had to take my suit off*
a **mir den Anzug ausziehen:** *take off* MY *suit* **Den** (not **meinen**) is used with **Anzug,** so **mir** is put in to clarify ownership. This is a standard pattern – **Zieh dir den Anzug aus:** *Take* YOUR *suit* off
b **ausziehen müssen** Once again, we find two INFINITIVES at the end of a perfect tense construction. When the perfect tense of a modal verb is used with a completing infinitive, the infinitive of the modal verb is used instead of a past participle. It is really the same type of construction as in N14b above, e.g.:
Ich muß in die Stadt gehen: *I must (have to) go into town.*
Ich *habe* in die Stadt gehen *müssen*: *I* HAD *to go into town.*

20 **und habe gewartet, bis er fertig war.** *and waited till it was ready.*
bis er fertig war This is a dependent clause introduced by **bis** and the verb (**war**) must go at the end.

21   Ich habe mir bloß die Haare färben lassen... *I've only had my hair tinted...*

a   mir die Haare (N19a above)   MY *hair* is indicated by **mir**. *Hair* is sometimes **das Haar** and sometimes **die Haare** (plural, of course). Both are generally acceptable.

b   färben lassen   Compare the construction dealt with in **N14b**.

22   Und wie haben sie dir aus deinen glatten Haaren solche Locken gedreht? *And how did they roll curls like that with (from) your straight hair?*

a   dir: *for you*   This kind of use of the dative of the personal pronouns is very common. It is not always necessary to translate it.

b   solche Locken: lit. *such curls*   **Solche** must often be translated as LIKE THAT. (**Solcher** is a **der** word).

23   Seht ihr denn nicht, daß ich mir eine Perücke gekauft habe? *Don't you see (that) I've bought myself a wig?*

daß ich mir eine Perücke gekauft habe   In a perfect tense construction in a **daß** clause, the auxiliary (**habe**) is placed last, remember, and the past participle immediately before it.

Part three

Kochkunst   *Haute cuisine*

24   Ich weiß nicht, wie ich das machen soll. *I don't know how to do it.*

wie ich das machen soll   This is the best way of saying *how to do it* (*how I should do it*). This is an 'indirect question' type of dependent clause, introduced by the question word **wie?:** *how?* The verb (**soll**) is separated from its subject (**ich**) and goes to the end, after the completing infinitive.

25   Ich habe vergessen, ob man das Wasser zuerst kochen muß. *I've forgotten whether one has to boil the water first.*

vergessen   This is the past participle, which happens to be the same as the infinitive. Firstly, **ver-** is an inseparable prefix, so **ge-** is dropped. Secondly, there is an **-en** instead of a **-t** at the end. This is the first example of a past participle of a strong verb, a distinctive feature of which is precisely this fact that the past participle ends in **-en** and not **-t** as in weak verbs. There are weak and strong verbs in English too:

WEAK	STRONG
walk – walked	*know – known*
play – played	*sing – sung*
cook – cooked	*make – made*

12

These are dealt with in detail in later lessons, and a full list of strong verbs (with their past participles) appears in Appendix **24**.

26 **wenn du nicht kochen kannst.** *if you can't cook.* If there is more than one dependent clause, they follow each other as independent units of the sentence, separated by commas and each obeying the rules within its own clause.

Endlich eine Antwort   *An answer at last*

27 **mich zweimal gefragt.** *asked me twice (two times).*   When **fragen** means *to ask (a person)*, the person is put in the accusative — here **mich**.

28 **warum haben Sie meine Frage nie beantwortet?** *why have you never answered my question?* (a DIRECT question with a perfect tense)
Beantwortet is the past participle of **beantworten**: *to answer.*
Be- is an inseparable prefix – no **ge-**. The stem ends in **-t** so an **e** must be inserted between the two **t**'s.

Da läßt sich nichts machen!   *There's nothing to be done about it!*

29 **Da läßt sich nichts machen!**
a **läßt**   **Lassen** is a vowel-changing verb.
b **machen:** (here) *be done*   The infinitive of a verb can mean *be +* past participle in certain circumstances, e.g.: **nichts zu machen** means *nothing to be done* not *nothing to do.*

30 **lasse ich sie mir vom Friseur machen.** *I have it done (for me) by the hairdresser.*
vom Friseur   *Done* BY a person is **von**.

31 **Deshalb lasse ich sie so, wie sie sind.** *That's why I leave it just as it is (leave it alone).*
a **Lasse** has a quite straightforward meaning here – *leave* or *let*.
b **so, wie sie sind**   In translation, **so** can be ignored. *Just as it is* (of anything): **so, wie es ist.** There is a comma after **so**, as **wie** begins a dependent clause.

13

Lektion dreizehn   Die Verlobung

Lesson thirteen   The engagement

What happens

The day of the engagement has arrived at last.

In Part 1 Eva explains why she was angry with Herbert. In Part 2 Herbert and Eva exchange rings, toasts are drunk and they all go off to a nightclub to celebrate the engagement.

New words in this lesson

der Jugendliche(-n) juvenile, young person
der Mantel(ˮ) coat
der Ring(-e) ring
der Schluß end
der Toast health, toast
der Wunsch(ˮe) wish

die Bestellung(-en) order
die Garderobe(-n) cloak-room
die Handarbeit(-en) handicraft and needlework
die Kindergärtnerin(-nen) kindergarten teacher (female)
die Zeremonie(-n) ceremony

das Beste best
das Examen(-) examination
das Gläschen(-) small glass
das Herz(-en) heart
das Jugendheim(-e) youth centre (residential)
das Kabarett(-s) cabaret, nightclub
das Leben life
das Singen singing
das Spielen play

bitten to ask
nennen to call
(sein) du bist gewesen (to be) you've been

(sollen) du solltest (should, ought) you should have
tun to do
verlieren to lose

beschäftigen to occupy
gratulieren (D) to congratulate
heiraten to marry
legen to put
liegen lassen to leave (something) lying
regnen to rain
reservieren to book, reserve
wünschen to hope

anstellen to employ
aufhören to give-up
entgegennehmen to accept, take (an order)

sich beeilen to hurry
sich duzen to say 'du' to each other
sich freuen über to be very pleased about

eifersüchtig jealous
fertig finished
gemütlich pleasant, comfortable
glücklich happy
letzt last
mancher, manche, manches some, quite a few

114

naß wet
wichtig important

inzwischen in the meantime
nirgends nowhere
überall everywhere

darauf on that
darüber about that
irgendwie somehow
obwohl although
sonst or else, otherwise
zwar actually, really, certainly

auf to

am liebsten möchte ich I'd like best to
auf keinen Fall on no account
drei Viertel sechs quarter to six
es ist mir egal I don't mind
im letzten Augenblick at the last moment
mein Examen machen to sit my exam
und dergleichen (u. dgl.) and such like
von jetzt ab from now on
wir haben es geschafft we have made it
zum Schluß finally

Notes

Part one

1 **Ich war nicht wirklich eifersüchtig auf Anne Green.** *I wasn't really jealous of Anne Green.*
  eifersüchtig auf *Jealous of* is **eifersüchtig auf** + accusative.

2 **weil ich in den letzten Wochen zu viel gearbeitet habe.** *because I've been working too hard in the last few weeks.*

a **Zu viel** means *too* MUCH, but **viel arbeiten** is *to work* HARD.

b **gearbeitet** Remember any past participle can mean *been doing* something as well as *done* something.

3 **Obwohl ich eigentlich Kindergärtnerin von Beruf bin,** *Although I'm really a Kindergarten teacher by profession,*
  Obwohl: *although* always introduces a dependent clause, so the verb (**bin**) is placed at the end of the clause.

4 **hat man mich in einem Jugendheim angestellt.** *I've been employed in a home for young people.*
  Hat man mich ... angestellt: *I have* BEEN *employ*ED is what is known as a PASSIVE construction in English. That is, something has BEEN DONE TO the subject (*I*); the subject is not the instigator of the action. Compare:
  Ich habe es ihm gezeigt: *I* SHOWED *it to him.*
  Man hat es mir gezeigt: *I* WAS SHOWN *it.* (*One has shown it to me.*)
  You see how neatly German can avoid a passive in form (though not in meaning) by the use of **man** (*one, they, someone*) plus an ACTIVE verb. (Active is the opposite of passive, grammatically speaking.) In English we then turn the object (**mich** in our sentence)

into the subject (*I*) and use a *be* or *been* + a past participle.
Do not, however, confuse a *been* + *-ing* (*been employing*)
construction (which is active) with a *been* + *-ed* (*been employed*)
construction (which is passive). In the past participles of verbs with
separable prefixes, the separable prefix precedes **ge-**.

5 **Dort tue ich mein Bestes.** *There I do my best.*
mein Bestes German makes the adjective **best** into a noun by
giving it a capital letter and a neuter classification – **das Beste.**
Note, however, that it must still be treated like an adjective as far
as endings are concerned. **-es** is the strong adjective ending,
after **mein**.

6 **Ich versuche, die Jugendlichen zwischen vierzehn und neunzehn
Jahren irgendwie zu beschäftigen:** *I try to occupy in some way the
youngsters between fourteen and nineteen:*

a This is an example of the possible distance in German between
the verb (**versuche**) and its completing infinitive with **zu** (**zu beschäftigen**) which must go to the end.

b **die Jugendlichen** This is really an adjective being used as a noun,
but requiring adjective endings. This word is used far more in the
plural (*young people*) than in the singular.

7 **mit Spielen, Singen, Lesen, Handarbeiten und dergleichen.** *with
playing, singing, reading, handicraft and the like.* You have already
encountered verbs used as nouns. They are written with a capital
and assigned a neuter classification. The English translation
nearly always ends in *-ing* – *playing, singing, reading.*
und dergleichen This phrase for *and the like* never changes in
any way and is frequently abbreviated to **u.dgl.**

8 **Ich weiß nicht, wie lange ich dort noch arbeiten werde.** *I don't know
how long I shall go on working there.*

a **wie lange ich dort noch arbeiten werde** This is an indirect question
(**wie lange**), so the verb (**werde**) is at the end, immediately preceded
by the completing infinitive (**arbeiten**).

b **noch arbeiten werde** **Werde** indicates the future (*I shall, I'll*) and
noch arbeiten: means literally *still work*. In English, we say *go on
working* or *continue to work*.

9 **An manchen Tagen möchte ich am liebsten gleich aufhören.** (*On*)
Some days I'd rather just give it all up.

a **an manchen Tagen** **Mancher/e/es** has endings like **dieser**. It can
mean *many a* (*on many a day*), although it is followed by a plural.
(See Appendix **1**.)

b am liebsten This is the stage after **lieber** (see L2, N46) and is called the superlative degree of the adverb. Used with a verb, then, **am liebsten** means (*would*) *like most or best*.
Ich trinke gern Bier: *I like beer.*
Ich trinke lieber Wein: *I prefer wine.*
Ich trinke am liebsten Kognak: *I like brandy best.*

Part two

Die Ringe *The rings*

10 **Aber Herbert! Wie kannst du im letzten Augenblick unsere Ringe verlieren?** *Herbert! How* CAN *you lose our rings at the last minute?*
aber Herbert! You cannot translate this **aber** into English except by tone of voice.

11 **Ich erinnere mich genau, wie die Verkäuferin sie eingepackt hat.** *I remember clearly the saleswoman wrapping them.*
wie die Verkäuferin sie eingepackt hat This is the only way of rendering the English construction. Herbert is not, strictly speaking, remembering HOW she did it, nor even the fact that it was done (which would be a **daß** clause). He is recalling watching her while she did it, or as she did it.

12 **Wo bist du gestern noch gewesen?** *Where else were you yesterday?*
bist du . . . gewesen?: lit. *have you been?* This is a perfect tense construction, but it has one strikingly different feature from those you have so far encountered – the auxiliary verb is **bist** and not **hast** as you would have expected. With certain verbs, the auxiliary used is **sein** and not **haben** and one of the most important of those is the verb **sein** itself. Its past participle is **gewesen** – quite irregular as you might expect of the verb **sein** by now. The category of verbs with which **sein** is used to form the perfect tense will be dealt with in the next few lessons, and you will find that this fact is mentioned in the list of parts of strong and irregular verbs in Appendix **24**.

13 **fürs Kabarett** *for the cabaret* **fürs** = **für** + **das.**

14 **mit ein paar Freunden telephoniert** *telephoned a few friends* *To phone someone* is either **anrufen** + accusative (or **bei** + dative (L9)) or **telephonieren** MIT + dative. **Ein paar** never changes, but the **-n** on **Freunden** indicates the dative.

15 **Um drei Viertel sechs solltest du deine Eltern abholen.** *At a quarter to six you were (supposed) to fetch your parents.*

117

13
a **um drei Viertel sechs** This is an alternative to **Viertel vor sechs.**
b **solltest du** This is the imperfect tense of **sollen,** and is formed just like that of **wollen** (L9, N4b). (See Appendix **12.**)

16 **Ich habe sie auch abgeholt.** *I* DID *fetch them.*
a **Auch** translates the emphasis on DID.
b **abgeholt** This is the past participle of **abholen.** Note where the **ge-** is placed, sandwiched between the separable prefix **ab-** and the rest of the past participle.

17 **Ja, jetzt weiß ich, wohin ich sie gelegt habe.** *Yes, now I know where I put them.*
a **wohin ich sie gelegt habe** This is an indirect question, so the verb phrase is placed at the end.
b **gelegt** The translation of *put* involves a little thought. So far you have met **stellen** (the lady in the cleaner's *put* Walter in the corner); **stecken** (did she try to *put* him into the machine with his suit) and **legen.** Briefly **stellen** is used for fairly large things which one *stands* somewhere; **stecken** for anything which is *enclosed* (perhaps rather unceremoniously) in a drawer, pocket, bag, etc. (like English *stick* used colloquially); and **legen** for fairly small things *laid* on a surface or even inside something.

Ein Toast *A toast*

18 **Und nun zum Schluß einen letzten Toast auf unsere beiden Verlobten.** *And now to end with, a last toast to our happy couple.*
a **einen** This is accusative because a subject and verb are actually not mentioned, but nevertheless implied.
b **auf unsere beiden Verlobten** *A toast* TO is **auf** + the accusative. **Verlobte** is another adjective (or past participle, really) used as a noun, but retaining adjective endings (**-en** after **unsere**).

19 **aber wir gratulieren euch von Herzen und wünschen, daß ihr zusammen glücklich sein werdet.** *but we congratulate you warmly and hope that you'll be happy together.*
a **euch** **Gratulieren** takes the dative case.
b **von Herzen**: lit. *from the heart* **Das Herz** has **-en** in the dative and **-ens** in the genitive. (See Appendix **8** on Mixed nouns.)

20 **... und werden uns eure Wünsche zu Herzen nehmen.** *... and will take your good wishes to heart.*
uns This is not strictly necessary, but indicates OUR *hearts.*

21 **Sobald ich fertig studiert habe, wollen wir heiraten.** *As soon as I have completed my studies, we intend to get married.*

a **Sobald:** *as soon as* introduces a dependent clause (of time) and the verb is placed at the end of the clause.

b **fertig studiert** **Studiert,** being an **-ieren** verb, has no **ge-** in the past participle. **Fertig** means *finished, at an end.* It is not a separable prefix, but is often used along with a verb meaning *to bring that activity to an end:* **fertig studieren:** *to finish studying;* **etwas fertig schreiben:** *to finish writing something.*

Noch ein Toast   *Another toast*

22 **Darf ich Sie und Ihren Mann bitten, mich statt „Fräulein Schultze" von jetzt ab „Eva" zu nennen?** *May I ask you and your husband to call me 'Eva' from now on, instead of 'Fräulein Schultze'?*

a **Bitten** means *to ask* in the sense of *request.* If one is requesting a person, the person is in the accusative case.

b **bitten,... zu nennen** Whatever the person(s) is requested to do, the verb form is the infinitive, which is placed at the end of the sentence preceded by **zu.**

23 **Ich freue mich sehr darüber.** *I'll be delighted to.* (*I'm delighted about that.*) **sich freuen** *über:* *to be very pleased about;* **sich freuen** *auf:* *to look forward to* (L7)

24 **Darauf müssen wir noch ein Gläschen trinken.** *We must have another drink to that.*
darauf **trinken auf:** *to drink* TO *something*

25 **ein kleines bißchen Zeremonie** *a little bit of ceremony* **Kleines** is agreeing with **bißchen** here since it is doing duty as a noun.

Im Kabarett   *In the nightclub*

26 **Kabarett** *nightclub* This word really means *cabaret,* so it is only used for nightclubs with a floor-show.

27 **Eben fängt es an zu regnen.** *It's just beginning to rain.* **Anfangen:** *to begin* requires **zu** + an infinitive, and infinitives go to the end of the sentence, thus taking precedence over the rule that separable prefixes go to the end. However, if whatever follows *begin(s)* is very short (as here) it is possible that you might hear **es fängt zu regnen an.** Variation occurs much more when **anfangen** is used in the perfect tense, however.

28 **Beeilt euch, sonst werdet ihr naß!** *Hurry up or you'll get wet!*

a **beeilt euch** The request form (familiar plural) of a reflexive verb always has the reflexive pronoun AFTER the verb: **Beeile** *dich!* (familiar singular) **Beeilen Sie** *sich!* (formal)

13

119

b **sonst:** *or else, otherwise* Its only effect on word order is to reverse subject and verb, if it is placed first.

c **werdet ihr** Remember **werden** means *to become* or *get* as well as being used as an auxiliary verb to form the future tense.

29 **Wir haben es gerade noch geschafft.** *We've only just made it.*
geschafft This use of **schaffen** is colloquial but very common.

30 **So klein und gemütlich habe ich es mir nicht vorgestellt.** *I didn't imagine it (to be) so small and pleasant.*
gemütlich Here is one of those 'atmosphere' words which is difficult to translate into another language – *comfortable, cosy* and *pleasant* are all implied by **gemütlich.**

31 **und nimmt Ihre Bestellung entgegen.** *and will take your order.*
Entgegennehmen is the word used for waiters or people in a similar situation 'taking' an order. The verb really means *receive* or *accept.*

Part three

Sie vergißt viel *She's very forgetful*

32 **läßt ihre Bücher ... liegen** *leaves her books lying ....* Here **lassen** is used in yet another sense – *to leave* a thing somewhere. Notice that in the phrase *she leaves ... lying, lying* is translated by the infinitive (**liegen**).

33 **wenn sie sie morgen wieder liegen läßt.** *if she leaves them lying about again tomorrow.*

a Note how the same verb phrase is handled in a **wenn** clause. As usual, the verb (**läßt**) goes last immediately preceded by the infinitive.

b **sie sie** The first one means *she* and the second *them*. This may sound awkward to English ears, but it happens quite often and one gets used to it.

Kein Grund *Insufficient reason*

34 **ich habe nicht gedurft.** *I wasn't allowed (given permission).*
gedurft The past participle of **dürfen** IS used this time because Renate does NOT use another verb (infinitive) along with it.

Lektion vierzehn Letzter Tag in Berlin

Lesson fourteen Last day in Berlin

What happens

The visit to Berlin is nearly over.

In Part 1 Herr Kühn mentions the highlights of their stay and announces their plans for the last day. In Part 2 Renate and Herbert discuss examinations, and Frau Kühn and Eva talk about a fashion show; finally the visitors leave for Munich.

New words in this lesson

der Abschied(-e) departure, farewell
der Berg(-e) mountain
der Professor(-en) professor

die Angst("e) fear, fright
die Boutique(-n) boutique
die Geschichte(-n) story
die Mensa (Mensen) student refectory
die Mode(-n) fashion
die Modenschau(-en) fashion show
die Musikhochschule(-n) college of music
die Suche(-n) search
die Zeitschrift(-en) magazine

das Drittel(–) third
das Faschingskleid(-er) fancy dress
das Kleid(-er) article of clothing, dress
das Konzert(-e) concert
das Schloß("sser) palace, castle
das Studium study

(essen) du hast gegessen you've eaten
(gefallen) (D) es hat uns gefallen we liked it
(helfen) (D) sie hat mir geholfen she's helped me
(nehmen) du hast genommen you've taken
(sehen) wir haben gesehen we've seen

(sollen) ich sollte I was to
(sprechen) ich habe gesprochen I've spoken
(trinken) du hast getrunken you've drunk

erlauben to allow, permit
hoffen to hope
passen (D) to fit
prüfen to examine
wiederholen to take again

(anfangen) er hat angefangen he's begun
(ausgeben) ihr habt (Geld) ausgegeben you've spent (money)
aussehen (er sieht aus) to look (he looks)
(einladen) sie (die Familie) hat eingeladen they (the family) have invited
fertig werden to finish
schwerfallen(D) to be difficult

sich fragen to ask oneself

arm poor
billiger cheaper
furchtbar terrible, terribly
gelb yellow
herzlich heartfelt, sincere
hübscher prettier
länger longer
liebst favourite

121

14

schneller quicker
weiß white

außerdem besides, also
meistens mostly, usually
noch also
trotzdem in spite of it
ungefähr about, approximately
wohl probably

bald einmal soon
neulich recently
schon wieder again

als than

selber oneself

an Weihnachten at Christmas

besser gesagt or rather
das heißt that means
das kommt darauf an it depends
das war sehr freundlich von Ihnen that was very kind of you
du bist eifersüchtig auf mich you are jealous of me
es ist bekannt it's a well known fact
es fällt mir schwer I find it hard
ich frage mich nur I wonder
in irgendeiner Zeitschrift in some magazine or other
ist dir bekannt? are you aware that?
mit etwas fertig werden to get finished with something
willst du mir Angst machen? do you want to frighten me?
zu Ende bringen to finish
zum Abschied to say farewell

Notes

Part one

1   **Jetzt sind wir länger als vierzehn Tage in Berlin gewesen.**
    Now we've been in Berlin more than a fortnight.
    länger als: *longer than*   When *more* refers to a period of
    time, one must use **länger,** not **mehr. Länger** is the comparative
    of **lang.** One adds an Umlaut and **-er.** Except with irregular
    adjectives (*good, better,* etc.) and adverbs, this is the standard
    procedure, though the addition of the Umlaut is not invariable.

2   **Es hat uns hier gut gefallen,** *We've enjoyed being here* (*we've
    liked it here*),
    Gefallen: *to please,* remember, requires an impersonal construction
    putting the English subject (*we*) into the dative (**uns**) in German.
    Gefallen in this sentence is obviously a past participle, yet its
    form is identical with the infinitive. This is because **ge-** is an
    inseparable prefix, and because **gefallen:** *to please* is a so-called
    strong verb; the past participles of strong verbs end in **-en** (**L12,**
    vergessen and **bekommen;** also Appendix **24**).

3   **trotzdem haben wir viel gesehen.** *in spite of that, we've seen a lot.*
    gesehen   This is the past participle of **sehen.** Note that
    although not all strong verbs are vowel-changing in the present

122

tense, any verb that does have such a vowel change is strong, and its past participle will end in -en.

4 **Der Besuch im Schillertheater** *The visit* TO *the Schillertheater* This is dative because one thinks of one's *being* there and not of *going* there.

5 **Familie Schultze hat uns zum Abschied noch einmal zum Mittagessen eingeladen.** *The Schultze family has invited us to lunch again as a farewell visit.*
eingeladen This is the past participle of **einladen**: *to invite.* As with weak verbs with separable prefixes, the separable prefix in strong verbs precedes the **ge-** (L13, N16b).

6 **wir haben uns alle gleich gut verstanden** *we got on well with each other*
verstanden This is the past participle of **verstehen**. Since **ver-** is an inseparable prefix, you would not expect a **ge-**. It is a strong verb, so the past participle ends in **-en**. But how does **-steh-** become **-stand-**? How does *under*STAND become *under-*STOOD*?* It may be easier to accept such difficulties if it is pointed out that the same difficulty exists in English.

Part two

In der Universität *In the university*

7 **wann hast du eigentlich zu studieren angefangen?** *when did you actually begin to study?*
This is the kind of sentence referred to in L13, N27. Depending on the length of the infinitive phrase (**zu studieren**) and to the same extent on the preference of the speaker, the infinitive phrase can be placed before the past participle (as here), or after it (**wann hast du angefangen zu studieren?**). If the infinitive phrase is rather long it is more often placed after the past participle, e.g. **Wann hast du angefangen, Psychologie in Berlin zu studieren?**: *When did you begin to study psychology in Berlin?*

8 **vor ungefähr viereinhalb Jahren.** *about four and a half years ago.*
viereinhalb This is how one adds *and a half* to any number except **eins**. *One and a half* is **anderthalb** or sometimes **eineinhalb**.

9 **Ist dir bekannt, daß fast ein Drittel aller Studenten in Deutschland das Studium nicht zu Ende bringt?** *Are you aware that nearly a third of all students in Germany don't complete their studies?*

a **ist dir bekannt, daß...**: *is (the fact) known to you, that...*

Grammatically speaking **ist dir bekannt,** is a clause without a subject as the 'subject' is the whole **daß** clause which follows. This is why it is necessary to say *it* or *the fact* when translating literally.

b **ein Drittel** Fractions are easy in German as one normally just adds **-tel** to the number (e.g. **Viertel:** *a quarter*). A *third* (as in English) is irregular, however.

c **aller Studenten** This is the genitive plural, and **aller** requires the strong adjective ending.

10 **Willst du mir Angst machen?** *Are you trying to (do you want to) frighten me?*
To frighten someone is **Angst** (*fear*) **machen** plus the dative.

11 **in irgendeiner Zeitschrift gelesen.** *read in some magazine or other.*

a **irgendein** This word is used to convey vagueness. It has the same endings as **ein.**
irgendwie: *somehow or other* **irgend etwas:** *something or other*

b **gelesen** This is the past participle of **lesen.**

12 **Ist es nicht erlaubt, das Examen zu wiederholen?** *Isn't one (it) allowed to resit the exam?*
zu wiederholen **Wiederholen** means *to repeat.* From the position of **zu** you will see that **wieder** is an inseparable prefix. But what about **ich freue mich sehr, dich wiederzusehen**?
Here, it is a separable prefix. By far the easiest way to remember when it is separable and when inseparable is to listen for the stress and get it right from the first time you hear it. As you already know, inseparable prefixes are always unstressed and separable prefixes stressed. **Wiedersehen** is therefore separable; **wiederholen** is inseparable. Fortunately there are few prefixes which can be either, and there need never be any doubt in your mind so long as you get the stress correct.

13 **Das kommt darauf an.** *It depends.* This is an idiom which you must just accept without analysis. It is a much used expression and quite easy to remember.

14 **Weißt du schon, welcher Professor dich prüfen wird?** *Do you already know which professor will be examining you?*
welcher This word you know already, though only in DIRECT questions (**Welcher Professor wird dich prüfen?**). This is an indirect question, but **welcher** used in this way behaves precisely as it does in direct questions – i.e. its endings will be dependent on the class of the following noun and the function

that noun fulfils in the **welch-** clause, e.g. **Weißt du, welchen Gürtel er gekauft hat?**: *Do you know which belt he bought?*

15 **Ich habe schon oft mit ihm über meine Arbeit gesprochen.** *I've often talked to (with) him about my work.*

a **mit ihm über meine Arbeit gesprochen** *To talk* TO *someone* ABOUT *something* – use **mit** and the dative of the person and **über** and the accusative of the subject of discussion.

b **gesprochen** This is the past participle of **sprechen** (L14, N6).

16 **Du, Herbert, ich habe schon wieder furchtbaren Hunger.** *I say, Herbert, I'm terribly hungry again.*

a **Du, Herbert** This is very colloquial and is only used with **du** (not with **Sie**), which indicates the familiarity of this opening gambit. The English rendering, *I say*, is quite inadequate but as near as one can get to the sense of it.

b **furchtbaren Hunger**: lit. *dreadful hunger* **Furchtbaren** has the strong adjective ending (**-en**), though it happens, in this case, to be the same as the weak one.

17 **Du hast seit zwei Stunden nichts gegessen und getrunken.** *You've had nothing to eat and drink for two hours.*
gegessen und getrunken **Gegessen** is the past participle of **essen**, and the only unusual feature is the extra **g** between the two **e**'s for reasons of sound harmony. **Getrunken** is the past participle of **trinken.**

Neue Kleider   *New dresses*

18 **Sicher habt ihr viel Geld ausgegeben.** *You've spent a lot of money, no doubt.*

a **sicher**: *certain, sure* This can often be translated as *no doubt.*

b **ausgegeben** This is the past participle of **ausgeben**, *to spend* (money). **Gegeben** is the past participle of **geben** and any separable prefix is simply attached to the beginning. Compare:– **aufgeben, aufgegeben; ansehen, angesehen; aussehen, ausgesehen.**

19 **Oder besser gesagt,** *or rather (better said)* The comma after **gesagt** avoids subject-verb inversion here.

20 **Sie sind ganz leicht selber zu machen.** *They are quite simple to make oneself.*
selber This word serves the same purpose as **selbst,** which you already know. **Selber** is the more colloquial version.

14

21 **Eva hat mir beim Suchen geholfen** *Eva helped me look*

  a **beim Suchen:** lit. *with the searching* **Beim** + a verb used as a noun means *in the doing of it* or *while doing it*, e.g. **beim Sprechen:** *while speaking, in speaking.*

  b **geholfen** This is the past participle of **helfen.**

22 **und hat zwei sehr nette Kleider gefunden.** *and found two very nice dresses.*

    gefunden This is the past participle of **finden.**

23 **Das weiße war vielleicht hübscher als das gelbe.** *The white one was perhaps prettier than the yellow one.*

    das weiße When you wish to use *one* in a phrase like *the white one,* you just use the appropriate form of **der/die/das** plus the adjective (with the weak ending).

24 **hat mir besser gepaßt.** *suited/fitted me better.* **Passen** can mean *to suit* or *fit.* **Besser** (like **gut**) can be both an adjective and an adverb. Here it is an adverb.

25 **Hast du es genommen?** *Did you take it?*

    genommen This is the past participle of **nehmen.**

26 **Hoffentlich sagst du nicht, daß es wie ein Faschingskleid aussieht.** *I hope you won't say it looks like a fancy dress costume.*

  a **Fasching** is carnival time in Munich, and everyone dresses in fancy dress.

  b **aussieht** Separable prefixes join the main verb when it comes at the end of a dependent clause.

Der Abschied   *Departure*

27 **es war sehr freundlich von Ihnen, uns zum Flughafen zu fahren.** *it was very nice (kind) of you to drive us to the airport.*

    uns zum Flughafen zu fahren An infinitive phrase must complete **es war freundlich von Ihnen.**

28 **Der Abschied fällt mir dieses Mal gar nicht schwer.** *I don't find leaving at all hard (to bear) this time.*

    Der Abschied fällt mir nicht schwer: lit. *The farewell doesn't fall heavily on me.* **Der Abschied fällt uns schwer:** *We find the farewell hard to bear/we feel it keenly.*

29 **geht's zum Skilaufen** *we'll be off ski-ing (it's off to the ski-ing)*

30 **Ich sollte Sie von meiner Tante, Frau Raffke, grüßen.** *I was to give you my aunt, Frau Raffke's, regards.* **Grüßen** (*to greet*) and the accusative of the person is *to give* (or *send*) *someone regards; from* is **von** + dative, e.g. **Grüßen Sie ihn von mir:** *Give him my regards.*

31 **Sie hofft, Sie bald einmal in Berlin wiederzusehen.** *She hopes to see you again soon in Berlin.*
    wiederzusehen **Wieder** is separable in **wiedersehen** (it is stressed).

32 **Sie waren seit langer Zeit ihre liebsten Gäste.** *You were her favourite guests in a long time.*
    liebst- This is the superlative of **lieb:** *dear,* and is always used (with the appropriate ending) to translate *favourite.*

Part three

Besser oder schneller?   *Better or quicker?*

33 **daß man in Deutschland nicht so schnell mit dem Studium fertig wird wie in England.** *that one doesn't complete one's course of study in Germany as quickly as in England.* **Fertig wird** completes the **daß** clause and the other half of the comparative phrase (**nicht so schnell ... wie in England**) follows.

Was soll ich tun?   *What shall I do?*

34 **Es ist bekannt, daß man dort billiger ißt und mehr bekommt als im Restaurant.** *It's a well-known fact (it's common knowledge) that you can eat more cheaply there and get more than in a restaurant.*
    The verb, or in this case, verbs (**ißt** and **bekommt**) in the **daß** clause are placed BEFORE the **als** phrase (i.e. the completion of the comparative).

Lektion fünfzehn   Schnee in München

Lesson fifteen   Munich in the snow

What happens

The Kühns are back in Munich and settled in Frau Riemer's flat, with which they are more than satisfied.

In Part 1 Frau Kühn describes the flat and the winter weather and plans an outing. In Part 2 the family discuss how to get to Nymphenburg Palace; they walk along the banks of a canal and Herr Kühn tells Renate something about the history of the Palace.

15 New words in this lesson

der Baum(¨e) tree
der Handschuh(-e) glove
der Kanal(¨e) canal
der Kurfürst(-en) Elector
der Schlittschuh(-e) skate
der Schnee snow
der Stiefel(–) boot
der Stil(-e) style
der Weg(-e) path
der Wintersport winter sports

die Burg(-en) castle
die Gegend(-en) area
die Gelegenheit(-en) opportunity
die Residenz(-en) residence
die Seite(-n) side
die Straße(-n) street, road

das Buch(¨er) book
das Eis ice
das Eisschießen curling
das Internat(-e) boarding school

(empfehlen) sie hat empfohlen she has
   recommended
fehlen to be missing
halten to stop
halten für to consider
kommen to get to
laufen to walk
liegen to lie
(schlafen) ich habe geschlafen I've slept
(schließen) es ist geschlossen it is closed
schneien to snow

(anrufen) ich habe angerufen I've telephoned
aufpassen to watch out
spazierengehen to go for a walk

sich (D) ansehen to watch, take a look at
(sich) anziehen (ich habe etwas angezogen) to dress (oneself) (I've put something on)
sich entscheiden to decide in favour of
(sich entschließen für) wir haben uns entschlossen we've decided

eigen own
fest hard, solid
froh pleased, happy, glad
glatt slippery
hohe high
kalt cold
langsam slow(ly)
trocken dry

am einfachsten easiest
am schnellsten quickest

einmal once
noch nie never
vorgestern the day before yesterday

dorthin to that place, there
um round
weg away

Achtung! take care! look out!
also dann los! right, let's go!
aus der Nähe from close up, nearby
es waren there were
genauso just as
gleich in a minute
mir ist etwas kalt I'm feeling a bit cold
um die Ecke round the corner
wie noch nie as never before
wissen ... noch to remember

Notes

Part one

1   **Ich bin froh, daß wir uns für Frau Riemers Wohnung entschlossen
   haben.** *I'm glad we decided on Frau Riemer's flat.*

128

entschlossen This is the past participle of **entschließen**. **Ent-** is an inseparable prefix.

2 **Aber es ist trockener und fester Schnee,** *But it is dry and hard snow,*
trockener und fester Schnee The **-er** on **trockener** and **fester** is the strong adjective ending (**der Schnee**) and not to be confused with **-er** of the comparative degree. An adjective in the comparative degree requiring a nominative singular masculine strong ending would end in **-erer**, e.g. **ein besserer Wagen:** *a better car.*

3 **spazierengehen** *to go for a walk* This is like **kennenlernen** – a compound verb in which the first one is treated like a separable prefix.

Part two

Nach Nymphenburg   *To Nymphenburg*

4 **Wie kommen wir am schnellsten nach Nymphenburg?** *What's our quickest way to Nymphenburg?*
am schnellsten: lit. *most quickly* This is where we see an obvious difference between the adjective and the adverb (apart from adjective endings). The adverb MUST be **am schnellsten.** (See Appendix **2.**)

5 **Wir brauchen nicht mit dem Auto zu fahren.** *We don't need to (have to) go by car.*
wir brauchen nicht... zu fahren This is the best way of saying *don't have to* do something – **brauchen nicht + zu +** infinitive.

6 **hält gleich hier um die Ecke.** *stops just round the corner from here.*

a **hält** **Halten:** *to stop* (vowel-changing) is unusual in the third person in that it is **hält** and NOT **hältet.**

b **um die Ecke** **um:** *round,* always takes the accusative.

7 **am einfachsten** *in the simplest way* Since this expression has **am** in front, it is immediately recognizable as an adverb. **Einfach** means *simple* (or *simply*); **am einfachsten:** *in the simplest way.*

8 **empfohlen** *recommended* This is the past participle of **empfehlen:** *to recommend.* **Emp-** is an inseparable prefix.

9 **brauchen wir nicht umzusteigen und nicht weit zu laufen.** *we don't have to change or walk far.*

a Any similar types of sentence, clause or phrase can be joined by **und.** Sometimes this cannot be literally translated into English, however, and one must choose another link word, like *or.*

b **laufen** The dictionary will give the first meaning as *to run.* In colloquial German, it also means *to walk* (i.e. go on foot).

10 **Jeder muß sich so warm wie möglich anziehen.** *Everyone must dress as warmly as possible.*

a **sich anziehen:** *to dress* (*oneself*) **Sich** is accusative.

b **so warm wie möglich** This is a standard pattern – *as...as possible* is **so ... wie möglich.**

11 **Ich habe mir schon meine hohen Stiefel angezogen.** *I've already put my high boots on.*

a **ich habe mir ... angezogen** Compare this with L15, N10a. **Mir** is dative because the direct object is **meine hohen Stiefel. Sich** (dative) **anziehen** here means *to put on* (a garment) and **mir** is to indicate that the speaker is putting on the garment herself.

b **angezogen** This is the past participle of **anziehen.**

12 **Ich bin auch gleich fertig.** *I'll be ready in a minute, too.*
Gleich normally means *immediately,* but also *almost immediately,* i.e. *in a minute.*

Den Kanal entlang *Along the canal*

13 **mit hohen Bäumen** *with tall trees*
hohen **Hoch** is *high, tall,* but the **c** drops out when it is used in front of a noun. This is the dative plural.

14 **es schneit immer noch.** *it's still snowing.* **Immer** intensifies the **noch,** and is used when something has been going on for quite a time and looks like continuing.

15 **Paß auf und lauf langsam!** *Watch out and walk slowly!* These are familiar (singular) request forms. Note that a separable prefix (**paß auf!**) comes after the main part.

16 **Was spielen die denn?** *What* (*game*) *are* THEY *playing?*
die This is used instead of **sie** here. It is a habit in the spoken language to use this pronoun (identical with **der** in nominative, accusative and dative singular) when you wish either to give emphasis (as here) or to indicate disapproval or even contempt.

17 **ein beliebter Wintersport** *a popular winter sport* **Beliebter** has the strong adjective ending after **ein** (it is NOT a comparative).

18 **Und hier vorn, direkt vor uns, laufen sie Schlittschuh.** *And here, just ahead of us, they're skating.*
laufen sie Schlittschuh **Schlittschuh laufen** means *to skate.* Although **Schlittschuh laufen** is written as two separate words, you can see that **Schlittschuh** is treated in the same way as a separable prefix.

130

19 **Früher bin ich auch viel Schlittschuh gelaufen.** *Once (formerly) I did a lot of skating too (I skated a lot).*
bin ich ... Schlittschuh gelaufen **Schlittschuh gelaufen** is the past participle of **Schlittschuh laufen** (L15, N18). Note that the auxiliary verb is **bin** and not **habe**.

Schloß Nymphenburg *Nymphenburg Palace*

20 **Erinnerst du dich, Renate, was ich dir einmal vom Schloß Nymphenburg erzählt habe?** *Do you remember what I once told you about (of) Nymphenburg Palace, Renate?*
vom ... erzählt habe **Erzählen von** means *to tell of* or *about*. **Erzählt** is the past participle. **Er-** is inseparable and the verb is weak, so one adds **-t** (not **-en**) to the stem.
21 **Dann weißt du sicher auch noch,** *Then no doubt you also remember,*
Wissen + noch (*still know*) must often be translated as *remember*.
22 **daß Nymphenburg die Sommerresidenz der bayerischen Kurfürsten gewesen ist.** *that Nymphenburg was (has been) the summer residence of the Bavarian Electors.*
der bayerischen Kurfürsten This dates from long before the unification of Germany, when Bavaria was ruled over by a princeling with the title of Elector.
23 **Aber ich lese hier gerade, daß die kleine Amalienburg im Park schon geschlossen ist.** *But I'm just reading here that the little Amalienburg in the park is already closed.*
 a **die kleine Amalienburg** A summer residence built by Elector Karl Albrecht for his wife.
 b **geschlossen** You will recognize this as a past participle from its form, though it is here serving as an adjective (like *closed* in English). Many past participles are used as adjectives and are treated in the same way as adjectives. **Geschlossen** is used after the noun here, so it requires no ending.
24 **vielleicht entscheidest du dich morgen schon für das Internat am Chiemsee.** *perhaps you'll decide by tomorrow on the boarding school at Lake Chiem.*
am Chiemsee **Der See** means *the lake*. The word **See** is usually attached to the name given to the particular lake.
25 **und wirst bestimmt Gelegenheit haben, noch einmal hierher zu kommen.** *and will certainly have the opportunity of coming here again.*

15

Gelegenheit haben   This expression requires completion by an infinitive phrase with **zu.**

26 **Glaubt ihr nicht, daß es jetzt Zeit ist, nach Haus zu gehen?** *Don't you think (that) it's time to go home now (time we went home now)?* Notice that a **daß** clause can be 'embedded' in the sentence, in the sense that the verb phrase of the **daß** clause is NOT the last item of the sentence, though it is the last item of the **daß** clause. Here, the **daß** clause is completed and the infinitive phrase with **zu** follows. N.B. the different placing of **jetzt** and *now* in the German and English sentences.

27 **mir ist auch etwas kalt.** *I'm feeling a bit cold, too.*
    mir ist kalt   This is how one says *I'm cold* (like **mir ist schlecht:** *I'm sick*). It is one of those odd sentences without a grammatical subject. The person feeling cold is always in the dative case, e.g. **Ist Ihnen kalt?:** *Are you cold?*

28 **Jetzt hat es aufgehört zu schneien.** *Now it's stopped snowing.*
    aufgehört zu schneien   **Aufhören zu** is treated in the same way as **anfangen zu:** *to begin* (L13, N27 and L14, N7).

Part three

Zum Englischen Garten   *To the English Garden*

29 **den Weg dorthin** *the way there (to that place)*   **-hin** indicates motion AWAY from the speaker.

Schlittschuh laufen   *Skating*

30 **jeder wollte noch schneller laufen als der andere.** *each one wanted to skate even faster than the other.* Notice that the infinitive (**laufen**), which normally goes to the end, appears before the second half of the comparative (**als der andere**). This is exactly what happens with **daß** clauses.

Lektion sechzehn   Schulbesuch

Lesson sixteen   Visit to a school

What happens

The matter of Renate's education must be settled fairly soon, since the school year begins after Easter in Germany.

In Part 1 the headmaster of the school the Kühns are considering talks about his school. In Part 2 Herr and Frau Kühn talk to the headmaster and Renate questions one of the senior boys, who is showing her round. Finally the family discuss it among themselves.

New words in this lesson

der **Direktor**(-en) headmaster, principal
der **Fehler**(–) mistake
der **Film**(-e) film
der **Leiter**(–) head, manager
der **Schulbesuch** visit to a school
der **Schüler**(–) pupil

die **Erziehung** education
die **Form**(-en) form
die **Freizeit** spare time, leisure
die **Klasse**(-n) class, form
die **Meinung**(-en) opinion
die **Möglichkeit**(-en) possibility
die **Privatschule**(-n) private school
die **Schule**(-n) school
die **Schülerin**(-nen) school-girl
die **Umgebung**(-en) surroundings
die **Welt** world

das **Abitur** secondary school leaving examinations ('A' Levels)
das **Ausgehen** going out
das **Gebiet**(-e) field
das **Heimweh** home-sickness
das **Interesse**(-n) interest
das **Tanzen** dancing
das **Wochenende**(-n) week-end

das **Fechten** fencing
der **Fußball** football
das **Schwimmbad**("er) swimming-pool
das **Schwimmen** swimming
das **Segeln** sailing
der **Sport** sport(s)
die **Sportart**(-en) type of sport
der **Sportler**(–) athlete, sportsman
das **Tauchen** diving
das **Tennis** tennis
das **Turnen** P.T., gymnastics

die **Alten** old ones
die **Älteren** older ones
die **Jungen** young ones
die **Jüngeren** younger ones

der **Finne**(-n) Finn (male)
die **Finnin**(-nen) Finn (female)
der **Italiener**(–) Italian (male)
der **Portugiese**(-n) Portuguese (male)
die **Portugiesin**(-nen) Portuguese(female)
der **Spanier**(–) Spaniard (male)
die **Spanierin**(-nen) Spaniard (female)

ausländisch foreign
brasilianisch Brazilian
portugiesisch Portuguese (language)

16

finden to find, to think of
gelingen (D) (es ist mir gelungen)
   to succeed, manage (I've succeeded)
liegen to lie
verbieten (es ist verboten) to forbid,
   prohibit (it is forbidden)
(werden) du bist geworden you've got

antworten auf to answer
(erlauben) es ist erlaubt it is allowed
schaffen to create, accomplish

herkommen to come here
herumführen to show round

sich gewöhnen (an) to get used (to)
sich wohl fühlen to feel at ease

anders different
best best
fanatisch fanatical
fleißig hard-working
fließend fluent

geboren born
gemischt mixed
meist most
satt satisfied
üblich usual

ganz really, very, quite, whole
gegen against

welche some, any

aus der ganzen Welt from all over the
   world
das hängt davon ab, ob that depends on
   whether
ich kann mir nicht denken I cannot
   imagine
meiner Meinung nach in my opinion
mir fällt etwas ein something has
   occurred to me
noch immer und überall no matter
   where or when
zu viert schlafen to sleep four to a room

Notes

Part one

1 **Meine Schule ist anders als die meisten.** *My school is different
from most.*
anders als: lit. *other than   Other* is used here in the sense of
different. From in this expression must be **als.**

2 **ist es mir gelungen,** *I have succeeded,* **Gelingen** means *to succeed.*
It must be used impersonally, like **gefallen,** e.g. **es gelingt** *mir:*
I succeed. The English subject is dative in German. **Gelungen**
is the past participle (**ge-** is an inseparable prefix). Note that the
auxiliary verb is **sein.**

3 **eine der besten Privatschulen Deutschlands zu schaffen.** *in creating
one of the best private schools in Germany.*
Gelingen is followed by an infinitive phrase with **zu.**
Deutschlands   This is genitive (*of Germany*). In German you
use the genitive frequently after a superlative, like *best* (*best
school* OF *Germany*).

134

4   **aus der ganzen Welt**   *from the whole world (from all over the world)* **Ganz** can be either an adverb or an adjective.

5   **Unser˙ganz besonderes Interesse liegt auf dem Gebiet des Sports.**
Our particular interest lies in the field of sport.
ganz besonderes   Ganz is used as an adverb here and means
quite or *very*, though it does not really need to be translated
in this phrase.

6   **Möglichkeiten zum Skilaufen,** *possibilities of ski-ing, (opportunities* would be permissible here) **Möglichkeiten zu** is followed by
the dative. All the sports which follow are verb infinitives used
as nouns, except **Fußball** and **Tennis.**

7   **Ich kann mir nicht denken, daß sich jemand bei uns nicht sofort
wohl fühlt.** *I cannot imagine anyone not immediately feeling at
home here.*
daß sich jemand bei uns nicht sofort wohl fühlt   A **daß** clause is
the only way of dealing with the English construction *imagine
anyone feel*ING, *be*ING, *do*ING etc.

Part two

Fragen der Eltern   *Parents' questions*

8   **Lassen Sie mich Ihnen zuerst unser neues Schwimmbad zeigen** . . .
Let me show you our new swimming-pool first . . .
lassen Sie mich. . .zeigen   Lassen meaning *let* is quite
uncomplicated. You just have to remember to put the infinitive
(here **zeigen**) at the end.

9   **wie viele Schüler Sie in Ihren Klassen haben?** *how many pupils
you have in your classes?* This is an indirect question (after
sagen) so the verb goes to the end. The question mark belongs
to the question (direct) **können Sie uns**. . .

10   **Gewöhnlich sind es ungefähr zwanzig,** *Usually, there are about
twenty (it's about twenty),*
sind es   English *there are* or *it's* must be **es sind** if it is followed
by a plural (here, **zwanzig**).

11   **gemischt** *mixed*   This is a past participle (of **mischen:** *to mix*).
It is used as an adjective AFTER the noun.

12   **Meiner Meinung nach ist das die beste Form der Erziehung.**
In my opinion, that is the best form of education.

a   **meiner Meinung nach**   This is an idiom meaning *according to
what I think.* **Nach** can mean *according to,* and when it does, it is
often placed AFTER the noun. Note that the noun is still dative.

16

b **der Erziehung** This is genitive, and it is not possible to omit *the* as it is in English. Generalized statements about whole concepts nearly always use the definitite article (**der/die/das**).

13 **Unsere Tochter ist vier Jahre lang in eine brasilianische Schule gegangen.** *Our daughter went to a Brazilian school for four years.*

a **vier Jahre lang** **Lang** is sometimes used after a period of time when the period of time in question is a long one. It expresses English *for* that period of time.

b **ist...gegangen** **Gegangen** is the past participle of **gehen**: *to go,* and the auxiliary used is **sein**.

14 **Glauben Sie, daß sie es in drei Jahren bis zum Abitur schaffen wird?** *Do you think she will manage the higher leaving certificate in three years?*

a **in drei Jahren** *Within* a period of time is **in** + dative.

b **bis zum Abitur**: *as far as* or *up to the 'Abitur'* The **Abitur** has no translation; it is the equivalent of the English 'A' Level.

15 **Es wird ihr gelingen, wenn sie fleißig ist, und es schaffen will.** *She will succeed, if she works hard and* WANTS *to manage it.*
es wird ihr gelingen (L16, N2) **Gelingen** must be used impersonally, so the English subject (*she*) will be dative in German (**ihr**). This is future tense.

Renates Fragen *Renate's questions*

16 **Ich bin Friedhelm Pirzl und soll dich ein bißchen herumführen** *I'm Friedhelm Pirzl and I'm to show you round a bit*
herumführen: *to take* or *lead round* **Herum** is separable.

17 **und auf Fragen antworten, wenn du welche hast.** *and answer questions, if you have any.*

a **auf Fragen antworten** **Antworten** cannot have a direct object as *answer* can in English. You must either use **beantworten** (L5) or **antworten** *auf* + accusative.

b **wenn du welche hast** Usually, you do not have to find a single word for *any* in German. You either just ignore it (as in **Hast du Zigaretten?**: *Have you any cigarettes?*) or it is covered by another word (**Nein, ich habe keine**: *No, I haven't any*). There is no getting round it in an expression like this, however, and **welche** is the word used.

c **du** Young people up to about sixteen call each other **du** irrespective of relationship or length of acquaintance.

18 **Bist du in Brasilien geboren?** *Were you born in Brazil?*

136

bist...geboren Geboren is a past participle form, but you will only require it in the perfect. Note that the auxiliary is **sein.**

19 **ich bin in der dreizehnten,** *I'm in the thirteenth (class),*
What classes are called can vary, especially between state schools and private schools. Schooling begins at the age of six in Germany, and if you go as far as you can (to **Abitur** level), it normally takes thirteen years.

20 **Das hängt davon ab, ob man zu den Jungen oder zu den Alten gehört.** *It depends on whether you belong to the juniors or the seniors.*

a **das hängt davon ab, ob...** Abhängen von means *to depend on,* e.g. **es hängt vom Alter ab:** *it depends on age.* Von is an essential part of the verb phrase, and its object (WHAT it depends on) is in the dative. The object of **von** in our sentence is the whole **ob** clause. In German, you cannot leave a preposition (**von, auf, in, an, zu,** etc.) hanging at the end of a sentence or clause (separable prefixes are a different matter entirely), so **da** is put in to complete the phrase, and **da** stands for the following clause. One could say in English *it depends on* THE FACT (*as to whether*).

b **ob man zu den Jungen oder zu den Alten gehört** Gehören requires **zu** when the subject is not POSSESSED by the following noun or pronoun – as in **Dieser Koffer gehört Herrn Kühn** – but is part of the category described by the following noun, as here – **man gehört zu *den Jungen.*** In English we would say simply *one* IS *a junior or a senior.*

c **den Jungen oder zu den Alten** This is not the dative plural of **der Junge,** but the adjective **jung:** *young,* used as a noun and given a weak adjective ending. **Den Alten** is the adjective **alt:** *old,* similarly used.

21 **Die Jüngeren schlafen zu viert.** *The younger ones sleep four to a room.*

a **die Jüngeren** jung: *young;* **jünger:** *younger* (This is one instance where you must add an Umlaut as well as **-er** to form the comparative.)

b **zu viert:** *in fours* This form (with **-t** added to the number) is used for *in twos, threes, fours,* or a *twosome, foursome* etc.

22 **Die Älteren zu zweit oder zu dritt in einem Zimmer.** *The older ones two or three to a room.*

a **die Älteren** alt: *old;* **älter:** *older* (Umlaut required here, too.)

b **zu zweit oder zu dritt** (L16, N21b) Note that **zu dritt** (like **dritte:** *third*) is slightly irregular.

23 Ich wohne z.B. mit einem Italiener und einem Finnen zusammen.
I, for example, share (live) with an Italian and a Finn.

a einem Finnen **Der Finne** is *the Finn* (male). There is a final **-n** in all cases except the nominative singular (See Appendix **8** on Weak nouns.)

b zusammen **Mit** is not enough here. When it sounds sensible to say *in company with* in English, you require **mit...zusammen** in German.

24 Ist es erlaubt, im eigenen Zimmer zu rauchen? *Is one allowed to smoke (is smoking allowed) in one's own room?*

a Ist es erlaubt: *is* IT *allowed,* can be used for *is* ONE *allowed,* AM I *allowed* etc. so long as what follows makes it clear who wants the permission.

b im eigenen Zimmer It is not always necessary to use a possessive adjective (**sein, mein, Ihr** etc.) with **eigen.** Often **der** or **ein** is used instead, e.g. **Wir möchten ein eigenes Haus haben:** *We'd like a house of our own.*

25 Nur im Freizeitzimmer wird geraucht, *Smoking is restricted to the common-room, (There is smoking only in the common-room,)*

a nur im Freizeitzimmer: lit. *only in the leisure-time room*

b Wird geraucht means literally *is smoked,* or *is there any smoking (done).* This is a passive construction (L13, Part 1 – **man hat mich angestellt**) – both in meaning and in grammatical form this time. Passive constructions are easy because they are formed, as in English, with an auxiliary verb, plus the past participle of the activity in question. In English, *be* is the auxiliary (*it* IS *done*), in German, **werden.** So you have no new forms to learn.
Wir verkaufen hier Zigaretten: *We sell cigarettes here.*
Zigaretten *werden* **hier verkauft:** *Cigarettes are sold here.*
The sentence here is rather special, however, since it is one of those German sentences without a grammatical subject (like **mir wird kalt, mir ist schlecht**). Such sentences in the passive are translated by *there is* + the *-ing* form of the verb, *there is smoking* but one often has to adapt them further in English.

26 sonst ist es verboten. *otherwise it's forbidden.*
verboten This is, in fact, a past participle – from **verbieten:** *to forbid.*

27 Unser „Benno" ist nämlich fanatischer Sportler und ist gegen Rauchen. *Our 'Benno', you see, is a fanatic about sport and is against smoking.*

Gegen is always followed by the accusative.

28 **Oh je! Und wie ist es mit dem Ausgehen?** *Oh, dear! And what about outings?*
wie ist es mit...? This is the simplest way of asking *what's the situation as regards...?*

29 **Ausgehen darf man jeden Samstag und einmal im Monat das ganze Wochenende.** *You are allowed to go out every Saturday and, once a month, for the whole weekend.*
einmal im Monat This is a standard pattern for a number of times in any given period: **zweimal im Jahr; einmal in der Woche** etc.

Die wichtigste Frage   *The most important question*

30 **Die wichtigste Frage**   The superlative of an adjective (*best, nicest, most important*) is formed simply by adding -st to the adjective (except for some irregular ones). Do not forget to add the normal appropriate ending after the -st. (See Appendix 2.)

31 **wie findest du das Internat?** *what do you think of the school?*
Finden, which means *find,* is very often used when expressing or requesting an opinion.

32 **ich werde mich wohl bald an die neue Umgebung gewöhnen.**
I'll probably soon get accustomed to the new surroundings.
mich an die Umgebung gewöhnen   **sich** (accusative) **gewöhnen an** + accusative: *to get used to something*

33 **alles..., was du wissen wolltest?** *all (that) you wanted to know?*
All that + a whole clause is **alles, was.** *Nothing that* (**nichts, was**) and *much that* (**vieles, was**) are treated in the same way.

34 **mir fällt gerade etwas ein!** *something has just occurred to me!*
a In German you use the present tense, because you speak almost as it actually occurs to you.
b **mir fällt etwas ein**   **Einfallen** + dative of the person means *to occur to the person* (i.e. *to enter his head*).

35 **Bis jetzt bist du noch immer und überall satt geworden, oder nicht?** *Up to now, no matter when or where, you've always been satisfied – or am I wrong?*
bist du satt geworden   **Satt werden** means *to get enough* (usually *to eat*), *to become replete.* **Geworden** is the past participle of **werden,** and the auxiliary verb used is **sein.**

Part three

Verboten! *Forbidden!*

36 Es ist zwar nicht erlaubt zu tanzen, aber es wird trotzdem getanzt. *Dancing is not allowed, in fact, but nevertheless (despite that) dancing goes on.*
   es wird getanzt This clause has a subject (**es**), but it is rendered in English in just the same way as the clause without **es** in L16, N25b (*there is dancing; dancing takes place*).

Ausländer *Foreigners*

37 einige unserer ausländischen Schüler und Schülerinnen *some of our foreign boys and girls*
   a To form a feminine from a masculine, add **-in** (**Schüler, Schülerin**), and to form the plural of such feminines, add **-nen** – **Schülerin***nen.*
   b einige unserer...: *some of our...* Notice the use of the genitive case here.

38 Ich bin Portugiese, und mein Freund...und sein Bruder José sind Spanier. *I'm Portuguese, and my friend ... and his brother José are Spanish.*
   ich bin Portugiese Remember there is never any word for *a* (*an*) when stating people's nationalities. **Portugiese** is a weak noun (it ends in **-en,** except in the nominative singular). (See Appendix **8.**)

39 eine Finnin *a Finnish girl* The **e** of **der Finne** is dropped before **-in** is added for the feminine.

Lektion siebzehn Geschäftskonferenz in Frankfurt

17

Lesson seventeen Business conference in Frankfurt

What happens

Herr Kühn has to go to head office in Frankfurt for an important conference at which he himself has to make a lengthy report.

In Part 1 a company driver, who has been sent to meet Herr Kühn, complains about his job. In Part 2 he drives Herr Kühn to the office, a colleague shows Herr Kühn the new buildings and Herr Kühn und Herr Schmidt discuss problems over a working lunch.

New words in this lesson

der **Angestellte**(-n) employee
der **Arbeiter**(–) worker
der **Beginn** start
der **Chauffeur**(-e) driver, chauffeur
der **Chef**(-s) boss
der **Clown**(-s) clown
der **Computer**(–) computer
der **Ersatzteil**(-e) spare part
der **Geschäftsbericht**(-e) business report
der **Kundendienst**(-e) after-sales service
der **März** March
der **Mitarbeiter**(–) colleague
der **Parkplatz**(ᵉe) car park
der **Techniker**(–) technician
der **Umsatz**(ᵉe) turnover
der **Verkehr** traffic

die **Branche**(-n) branch
die **Fabrik**(-en) factory
die **Fachkraft**(ᵉe) skilled worker
die **Firma** (**Firmen**) firm, company, factory
die **Geschäftskonferenz**(-en) business conference
die **Kantine**(-n) canteen
die **Konferenz**(-en) conference
die **Lieferzeit**(-en) delivery date

die **Mitternacht** midnight
die **Montage**(-n) assembly
die **Reparaturwerkstatt**(ᵉen) repair shop
die **Schnellstraße**(-n) clearway
die **Sorge**(-n) trouble, worry
die **Sprachkenntnis**(-se) knowledge of the language
die **Verwaltung**(-en) administration
die **Werkskantine**(-n) factory canteen

das **Bett**(-en) bed
das **Gebäude**(–) building
das **Hauptwerk**(-e) main factory
das **Lager**(–) warehouse
das **Plakat**(-e) poster
das **Tausend**(-e) thousand
das **Werk**(-e) works, factory

die **Geschäftsleute** (**Pl.**) businessmen business people

irgend etwas something, anything

(**beginnen**) **sie haben begonnen** they've begun
besprechen to discuss

141

(bitten) **er hat (mich) gebeten** he has asked (me)
leiden to suffer
scheinen to seem, appear
(tun) **etwas läßt sich tun** something can be done
unterhalten to entertain
(werden) **würden Sie?** would you?
(wissen) **ich habe (es) gewußt** I've known (it)

führen to guide, conduct

abhalten to hold
(ankommen) **er ist angekommen** he's arrived
anlernen to instruct, train
einrichten to install
herumstehen to stand around
hochhalten to hold up
stecken bleiben (ich bin stecken geblieben) to get stuck (I got stuck)
vorbeifahren (ich bin vorbeigefahren) to drive past (I drove past)

sich ändern to change
sich (D) denken (das habe ich mir gedacht) to think (I thought so)

ausgebildet trained
ausgezeichnet excellent
dicht thick, dense
dümmst stupidest
fehlend lacking
hochqualifiziert highly trained

lächerlich ridiculous
lokal local
niedrig low
oberst top, highest
privat personal, private
riesig huge
spät late
übrig remaining, other

rechtzeitig on time
stundenlang for hours
vorhin a short while ago

nahe, näher close, closer

da drüben over there
daneben next to it
darunter under it, as a result of it
dazu for that

durch round, through

damit beginnen to begin on (something)
er läßt sich entschuldigen he sends his apologies
es fehlt an (D) there is a lack of
es handelt sich nicht um it is not a question of
Gott sei Dank! thank heavens!
leidet dárunter suffers as a result of that
mehr oder weniger more or less
mindestens at least
sozusagen so to speak
unter uns between ourselves
würden Sie bitte mitkommen? would you come this way please?

Notes

Part one

1 **Es ist kein Vergnügen, mehrere Male in der Woche zum Flughafen zu fahren und Geschäftsleute abzuholen.** *It's no pleasure to drive to the airport several times a week to meet business people.*

a More than one infinitive phrase with **zu** may follow the comma, linked by **und,** each one being completed before another is added.

b **Geschäftsleute** This is the plural of **Geschäfts*mann*.**

2 **Ist es wirklich nötig, wie ein Clown stundenlang herumzustehen und ein Plakat mit ihrem Namen hochzuhalten?!** *Is it really necessary to stand around like a clown for hours holding up a notice with their name on it?!*

a Note that when two infinitive phrases are joined by **und,** the second infinitive (**hochhalten**) is often translated by the *-ing* form of the English verb (*hold*ING *up*).

b **mit ihrem Namen   Ihrem:** *their* is the 'vague third person plural' which is used in English, too. The singular of **Name** must be used, as there is only one name on the notice, yet to say *his* (**sein**) would be unjustified as no one person has been mentioned to whom it could refer.

3 **Es scheint mir die dümmste und lächerlichste Arbeit auf der Welt zu sein.** *To me it seems the most stupid and ridiculous job in the world.*

a **es scheint mir ... zu sein:** *it seems to me to be*   **Es scheint** is followed by an infinitive phrase with **zu** provided the English version is *it seems* TO and not *it seems* THAT.

b **die dümmste und lächerlichste Arbeit   Dumm:** *stupid* and **lächerlich:** *ridiculous* are used in the superlative degree here. As in English, **-st** is a sign of the superlative (*most, nicest, fastest, best* etc.). Forming the superlative of the adjective is very easy. One simply adds **-st** to the basic adjective: **schön – schönst; neu – neuest.** Sometimes for reasons of sound harmony, one must add **-est,** as with **neu, nett** (**nett***est*), **weit** (**weit***est*). As with the comparative degree, an Umlaut must sometimes be added if the vowel sound of the stressed syllable is **a, o, u** or **au** (though there are exceptions to this rule). Hence **dumm – dümmst.** After adding the **-st** or **-est,** do not forget to add the necessary adjective ending.

c **auf der Welt**   It is not compulsory to translate IN *the world* by **auf** but **auf** IS used very often after a superlative.

4 **Da die Firma Branchen in vielen Ländern hat,** *As the company has branches in many countries,*
Da: *as, since* (meaning *as a result of the fact that*) belongs to the category of link words (or conjunctions) which force the verb to the end of the clause.

5 **kommen jedes Jahr Tausende von Mitarbeitern und Kunden.** *thousands of executives and customers come every year.*

a **Tausende von**   Although **tausend:** 1,000 is written with a small

t, it is being used in the plural as a noun here, so it has a capital **T.** Note that *thousands* OF and *hundreds* OF require **von** + dative.

b **Mitarbeitern und Kunden** These are both dative plural, although **Kunden,** a weak noun, would have **-n** anyway in every case except the nominative singular. (See Appendix **8** on Weak nouns.) **Mitarbeiter** literally means a *colleague,* but it has acquired the status of *executive,* the holder of a post of responsibility.

6 **Sie halten hier ihre Konferenzen ab** *They hold their conferences here*

halten ... **ab** This form is used instead of just **halten** when speaking of a gathering of people.

7 **oder wollen durch das Werk geführt werden.** *or want to be taken round the factory.*

a **wollen** ... **geführt werden** This is a passive construction. You will recall examples of passive constructions from Lesson **16** (**wird geraucht; wird getanzt**). Here we have to contend with the modal verb **wollen** in the passive construction, and you will note that the rules about modals plus the infinitive apply here just the same. *To be,* however, is **werden** (since the phrase is *to be taken*) which goes to the end, immediately preceded by the past participle (**geführt**). Compare:

Sie *werden* durch das Werk *geführt*: *They are (being) taken round the factory.*

Sie wollen durch das Werk *geführt werden*: *They want to be taken round the factory.*

(See Appendix **15.**)

b **durch das Werk** Durch means *through* (L9, N6e). English often uses *round* where German uses **durch.**

8 **Einige von ihnen müssen abends unterhalten werden.** *Some of them have to be entertained in the evening.*

a **müssen** ... **unterhalten werden** This is another passive construction with a modal verb (**müssen**) and is exactly the same sentence pattern as that dealt with in N7 of this lesson.

b **unterhalten** This is a past participle here, though it happens to be identical in form with the infinitive, like a number of other strong verbs with inseparable prefixes (**vergessen, bekommen, gefallen**). The prefix **unter-** can be separable or inseparable, depending on whether it is stressed or unstressed. Here it is unstressed, therefore inseparable (L14, N12).

9 **Dann wird es oft Mitternacht und noch später, bis ich selbst ins Bett komme.** *Then it's often midnight and even later before I get to bed myself.*

a **wird** This is used in the sense of *become* here, not as an auxiliary verb. You could say it GETS *to midnight.*

b **noch später** Spät means *late;* **später:** *later.* **Noch** + any adverb (or adjective) in the comparative degree means *even.*

c **bis ich selbst ins Bett komme** Bis introduces a dependent clause here, therefore the verb goes to the end.

d **ins Bett komme** Ins is used because movement is indicated. **Ins Bett** *kommen* (*to get to bed*) is used instead of **ins Bett** *gehen* (*to go to bed*) when you wish to indicate that something has prevented you from going earlier.

Part two

Fahrt zur Firma *Driving to the factory*

10 **Würden Sie bitte mitkommen?** *Would you come this way, please?*
würden Sie This form of **werden** which you will be dealing with thoroughly later in the course is used here as a courtesy form.

11 **Aber vor einer Dreiviertelstunde war er so dicht, daß ich mehrere Male stecken geblieben bin.** *But three quarters of an hour ago it was so dense that I got stuck several times.*
stecken geblieben bin Stecken bleiben: *to get stuck,* though written as two words is treated as one verb. **Stecken** is like a separable prefix; **bleiben** is therefore the part which changes, and which decides what the auxiliary verb in the perfect tense will be. **Bleiben** (*to remain*) always has **sein** as auxiliary and the past participle is **geblieben.**

12 **Die neue Fabrik ist ganz nahe beim Flughafen,** *The new factory is quite close to the airport,*
nahe beim Flughafen nahe bei + dative: *close to, near to*

13 **Sie ist viel näher als die alte.** *It is much nearer than the old one.*
viel näher als Nah means *near;* **näher:** *nearer. Than* is always **als** after a comparative.

14 **das nächste Mal** *the next time* Although you have seen **nächste** before (**nächste Woche:** *next week*), you will now for the first time realize where it stems from; it is, in fact, the superlative degree of **nah.** Its basic meaning is *nearest.*

15 **wird es wohl nicht länger als fünf Minuten dauern.** *it probably won't take longer than five minutes.*
nicht länger Länger is the comparative degree of **lang.**

16 **Dann soll nämlich die Schnellstraße endlich fertig sein.** *By then, you see, the clearway should at last be finished.*
Schnellstraße This is not precisely the same thing as the **Autobahn** which is a highway link between major cities. A **Schnellstraße** has many features of the **Autobahn** but is an urban clearway, a bypass, or simply a direct route from airport to city.

17 **Ich bin schon gespannt, was sich alles geändert hat.** *I'm eager to see what changes have taken place.*

a **was sich alles geändert hat** This is an indirect question introduced by **was,** therefore the verb is at the end. **Sich ändern** means *to change (oneself, itself).* This is used with a reflexive pronoun when some change is taking or has taken place in the subject of the verb.

b **was ... alles** This does not mean exactly the same as **alles, was** though it may well come to the same in the end. Its literal translation *what all has changed* is hardly correct in English.

Die neue Fabrik *The new factory*

18 **Bis zum Beginn der Konferenz haben wir noch etwas Zeit,** *We've still got some time till the start of the conference,*
bis zum Beginn *Till* before a noun preceded by *the* is usually translated by **bis zu** + dative case, although **bis** by itself means *till,* e.g.:
bis Freitag!: *till Friday!*
bis zum nächsten Mal: *till the next time.*

19 **Ist Herr Schmidt denn noch nicht angekommen?** *Has Herr Schmidt not yet arrived then?*
ist ... angekommen Angekommen is the past participle of **ankommen:** *to arrive.* As you see, the auxiliary required is **sein** and not **haben.**

20 **Er läßt sich entschuldigen.** *He sends his apologies.* This is the same kind of construction with **lassen** as you met in **L12, N14b** (**ich lasse meinen Anzug reinigen:** *I'm having my suit cleaned*) although the English idiom uses a quite different one.

21 **Deshalb hat er mich gebeten, Sie in unserer neuen Fabrik herumzuführen.** *For this reason he asked me to take you round our new factory.*

a **mich gebeten** **Gebeten** is the past participle of **bitten**: *to request* or *ask*. This word should not be confused with **fragen**: *to ask* (meaning *to seek information*). It is followed by an infinitive phrase with **zu.**

b **Sie in unserer neuen Fabrik herumzuführen** Here is an alternative to **durch das Werk** *führen.* Note that, literally, it means TAKE *you around* IN *our new factory.*

22 **Ist ja wunderbar!** *That's really wonderful!* The subject is often omitted in this sentence type, where the verb is **sein** and the subject can be clearly understood by the listener.

23 **Das habe ich noch gar nicht gewußt.** *I had no idea.*
gewußt This is the past participle of **wissen**: *to know.* It has a vowel change, like a strong verb, but a **-t** suffix, like a weak verb. There are a very few common verbs which combine aspects of both types of past participle. **Gewußt** is one of the most frequently required ones.

24 **An den riesigen Parkplätzen für die Arbeiter und Angestellten bin ich vorhin schon vorbeigefahren.** *Just a few moments ago I drove past the huge carparks for the workers and employees.*

a **für die Arbeiter und Angestellten** The distinction between *workers* and *employees* sounds odd in English, but **Angestellte** is used for clerical workers as opposed to manual workers. Remember **Angestellte** is a past participle used as an adjective and requires adjective endings. **Angestellten** shows the weak ending after **die,** but as **die** is a little far away, this may not have been immediately obvious to you.

b **an den riesigen Parkplätzen bin ich vorbeigefahren** **Vorbeifahren an** + dative means *to drive past something.* **Vorbeigefahren** is the past participle. The only point difficult to remember is that the auxiliary verb is **sein.** The collection of **sein** verbs is now as follows:
passieren: *to happen* (**passiert**)   **sein**: *to be* (**gewesen**)
laufen: *walk/run* (**gelaufen**)
Schlittschuh laufen: *to skate* (**Schlittschuh gelaufen**)
gehen: *to go* (**gegangen**)   **werden**: *to become* (**geworden**)
ankommen: *to arrive* (**angekommen**)
bleiben: *to remain* (**geblieben**)   **fahren**: *to drive* (**gefahren**)
Out of those nine, there are five which could be said to have something in common – **laufen, Schlittschuh laufen, gehen, ankommen** (and therefore **kommen**), **fahren.** The common factor

17

is that they all describe movement of some kind. But then most verbs do! The point is that the subject is moving from one point to another. This is not, however, an infallible rule. As you see, four out of our nine verbs cannot be accounted for in this way. A more useful method is to think of subject, verb and direct object as 1, 2, 3 respectively. Verbs which cannot have a 3 have **sein** as auxiliary. Only sentences of the types 1 2 or 1 2 1 (where item 3 is called 1 because it refers back to the subject – with the exception of all reflexive verbs!) can have **sein** as auxiliary. This works fairly well. For instance, one cannot arrive *something;* but one can become (**werden**) an engineer; one can remain (**bleiben**) a bachelor; one can be (**sein**) an excellent German speaker.

25 **Eben hat man damit begonnen, eine zweite Kantine einzurichten.**
They've just begun to install a second canteen.

a This construction, whereby **da** is used as a 'stand-in' for what follows, was encountered in L16, N20a. **Da** here stands for the following infinitive phrase because the main verb phrase (**beginnen** *mit*) like **abhängen** *von* in Lesson **16**, ends in a preposition.

b **Begonnen** is the past participle of **beginnen. Be-** is an inseparable prefix, so there is no **ge-**.

26 **Ich möchte, daß Sie rechtzeitig in Ihre Konferenz kommen.**
I want you to be in time for your conference.

a **ich möchte, daß Sie** In German there is no way of saying someone wants someone else to do something except by using a **daß** clause.

b **rechtzeitig ... kommen** *to be in time* and *to be late* use the verb **kommen** (and not **sein**) when the English version is some part of the verb *to be.*

Geschäftliches beim Mittagessen *A working lunch*

27 **Geschäftliches** This is the adjective or adverb **geschäftlich** turned into a collective neuter noun meaning *business matters.*

28 **Ihren ausgezeichneten Geschäftsbericht über den Umsatz haben wir nun gehört.** *We've now heard your excellent sales report.*
über den Umsatz A report *on* or *about* something is **über** + the accusative. **Umsatz** can mean *turnover, sales, returns.*

29 **Es handelt sich nicht um Sorgen mit den Lieferzeiten der Ersatzteile.**
It is not a matter of troubles over the delivery dates of spare parts.

148

30 **Das habe ich mir gedacht.** *I thought as much.* (*So I thought. So I suspected.*)

Gedacht is the past participle of **denken,** and is like **gewußt** in that it has a root change (like strong verbs) and a -t suffix (like weak verbs). **Sich denken** means *to imagine, conceive, suspect* (L16, Part 1, last sentence – **ich kann mir nicht denken**). This idiom is worth learning by heart, together with **Das kann ich mir denken:** *I can well imagine.*

31 **Aber es fehlt einfach an hochqualifizierten Technikern für die Montagefabrik und die Reparaturwerkstätten.** *But there is a lack of highly qualified technical experts for the assembly factory and the repair workshops.*

es fehlt an Technikern **es fehlt** *an* + dative case: *there is a lack of* (or here, *we lack*)

32 **Der Kundendienst leidet darunter.** *After sales service is suffering as a result of that.*

leidet darunter **Leiden unter etwas** means *to suffer on account of* or *as a result of something.* Remember any preposition (here **-unter**) can be combined with **da(r)** as its 'object' or 'complement' provided this is not a person (or persons).

33 **Sind die lokal angestellten Leute nicht qualifiziert genug?** *Are the locally employed people not qualified (skilled, experienced) enough?*

die lokal angestellten Leute The adjective **angestellten** is separated from **die** by a word here. Frequently, the article (*the*) is separated from a following adjective by more than one word. In such phrases (known as the extended adjectival phrase) it is difficult to hold the proper ending for the adjective in your mind till you reach it.

34 **Ich brauche mindestens drei hier bei Ihnen im Hauptwerk ausgebildete Fachkräfte.** *I need at least three experts trained here with you in the main factory.*

a **drei hier bei Ihnen im Hauptwerk ausgebildete Fachkräfte** This extended adjectival phrase illustrates precisely the point made in N33 above. In German it reads literally, *three* HERE WITH YOU IN THE MAIN FACTORY *trained experts.* The part in capital letters separates *three* (which occupies the position of a **der** or **ein** type of word here) from *trained* (**ausgebildete**), which must show the appropriate adjective ending according to what precedes or follows it, namely **drei** and **Fachkräfte.** The speaker has to remember that **drei** is like any other adjective, so **ausgebildet-**

will have to show the STRONG adjective ending to agree with the accusative plural **Fachkräfte.**

b **Fachkräfte Fach** means *subject, speciality;* **Kraft** (=e): *power, strength.* **Kräfte** is very often used in business and professional jargon as *personnel* or *staff* (**Schreibkräfte:** *clerical staff;* **Lehrkräfte:** *teaching staff*). **Fach-** as a first component in a compound noun means *technical, expert, highly skilled.* (**Fachmann:** *expert;* **Facharzt:** *specialist doctor*).

35 **Sie sollen die Leute dort besser anlernen und dazu natürlich die nötigen portugiesischen Sprachkenntnisse haben.** *They are to (their job will be to) train the people there better and for that purpose they should, of course, have the necessary knowledge of Portuguese.* Notice how in English we have to translate **sollen** twice, in a different way in each part of the sentence.

36 **Tja, Herr Kühn, was sollen wir da machen?** *But, Herr Kühn, what are we to do (about it)?*

a **tja** This is a noise rather than a word, indicating helplessness, resignation, bewilderment, depending on the tone of voice.

b **da** In this instance **da** means *about that.*

37 **Fehlende Fachkräfte sind auch unser Problem hier im Hauptwerk.** *Insufficient skilled staff are our problem here in the main factory too.*
fehlende This is an adjective formed from **fehlen:** *to lack* and is equivalent to English *-ing* adjectives.

38 **Trotzdem will ich sehen, ob sich nicht irgend etwas für Sie tun läßt.** *However, I'll make a point of seeing whether something can't be done for you.*

a **will ich sehen** Will is very strong here, indicating firm intention, which is why the English version is not just *I'll see.*

b **ob sich nicht irgend etwas für Sie tun läßt** **Ob** introduces an indirect question, so the main part of the verb appears last (**läßt**). This clause is difficult because of the verb phrase (**sich tun läßt**). As you know, **lassen** with another infinitive means *to have something done* (**tun lassen:** *to have something done*). But it is used IMPERSONALLY here, that is, **irgend etwas** is really the subject; this accounts for the presence of **sich.** Literally, **sich tun lassen** means *to have itself done,* therefore we can change it into a passive form in English and say CAN BE *done.* **ob sich irgend etwas tun läßt:** *whether anything can be done.*

Denken und Wissen *Thinking and knowing*

39 **Denken und Wissen** These are infinitives of verbs used as nouns and are not to be confused with ADJECTIVE forms made from infinitives (**fehlend**) which are also rendered by an *-ing* suffix in English.

40 **Ich habe nicht gewußt, daß du auch Chauffeur bist.** *I didn't know you were a driver too.*

Bist is translated as *were* not *are*. This sequence of tenses is tricky at first. Even if the verb in the main clause is in a past tense, if the fact stated in the dependent clause is still true at the time of saying so, then the verb is in the present tense.

Lektion achtzehn **Frau Kühn besucht eine Freundin** 18

Lesson eighteen **Frau Kühn visits a friend**

What happens

While Herr Kühn is at the conference in Frankfurt, Lore takes the opportunity of visiting a childhood friend at Lake Constance.

In Part 1 Frau Kühn's friend Klara Häfner talks about herself and Frau Kühn. In Part 2 Frau Kühn gives a fellow passenger on the train some advice, reminisces with Klara and tells her family news.

New words in this lesson

der **Aufenthalt**(-e) stop
der **Eilzug**("e) fast train
der **Fahrplan**("e) time-table
der **Kopf**("e) head
der **Mitreisende**(-n) fellow passenger
der **Personenzug**("e) local train
der **Schaffner**(-) guard

der **Schrank**("e) cupboard
der **Tischler**(-) carpenter
der **Tischlermeister**(-) master carpenter

die **Freundin**(-nen) girl-friend
die **Hand** ("e) hand
die **Handtasche**(-n) handbag

18

die **Kindheit** childhood
die **Lehre(-n)** apprenticeship
die **Lehrerin(-nen)** teacher (woman)
die **Luft** air
die **Meisterprüfung(-en)** exam. for the title of 'master' of a trade
die **Mitreisende(-n)** fellow passenger (female)
die **Schneiderin(-nen)** dressmaker
die **Schreibkraft("e)** typist
die **Schwierigkeit(-en)** difficulty
die **Sekretärin(-nen)** secretary
die **Wand("e)** wall

das **Abteil(-e)** compartment
das **Ding(-e)** thing
das **Glück** luck
das **Kursbuch("er)** railway guide
das **Weihnachtsfest(-e)** Christmas festivities

die **Möbel (Pl.)** furniture

finden to find, have an opinion about
(fliegen) er ist geflogen he has flown
hängen to hang, to be hanging
es hat gehangen it hung, it used to hang
(sein) es wäre gewesen it would have been
(sitzen) ich habe gesessen I have been sitting
stellen to put
stören to inconvenience, to disturb
verdienen to earn

sich verheiraten to get married
sich waschen to wash

eintreten to enter
mitbringen to bring (with one)
vorbereiten to prepare

dabei sein to be present
eine Lehre machen to be apprenticed
Glück haben to be lucky
recht haben to be right

befreundet friendly
dreijährig lasting three years
eiskalt cold as ice
falsch wrong
frisch fresh
froh glad, pleased
gesund healthy
modisch fashionable

erst for the first time
kürzlich recently
schon immer always

als when

anders differently
gegenseitig each other
jedoch however
miteinander together, jointly
sogar even
sowieso anyway

an against
auf in
bei while having
über via

ach du meine Güte! good gracious!
aus dem Kopf from memory
danke no thank you
ganz im Gegenteil on the contrary
im Ausland abroad
in Ruhe undisturbed
stört es Sie? do you mind?
wie finden Sie...? how do you like...?

Notes
Part one

1 **Unsere Eltern lernten sich kennen, als sie noch in Konstanz am Bodensee wohnten.** *Our parents got to know each other when they were still living in Konstanz on Lake Constance.*

152

a lernten sich kennen Remember **kennen** is treated like a separable prefix, therefore goes to the end of the clause. **Lernten** is the imperfect tense of **lernen.** You are already familiar with the imperfect tense of **sein, haben, wollen, müssen** and **können,** which are very frequently used. The use of the imperfect tense of other verbs in the spoken language varies considerably. Apart from **sein, haben** and the modal auxiliaries, it is hardly ever used in speech in South Germany and Austria. In North Germany, however, it is used as an alternative to the perfect in speech. It is widely used in the written language in description of all kinds of action and situations in the past, so it must be learned. This situation, in which Klara is narrating events that happened or situations which existed long ago is one in which the imperfect is preferable to the perfect – indeed in some instances it is essential. With weak verbs, the formation of the imperfect tense is easy and the endings are the same as in the present tense, except that the third person singular (after **er, sie, es, man,** a noun or a person's name) is the same as the first person singular (after **ich**). (See Appendix 12.) The basis of the imperfect of WEAK verbs is the stem + -t, e.g. **lernen: lern + t** + appropriate ending. *He got to know her:* **Er lernte sie kennen.**

b als sie noch...wohnten **Wohnten** is the imperfect of **wohnen,** formed as described above. This is a dependent clause, since the verb **(wohnten)** is at the end. **Als** has a different meaning here from the one you already know (*than* as in **besser als**). It means *when.* It is used when past time is being referred to, and it introduces a dependent clause. Remember, *when* referring to future time is **wenn.**

2 Lore interessierte sich schon immer für modische Dinge und wollte Schneiderin werden. *Even then Lore was always interested in fashion (fashionable things) and wanted to become a dressmaker.* **interessierte sich** This is the imperfect tense of **sich interessieren** and is quite regular.

3 Deshalb machte sie eine dreijährige Lehre und danach sogar die Meisterprüfung. *Therefore she served a three year apprenticeship and afterwards even sat the final professional examination.*

a dreijährige Lehre It is possible to use one word for *lasting for three years* (or any number of years) simply by adding **-jährig** and the right adjective ending to the number.

b machte...Lehre und...Meisterprüfung The same verb

153

18

(**machte**) in German is used for *serving* an apprenticeship and *sitting* an exam. This form is the imperfect of **machen. Die Meisterprüfung** is the examination for the title of 'master' of a trade or craft.

4   **Ich sollte eigentlich Lehrerin werden,** *I was really going to be a teacher,* **ich sollte. . .werden   Ich sollte** is the imperfect of **sollen** and means *I was to* or *I was supposed to,* but *I was going to* is often an acceptable English version if it carries the sense that one *was expected to.*

5   **wollte aber lieber sofort Geld verdienen**   *but preferred to start earning money immediately*   **Aber** is placed after the verb from whim and for no grammatical reason. It is, however, the conjunction linking the two statements, and you will remember that **aber, und** and **oder** do not affect word order.

6   **und arbeitete deshalb in verschiedenen Büros als Schreibkraft.** *and so worked in various offices as a typist (clerical assistant).*

a   **Arbeitete** is the imperfect tense of **arbeiten.** As usual, when the verb stem ends in a **-t** (or **-d**) and another is to be added, an **e** is inserted between them.

b   **als Schreibkraft   Als** means *in the capacity of* in this case. You now know three possible meanings for **als:**
   i *than*   (**besser als**)
   ii *as*   (**als Lehrerin; als Schreibkraft**)
   iii *when* (referring to past time).

7   **Als Lore sich verheiratete, besuchten wir uns gegenseitig mindestens einmal im Jahr.** *When Lore got married, we visited each other at least once a year.*
   Gegenseitig means *mutually* or *reciprocally.* It is not strictly necessary (**uns** conveys the meaning), but reinforces or intensifies **uns.**

8   **Seit vier Jahren haben wir uns jedoch nicht mehr gesehen,** *For four years, however, we haven't seen each other,*
   nicht mehr   This is used instead of just **nicht** when an action or situation was (or is) discontinued.

Part two

Im Zug   *In the train*

9   **Stört es Sie, wenn ich das Fenster schließe?** *Do you mind if I shut the window?*

Stört es Sie?: *Does it disturb* (or *inconvenience*) *you?* This is a phrase one requires so often that it is worth learning by heart.

10   **Da sitze ich ja im falschen Zug.** *Then I'm* (*sitting*) *in the wrong train.*
   da   This word is very colloquial here, and is often used when it is quite unnecessary. Non-native speakers should not use it too much.

11   **Ich glaube es, aber fragen Sie lieber den Schaffner!** *I think so, but you'd better ask the guard.*
   fragen Sie lieber...!: lit. *rather ask...!* Where in English we use phrases like *you'd better* or *you'd best* German uses the request form plus **lieber** (*better*) or **am besten**.

12   **Wenn wir über Memmingen fahren, habe ich wahrscheinlich Glück.** *If we go via Memmingen, I'll probably be lucky.*
   habe ich...Glück: *I'm* (or *I'll be*) *lucky* (*I have luck*)   You have met expressions where in English we use *be* and in German **haben:** *have* before. (**Sie haben recht:** *You're right.* **Sie haben Hunger:** *You're hungry.*) **Glück haben** is a very common one.

13   **Die meisten Eilzüge haben dort ein paar Minuten Aufenthalt.** *Most fast trains stop there for a few minutes.*
   die meisten Eilzüge   This is treated just like an ordinary adjectival phrase, **meisten** having a weak adjective ending after **die. Meisten** is an irregular superlative form (**viel – mehr – meist**).

In der Wohnung   *In the flat*

14   **Endlich sind wir zu Haus angekommen!** *At last we've arrived home!*
   a   **sind wir...angekommen**   Angekommen is the past participle of **ankommen.** Note it has **sein** as auxiliary.
   b   **zu Haus**   As you know this phrase means *at home* and is used as a location and not as a destination. Yet it is used with **ankommen** – an apparent contradiction! **Ankommen** (with **in,** or **an**) is, in fact, used with the dative, as the Germans think of the precise moment of arrival in this connection as the cessation of movement.

15   **Tritt ein, Lore!** *Come in, Lore!* This is the familiar request form, and **treten** (therefore also **eintreten**) is a vowel-changing verb. The **e** changes to **i** and the **t** is doubled.

16   **Es hat sich nichts geändert.** *Nothing has changed.* The Germans

prefer to invent an impersonal subject (**es**) as a kind of parallel to **nichts**.

17 **Alles ist so geblieben, wie es früher war.** *Everything has stayed just as it used to be (was before).*

ist so geblieben So bears out the German tendency to complete the sense of a clause by making something stand in for the following clause (**wie es früher war**) which is the real completion. (Remember **es hängt davon ab, ob**...in L16.)

18 **Nur die Möbel stehen etwas anders.** *Only the furniture is arranged somewhat differently.*

stehen This is a plural form, of course, since **Möbel** is also plural. **Möbel** is not a collective like *furniture*. Literally, **stehen** means *stand*.

19 **Dieser Schrank z. B., hat der nicht immer auf der anderen Seite gestanden?** *This cupboard, for instance, didn't it use to be on the other side?*

hat der nicht immer...**gestanden** **Gestanden** is the past participle of **stehen** and is used here in the same sense as in N18 above. The English phrase *used to* + verb is the best way of rendering the German here, although it is usually associated with the IMPERFECT tense. The presence of **immer** in this sentence affects the translation since it gives duration to the situation in the past.

20 **Wir haben ihn hier an diese Wand gestellt,** *We put it here against this wall,*

wir haben ihn gestellt **Gestellt** is used for *put* (as past participle) when one is speaking of putting things somewhere in an upright position.

21 **weil man dann die Türen besser aufmachen kann.** *because one can open the doors more easily then.*

a This is a dependent clause (of reason) and shows what happens when there is a modal verb with a completing infinitive with a separable prefix – the modal is placed last, immediately preceded by the infinitive with the separable prefix attached.

b **besser aufmachen kann** **Besser** is often used to translate *more easily*.

22 **Und ein neues Bild hängt auch an der Wand.** *And a new picture is hanging on the wall too.*

hängt an der Wand **Hängen:** *to be hanging,* describes a situation and not an action, so the dative is used after **an**.

23 **Hat das nicht schon dort gehangen, als du das letzte Mal hier warst?** *Wasn't it already (hanging) there when you were last here?*

a **Gehangen** is the past participle of **hängen** (L18, N22).

b **als du hier warst** **Als**: *when* (in past time) introduces a dependent clause (L18, N1b). **Warst** is the familiar singular imperfect form of **sein**: *to be* (L18, N1a).

24 **Willst du dich nicht setzen?** *Won't you sit down?* Note the order of the reflexive pronoun (**dich**) and **nicht** in this sentence pattern.

25 **Danke! Ich habe den ganzen Tag im Zug gesessen.** *No, thank you! I've been sitting in the train all day (the whole day).*

a **Danke!** can often mean NO, *thank you!*

b **ich habe...gesessen** **Gesessen** is the past participle of **sitzen**: *to be sitting,* and is so irregular that it calls for extra attention.

26 **Ich wasche mir nur schnell die Hände,** *I'll just give my hands a quick wash,*

ich wasche mir...die Hände This is the same type of construction you met in Lesson **15** with **sich anziehen**: *to dress,* or (where **sich** is dative) *to put on a garment.* **Sich waschen** means *to wash oneself.* **Sich (D)** *etwas* **waschen**: *to wash* SOME PART *of oneself,* where the dative is a reflexive pronoun indicating the owner of the part washed.

Bei einer Tasse Kaffee *Chatting over a cup of coffee*

27 **bei** *while having* Used with an expression like this **bei** has a special meaning – *while having* (a cup of coffee, a glass of wine, etc.), and refers to the conversation going on at the same time.

28 **Was für eine hübsche Handtasche hast du mir da mitgebracht!** *What a pretty handbag you brought me!*

a **was für...!** When used with an exclamation mark this has nothing to do with **was für...?** meaning *what kind of?*

b **Mitgebracht** is the past participle of **mitbringen**: *to bring* (*with one*). It is a mixture of weak and strong procedures, like **gewußt** (from **wissen**) and **gedacht** (from **denken**) which both occurred in Lesson **17**.

29 **Das wäre aber wirklich nicht nötig gewesen,** *That really wasn't necessary,*

wäre gewesen **Wäre** (*would be*) coupled with **gewesen** means *would have been,* literally, but it is used here merely as a courtesy form.

30 **Vorgestern ist er zu einer Geschäftskonferenz nach Frankfurt geflogen.** *The day before yesterday he flew to Frankfurt, for (to) a business conference.*

ist...geflogen **Geflogen** is the past participle of **fliegen:** *to fly.* The auxiliary is **sein.**

31 **Aber wenn Renate weg ist, werde ich viel allein sein.** *But when Renate is away, I'll be on my own a lot.*
wenn Renate weg ist **Wenn** can mean *when* as well as *if.*

32 **Warum ist Renate heute nicht mitgekommen?** *Why did Renate not come with you today?*
ist...mitgekommen The auxiliary is **sein** in the perfect tense of **kommen** and any compound of **kommen** (i.e. **kommen** with any SEPARABLE prefix).

33 **Sie wollte lieber in München bleiben und unser Weihnachtsfest vorbereiten.** *She preferred (wanted rather) to stay in Munich and make preparations for our Christmas festivities.*

  a **sie wollte** The third person (the form matching **er, sie, es,** a name etc.) is exactly the same as the first person (the **ich** form) in the imperfect tense. (See Appendix **12.**)

  b **und unser Weihnachtsfest vorbereiten** **Das Fest:** *feast* or *festival* may be added to a noun, thus describing the particular **Fest** in question.

34 **Sicher ist sie froh, es dieses Jahr in Deutschland feiern zu können.** *She must be happy to be able to celebrate it in Germany this year.*

  a **sicher ist sie froh:** lit. *certainly she is happy* When the speaker is just assuming something which is as good as a certainty *must be* should be translated by **sicher.**

  b **es...feiern zu können** This infinitive phrase is different from those encountered up to now. Here we have two infinitives linked by **zu.** **Feiern** is the completing infinitive of the modal verb **können,** which is itself an infinitive (the completion of **ist froh,...zu...**). This pattern occurs quite frequently, as a modal verb is often the completing infinitive phrase preceded by **zu,** and itself requires a completing infinitive (without **zu**), e.g.: **Es freut mich, Ihnen** *sagen zu dürfen*: *I am pleased to be able to tell you.* **Es ist kein Vergnügen, eine halbe Stunde hier** *warten zu müssen*: *It's no pleasure to have to wait here half an hour.*

35 **Herbert und Eva werden auch dabei sein.** *Herbert and Eva will also be there.*
dabei sein: *to be present* Although it is normally written as two words, **dabei** behaves like a separable prefix, as regards position.

36 **Als ihr in Berlin wart?** *When you were in Berlin?*
Ihr wart is the familiar plural imperfect of **sein.**

37 **Hast du Eva vorher schon gekannt?** *Did you know Eva before that?*
Gekannt is the past participle of **kennen:** *to know.* It belongs
to the **gewußt, gedacht, gebracht** group. You now know the past
participles of the four most common verbs of this so-called
'mixed' type.

38 **ich habe sie erst dort kennengelernt.** *I only got to know her there.*
Kennengelernt is the past participle of **kennenlernen. Kennen** is
treated like a separable prefix.

39 **Sie scheint das richtige Mädchen für ihn zu sein.** *She seems to
be the right girl for him.*
scheint...zu sein **Scheinen** means *to seem,* when it has nothing to
do with appearance, which would be **aussehen.** The completing
infinitive preceded by **zu,** goes to the end of the sentence.

Part three

Zugauskunft *Train information*

40 **Reisende** *passenger* This is a noun formed from what is called
the present participle of a verb, which ends in **-end.** It is a noun,
but behaves like an adjective as far as endings are concerned, e.g.:
der Reisende   die Reisende
ein Reisender   eine Reisende

Aus der Kindheit *Childhood memories*

41 **aus der Kindheit:** FROM *childhood* **-heit** is a common ending for
abstract nouns and it is a FEMININE ending.

42 **Was wolltest du früher einmal werden?** *What did you use to
want to be?*
wolltest du Here is the familiar singular imperfect of **wollen,**
which is quite regular.

43 **Als Fünfjähriger wollte ich immer Schaffner werden.** *As a five
year old I always wanted to be a (railway) guard.*
Fünfjähriger A noun of this kind can be made by preceding
-jährige(r) with the required number. Its endings are like those
of an adjective.

18 Ihr Beruf? *Your profession?*

44 **Mitreisender** *fellow passenger* You must have noticed how often **mit** is attached to a noun or verb in German to indicate being involved or included in the same activity (**Mitarbeiter, mitkommen**).

45 **zur gleichen Zeit, als ich meine Frau kennenlernte.** *at the same time as I got to know my wife.*

a **zur gleichen Zeit** **Gleich** is used for *same* in this expression referring to the concurrence of two events.

b **zur gleichen Zeit, als** **Als** seems to serve double duty here as

   i introduction to the second half of the comparison,

   ii the introduction to a dependent time clause, which ıs the second half of the comparison.

It really means *when* but is translated into English by *as* or *that*.

---

19 **Lektion neunzehn** **Renates Freunde**

Lesson nineteen **Renate's friends**

What happens

While her father is at the conference in Frankfurt and her mother is visiting her friend at Lake Constance, Renate is left on her own in the Munich flat.

In Part 1 Frau Rupf, the caretaker, is disturbed by the noise coming from the Kühn's flat. In Part 2 Renate tries to quieten the party down, Bruno Weigandt recognizes Fräulein Stiegler and Frau Kühn arrives back unexpectedly.

New words in this lesson

der Dummkopf(ˮe) idiot
der Flur(-e) corridor, hall
der Krach noise, din
der Platz(ˮe) square
der Rotwein(-e) red wine

die Hausmeisterin(-nen) caretaker (female)
die Party(-s) party
die Pause(-n) break, rest
die Rückkehr return

160

das Schloß(⸗sser) lock

(bringen) wir haben gebracht we've brought
(fliegen) sie flog she flew
leiden to bear
sprechen to talk
(treffen) ich habe dich getroffen I've met you
(tun) sie hat (es) getan she's done (it)

klingeln to ring (bell)
machen to have, give
stecken to stick

bekanntmachen to introduce
loswerden (sie ist ihn losgeworden) to get rid of (she got rid of him)
(mitbringen) du hast mitgebracht you've brought along
stehenbleiben to stay, to stop
wegfahren (sie sind weggefahren) to go (drive) away (they've gone away)
zusammenfallen to collapse

(einem) Gesellschaft leisten to keep (someone) company
Pause machen to have a break, rest

Spaß machen to joke
stecken lassen to leave (sticking in)

laut noisy
plötzlich sudden
selb same
unangenehm unpleasant

auf einmal all at once
hinterher afterwards
schon wieder again

außen outside
tiefer below

bloß really, only, merely

an up against
über on top of

du lieber Himmel! good heavens!
ein Kommen und Gehen a coming and going
hör mal! listen!
ich kann das nicht leiden I can't stand that

lassen Sie mich in Ruhe! leave me alone!
mein Gott! good heavens!, Lord!
Menschenskind! good gracious!
Moment mal! just a moment!
nach Haus home(ward)
sag bloß . . . don't tell me . . .

19

Notes

Part one

1 **Ich möchte bloß wissen, was heute in Frau Riemers Wohnung los ist.** *I'd just like to know what's going on in Frau Riemer's flat today.*

was . . . los ist Used with some part of **sein, los** means *going on, happening,* as it does here. It can also mean *to be wrong, to be the matter,* in a context where things are clearly not going well. **Was ist los?:** *what's up? what's going on? what's wrong? what's the matter?*

2 Es ist ein Kommen und Gehen und ein Krach, daß man sein eigenes Wort nicht mehr versteht. *There's a coming and going and such a din that you can't hear yourself think.*

daß man sein eigenes Wort nicht mehr versteht   The meaning of this idiom is *that one no longer understands one's own words.* This must be converted into the precise idiom used in English in an identical situation.

3 Eine Familie Kühn aus Brasilien mietete ihre Wohnung am selben Tag, als sie zu ihrer Tochter in die Vereinigten Staaten flog. *A family called Kühn from Brazil rented her flat on the same (very) day (that) she flew to her daughter in the United States.*

a Mietete is the imperfect tense (3rd person singular) of **mieten**. An **e** is put before the ending as the stem **miet-** ends in **t**. (L18, N1a).

b **am selben Tag, als**   *On the same day when/as* followed by a whole clause. This is a similar construction to the one dealt with in L**18**, N**44b**. It is really a time clause, but *as, that* or no word at all for **als** are the only possibilities in English.

c **in die Vereinigten Staaten**   In is followed by the accusative because motion is described. *To* most countries, as you already know, is **nach,** but if the country happens to be feminine or plural, as here, in + accusative must be used.

d Flog is the imperfect of **fliegen:** *to fly.* Apart from **sein,** this is the first imperfect of a strong verb which you have encountered. Notice the difference between **flog** and **mietete** with regard to form and endings. Firstly, there is a vowel change from **ie** to **o,** and secondly, there is no addition of **-t** and no ending at all. (Compare English *I flew* with *I hired* or *I rented.*) A comparison with English strong verbs in the past tense may help you to remember that first person (**ich** form) and third person (**er** form) singular of German strong verbs in the imperfect tense have no ending, and have a vowel change. The vowel change from **fliegen** to **flog** happens to be the same as the vowel change in the past participle (**geflogen**), but, unfortunately, this cannot be assumed. When you are learning to use a verb in all three tenses (present, perfect and imperfect) the only way is to learn the three forms listed in the strong verb list in Appendix **24,** namely – the infinitive, the third or first person singular of the imperfect, and the past participle, e.g.:

fliegen   flog   geflogen

sein   war   gewesen
kommen   kam   gekommen

19

4 Soviel ich weiß, sind Herr und Frau Kühn auch weggefahren.
As far as I know, Herr and Frau Kühn have also gone away.
Weggefahren is the past participle of **wegfahren:** *to go away*
(sufficient distance to involve travelling in a vehicle). **Fahren**
requires **sein** as auxiliary (verbs of motion principle), therefore
so does any compound of **fahren** with a separable prefix.

5 Es ist schrecklich, wie man auf alles und jeden aufpassen muß!
*It's dreadful how one must keep a wary eye on everything and
everyone.*
wie man auf alles und jeden aufpassen muß   Aufpassen auf +
accusative means *to pay attention to* or more colloquially,
keep an eye on something. Sometimes a separable verb requires
the use of a preposition (**an, auf, in, von, aus**) after it which
happens to be identical with the separable prefix. This is the
case here with **auf.**

Part two

Auf dem Flur   *In the entrance hall*

6 Ich war's, Franz. *It was me, Franz.* The apostrophe stands for
the missing **e** in **ich war (e)s.** Remember that in such phrases
(e.g. **das bin ich:** *that's me*) the person is the SUBJECT in German.
7 Du bist's! *It's you!* **Du bist's = du bist es (L19, N6)**
8 Ich habe doch den Schlüssel außen im Schloß stecken lassen.
But I left the key sticking in the lock on the outside.
stecken lassen   It is possible that the construction used here –
when **lassen** means *to leave* – developed by analogy with those
occurring in **L12 (N14b).** It is similar to **liegen lassen (L13, N32).**
In such expressions, **lassen** has come to be treated like a
modal verb (followed by a completing infinitive) in the perfect
tense. The infinitive replaces the past participle.
9 Ihr braucht nicht hier im Flur stehen zu bleiben. *You don't have
to stand (stay standing) out here in the passage.*
a ihr braucht nicht ... zu   Brauchen nicht + **zu** and infinitive
is the best way of saying *don't have to do something.*
b stehen zu bleiben   Stehen bleiben: *to remain standing, (stand
still)* is a combination like **liegen lassen** (or **stecken lassen**)

163

19

where the first verb (even if written separately) behaves like a separable prefix.

10 **Kommt doch rein!** *Do come in!* This is the familiar request form. **Rein** is short for **herein (hereinkommen:** *to come in).*

11 **Wir haben eine Flasche Rotwein gebracht.** *We've brought a bottle of red wine.*
eine Flasche Rotwein There is no word for *of,* remember, in expressions of quantity. The adjectives **rot** (*red*) and **weiß** (*white*) when applied to wine have become so much part of the noun that they have been incorporated into it.

12 **Wie nett, daß jeder mir Gesellschaft leisten will!** *How nice that everyone wants to keep me company!* **Gesellschaft leisten** (with dative) is *to* KEEP *someone company.*

Unangenehme Überraschung *An unpleasant surprise*

13 **Unangenehme Überraschung** You may have noticed how often the article (*a, an, the*) can be omitted from titles in German.

14 **Seid doch ein bißchen ruhiger!** *Do be a bit quieter!*
Seid is the familiar plural imperative or request form of **sein.**

15 **Macht mal Pause, Kinder!** *Have (make) a break, folks!* **Macht** is also the familiar plural request form. **Pause machen** means *to have* or *take a break.* **Kinder!** is used by young people (and even not so young people) to their contemporaries. American usage – *kids!* – probably approximates to it better than any English phrase.

16 **Es wird nicht mehr getanzt.** *No more dancing!* This is the passive construction explained in Lesson **16.** Here, however, there ıs a subject, **es,** and the full translation would be *there is to be no more dancing.*

17 **Sonst fällt der armen Frau Rupf das Haus über dem Kopf zusammen.** *Or the house will collapse over poor Frau Rupf's head.*

a **der armen Frau Rupf ... über dem Kopf** Compare the construction in L18, N26. The definite article (*the:* **dem**) is used with the part of the body in question, and the dative of the person (**der armen Frau Rupf**) indicates to whom it belongs.

b **fällt ... zusammen Zusammenfallen:** *to collapse* is a vowel-changing verb, so the third person singular is **fällt.**

18 **Ich wohne ja hier, das heißt (d.h.) einen Stock tiefer, unter Frau Riemer oder jetzt Familie Kühn.** *I do live here, after all, that is,*

164

one floor down, underneath Frau Riemer, or for the time being,
the Kühn Family.

a **das heißt (d. h.):** *that's to say,* or *that is* The abbreviation **d. h.** is equivalent to English *i.e.*

b **einen Stock tiefer** **Tief** literally means *deep* or *low,* and **tiefer** is the comparative degree. *One floor lower down* or just *one floor down* is the translation. Adverbial phrases of place (like those of time), are put in the accusative, provided there is no word present (**in, an, auf** etc.) which would necessitate a dative or a genitive.

19 **Gut, daß ich dich getroffen habe,** *It's a good thing I met you,*
Getroffen is the past participle of **treffen:** *to meet.*

20 **Machst du Spaß?** *Are you joking?* This phrase is not to be confused with those including a dative (person) after **Spaß machen,** e.g. **Das macht mir keinen Spaß:** *That's no pleasure (fun) to me.*

21 **Herr Lenz hat es von mir bekommen.** *Herr Lenz got it from me.*
hat ... bekommen This is the past participle of **bekommen,** **be-** being an inseparable prefix. (Only compounds of **kommen** with SEPARABLE prefixes have **sein** as auxiliary in the perfect tense.)

22 **Wie hat sie denn das getan?** *How did she do that?*
Getan is the past participle of **tun:** *to do.*

23 **Ganz einfach. Statt um die Ecke zu fahren, ist sie an dem Baum gelandet.** *Quite simply. Instead of driving round the corner, she landed up against the tree.*

a **statt um die Ecke zu fahren** **Statt** + **zu** + infinitive translates *instead of doing something.*

b **ist sie an dem Baum gelandet** **Landen** requires **sein** as auxiliary in the perfect tense. (It is a verb of motion.)

c **an dem Baum gelandet** The dative case is used here for the same reason as it is used with **ankommen:** *to arrive.* The moment of landing is the moment movement ceases.

24 **Aber frag sie doch selber!** *But ask her yourself!*
Frag is the familiar singular request form.

Plötzliche Rückkehr   *Sudden home-coming*

25 **Ich habe gewußt, daß wir uns irgendwo wiedersehen werden.**
I knew we would see each other again somewhere.
werden This form is, no doubt, unexpected as a translation of

would. This is another example of the sequence of tenses in German being different from the sequence of tenses in English (L17, N40). In German, you have to think of what the speaker would have said to himself at the time, in this instance *we* SHALL *see each other again.*

26   **In Berlin ist er schon hinter mir her gewesen.** *He was already chasing after me in Berlin.*
hinter mir her: lit. *along behind me*   **Hinter** is followed by the dative in this expression.

27   **Fräulein Stiegler ist ihn auch kaum losgeworden.** *Fräulein Stiegler could hardly get rid of him either.*
ist ihn kaum losgeworden   **Loswerden** means *to get rid of.* **Ich werde ihn nicht los:** *I can't get rid of him.* **Werden** has **sein** as auxiliary, remember.

28   **Ich kann mir gar nicht vorstellen, wer ihn eingeladen hat.** *I can't imagine who invited him.*
Eingeladen is the past participle of **einladen.**

29   **Das sind alle meine Freunde.** *These are all my friends.*
das sind   Here is the plural of **das ist:** *this is/that is.* **Das** does not change in this construction even when what follows is not singular.

30   **Darüber können wir morgen noch sprechen.** *We can talk about that tomorrow.*
darüber   **Sprechen über** means *to talk about,* and **über** may be combined with **da(r)** provided the topic is not a person.

Part three

Zu laut!   *Too loud!*

31   **Ruhe! Macht doch nicht solchen Krach!** *Be quiet! Don't make such a noise!*
solchen Krach   **Solch** is declined like **der,** therefore it requires an **-en** (accusative singular masculine) ending here.

Lektion zwanzig   Weihnachten

20

Lesson twenty   Christmas

What happens

Herr Kühn returns from his conference in good spirits only to be depressed by the stony silence between Renate and her mother.

In Part 1 Herr Kühn describes the situation and admits he sympathizes with Renate. In Part 2 Renate and her mother are reconciled. Preparations are made for the Christmas party, the Pfaffingers arrive and they all sit down to Christmas dinner.

New words in this lesson

der Gänsebraten roast goose
der Genuß(=sse) treat, enjoyment
der Glühwein mulled wine
der Weihnachtsbaum(=e) Christmas tree

die Kerze(-n) candle
die Nuß(=sse) nut
die Versöhnung(-en) reconciliation

das Fest(-e) festival, feast
das Gebäck pastries, biscuits

(bleiben) sie sind geblieben they've stayed

hängen an (gehängt) hang (something) on
meinen to think

schmücken to decorate

(sich entscheiden) ich habe mich entschieden I've decided
sich fühlen to feel

fränkisch Franconian
wenig few
wichtiger more important

daran on it

so so

allerseits to all (of you)
es war mir nicht recht I didn't want it
frohe Weihnachten! Happy Christmas!
ich tue mein Bestes I'm doing my best
nicht so schlimm don't worry

Notes

Part one

1   **aber sie haben kein Wort miteinander gesprochen.** *but they hadn't a word to say to each other.*

a   **miteinander:** *to each other*   The reciprocal pronoun **sich** is inadequate when a verb has a preposition after it to complete the sense in which it is being used (e.g. **sprechen** *mit*). In such

167

20

cases **einander:** *one another* is used, preceded by the appropriate preposition as a prefix. Hence **zueinander, voneinander** etc.

b **Gesprochen** is the past participle of **sprechen.**

2 **Ich hatte zuerst keine Ahnung, was passiert war.** *At first I had no idea what had happened.*

was passiert war This is called the pluperfect tense and simply means that the auxiliary means *had* instead of *has.* You therefore use the imperfect tense of **sein (war/waren)** or **haben (hatte/hatten)** plus the past participle:

ich habe gesagt: *I (have) said* **ich hatte gesagt:** *I had said*
ich bin gewesen: *I have been* **ich war gewesen:** *I had been*

3 **Später erzählte mir Renate, daß sie sich gezankt haben.** *Later, Renate told me that they (had) quarrelled.*

a **Erzählte** is the imperfect of **erzählen.** Remember the first and third persons (**ich** and **er** forms) are the same in the imperfect.

b **daß sie sich gezankt haben** The English translation would be *had quarrelled.* This is the matter of sequence of tenses referred to in Lesson **19.** In German, you think of what the speaker would have said to the person reporting what was said. Renate would have said *we* HAVE *quarrelled* so the perfect tense is used.

4 **ein paar andere Leute** *a few other people* Adjectives after **ein paar** have a strong ending.

5 **haben sich über den großen Krach beschwert.** *complained about the terrible noise.* **sich beschweren *über*** + accusative: *to complain* ABOUT (*something*)

6 **Ich habe jedoch nicht mit Renate zanken können,** *I couldn't, however, go on at Renate,*

mit Renate zanken: *have words with Renate* **Zanken** is usually used reflexively or rather with reciprocal **sich,** but since both parties would not be equally involved here, it has more of the sense of *reproach.*

Part two

Die Versöhnung *The reconciliation*

7 **Es war mir selber nicht recht, daß alle Freunde auf einmal gekommen sind und bis Mitternacht geblieben sind.** *I myself didn't like the idea of them all coming at once and staying till midnight* (... *it was not all right with* ME, *that*... etc.). A participial phrase in English (*them all* COMING *at once and* STAYING *etc.*) has to be rendered in German by a **daß** clause.

8   **Schon gut, Renate!** *That's all right then, Renate.* The use of this phrase usually means that the speaker considers the subject closed.

Vorbereitungen für das Fest   *Preparations for the Christmas party*

9   **Beeil dich, Renate!** *Hurry up, Renate!* The request or command form of a reflexive verb has the reflexive pronoun after the verb in the familiar forms. In the formal request form, it follows **Sie** (**Beeilen Sie sich!**).

10   **Sonst werden wir nicht fertig, bis Pfaffingers kommen.** *Otherwise (or else) we won't be ready by the time the Pfaffingers come.* **Bis** usually means *till* (*until*), but it can also mean *by* a certain day or date, or *by the time* a certain event occurs.

11   **Und der Tisch ist auch noch nicht gedeckt.** *And the table isn't laid yet either.* **Gedeckt** is a past participle, used here as an adjective after the noun (**Tisch**).

12   **mein Bestes**   This is used as a noun (**das Beste**) but requires a strong adjective ending.

13   **für nichts anderes**   After **nichts,** the adjective has a strong neuter ending (**-es**).

14   **Zuerst muß ich Eva fragen, welches Kleid ich anziehen soll.** *First I must ask Eva which dress I should put on.* **anziehen**   This verb need not always have a reflexive pronoun. It is not necessary here, though people do often put in a dative reflexive pronoun with **anziehen** when it is not really necessary.

Ankunft der Pfaffingers   *The arrival of the Pfaffingers*

15   **Eva werdet ihr auch sofort kennenlernen.** *You'll meet* EVA *too, in a minute.* The inverted order (object–verb–subject) gives EVA the desired stress.

16   **jetzt fängt es auch noch zu regnen an.** *and now it's starting to rain as well.* Remember that with **anfangen** and **aufhören** (*to stop*) it is possible to place the infinitive with **zu** BEFORE or AFTER the separable prefix:
Es fängt zu regnen an.   Es fängt an zu regnen.
The choice is at least partly dependent on the fact that the prefix (**an**) must not be too far removed from the main part of the verb.

17   **ein Glas heißen Glühwein** *a glass of hot mulled wine*

20 Ein Glas is in the accusative case, as the direct object of bieten, and heißen Glühwein is put in the same case. (L11, N31b)
ein Glas helles Bier   ein Glas warme Milch
ein Glas guten Wein

18 **richtig gemütlich** *very cosy* **Richtig** is used colloquially as an expressive substitute for **sehr** (compare Yorkshire use of *right* before an adjective, or general colloquial American English *real*).

19 **Ihr habt sogar Äpfel, Nüsse und Weihnachtsgebäck daran gehängt.** *You've even hung apples, nuts and Christmas sweetmeats (fancy biscuits) on it.*
daran gehängt **Gehängt** is the past participle of **hängen (an):** *to hang (something ON something)* and is not to be confused with **gehangen,** which is the past participle of **hängen:** *to be hanging.*

Das Festessen   *Christmas dinner*

20 **Setzt euch!** *Sit down!* (the familiar plural of a reflexive verb)

21 **Es gibt Gänsebraten...** *There's roast goose...* **(Der) Braten** is a roast of any kind. To describe what kind of roast, put the name of the animal (or meat, if the word happens to be different) in front. English uses *roast* as an adjective in this kind of expression, German uses **Braten** as a noun.

22 **... und als besonderen Genuß einen echten fränkischen Rotwein dazu.** *... and as a special treat, a real Franconian red wine to go with it.* These adjectives all have accusative endings because their nouns are objects of **es gibt** from the beginning of the interrupted sentence.

23 **uns allen** *us all* **Uns** is dative, of course, and so also is **allen** (strong adjective ending).

24 **guten Appetit!** That is, **(Ich wünsche euch) guten Appetit** – hence the accusative ending. There is no equivalent for this phrase in English because we do not have the charming custom of wishing everyone at table 'a good appetite' before beginning a meal.

Part three

Zwei verschiedene Weihnachtsbäume   *Two different Christmas trees*

25 **so viele hübsche Sachen** *so many pretty things* **Viele** requires any other adjective following it to have a strong ending.

Lektion einundzwanzig   Skiurlaub zu viert

21

Lesson twenty-one   Skiing holiday for four

What happens

After the Christmas festivities and before Herbert and Eva return to Berlin, they go off to the mountains, accompanied by Renate and Franz, for a few days' skiing.

In Part 1 a petrol pump attendant talks about his job. In Part 2 Herbert has his non-skid chains checked, and Renate complains that the mountain hut is uncomfortable. Later Herbert, Renate and Franz discuss Renate's skiing.

New words in this lesson

der **Automechaniker**(–) motor mechanic
der **Fortschritt**(-e) progress
der **Hochbetrieb** rush, busy season
der **Hosenboden**(⸚) seat of trousers, bottom
der **Kilometer**(–) kilometre
der **Luftdruck** pressure
der **Preisunterschied**(-e) difference in price
der **Reifen**(–) tyre
der **Schlafsack**(⸚e) sleeping bag
der **Ski**(-er) ski
der **Skikurs**(-e) ski course
der **Skilehrer**(–) ski instructor
der **Tankwart**(-e) garage attendant
der **Versuch**(-e) attempt

die **Art**(-en) type, sort
die **Berghütte**(-n) mountain hut, refuge
die **Einfachheit** simplicity
die **Ferienzeit**(-en) holiday period
die **Garage**(-n) garage
die **Generation**(-en) generation
die **Größe**(-n) size
die **Hütte**(-n) hut
die **Kritik** criticism

die **Panne**(-n) breakdown
die **Reparatur**(-en) repair
die **Schneekette**(-n) non-skid chain
die **Schuld** fault

das **Benzin** petrol
das **Dorf**(⸚er) village
das **Öl** oil
das **Schlimmste** the worst
das **Wasser** water

die **Ferien** (Pl.) holidays
die **Großeltern** (Pl.) grandparents

das **Neujahr** New Year
(das) **Ostern** Easter

(dürfen) ich **durfte** I was allowed to
fallen (ich **fiel**) to fall (I fell)
(geben) er **gab** he gave
(gefallen) es **gefiel mir** I liked it
(gehen) es **ging** it went
(liegen) ich **lag** I lay
mögen (du **magst**) to like (you like)
(scheinen) sie **schienen** they seemed

(sehen) **ich sah** I saw
(sein) **es war gewesen** it had been
(sitzen) **ich saß** I sat
(wissen) **ich wußte** I knew
ziehen (Sie werden gezogen) to pull (you are pulled)

kontrollieren control, check
lernen to learn
prüfen to check
spannen to tighten
tanken to refuel

Angst haben to be afraid
ausleihen to hire out
ernst nehmen to take seriously
nachfüllen to refill
saubermachen to clean
stecken bleiben to break down
(sie sind stecken geblieben) (they've broken down, got stuck)
übrig haben to have left over
zurückgehen to go back, return

sich (D) etwas ausleihen (ich habe sie mir ausgeliehen) to borrow something (I've borrowed them)
sich (D) leisten to afford

böse angry
dunkel dark
dunkler darker
fest tight
genannt called

höher higher
primitiv primitive
steil steep
teurer dearer
übrig left
unzufrieden discontented

daran of it
hinauf up
hinunter down
höher hinauf higher up

halt just, simply
überhaupt at all
wenigstens at least
wert worth

ab und zu now and then, from time to time
aufs = auf + das to the
das wundert mich gar nicht I'm not at all surprised
es gehört dazu it's all part of it
ich hatte schreckliche Angst I was terribly afraid
nicht der Rede wert not worth mentioning
oh je! oh dear!
sei mir nicht böse! don't be cross with me!
seien Sie bitte so gut please be so kind as to
vor allen Dingen above all

Notes

Part one

1 **in einem kleinen Dorf, genannt Hohenfeld am Arlberg.** *in a little village called Hohenfeld am Arlberg.*
   Genannt is the past participle of **nennen:** *to name.* It belongs with the 'mixed' group (**gewußt, gedacht, gekannt, gebracht**).
2 **Während des ganzen Jahres wird bei uns nicht halb so viel gearbeitet wie jetzt in den Wintermonaten.** *During the whole year there isn't half as much work done here as now in the winter months.*

wird ... nicht halb so viel gearbeitet: lit. *is not half so much worked* This is a passive construction (*work is being done*) without a subject (like **hier wird getanzt** or **hier darf nicht geraucht werden**). In English we invent a kind of subject: *there is...* (See Appendix 15.) Note that the **past** participle completes the first part of the comparison (**halb so viel**) before the second half begins. This is the usual order with comparative constructions involving a verb phrase.

3 **Hochbetrieb** *busy season* This is a word used by businesses, shops, travel agencies etc. to describe their busiest time. It means *intense activity,* literally.

4 **Gewöhnlich wird nur Benzin getankt;** *Usually, it's just a matter of supplying petrol;*

a This is another passive construction (*petrol is just supplied*).

b **Benzin getankt** **Benzin tanken** must be taken together to mean *refuel.* **Getankt** is the past participle.

5 **manchmal muß der Luftdruck in den Reifen geprüft werden,** *sometimes the pressure in the tyres must be checked (tested),*

a Note the word order.

b **muß geprüft werden:** *must be checked* **Werden** means *be* in passive constructions. Here it is the infinitive (**werden**) which is required to complete the modal verb **muß. Geprüft** is the past participle required to complete **werden.** This pattern (*something must be done*) is very common, as you may imagine, and it is worth learning an example by heart.

6 **und ab und zu sollen das Öl und das Wasser kontrolliert und nachgefüllt werden.** *and now and then the oil and water are to be checked and filled up.*

kontrolliert There is little difference in meaning, for practical purposes, between **prüfen** and **kontrollieren** used in this sense, though they are not always interchangeable. **Kontrollieren** is *to exercise a control;* **prüfen** is *to test for* something. Here are more examples of the same pattern as in N5b above: **sollen kontrolliert werden, sollen nachgefüllt werden.**

7 **wenn sie stecken geblieben sind.** *when they have got stuck.* (L17, N11)

wenn Having been told to use **als** for *when* if referring to a past event, a possible misunderstanding could arise here; **wenn** means *whenever* in this instance. If you can substitute *whenever* for *when* in English, you must use **wenn** in German.

Part two

Kleine Panne   *A slight hitch*

8   Seien Sie doch bitte so gut, und   *Please be so kind as to*

a   This is a stock phrase – learn it by heart!

b   **seien Sie**   This is the request form (polite or formal version)
of **sein,** and is quite irregular. You already know the familiar
forms **seid!** (plural) and **sei!** (singular).

9   Das wundert mich gar nicht. *I'm not at all surprised (at that).*
Es wundert mich is an impersonal expression (i.e. subject is
es/das) meaning *it surprises me.* The person surprised is always
in the accusative, e.g.: **Es wundert *uns*:** WE'RE *surprised.*

10   Ich habe sie mir von einem Freund ausgeliehen. *I borrowed
(hired) them from a friend.*
Ausgeliehen is the past participle of **ausleihen.** Very often a
verb which has **ei** in the infinitive changes to **ie** in the past
participle (**bleiben, geblieben**).

11   Das wußte ich nicht. *I didn't know (that).*
wußte   This is the imperfect of **wissen,** and you will note that
the imperfect, like the past participle (**gewußt**), is a mixture of
the weak and strong systems. It changes its vowel (**i** becomes **u**)
and adds the weak ending **-te** as well. This is true of all other
verbs in the same group and it may also be assumed that
whatever internal change was made to form the past participle,
the same internal change takes place to form the imperfect.

**12   Als mein Freund sie mir gab, schienen sie die richtige Größe zu
haben.** *When my friend gave them to me, they seemed to be the
right size.*

a   **Gab** is the imperfect tense of **geben:** *to give.* As you learned in
L19, N3d strong verbs have no **-te** in the imperfect tense
(singular) and the root vowel (the one bearing the stress)
changes as with the past participle.

b   **Schienen** is the imperfect of **scheinen:** *to seem* (the **Sie** and
plural forms). Notice we have an **ei** to **ie** change here again.
Note also that the **-t-** of the imperfect of weak verbs has
vanished, as there is no need for it as a means of distinction
from the present tense. The vowel change is enough.

13   Das ist alles, was ich für Sie tun kann. *That's all (that) I can do
for you.*
alles, was   English does not need the link word (*that*) between the

two clauses. In German, however, you are very conscious of the fact that there are two clauses; the second one must have an object, so **was** cannot be omitted. Why **was?** (and not **das**). Think of *That is what I can do for you.* **Alles** is the completion of the first clause (*that is* ALL) and is 'standing in' in the first clause, for **was** in the second one. Just try to remember that if **alles** is followed immediately by another whole clause, the link word is **was**. And, of course, as it is a kind of dependent clause, the verb (**kann**) is at the end.

14 habe ... übrig **Übrig haben** means *to have left* (*left over*). Although it is a separate word, **übrig** behaves like a separable prefix and goes to the end of this sentence.

15 Das wäre nett von Ihnen. *That would be kind of you.* This is the 'courtesy' subjunctive again, reinforced by the fact that he has not yet carried out the action referred to.

16 höher hinauf zur Berghütte *higher up to the mountain hut*
a **Höher** is the irregular comparative of **hoch:** *high.*
b **hinauf** denotes direction away from the speaker, and **herauf** direction towards the speaker (see **hereinkommen L6** and **herkommen L16** vocabularies).

17 müssen Sie halt aus dem Schnee gezogen werden, *you'll just have to be pulled out of the snow,*
a This is another passive construction with a modal (*must be pulled*) (L21, N5b).
b **Gezogen** is the very irregular past participle of **ziehen:** *to pull.*

18 wie schon so viele andere vor Ihnen. *like so many others before you.*
a **viele andere** *People* is understood here; **andere** is really an adjective and has the strong ending after **viele.**
b **vor Ihnen** **Vor** here means *before, prior to* (L7, N44).

In der Berghütte *In the mountain hut*

19 Wann wurde denn hier zum letzten Mal saubergemacht? *When was this place last cleaned?*
wurde ... saubergemacht This is a passive construction (with no subject) in the imperfect tense. All that is required to change a present tense passive into an imperfect passive is to change the auxiliary (**werden**) into the imperfect. **Wurde** is the imperfect tense of **werden** (irregular) and **saubermachen** means *to clean* (*make clean*). **Hier** has been made into a subject – *this place* – which is necessary in English sentence structure.

20 So primitiv habe ich mir diese Hütte nicht vorgestellt. *I didn't*

175

think (imagine) this hut would be so primitive.

habe ich mir ... vorgestellt **Sich vorstellen** means *to imagine, picture to oneself,* so it may be translated as *think.* The reflexive pronoun must be dative (**mir**). Having chosen to translate **sich vorstellen** as *think* here, you must complete it with *would be* in English. When you want to say something is somehow different from what you were expecting it to be, this pattern of sentence using **sich vorstellen** is the best way to express it.

21 **Mir gefiel sofort alles, was ich sah.** *I liked everything (that) I saw immediately.*

mir gefiel Here is the imperfect tense of **gefallen. Mir** placed at the beginning of the sentence gives it emphasis.

22 **Du magst diese Einfachheit vielleicht.** *Perhaps you like this simplicity.*

du magst Here, at last, is the present tense of **mögen:** *to like.* The fact that you have had to wait so long for its appearance is evidence of its low frequency in comparison with **möchte/ möchten** (WOULD *like*) which was introduced very early in the course. The present tense has other shades of meaning – e.g. it is often translated as *may.*

23 **warmes Wasser zum Waschen** *warm water for washing* **Zum** + a verb used as a noun usually means FOR *doing* something.

24 **mag ich auch lieber als kaltes.** *I like better than cold (water), too.* **Mag lieber** is used when one is speaking in general terms, whereas **möchte lieber** expresses a preference (which is likely to be fulfilled) in a particular situation. **Mag** is the **ich** form of **mögen** (and also the **er** form, since the two are the same in ALL the modal verbs).

25 **Vergiß nicht, daß andere Leute diese Art von Ferien besonders gern mögen!** *Don't forget that other people are particularly fond of this kind of holiday!*

a **Vergiß** is the familiar singular command form of **vergessen.** When a verb is vowel–changing, the familiar singular command form has such a vowel change.

b **gern mögen** **Mögen** is the **sie** (*they*)/**Sie** form – identical with the infinitive. Note that **mögen,** like any other verb, can be combined with **gern** to intensify the liking.

26 **Und denke auch daran, daß Hotels viel teurer sind!** *And bear in mind the fact that hotels are much dearer!*

a **denke auch daran, daß** **Denken an** means *to think about, reflect* *on.* The whole **daß** clause is the completion of **an,** but it must have a 'stand in' for it within its own clause – hence **daran** – translated by *the fact* (**es hängt davon ab, ob**... L16, N20a).

b **Teurer** is the comparative of **teuer.** The second **e** drops out when any ending is added to the word.

27 **Wir können uns keinen so teuren Urlaub leisten.** *We can't afford such an expensive holiday.*

a **teuren** The second **e** of **teuer** usually drops out when any ending is added.

b **uns ... leisten** **Sich leisten** means *to afford.* The reflexive pronoun is dative.

28 **Sei mir nicht böse, Eva!** *Don't be cross with me, Eva! With me* is translated by the dative – **mir** – and no word for *with* is required.

Erste Skiversuche *First attempts at skiing*

29 **was wurde ... gelernt?** *what was learned?* This is the passive imperfect again (L21, N19).

30 **Ging es schon ein bißchen besser als gestern?** *Did it go a little (a bit) better than yesterday?*
Ging is the imperfect tense of **gehen** and is very irregular.

31 **Ich durfte zum ersten Mal einen kleinen Berg hinunter.** *I was allowed to go down a small mountain for the first time.*

a **ich durfte** This is the imperfect of **ich darf:** *I may.* It is formed like the imperfects of most modal verbs (**konnte, wollte, mußte, sollte**) – that is, like a weak verb, except for the disappearance of the Umlaut in **dürfen** (infinitive).

b **hinunter** This is really a separable prefix with the main part of its verb missing; it is unnecessary to add, for example, **laufen** or **fahren** as the context makes the meaning clear (N16b).

c **einen kleinen Berg** This is accusative, and therefore makes it clear that the infinitive is understood though not mentioned, this phrase being the object of that missing infinitive.

32 **Das nenne ich einen großen Fortschritt.** *I call that great progress.*
einen Sometimes the word **ein:** *a* is used with a type of word (**Fortschritt:** *progress;* **Rat:** *advice*) which the words *a* or *an* could not precede in English. This is often because the German word has a literal meaning which the word *a* could precede in English. **Fortschritt** really means a *step forward.*

33 **Ich fiel ... auf meinen Hosenboden** *I fell ... on my bottom*

fiel auf Fiel is the imperfect of **fallen:** *to fall. To fall* ON is **fallen auf** + accusative.

34 **aber lange stand ich nie auf meinen Skiern.** *but I never stood up on my skis for very long.*
Stand is the imperfect of **stehen:** *to stand.*

35 **Wenn man Skilaufen lernt, gehört das dazu.** *When you're learning to ski* (*skiing*), *that's all part of it.*
gehört das dazu **Gehören zu** means *to be part of* (a process), *to belong within* (a certain category). **Das gehört dazu** is a common idiom, which can usually be translated by *that's usually the way of it.*

36 **saß oder lag ich ... immer** *I was always sitting or lying...*
This sounds better in English than *I sat, I lay* because the action was recurrent! Although this COULD have been put in the perfect tense in German, it is more correct to use the imperfect here, because expressing repeated action in the past is precisely one of the functions of the imperfect tense. **Saß** is the imperfect of **sitzen:** *to be sitting.* **Lag** is the imperfect of **liegen.**

37 **Und danach habe ich auf Skiern wieder hinauf gesollt.** *And then* (*after that*) *I was supposed to* (*expected to*) *climb back up again on my skis.*
gesollt This is the straightforward past participle of **sollen,** used when there is NO completing infinitive mentioned. (**Hinauf** is really a separable prefix used in the same way as **hinunter** in L21, N31b). Although all the modal verbs have ordinary past participles (**gewollt, gekonnt, gemußt** etc.), they are much less used than their infinitives used as past participles.

38 **Das war das Schlimmste.** *That was the worst thing.*
das Schlimmste **Schlimm** means *bad;* **schlimmst-:** *worst.* This, then, is the superlative of **schlimm** used as a noun.

39 **Es ist spät geworden** *It's late* Lit *it has got late*
Ist geworden is the perfect tense of **werden:** *to become, to get.*

40 **und wird immer dunkler.** *and it's getting darker and darker.*
immer dunkler When a comparative is repeated in English, (*better and better, worse and worse*) one simply uses the German comparative once, preceded by **immer.**
dunkel: *dark* (the **e** of **dunkel** drops out when any ending is added to the word (N26b)): **dunkler:** darker

41 **Laßt uns ... zurückgehen!** *Let's go back!* **Laßt** is the familiar plural request form of **lassen.**

Kein Preisunterschied   *No difference in price*

42   nicht der Rede wert.   *not worth mentioning.*   **Rede** means *talk, speech.* Any noun followed by **wert** is in the genitive case, e.g. **eines Besuches wert**: *worth a visit.* **Wert** always comes AFTER the noun.

Bessere Möglichkeiten?   *Better opportunities?*

43   Warum scheinen es die Leute in Österreich dann so viel besser zu können? *Why do the people in Austria seem to be so much better at it?* **es ... besser zu können**   **Etwas gut können** means *to be good at something,* therefore this phrase means *to be better at it.*

44   und man schon als kleines Kind und dann sein ganzes Leben lang regelmäßig Ski läuft. *and one begins as a small child and skis regularly all one's life.* This is a second part of the **weil** clause joined to the first part by **und.** So **Ski läuft** is at the end of the clause.

Langsame Fortschritte   *Slow progress*

45   meine Skier sind immer stecken geblieben. *my skis kept getting stuck (always got stuck).*
stecken geblieben   **Stecken bleiben** means *to get stuck.* **Stecken,** although a separate word, behaves like a separable prefix as far as word order is concerned.

46   Es muß alles gelernt werden   *Everything has to be learned*
a   This is a passive construction with a modal verb (**muß**) (L21, N5b).
b   **es ... alles**   Both of these words are fulfilling the same rôle, really, – that of the subject. This construction is often used when **nichts, alles, viel** is the subject of the sentence.

Lektion zweiundzwanzig   Eine Bewerbung   **22**

Lesson twenty-two   An application for a job

What happens

Herr Kühn is now intent on finding a suitable person for the post of his secretary.

22

In Part 1 Margot Stiegler, who has applied for the job, talks about her application and forthcoming interview. In Part 2 Renate remembers that she has met Fräulein Stiegler. Herr Kühn interviews Fräulein Stiegler.

New words in this lesson

der **Besuch**(-e) attendance
der **Betrieb**(-e) firm, office
der **Eindruck**(¨e) impression
der **Elektrobetrieb**(-e) electrical firm
der **Flug**(¨e) flight
der **Hinflug**(¨e) outward flight
der **Lebenslauf**(¨e) curriculum vitae,
  personal record
der **Rückflug**(¨e) return flight
der **Zufall** coincidence

die **Arbeitsbedingung**(-en) condition of
  work
die **Bewerberin**(-nen) applicant (female)
die **Bewerbung**(-en) application
die **Empfehlung**(-en) recommendation
die **Entscheidung**(-en) decision
die **Fähigkeit**(-en) capability, ability
die **Handelsfirma** (-firmen) commercial
  firm
die **Höhere Handelsschule**(-n) College of
  Commerce
die **Information**(-en) information
die **Korrespondenz**(-en) correspondence
die **Schreibmaschine**(-n) typewriter,
  typewriting
die **Stellung**(-en) position, situation, job
die **Stenographie** shorthand

das **Gespräch**(-e) talk, meeting, interview
das **Interview**(-s) interview
das **Zeugnis**(-se) certificate

die **Kosten** (Pl.) costs, expenditure

(das) **Portugal** Portugal
die **Schweiz** Switzerland

(das) **Spanien** Spain

bieten (sie werden geboten) to offer
  (they are offered)
(**bitten**) **ich wurde gebeten** I was asked
(**fahren**) **Sie fuhren** you went
(**kommen**) **ich kam** I came
(**lesen**) **ich las** I read
(**schreiben**) **ich schrieb** I wrote
tragen to meet (costs)
treffen to take (decision)

erledigen to see to, carry out, take care of
fürchten to be afraid
verbessern to improve
verlangen to demand

aufwachsen to grow up

sich erinnern an to remember
(**sich kennen**) **sie haben sich gekannt**
  they have known each other
sich verabreden to make an appointment
sich verlassen auf to rely upon

bekannt well-known, known
bereit prepared
dortig local
Frankfurter of/from Frankfurt
französisch French
größte greatest
höchste highest
interessant interesting
komisch strange, funny
passend suitable
praktisch practical
selbständig independent

180

technisch technical
überrascht surprised
unfreundlich unpleasant
verantwortungsvoll responsible
vielseitig varied
zuverlässig reliable
zweieinhalb two and a half

dorthin there

regelmäßig regularly

ein Gespräch führen to have a talk
höchste Zeit high time
ohne weiteres easily, readily
schon längst for a very long time
sowohl...als auch both...and
zum größten Teil for the most part

22

Notes

Part one

1 **Mein Name...ist Ihnen schon längst bekannt.** *My name...has been familiar to you for a very long time.*
a **ist Ihnen bekannt:** *is known to you* **Ist Ihnen etwas bekannt?** is an alternative to **Kennen Sie etwas?**
b **Längst** is the superlative of **lang(e).** As well as *long*EST, it can mean VERY *long,* in this instance, *a very long time.* Many idiomatic superlatives mean *very* – rather than the *-est* version.
2 **Ich kam vor zweieinhalb Monaten nach München,** *I came to Munich two and a half months ago,*
   ich kam This is the imperfect tense of **kommen.** The use of the imperfect or perfect here is a matter of choice.
3 **um mir eine neue Stellung zu suchen.** *in order to look for a new job (for myself).*
   um ... zu suchen **Um** means *in order to,* and goes in the same place as *in order to* in the English sentence. It is completed by an infinitive at the end, preceded by **zu.**
4 **Bis jetzt habe ich noch nichts Passendes gefunden.** *Up to now I haven't found anything suitable.*
a **nichts Passendes** After **etwas** and **nichts,** an adjective used as a noun has a strong neuter ending (and a capital letter, of course).
b **habe ich ... gefunden** **Gefunden** is the past participle of **finden.**
5 **las ich** *I read* **Las** is the imperfect tense of **lesen:** *to read.*
6 **eine Sekretärin, die ...haben soll.** *a secretary, who should have...* **Die** means *who* in this sentence, referring back to **eine Sekretärin.** *Who* in this sentence is not a question word; it is a link word between two clauses, to save having to make two separate sentences in which the element common to both is the secretary.

It is called a RELATIVE pronoun, because it is doing duty for a noun in the previous clause; and the *who* (or *which*) clause is called a relative clause.

The relative pronoun has the same effect on the position of the verb as words like **wenn, daß, weil** etc. – i.e. the verb must go to the end of the *who* clause. If the verb happens to be composed of more than one word, they are arranged in the usual way: past participle/infinitive, auxiliary. In this clause, we have an infinitive (**haben**) and a modal auxiliary (**soll**).

The relative pronouns are very easy to learn because, with the exception of the genitive case and the dative plural, their forms are identical with the definite article (**der, die, das**).

The classification (**der, die, das**) of the relative pronoun, and whether it is singular or plural are decided by the word it refers to, which is called its antecedent. **Sekretärin** is the antecedent of **die**. Since the relative pronoun may play a different rôle in the relative clause from the rôle of the word it refers to in the main clause, its CASE is decided by its function in the relative clause. **Sekretärin** is accusative, (it is the object of **sucht**); **die** is nominative, (it is the subject of **haben soll**).

7 **werden geboten** *are offered* This is a passive construction in the present tense (i.e. the auxiliary, **werden,** is in the present tense). **Geboten** is the past participle of **bieten:** *to offer.*

8 **Ich schrieb** *I wrote* **Schrieb** is the imperfect of **schreiben.**

9 **legte … dazu** *enclosed* **Legte** is the imperfect of **legen:** *to put.* **Dazu** combined with it means *to add to it,* therefore in this context, the phrase means *enclosed.*

10 **Zu meiner größten Überraschung wurde ich heute morgen von einem Herrn Kühn angerufen** *To my very great surprise, I was telephoned by a Herr Kühn this morning*

a **größten** (L22, N1b) **Größt** is the superlative form of **groß.** For obvious reasons, another **-ss** sound is NOT added to form the superlative. There is no danger of ambiguity, since the Umlaut distinguishes it from **groß.**

b **wurde ich … angerufen** This is the passive imperfect.

c **von einem Herrn Kühn** In passive constructions, the action is carried out BY someone or BY MEANS OF something. When the 'doer' is a person, *by* is always translated by **von.**

11 **zu einem Interview gebeten.** *requested to attend an interview.* **Gebeten** is the past participle of **bitten:** *to request.* As you see, it

can be used in German without a completing infinitive, in which
case it has the sense of *invited* or even *bidden.*

Part two

Partygast als Bewerberin!   *Party guest as an applicant!*

12   **denn ich habe mich für heute um 1 Uhr mit einer Dame zu einem
Gespräch verabredet.** *because I've made an appointment with a lady
for an interview (talk, meeting) at one o'clock today.*

a   **ich habe mich für heute ... verabredet**   **Sich verabreden** *für* means
to make an appointment FOR a certain time (not purpose).

b   **zu einem Gespräch**   This translates the purpose – **zu:** *for.*

13   **auf der Party, die ich vor Weihnachten hier hatte.** *at the party
(which) I had here before Christmas.*
Die is a relative pronoun (L22, N6), therefore **hatte** is at the end
of the clause. Note that the relative pronoun can easily be
missed out of the English sentence altogether. It can NEVER
be omitted from the German sentence. **Die** is feminine singular
(agreeing with **Party**) and accusative as it is the object of **hatte.**

14   **Gewundert habe ich mich auch über ihr gutes Portugiesisch.** *I was
also amazed at her good Portuguese.*

a   This word order is not common, as one rarely needs to stress
a past participle so much as to put it in first position.

b   **Portugiesisch** has a capital letter because it is a noun here.

15   **höchste Zeit** *high time*   **Höchst** is the superlative of **hoch.**

16   **Das Restaurant, das ich gewählt habe, liegt in der Nähe vom Rathaus.**
The restaurant I've chosen isn't far from the Town Hall.
das ich gewählt habe   This is the relative clause in this sentence.
Note that it is embedded in the middle of the main clause. This
does NOT break the primary rule of 'verb second or last in the
German sentence' since the relative clause is considered an exten-
sion of **das Restaurant,** which is item one; therefore **liegt** is still in
position two. **Das** is neuter singular agreeing with **Restaurant** and
accusative because it is the object in its own clause.

Das Gespräch   *The interview*

Gespräch means *talk, conversation,* but is used here in the sense
of *interview.* **Das Interview** exists in German, but is associated
with press and television.

17   **Nach dem Besuch der dortigen Höheren Handelsschule** *After*

22

attending the local College of Commerce
nach dem Besuch **Besuchen** is the word used for *attending* or *going to* a school or college. Note once again the German preference for a noun **(Besuch)** rather than a verb phrase.

18 **in einem kleineren Elektrobetrieb** *in a rather small electrical firm*
The comparative form **(kleiner)** can sometimes be used to render *rather* or *fairly* before the adjective.

19 **Wie lange wären Sie bereit, in Brasilien zu bleiben?** *How long would you be prepared to stay in Brazil?*
wären Sie bereit **Wären** means WOULD *be.* You have encountered this form of **sein** before, mostly in 'courtesy' phrases. Its real use is in situations like this, which are hypothetical, and all verbs have forms for this kind of situation. It is dealt with in detail in later lessons.

20 **der Hin- und Rückflug** *outward and return flight* When the second component of two compound nouns mentioned together is common to both, a hyphen is substituted for it in the first noun.

21 **wird von uns bezahlt werden.** *will be paid by us.* This is a FUTURE passive construction, which you may find somewhat confusing at first, since **werden** is used in two capacities within the verb phrase: as the auxiliary used to form the future tense **(wird)** and as the auxiliary used to form the passive **(werden)**. In future passive constructions, it is the one that means *will* (*shall*) which agrees with the subject, and the one that means *be* which is the completing infinitive.

22 **Die wenigen Möbelstücke, die ich mir bis jetzt gekauft habe, kann ich ohne weiteres bei meinen Eltern lassen.** *The few bits of furniture (which) I've bought so far, I can quite easily leave with my parents.*

a **die ich mir ... gekauft habe** **Die** is plural, agreeing with **Möbelstücke** and accusative as the object of **gekauft habe.** Note that the relative clause is again embedded within the main clause. The reflexive pronoun is often used with **kaufen (mir ... gekauft habe:** *bought* MYSELF), but is not grammatically necessary in German any more than it is in English.

b **ohne weiteres** This is a very common idiom meaning *without any trouble at all!*

23 **Bei dieser Stellung** *In this job* **Bei** is used because the sense is *in the doing of this job.*

24 **die sowohl technische als auch praktische Fähigkeiten verlangt.**

184

which demands not only technical knowledge but also practical skills.

a   **Die** is feminine singular, agreeing with **Arbeit,** and nominative as the subject in its own clause.

b   **sowohl technische als auch praktische Fähigkeiten**   One noun (**Fähigkeiten**) is sufficient in German because it will do for both knowledge and skill, and the adjectival contrast (**technische** and **praktische**) is enough.

25   **Vielseitige Arbeit ist gerade das, was ich suche.** *Varied work is precisely what I'm looking for.*
  das, was: *that which,* or *the thing that*   The **was** clause is really a relative clause in German, as it refers back to **das** in the main clause. It has to be put in this way in German for the same reason that one must say **alles, was** (L21, N13); that is, the main clause must be COMPLETED by something which 'stands in' for the whole of the **was** clause. The relative pronoun **was** is used wherever the antecedent is indefinite, vague – words like **alles, nichts, etwas** – where nothing specific (which can be given a **der/die/das** classification and a singular or plural) has been mentioned.

26   **Die Korrespondenz wird zum größten Teil von Ihnen selbst erledigt werden.** *The correspondence will be dealt with for the most part by you independently.*

a   **zum größten Teil:** lit. *for the biggest part*

b   **von Ihnen selbst:** BY *you on your own* (L22, N10c)

27   **Ich glaube sagen zu dürfen, daß Sie sich auf mich verlassen können.** *I think I can say that you can rely on me.*
  sagen zu dürfen: lit. *to be able to say*   This very idiomatic way of putting it avoids having to make another **daß** clause, which would make the sentence very clumsy.

Part three

Sie haben sich schon gekannt   *They have met before*

28   **das die Verkäuferin ... mir geben wollte.** *that the salesgirl wanted to give me.*

a   **Das** is a relative pronoun, accusative case, as it is the object of **geben wollte.**

b   **Wollte** has a rather special shade of meaning here – *was about to.*

29   **jetzt erinnere ich mich daran.** *now I remember (it).*   **An** is really a part of the verb phrase and has to have a completion; since it is

not a person, **da-** may be used in combination with **an.**

Auch eine Empfehlung   *A further recommendation*

30   **Wie war das Gespräch, das du mit Fräulein Stiegler geführt hast?**
How was the talk you had with Fräulein Stiegler?
Das is neuter singular agreeing with **Gespräch,** accusative as the object of **geführt hast.**

So schnell geht es nicht   *These things take time*

31   **So schnell geht es nicht**   The translation is very free, and the German is another example of the range of meaning of **es geht.** A more literal translation would be *it doesn't happen as quickly as that.*

32   **Das geht schnell bei ihm.** *He makes decisions quickly.*

a   This is a use of **das geht** similar to that described above in N31.

b   **Bei ihm** has a rather special meaning here. It is used when one wants to indicate that it is a habit or a characteristic way of behaving.

---

23 **Lektion dreiundzwanzig**   **Beim Winterschluß-verkauf**

Lesson twenty-three   **At the winter sale**

What happens

Lore and Grete are planning a visit to a winter clearance sale. Walter has another lunch appointment with Fräulein Stiegler, whom he has now appointed to the post of his secretary.

In Part 1 a sales assistant in the millinery department describes the annual sale. In Part 2 the Kühns and Frau Pfaffinger plan to meet later and Frau Kühn needs some money. Frau Kühn loses her hat in the sale and buys a new one.

der Einkauf(¨e) purchase
der Hut(¨e) hat
der Ochs(-en) ox
der Rand(¨er) brim
der Schlußverkauf(¨e) sale
der Stoff(-e) material
der Treffpunkt(-e) meeting place

die Borte(-n) trimming
die Hutabteilung(-en) millinery department
die Ware(-n) goods

das Bargeld cash
das Konto (Konten) account
das Scheckbuch(¨er) cheque book

(beginnen) er begann it began
(haben) ich hatte I had
(mögen) ich mochte nicht I didn't want to
(tragen) man trug one wore
(verlieren) ich habe verloren I've lost

verkaufen to sell
wirken to have an effect

sich versammeln to rally, assemble

(abnehmen) ich habe ihn abgenommen I took it off
anprobieren to try on
aufstehen to get up
ausgeben to spend (money)
einkaufen to buy
herabsetzen to lower (price)
hereinströmen to flock in, stream in

dazwischen kommen to come between, to intervene
liegen lassen to leave, forget

auffallend striking, showy
beige beige
breit broad, wide
dick fat
elegant elegant
farben coloured
geschlossen closed
hell light
lila(farben) lilac coloured
schönst nicest, most beautiful
schwach weak
stark strong
ungeduldig impatient
unmodern old-fashioned
verloren lost
weich soft

bevor before
nachdem after

äußerst extremely
dafür instead
falls in case
unbedingt whatever happens, at all costs
ungern unwillingly, reluctantly

dazwischen between it

nach meinem Geschmack to my taste
nicht einmal not even
vor der Nase in front of my nose
weder ... noch ... neither ... nor ...

Notes

Part one

1 **Am liebsten wäre ich heute im Bett liegen geblieben.** *I'd sooner* (lit. *soonest*) *have stayed in bed today.*
a **Am liebsten** is the superlative of **gern** (L13, N9b).

23   **b**   **wäre ich … liegen geblieben**   **Liegen bleiben** means *to remain lying*. It is usual to use **liegen** for *to be in bed*, so **liegen bleiben** means *to* STAY *in bed*. **Bleiben** is the changing verb; **liegen**, though a separate word, behaves like a separable prefix. **Bleiben** has **sein** as auxiliary in the perfect tense, and **wäre**, which usually means *would be*, here means *would have*. This form **wäre/wären** is used when the action referred to is unlikely to happen. When it is used as an auxiliary with a past participle, the action did not happen at all, though it might have in different circumstances.

2   **Ich mochte einfach nicht aufstehen.** *I just didn't want to get up.* **ich mochte** Is the imperfect of **mögen** (irregular). **Mochte nicht** rather than simply **wollte nicht** indicates more distaste.

3   **Wegen des Winterschlußverkaufs, der heute morgen begann, mußte ich nämlich eine halbe Stunde früher als gewöhnlich zur Arbeit.** *Because of the winter sale, which began this morning, I had to go to work half an hour earlier than usual.* **mußte ich zur Arbeit**   **Mußte** (imperfect of **müssen**) can be used without **gehen** just as **muß** (present tense) can.

4   **Es gibt nichts, was ich so ungern tue, wie früh aufzustehen.** *There's nothing I dislike as much as getting up early.* **wie früh aufzustehen**   The infinitive with **zu** (*as to get up*) is used in the comparative phrase, where English has the *-ing* verb form.

5   **Ich hatte nicht einmal genug Zeit, um zu frühstücken.** *I hadn't even enough time to have breakfast.* **um zu frühstücken**   **Um … zu** expresses purpose: *for the purpose of (having breakfast).* N.B. **frühstücken** is NOT separable.

6   **lief ich zur Haltestelle,** *I ran to the bus-stop,* **Lief** is the imperfect of **laufen**: *to run*.

7   **wo mir natürlich der Bus vor der Nase wegfuhr.** *where I was just in time to see the bus drive away, of course.* (*where, of course, the bus drove off in front of my nose.*)

a   This is a relative clause, linked by *where* (**wo**) instead of *which*. **Wo** refers back to **Haltestelle**.

b   **mir … vor der Nase**   **Der** is used instead of **meiner**, and **mir** is put in to show to whom the nose belonged. This is a general pattern with parts of the body.

c   **wegfuhr**   **Fuhr** is the imperfect of **fahren**.

8   **Viele ungeduldige Kunden hatten sich schon vor den geschlossenen Türen versammelt.** *Many impatient customers had already gathered in front of the shut doors.*

188

a **viele ungeduldige Kunden**   When **viele** is followed by another adjective, that adjective has a STRONG plural ending.

b **hatten sich ... versammelt**   This is the pluperfect again (L20, N2).

9 **Hunderte, wenn nicht Tausende, werden in den nächsten vierzehn Tagen zu uns hereinströmen, um etwas Preiswertes einzukaufen.** *Hundreds, if not thousands, will pour in here in the next fortnight, looking (in order to shop) for a bargain.*

a **Hunderte – Tausende**   These words are used as nouns here and are given capital letters and a strong adjective ending.

b **in den nächsten vierzehn Tagen**   *In the course of* any period of time is **in** + the dative. German has no one word for *fortnight;* one says either **vierzehn Tage** or **zwei Wochen**.

c **um ... einzukaufen**   It is sometimes difficult to know when you have to precede the infinitive phrase with **um**, especially when English does not compel you to say *in order to,* and *to* conveys the meaning adequately. A working guide is that if it seems necessary to stress the notion of purpose, **um** should be used.

10 **Sie werden deshalb bei uns vieles finden, was billiger ist als in jedem anderen Geschäft.** *So they'll find a lot in our shop that's cheaper than in any other one.*

vieles, was billiger ist   **Vieles** means *a lot of things*. These words – **vieles, alles, etwas, nichts** –, sometimes called INDEFINITE numerals, have much in common as regards the way they affect other words associated with them, e.g. the relative pronoun following all of them is **was** (L21, N13 and L22, N25).

Part two

Treffpunkt: „Zum bayerischen Ochsen"   *Rendez-vous (meeting point) at the 'Bavarian Ox'*

11 Names of inns, pubs and restaurants which resemble this one (Red Lion, White Hart etc.) include **zum** as part of the name. **Ochs** is a weak noun.

12 **In dasselbe Kaufhaus, in dem wir damals die Geschenke für Herbert und Eva kauften.** *To the same store in which we bought the presents for Herbert and Eva that time.*

a **dasselbe:** *the same*   This adjective is composed of the word for

23
the plus **selb-** and both parts have to be changed according to the following word. The first part is treated exactly as **der/die/das** would be if it stood alone, and **selb-** gets a weak adjective ending.

b **in dem:** *in which* **Dem** is a relative pronoun referring to **Kaufhaus** (therefore neuter singular), and dative after **in** where no movement is involved. (**Wo** could also be used here.)

13 **Nachdem ihr eure Einkäufe erledigt habt, können wir uns vielleicht zum Mittagessen treffen.** *After you've made your purchases (done your shopping), perhaps we can meet for lunch.*

a **Nachdem:** *after* when a clause (and not just a noun) follows it, is like **als** (*when*) in that it always introduces a dependent clause, and the verb must go to the end.

b **erledigt** This is a weak past participle. **Er-** is an inseparable prefix, so there is no **ge-**.

14 **Wartet aber nicht auf uns, falls wir es nicht rechtzeitig schaffen!** *But don't wait for us, in case we don't make it in time.*
Falls: *in case,* or *lest* introduces a dependent clause, so the verb (**schaffen**) goes to the end.

15 **Man weiß nie, was einem dazwischen kommen kann.** *You never know what might happen.*
einem dazwischen kommen **Dazwischen kommen** means *to intervene, to come between,* so **einem dazwischen kommen** implies here *prevent one carrying out one's intention.* This is very idiomatic. **Einem** is the dative case of **man**.

16 **Gib mir aber bitte noch unsere Kontonummer, bevor du weggehst!** *But please give me our account number before you go!*

a **Gib** is the familiar singular request form of **geben**. When a verb is vowel-changing, remember, this form always has such a change.

b **bevor du weggehst** **Bevor** introduces a dependent clause of time like **als:** *when* and **nachdem:** *after.*

Der verlorene Hut *The lost hat*

17 **Wir haben vorhin einen Hut bei Ihnen liegen lassen.** *A little while ago we left a hat (lying) here.*
liegen lassen (L13, N32, L19, N8). You may also encounter **liegen gelassen,** because some people do say it.

18 **Nachdem wir in der Lederwarenabteilung gewesen waren, kamen wir direkt zu Ihnen.** *After we had been in the leather goods department, we came straight here.*
nachdem ... gewesen waren This clause is in the pluperfect tense

190

(L23, N8b). **Gewesen** (*been*) requires **sein** as auxiliary, and the pluperfect tense requires the auxiliary in the imperfect (**waren**).

19 **Aber der Hut, den ich verloren habe, war mein eigener.** *But the hat* (*which*) *I've lost was my own.*

den ich verloren habe Verloren is the past participle of **verlieren**: *to lose*. It is used in the title of this section as an adjective (**der verlorene Hut**). Den is masculine singular, agreeing with **Hut** and accusative as the object of **verloren habe.**

20 **...ja, dann habe ich ihn abgenommen, um einen neuen anzuprobieren.** ... *yes, then I took it off to try on a new one.*

Abgenommen is the past participle of **abnehmen**: *to take off* if you could reasonably substitute LIFT *off*. It can only be used for taking off HATS; for other garments use **ausziehen.**

21 **Dann muß er eigentlich irgendwo auf dem Tisch bei allen anderen liegen.** *Then it must actually be (lying) somewhere or other on the table beside all the others.*

bei allen anderen Allen is a dative plural ending, and **anderen** has a weak adjective ending.

22 **Oder dieser lilafarbene?** *Or this lilac (coloured) one?* Certain colours (**lila, rosa**), because they end in **-a** just cannot have normal adjective endings. **-farben** is often added on to the name of the colour, and the appropriate adjective ending is attached.

23 **Weder der eine noch der andere.** *Neither the one nor the other.*

weder ... noch: *neither ... nor* The case of the words which **weder** and **noch** precede depends, of course, on what has gone before. **Weder ... noch** have no effect whatever on the case used.

24 **Große auffallende Hüte trug man früher leider nicht.** *Large, striking hats were, unfortunately, not worn then (one didn't used to wear large, striking hats then).*

Trug is the imperfect of **tragen**: *to wear* (in this instance).

25 **Nein, der lila Hut wirkt äußerst elegant.** *No, the lilac hat has an extremely elegant (chic) effect.*

Äußerst is a superlative form but is translated as *extremely*.

26 **Ich muß ihn unbedingt haben.** *I must have it at any price (I've got to have it).*

Unbedingt is a very common German word indicating that the speaker (or the subject, if it does not happen to be the speaker) is not to be deterred.

27 **Na und? Ich bin von dem vielen Suchen schwach geworden,** *So what? I'm worn out with all the searching,*

23

von dem vielen Suchen: lit. *from the much searching* Suchen is a verb used as a noun (given a capital S and a **das** classification) and **vielen** is an adjective with a weak ending after **dem.**

Part three

Ohne Geld keine Tasche   *No money, no bag!*

28 **Wo wart ihr heute vormittag?** *Where were you this morning?*
wart ihr This is the familiar plural of the imperfect tense of **sein.**

29 **seid ihr ... gegangen** *did you go* Gegangen is the past participle of **gehen**; the auxiliary is **sein.**

30 **Was denkst du?** *Why do you think?* **Was** must be used in German for this idiom as **warum denkst du?** would mean *why are you thinking?* which is not the sense at all.

31 **Bevor wir Geld ausgeben konnten, mußten wir welches haben.** *Before we could spend any money we had to have some.*
welches This is the only sort of phrase in which it is necessary to translate *some* or *any* – that is, when either is used as a pronoun i.e. there is no noun following. When this happens, you use **welch-** giving it the strong (**der, die, das**) ending to suit the word it is standing for, and whatever case ending is required by its function in the sentence. Here **welches** is neuter singular agreeing with **Geld,** and accusative as the object of **mußten ... haben.** The corresponding negative (*not any, none*) is **kein-.**

Nichts, was ihm gefällt   *Hard to please*

32 **Weder der eine noch der andere ist nach meinem Geschmack.** *Neither is to my liking.*
There is no way of avoiding saying the whole phrase **weder der eine noch der andere** in German; you cannot use **weder** on its own as you can *neither* in English.

33 **Wie finden Sie den blauen?** *What about the blue one? (What do you think of the blue one?)* **Finden** has nothing to do with *finding* here. It means *what is your opinion of?*

Lektion vierundzwanzig   Eine Erkältung

Lesson twenty-four   A chill

24

What happens

Herr Kühn has been caught in a heavy shower without a raincoat
and begins to show signs of a very nasty cold during the night.
In Part 1 the doctor's secretary describes her work. In Part 2
Frau Kühn talks to the secretary on the telephone about her husband's symptoms, and medical fees. The doctor visits the house and
examines the patient.

New words in this lesson

der Arzt(⸚e) doctor, medical practitioner
praktischer Arzt general practitioner
(G.P.)
der Doktor(-en) doctor, physician
der Grund(⸚e) cause
der Hals(⸚e) neck, throat
der Hustensaft(⸚e) cough mixture
der Inhalt(-e) sense, meaning
der Körper(-) body
der Mund(⸚er) mouth
der Patient(-en) patient
der Puls(-e) pulse
der Regen rain
der Schmerz(-en) pain
der Schnupfen(-) cold (sniffles)
der Zahnarzt(⸚e) dentist

die Erkältung(-en) cold, chill
die Freude(-n) satisfaction, pleasure
die Kälte cold (weather)
die Kasse(-n) insurance
die Krankenversicherung(-en) sickness
and accident insurance
die Krankheit(-en) illness
die Lunge(-n) lung
die Sprechstundenhilfe(-n) receptionist
die Tablette(-n) tablet

die Temperatur(-en) temperature

das Fieber(-) temperature, fever
das Getränk(-e) drink
das Heilmittel(-) remedy
das Rezept(-e) prescription
das Wartezimmer(-) waiting-room

(bitten) er bat um he asked for
(halten) ich hielt I considered
(helfen) es half it helped
(lassen) ich ließ I left
messen to measure, take (temperature)
(schlafen) er schlief he slept
(tun) es tat it did
verschreiben to prescribe
werden to become

behandeln to treat
decken to cover
fehlen (D) to be the matter, to be
wrong with
gurgeln to gargle
holen to catch
husten to cough
lachen to laugh
niesen to sneeze
rechnen mit to reckon on, to bargain for

24

schlucken to swallow
schwitzen to sweat, perspire
strömen to pour
zittern to shiver

an in
bei for
um for

abhorchen to listen to (with stethoscope)
(anrufen) ich rief an I telephoned,
  rang up
weggehen to leave
weh tun (D) to hurt

frei available
heiser hoarse
krank ill, sick
leicht light
leidend suffering, ailing
normal normal
schwer heavy
unvernünftig foolish, unreasonable
vergangen past
voll full

damit with it
darüber about it
darum for it
davon of it

bisher until now
je at a time
mal just
solange as long as
unbedingt come what may, necessarily,
  without fail
vorübergehend temporarily

am ganzen Körper all over, in the whole
  body
das liegt daran, daß that's because
durchaus nicht absolutely not, by no
  means
er muß sich eine Erkältung geholt haben
  he must have caught a cold
erzählen von to tell about
es geht ihm schlecht he is not well
es schadet aber nichts it does no harm
es tat ihm alles weh he was sore all over
Freude haben an to find pleasure in
gute Besserung! I hope you will soon be
  well
irgendwie in any way
kein Wunder! no wonder!
nicht oder kaum little or nothing
nichts Schlimmes nothing serious
sich eine Erkältung holen to catch cold
sich halbtot lachen to split one's sides
  laughing
so gut wie gar nicht hardly at all, little
  or no
sonst noch etwas? anything else?
was fehlt mir? what's the matter with
  me?
was noch? what else?
zitternd vor Kälte shivering with cold

Notes

Part one

1 **Doktor Ignaz Lodenhuber, dessen Sprechstundenhilfe ich bin, ist
praktischer Arzt.** *Doctor Ignaz Lodenhuber, whose receptionist I
am, is a general practitioner.*
dessen Sprechstundenhilfe ich bin This is a relative clause and
dessen is the masculine (and neuter) genitive of the relative
pronoun. When relative pronouns were first introduced, it was
mentioned that they differed in form from the definite article
(**der/die/das**) ONLY in the genitive and in the dative plural.

194

2 **Doktor Lodenhuber, dem ich davon erzählte, lachte sich halbtot darüber.** *Doctor Lodenhuber, whom I told about it, split his sides laughing at it.*

Dem is a dative masculine relative pronoun – *whom*. **Erzählen** (*to tell*) requires that the person who is told be in the dative.

3 **Ich habe aber durchaus Freude an meinem Beruf.** *I am extremely happy in my job.*

Freude an meinem Beruf **Freude an** + dative: *joy* or *pleasure* IN

4 **Es gibt einige kranke und leidende Menschen, denen nicht oder kaum geholfen werden kann.** *There are some sick and suffering people for whom little or nothing can be done.*

a **leidende** This kind of adjective is really a form of the verb – called the present participle – being used as an adjective. Its equivalent form in English is that which ends in *-ing* (*suffering*) and which is also often used as an adjective. German present participles are formed by adding **-end** to the stem. Apart from their use as adjectives and also as nouns (**der Reisende**: *traveller/ travelling person*), they are not much used.

b **Denen** is the dative plural relative pronoun, the other form which differs from the definite article (N1 above). **Helfen** (of which **geholfen** is the past participle) is always followed by the dative of the person helped.

5 **Das liegt daran, daß es immer noch genug Krankheiten gibt, deren Gründe man nicht kennt.** *That stems from the fact that there are still a good many diseases, the causes of which are unknown.*

a **das liegt daran, daß**: *that lies in the fact that.* This is one of those verbal phrases ending in a preposition (**an**), the completion of which is really the whole following **daß** clause. Just as we insert *the fact that,* the Germans complete the phrase in the first clause with **da(r)**.

b **deren Gründe man nicht kennt**: lit. *whose causes (reasons) one does not know* **Deren**: *whose, of which* is the genitive plural relative pronoun.

6 **Solange man die Gründe für Krankheiten und die Heilmittel dagegen nicht gefunden hat,** *As long as the causes of diseases, and the means of curing them have not been found,*

a **Solange** introduces a dependent clause – so the verb phrase is at the end (**nicht gefunden hat**).

b **man ... nicht gefunden hat**: lit. *one has not found* A complicated passive can sometimes be avoided by using an active construction with **man** as subject. **Gefunden** is the past participle of **finden.**

c **die Heilmittel dagegen:** *the cures for them* (*means of healing them*) **Dagegen** really means AGAINST *them,* which is really more logical than a cure for. *Something* FOR (i.e. *to cure*) a pain is **etwas gegen.**

Part two

Krankenversicherung *Sickness insurance*

7 **Könnte ich bitte mit Doktor Lodenhuber sprechen?** *Could I please speak to Doktor Lodenhuber?*
könnte ich Here is a form of the verb you are gradually becoming familiar with (**wäre, möchte**) used as a courtesy form in preference to **kann ich?** which is less formally courteous.

8 **weil er gerade einen Patienten behandelt.** *because he is treating a patient just at the moment.*
einen Patienten **Patient** is a weak noun and has **-en** in every case except the nominative singular.

9 **Meinem Mann geht es seit der vergangenen Nacht sehr schlecht.** *My husband has not been at all well since during the night.*

a **meinem Mann geht es sehr schlecht** When you are talking of how your health is, remember to use **gehen** with the dative.

b **seit der vergangenen Nacht** **Vergangen** is really a past participle used as an adjective (**vergehen:** *to pass* (of time)). Hence, *the past night.*

10 **Dr. Lodenhuber ist uns von meiner Schwägerin, Frau Pfaffinger, als ein guter und zuverlässiger Arzt empfohlen worden.** *Dr. Lodenhuber has been recommended to us by my sister-in-law, Frau Pfaffinger, as a good and reliable doctor.*
Dr. Lodenhuber ist uns empfohlen worden This is a passive construction in the perfect tense. **Empfohlen** is the past participle of **empfehlen:** *to recommend.* In this construction we require two past participles: *been* and *recommended,* and *been* in the PASSIVE sense (a part of **werden**). The past participle of **werden** is **geworden,** as you know. But **geworden** means *become.* We must distinguish between the past participle of **werden** meaning *become* and the past participle of **werden** (used as passive auxiliary) meaning *been.* The **ge-** is simply dropped, so we have

a SPECIAL past participle of **werden** for exclusive use in passive constructions in the perfect tense:

er wird empfohlen: *he is recommended*
er wurde empfohlen: *he was recommended*
er ist empfohlen worden: *he has been recommended.*

11 **Sobald der Herr Doktor frei ist, werde ich ihm Bescheid sagen.** *As soon as the doctor is free, I'll inform him.*

der Herr Doktor When not referring to the doctor by name Brigitte says **der *Herr* Doktor** or addresses him as ***Herr* Doktor**. Distinguish between **Arzt** which is a description of a profession, and **Doktor** which is a title.

Der Arzt kommt *The doctor comes*

12 **Ich habe nicht damit gerechnet, daß Sie herkommen.** *I wasn't counting on your coming.* **Rechnen mit** is another verb phrase ending in a preposition (**mit**) and the **daß** clause following is its completion. In English, we have the pattern *count on* YOUR COMING. There is no such construction in German, so a **daß** clause must be used, completing the **mit** with **da** in its own clause (**L24, N5a**).

13 **Ich hielt es für das Beste, mir den Patienten selbst anzusehen.** *I considered it best to take a look at the patient myself.*

a **ich hielt es für das Beste** **Halten für** means *to consider to be*. **Hielt** is the imperfect tense. **Das Beste** is *the best thing*.

b **mir den Patienten selbst anzusehen** The expression used above requires an infinitive with **zu** to explain **es**. **Sich** (dative) **ansehen** means: *to take a look at*.

14 **Was fehlt ihm denn?** *What's the matter with him, then?* **Fehlen** is used impersonally (with the dative of the person referred to) meaning *to be the matter, to be wrong with*.

15 **Er muß sich gestern bei dem strömenden Regen eine schwere Erkältung geholt haben.** *He must have caught a bad cold in the pouring rain yesterday.*

a **er muß sich ... geholt haben** **Sich** (dative) **holen** means *to catch*. **Muß sich geholt haben** means *must have caught*. **Must have** + a past participle is translated by the present tense of **müssen** + past participle and **haben** (or **sein**, if the past participle is a verb which has **sein** as auxiliary).

b **bei dem strömenden Regen** **Strömend** is a present participle, here used as an adjective (**L24, N4a**).

197

16 **ohne einen Mantel anzuziehen** *without putting on a coat* This construction – *without doing* something must be dealt with by **ohne** + **zu** + infinitive.

17 **zitternd vor Kälte** *shivering with cold*

a **Zitternd** is a present participle used as such this time. Note that there is no **e** before the **n** of the infinitive.

b **vor Kälte:** WITH *cold* **Vor** is used when the following noun is the cause of the action (*shivering*). **Zitternd vor Angst** means *trembling* WITH *fear*.

18 **Nachts schlief er so gut wie gar nicht.** *In the night he had little or no sleep (he slept as well as not at all).*
Schlief is the imperfect of **schlafen.**

19 **tat ihm alles weh?** *he was sore all over (everything was hurting him)?*
tat ihm weh Here is another impersonal expression (the subject is not a person) with a following dative. **Weh tun:** *to hurt, be sore,* is like a separable verb, although it is two words.

20 **Ich ließ ihn natürlich im Bett** *I kept him in bed* This is an idiomatic use of **lassen** – i.e. it only means *kept* in this particular expression.

21 **rief Sie . . . an** *rang you up* **Rief** is the imperfect of **rufen.**

22 **Er bat mich darum, ihm ein Glas eiskaltes Bier zu bringen.**
He asked me to bring him a glass of ice-cold beer. This is a construction similar to that in L24, N5a in that the verb phrase in the first part (**bitten um:** *to ask* FOR) is completed by **da(r)**, standing for the following infinitive phrase, instead of by a **daß** clause. This type is much less common than the type completed by a **daß** clause.

23 **Das hätten Sie nicht tun sollen.** *You ought not to have done that* (or *shouldn't have*). The pattern here is basically that of the perfect tense of a modal verb (**sollen**) followed by a completing infinitive. The difference in form is in the auxiliary – **hätten.** These verb forms with Umlaut, which is not normally there in the imperfect (**wäre, könnte, hätte**) are forms of the SUBJUNCTIVE. Much more will be said of its uses in later lessons; in form, the endings are the same as for the imperfect tense; the only difference is the Umlaut. You will find it quite simple to memorize verb phrases like **hätte . . . sollen:** *ought to have* done.

24 **Ein heißer Tee wäre besser gewesen.** *A hot (cup of) tea would have been better.*

wäre besser gewesen Wäre (subjunctive) means *would be;*
wäre . . . gewesen: *would have been.*

Am Krankenbett *At the sick bed*

25 **Und das Bier, das Ihnen von Ihrer Frau gebracht worden ist, half
nicht dagegen?** *And the beer brought you by your wife didn't help?*

a **das Bier, das . . . gebracht worden ist** The second **das** is a relative
pronoun; therefore the verb phrase goes to the end and its three
components – two past participles and an auxiliary must be
arranged thus:
1 past participle of action described (**gebracht**)
2 special past participle **worden** for perfect passive
3 auxiliary, which is always some form of **sein.**
This is the arrangement of a perfect passive in a dependent
clause.

b **half nicht dagegen** Half is the imperfect of **helfen. Dagegen:**
against it requires no translation into English.

26 **je zwei!** *two at a time* This word **je** is always used when
prescribing, for the sake of precision.

Part three

Im Wartezimmer *In the waiting-room*

27 **Wo ist die Dame, deren Kind eine Erkältung hat?** *Where's the
lady whose child has a cold?*
deren Kind **Deren** is the genitive singular feminine of the
relative pronoun. You now know all the forms that are different
from **der/die/das** (*the*), namely all the genitives and the dative
plural:
GEN: MASC./NEUT. SING. **dessen**; FEM. SING. **deren**; PL. **deren**
DAT. PL: **denen** (See Appendix 6.)

Freude am Beruf *Happy in one's work*

28 **dasselbe werden, was sein Vater war?** *become the same as his
father?* The German here reads literally *become that same thing
which his father was.*
Was is a relative pronoun here. **Dasselbe** (like **alles, nichts,
vieles**) is too indefinite to be given a proper gender (**der, die,
das**); in such instances, the relative pronoun must be **was.**

25 Lektion fünfundzwanzig   Fasching
Lesson twenty-five   Carnival

What happens

Fasching is a very special festival in Germany, and Munich is the focal
point of it. During the final celebrations people traditionally dress
up in fancy costumes, there are magnificent processions, parties,
balls, dancing, even in the streets, and of course a great deal of
drinking.

    In Part 1 Franz Pfaffinger talks about all the festivals which are held
in Bavaria. In Part 2 Renate is given some parental advice, and she
and Franz meet some friends at a jazz club.

New words in this lesson

der Amerikaner(–) American
der Bilderrahmen(–) picture frame
der Boden(⸚) floor
der Engländer(–) Englishman
der Fasching Carnival
der Feiertag(-e) holiday, festival
der Jazzkeller(–) jazz club
der Kaffeebaum(⸚e) coffee-tree
der Lehrling(-e) apprentice
der Ratschlag(⸚e) advice, piece of advice
der ,Tintenfischkeller' 'Cuttlefish Cellar'

die Bar(-s) bar, counter
die Frucht(⸚e) fruit
die Kaffeebohne(-n) coffee bean
die Kette(-n) chain
die Kusine(-n) cousin (female)
die Lederhose(-n) leather trousers
die Musik music
die Norwegerin(-nen) Norwegian
  (female)
die Phantasie(-n) imagination
die Treppe(-n) stairs

das Blatt(⸚er) leaf
das Kostüm(-e) fancy-dress

das Nachthemd(-en) nightdress
das Oktoberfest October beer festival

fallen (fällt) to fall
(kommen) sie ist gekommen she's come

brauchen to have to
kritisieren to criticize

austrinken to empty (glass, bottle etc.)
herunterkommen to come down
hingehen to go (to)
mitgehen to go along (with)

bemalt painted, coloured
dänisch Danish
echt true, real
geblümt flowery
lächerlich ridiculous
lieber better
lustig funny, gay
schwedisch Swedish
unglücklich unfortunate, unsuccessful
vorsichtig careful

jedenfalls in any case
offiziell officially
überhaupt after all

übrigens by the way
zueinander together, to each other

oben at the top, above
unten at the bottom, below

an about

also gut all right then
auf der ganzen Welt throughout the
  whole world
bis auf down to
das ist doch klar! but of course!
es läßt sich gar nicht richtig tanzen it's
impossible to dance properly
frei haben to have a holiday (time off
  from work, school etc.)
gar nichts nothing at all
geöffnet sein to be open
geöffnet werden to be opened
halt deinen Mund! hold your tongue!
jeder kann tun und lassen, was er will
  everybody does just what he likes
jeder nach seinem Geschmack everybody
  to his liking
nebenbei gesagt by the way, incidentally
viel Vergnügen! have a good time!
von oben bis unten from top to bottom

Notes

Part one

1 **Das Schönste an Bayern und an München ist, daß so viel gefeiert wird.** *The nicest thing about Bavaria and Munich is that there are so many festivities.*

a **das Schönste an** **Das Schönste** is a 'noun' of the same category as **das Beste** – made from an adjective and given adjective endings. *About* coming after such an expression is **an** with the dative.

b **daß so viel gefeiert wird** This is a passive without a subject within a **daß** clause. **Feiern** means *to celebrate;* **wird gefeiert:** *is celebrated, there is celebrating, there are festivities.* **So viel** is an adverbial phrase, NOT the subject of **wird.**

2 **und das nicht nur zur Zeit des Oktoberfestes, das auf der ganzen Welt dafür bekannt ist.** *and that doesn't only apply to the time of the Munich beer festival (in October), which is world famous in this respect.*

a **Zur Zeit des Oktoberfestes** **Zur Zeit** + genitive means *at the time of.* The beer festival is referred to as **das Oktoberfest.**

b **das auf der ganzen Welt dafür bekannt ist** This is a relative clause. The antecedent of **das** is **Oktoberfest(es).** **Auf der ganzen Welt** means *throughout the world;* **dafür:** *for it (that),* i.e. for doing what you like. *In this respect* sounds better than *for that.*

3 **Während des ganzen Jahres gibt es Feste, Feiertage und Ferien, an denen man frei hat.** *During the whole year (throughout the year) there are feasts, festivals and holidays on which one doesn't work (which are public holidays).*

an denen man frei hat   This is a relative clause. **An** + dative, you remember, is used for ON *a day* (*days*); **denen** is the dative plural relative pronoun.

Part two

Gute Ratschläge   *Good advice*

4   **Und ich verlasse mich darauf, daß kein Alkohol getrunken wird.**
And I trust that no alcohol will be drunk.
ich verlasse mich darauf, daß: *I'm relying on* THE FACT *that*   **Sich verlassen** *auf* means *to rely* ON. When it takes a whole **daß** clause to say what one is relying on, as usual in these constructions, **da** stands for the other clause within its own. cf. **das liegt** *daran,* **daß**...(L24); **ich habe nicht** *damit* **gerechnet, daß**...(L24).

5   **Wir wollen nur ein bißchen tanzen gehen.** *We just want to go dancing for a while.*
tanzen gehen   This is like **spazieren gehen:** *to go walking* (*for a walk*). *To go ... ing* is always expressed in German by using the infinitive of the activity + **gehen.** The infinitive of the other verb behaves like a separable prefix, e.g.: **Wir gehen tanzen:** *We're going dancing.* **Wir wollen tanzen gehen:** *We want to go dancing.* **Wir sind tanzen gegangen:** *We went dancing.*

6   **Das hängt davon ab, wo gute Musik gemacht wird und richtig getanzt werden kann.** *It depends on where good music's played and one can dance properly.*

a   This sentence is of the same pattern as that discussed in several notes in recent lessons. **Abhängen von** means *to depend* ON. **Da** in **davon** stands for the whole **wo** clause.

b   **wo gute Musik gemacht wird:** *where there is good music,* or *where good music is played*   Note that you use **machen** with **Musik,** meaning *play music.*

c   **und richtig getanzt werden kann:** lit. *and can be danced properly* It is a passive construction without a subject, which should be quite familiar to you now. **Getanzt werden kann** – the verb phrase is arranged thus because it is still the dependent clause introduced by **wo.**

7   **ihr müßt euch ... treffen.** *you must be meeting* (*each other*).
Euch cannot be omitted when *each other* is implied (though not mentioned) in the English sentence.

8 **weil der schon ab sieben Uhr geöffnet ist.** *because it's open from seven onwards.*
Geöffnet is the past participle of **öffnen**: *to open.* Here it is serving as an adjective, therefore it can be used with **ist.**

9 **Die anderen werden meistens erst um acht oder halb neun geöffnet.** *The others* (clubs) *don't usually open till eight or eight – thirty.*
werden geöffnet: lit. *are open*ED   Oddly enough, one must use a non-passive in English *(they)* OPEN. **Geöffnet sein**: *to be open* describes the STATE or CONDITION of something. **Geöffnet werden**: *to be open*ED, *to open* describes what HAPPENS.

10 **Darunter kann ich mir gar nichts vorstellen.** *Goodness knows what that may mean! (from that (name) I can imagine nothing).*
This is so idiomatic and so confined to context that only a very free translation will convey the right reaction.

11 **Sonst sind deine Freunde weg, bis du dort ankommst.** *Otherwise* (or, *or else) your friends will be gone by the time you get there.*
Sonst only has the effect of inverting subject and verb. It does not introduce a dependent clause.

Faschingskostüme   *Fancy dress*

12 **Ich glaube, ich sehe sie gerade die Treppe herunterkommen.**
I think I see her just coming down the stairs.
ich sehe sie ... herunterkommen   The infinitive (**herunterkommen**) is used for the English participle *-ing (com*ING *down)* after **sehen,** i.e. when one sees someone else *do*ING something. **Herunterkommen** means *to come down.*

13 **sie ist voll von bunt bemalten Kaffeebohnen.** *it's full of brightly painted coffee beans.*

a **voll von**   This is not the only way of saying *full of,* but it is acceptable when followed by a plural, and is easy to use, since **voll** has no ending and **von** is always followed by the dative.

b **bunt bemalten Kaffeebohnen**   **Bemalt** is a past participle used as an adjective. This is the strong dative plural ending (**bemalen**: *to paint, colour over).*

14 **Und Ketten aus Kaffeebohnen, die bis auf den Boden hängen.**
And chains (made) of coffee-beans, hanging right down to the floor.

a **die bis auf den Boden hängen**   This is a relative clause. Compare

25 with the English translation (*hang*ING). The relative clause is the ONLY way to say such things in German.

b **bis auf:** *as far as, right down (up, along) to* Notice the accusative after **bis auf.**

15 **Er steckt in einem leeren Bilderrahmen.** *He is (stuck) inside an empty picture frame.*
er steckt **Stecken** can describe just where someone or something *is,* if the context is appropriate, as it certainly is here.

16 **Sei du lieber ruhig und halt deinen Mund!** *You'd do better to keep quiet and hold your tongue!* These are command forms (familiar singular) and if **du** is included in the phrase, it is either for emphasis or implies disapproval.

17 **Dein geblümtes Nachthemd und die Lederhosen passen auch nicht zueinander.** *Your floral nightdress and leather shorts hardly go together either (don't match each other).*

a **die Lederhosen** **Hose** means *trousers,* but **Lederhosen** are something quite specific, originating in Bavaria. They are leather shorts with shoulder straps.

b **passen ... zueinander** **Passen zu** means *to match, go with;* **einander:** *one another.* You have had other examples of little words like **mit** and **zu** joined to **einander** (**miteinander:** *with one another*).

18 **Ich dachte immer, im Fasching paßt alles zu allem.** *I always thought anything went with anything at Carnival time.*

a **paßt** Note the tense of **paßt** (present); it has to be past in English. The German is quite logical here, in that Anne is speaking generally, and not of something that has already taken place.

b **ich dachte** **Dachte** is the imperfect of **denken.** This verb is one of the mixed group with internal changes, yet weak endings.

19 **Alles, was ein bißchen Phantasie zeigt, ist erlaubt und willkommen.** *Everything (anything) that shows a bit of imagination is allowed and welcome.*
alles, was The **was** clause is a relative clause. Remember **was** is the relative pronoun when the antecedent is **alles, nichts,** or anything so vague and indefinite that it cannot be dealt with by the **der/die/das** relative pronoun.

Ausländer *Foreigners*

20 **läßt es sich gar nicht richtig tanzen.** *it's impossible to dance properly.*

204

läßt es sich ... tanzen Es läßt sich + an infinitive means *it can be done* (past participle in English). **Es läßt sich trinken** means *it can be drunk.*

21 **Karin, mit der du gekommen bist?** *Karin, with whom you came?* **Der** is the dative singular feminine relative pronoun.

22 **Sie bleibt gern sitzen und sieht lieber andere tanzen.** *She prefers to sit and watch other people dancing.*
sieht lieber andere tanzen The infinitive (**tanzen**) is used after **sieht** (L25, N12).

23 **Nebenbei gesagt,** *by the way,* There is no inversion of subject and verb after this, because of the comma. Inversion can always be avoided after an introductory word or phrase by using a comma, but this is rarely desirable. It is sometimes preferable to have the comma (which can only be rendered by a slight pause when speaking), notably in instances where the relationship between item one and the rest of the sentence is very tenuous.

24 **ich setze mich jetzt zu ihr und den anderen an den Tisch** *I'm going to sit down at the table beside her and the others*
ich setze mich zu **Zu** is used with **sich setzen** when one *joins* others who are already seated.

25 **und helfe ihnen die Gläser austrinken.** *and I'll help them (to) empty (drain) the glasses.*
helfe ihnen ... austrinken Note that no **zu** is necessary after **helfen** with a completing infinitive.

26 **Ich höre sie über irgendeinen Jazzkeller in der Leopoldstraße sprechen.** *I hear them talking about some jazz club in the Leopoldstraße.*

a **irgendeinen** Remember **irgend** in front of any element indicates vagueness – *some ... or other:*
irgendwo: *somewhere or other*
irgend etwas: *something or other*
irgendwie: *somehow or other.*

b **ich höre sie ... sprechen:** *I hear them talk*ING Infinitive in German, *-ing* form in English. **Hören** is exactly like **sehen** in this respect (L25, N12 and N22).

26 Lektion sechsundzwanzig Ein Unfall

Lesson twenty-six An accident

What happens

In this lesson there is drama and excitement. Renate and Franz happen
to be on the spot when a car with three passengers accidentally
goes off the road into the river Isar. Renate and Franz plunge into
the water and help to rescue the man, woman and child in the car.

In Part 1 the driver of the ambulance describes his job. In Part 2
passers-by give a description of the accident, the police and the
ambulance arrive and a reporter invites Renate and Franz to appear
in a television interview.

New words in this lesson

der **Bursche**(-n) youth, lad
der **Fußgänger**(–) pedestrian (male)
der **Kranke**(-n) sick person, patient
der **Krankenwagen**(–) ambulance
der **Mut** courage
der **Punkt**(-e) point, dot
der **Reporter**(–) reporter
der **Retter**(–) rescuer
der **Schreck** fright
der **Stadtplan**("e) street map
der **Stadtteil**(-e) district (of town or
  city)
der **Transport**(-e) transportation
der **Unfall**("e) accident
der **Verunglückte**(-n) casualty, victim
der **Zeuge**(-n) witness

die **Anerkennung**(-en) appreciation
die **Brücke**(-n) bridge
die **Decke**(-n) blanket
die **Einzelheit**(-en) detail, particular
die **Feuerwehr** fire brigade
die **Fußgängerin**(-nen) pedestrian
  (female)
die **Hosentasche**(-n) trouser pocket
die **Polizei** police

die **Polizeiwache**(-n) police station
die **Rettung**(-en) rescue
die **Sirene**(-n) siren

das **Brot**(-e) bread
das **Fernsehstudio**(-s) TV studio
das **Protokoll**(-e) record, report

(**dürfen**) **dürfte ich?** may I?
(**fahren**) **es ist gefahren** it has driven
(**fallen**) **er ist gefallen** he's fallen
frieren to feel cold
(**können**) **könnte ich?** could I?
(**schließen**) **ich schloß** I closed
schwimmen to swim
sinken to sink
springen (**er sprang**) to jump (he jumped)
sterben (**er stirbt**) to die (he dies)
treten to step, go
(**wissen**) **ich hätte gewußt** I would have
  known
(**ziehen**) **sie zogen** they pulled

lächeln to smile
retten to save
verdienen to deserve

(**anfangen**) **es fing an** it started

206

fortsetzen to continue

sich erholen to recover

anwesend present
lächelnd smiling
sauer sour
schwer serious

wohl well (in good health)

auf einmal suddenly
dort oben up there
vorbei past, over

damit so that, in order that
oder aber or else
so ... wie ... as ... as ...

ach Unsinn! nonsense!
auf dem Transport on the way
das mag it might
ein sauer verdientes Brot a hard-earned living
erste Hilfe leisten to give first aid
los! stand back!
Punkt 12 Uhr on the stroke of 12
so gut wie meine eigene Hosentasche like the back of my hand
um Hilfe rufen to shout for help
vor Freude with joy
zu jeder Jahreszeit in every season of the year
zu Protokoll nehmen to make out an official report
zum Glück luckily, fortunately

Notes

Part one

1 **bei schlechtem oder schönem Wetter,** *in bad or good weather,* In any kind of conditions relating to weather, *in* is translated as **bei.** (Remember **bei dem strömenden Regen:** *in the pouring rain* – L24.)

2 **von ganz München** *in the whole of (throughout) Munich* **Ganz** used with the name of a town or country can always be translated by *the whole of;* **ganz** never changes in form in such expressions, e.g.: **für ganz Deutschland:** *for the whole of Germany.*

3 **ein sauer verdientes Brot.** *a hard-earned living.* **Sauer** is used as an adverb here and has, therefore, no ending.

4 **Außer den regelmäßigen Transporten von Kranken und alten oder zu schwachen Menschen** *In addition to regular transportation of the sick and aged or infirm people* (lit. *too weak people*) **von Kranken** **Der Kranke:** *sick person,* is an adjective used as a noun, but treated as an adjective as regards endings. Since there is no **der** word preceding it, **Kranken** has a strong (dative plural) ending.

5 **werden wir fast stündlich zu Unfällen aller Art gerufen.** *we are called almost every hour to accidents of every kind.*

a **Gerufen** is the past participle of **rufen:** *to call, summon.*

b **aller Art** This is unusual, since **Art** is singular and **alle** is, of course, nearly always used with plurals, except for a few idiomatic exceptions. **Aller** is genitive singular.

6 **die Verunglückten:** *the injured* This is really a past participle used as a noun, but requiring adjective endings.

7 **Manchmal stirbt sogar jemand auf dem Transport, oder aber es wird ein Kind geboren, wie gestern zum Beispiel, Punkt 12 Uhr, um Mitternacht.** *Sometimes even, someone dies on the way (to hospital) or else a baby is born, like yesterday, for example, on the stroke of twelve midnight.*

a **stirbt** **Sterben** is a strong vowel-changing verb.

b **auf dem Transport** From this phrase, you will understand more clearly the meaning of the German word **Transport:** the act of *conveying* the patient to hospital, rather than the vehicle.

c **es wird ein Kind geboren** This is a passive construction.

Part two

Was ist passiert? *What has happened?*

8 **Jemand ist ins Wasser gefallen.** *Someone has fallen into the water.* **ist ... gefallen** **Fallen:** *to fall* has **sein** as auxiliary in the perfect tense. The past participle is identical with that of **gefallen:** *to please,* but that has **haben** as auxiliary and the context is unlikely to leave any possibility of ambiguity.

9 **ein Auto ist in die Isar gefahren.** *a car went into the river.* **die Isar** This is the river on which Munich lies. In Germany, the local inhabitants always refer to their river by its name, even in a case like this, where an English person would almost certainly just say *the river.*

10 **Ich hab's genau gesehen.** *I saw exactly what happened. (I saw it precisely* – meaning *as it was happening.)* **ich hab's** This is how one spells the spoken abbreviation of **ich habe es.** An apostrophe in German always means a letter has been omitted.

11 **Ich ging gerade spazieren.** *I just happened to be walking along.* **gerade** This is the word which both compels and permits the particular English rendering. **Gerade** is not new to you, of course. *To* HAPPEN *to be doing something* must be adapted in German, and this is one way of doing it.

12 **Auf einmal sah ich von der Brücke dort oben aus ein Auto im Wasser schwimmen.** *Suddenly, from up there on the bridge, I saw a car floating (swimming) in the water.*

von der Brücke aus Aus in this sort of phrase fixes the vantage point. **Von** alone is not enough.

13 **Es fing schon zu sinken an.** *It was already beginning to sink.*
es fing ... an Fing an is the imperfect of **anfangen**. Remember from earlier lessons that **an** is sometimes at the very end and sometimes precedes the infinitive phrase.

14 **hinter ihr her.** *after her.* **Hinter ... her** is used when someone is carrying out an ACTIVITY after or behind someone else who is doing/has done it first. Note that **hinter** takes the dative case.

15 **Zogen sie jemanden aus dem Wasser?** *Did they pull someone out of the water?*

a **Zogen** is the imperfect of **ziehen:** *to pull.*

b **Jemanden** is the accusative of **jemand.** It has **der** endings. Nowadays, however, you might hear it used without its proper endings.

16 **Es waren zwei Leute:** *It was two people:*
es waren The plural forms of **sein** can follow **es** (which is singular). This happens when what follows is a plural. (**Das sind meine Eltern. Es sind viele Plätze frei.**)

17 **Wurde die Polizei schon von jemandem gerufen?** *Did someone call the police?*

a The German is a passive construction (*were the police called by someone*), but an active construction is better in English.

b **von jemandem** Jemandem is dative of **jemand** (N15b above).

18 **damit sie das Auto wieder aus dem Wasser zieht.** *so that it can pull the car out of the water.*
damit: *in order that* If **damit** stands at the head of a clause, the verb goes to the end. (Do not confuse this word with **damit** meaning *with it* or *with them.* Context and verb placement should rule out any possibility of ambiguity.)

Polizei- und Krankenwagen *Police-car and ambulance*

19 **Zur Seite treten, bitte!** *Step aside, please! (Make way, please!)*
The infinitive is used as a command form in official situations, where the general public is being addressed.

20 **Los! Machen Sie bitte Platz, damit der Krankenwagen durch kann.**
Stand back! Make way, please, so that the ambulance can get through.
durch kann Sometimes a preposition (**durch**) is enough on its own in German when accompanied by a modal (**kann**). That is, it is unnecessary to say **durch***fahren,* but the completing verb form (usually *get, go, come, pass*) must be added in English.

26

21 Könnte ich bitte zu den Verunglückten? *Could I please get to the victims (injured)?*

a Another example of omission of the completing infinitive (N20).

b **könnte ich** This form (more courteous than **kann ich**) is not new to you. It is called the subjunctive, remember.

22 Neben mir stehen auch die Retter der Verunglückten. *The rescuers of the victims are (standing) here beside me as well.*
stehen Note the German is, if possible, more precise than English. We would just say *are*.

23 aber glücklich lächelnd vor Freude über die gelungene Rettung. *but smiling happily with joy at the successful rescue.*

a **Lächelnd** is the present participle of **lächeln**: *to smile.*

b **über die gelungene Rettung** **Lächeln** *über* + accusative means *to smile* AT *(about)*. **Gelungen** is the past participle of **gelingen**: *to succeed,* used here as an adjective.

24 Dürfte ich bitte Ihre Namen wissen? *May I be permitted to know your names?*
Dürfte is a subjunctive – here, simply a courtesy form. Note that it is formed in the same way as **könnte** *(could),* i.e. identical with the imperfect, except that the Umlaut is necessary.

25 Ich hätte nur gern gewußt, ... *I would just have liked to know ... (I would just like to have known...)*
hätte ... gewußt This is a subjunctive form, meaning *I* WOULD HAVE *known.* This subjunctive (**hätte**) is formed in the same way as **könnte** and **dürfte** – just add an Umlaut to the imperfect (L24, N23). (**Möchte:** WOULD *like,* is a form you have been using for a long time.) When the English verb phrase contains WOULD, it is usually necessary to have a subjunctive form in German. If the English phrase is *would have* + a past participle, then you use this subjunctive form of the auxiliary (**hätte** or **wäre**) plus the past participle. The situation here is complicated by the presence of **gern** which is idiomatic, of course, and the simplest way of coping with this type of phrase (**ich hätte gern** + past participle) is to memorize an example.

26 Wäre es nicht möglich, wenigstens ... *Would it not be possible at least...*
Wäre: WOULD *be* is the same kind of subjunctive, the one formed from the imperfect + an Umlaut. In the case of **sein,** however, for the **ich** and **er** forms you must also add the same endings as for the imperfect of any weak verb. (See Appendix **16**)

210

27 **Würden Sie mir bitte noch erzählen, ob Sie Angst gehabt hatten?**
Would you please tell me if you were frightened?
würden Sie This is the subjunctive of **werden,** and is very often
used to translate WOULD *do something*, especially if the following
infinitive happens to be a weak verb. This is because the subjunctive form of weak verbs (which would be the only possible
alternative) happens to be the very same as the imperfect.
The subjunctive of the weak verb would not do here, in any case,
as this *would* is a particular request form and simply means
be kind enough to – that is, it has nothing to do with the
hypothetical kind of *would* which describes what might happen in
given circumstances.

28 **Ich schloß einfach die Augen und bin gesprungen.** *I simply shut my
eyes and jumped.*
a **Schloß** is the imperfect of **schließen.**
b **bin gesprungen** Springen has **sein** as auxiliary in the perfect tense.

29 **Haben Sie jemanden im Auto sitzen sehen?** *Did you see someone
sitting in the car?* This is the perfect tense form of a verb phrase
with **sehen** + an infinitive (**sitzen**). Note that it is exactly the same
pattern as with the perfect tense of a modal verb followed by a
completing infinitive; one uses the infinitive of **sehen** and NOT
the past participle.

30 **Wir haben nur jemanden um Hilfe rufen hören.** *We just heard
someone shouting for help.*
This is the same pattern, with **hören** instead of **sehen** (N29).

31 **Eigentlich habe ich nicht viel zu tun brauchen.** *Actually, I didn't
need to do very much.* This again is a similar verb phrase pattern
to N29 and N30 above. **Brauchen (nicht)** is treated here like a
modal verb. The infinitive is used instead of the past participle.
Note, however, that **zu** is necessary before the infinitive.

32 **Franz hat mir das Kind aus dem Fenster ziehen helfen.** *Franz helped
me to pull the child out through the window.*
hat mir … ziehen helfen This is yet another example of the
infinitive used in the perfect tense instead of the past participle,
where there are two verbs dependent on each other. To sum up,
this happens when the main verb of the two is (a) a modal (thus
ich muß warten becomes in the perfect tense **ich habe warten
müssen**) or (b) **sehen** (L26, N29), **hören** (L26, N30), **helfen** or

33

brauchen – the last nearly always in the negative.

In Ihren Augen mag das alles ganz einfach gewesen sein. *In your eyes (as you see it) that may all have been perfectly natural (simple).*
mag . . . gewesen sein: *may have been* **Mag** (present tense of **mögen**) is frequently used in this sense, also in the present tense – **das mag sein:** *that may be.* **Gewesen:** *been* requires **sein** as auxiliary, and **sein** is the infinitive completing **mag.** It is the same pattern as **es muß gewesen sein:** *it must have been* (L23).

34 **Sie haben aber wirklich großen Mut gezeigt, der höchste Anerkennung verdient.** *But you have really shown great courage, which deserves the greatest appreciation (recognition).*

a **der . . . verdient** This is a relative clause, the antecedent of **der** being **Mut. Verdienen** here means *to deserve.*

b **höchste Anerkennung** Höchste has no **die** in front of it, but if it is literally translated as a superlative form *the* must be inserted in English. Otherwise, it must be translated as *very great.*

35 **Ich würde Sie gern für heute abend ins Fernsehstudio einladen,** *I'd like to invite you to the television studio this evening,*
würde gern This is really just another way of saying **ich** *möchte* **gern.** It is a polite expression of intention, relating to events that will probably happen.

Part three

Ein schwerer Unfall *A serious accident*

36 **Als ein Bus voller Touristen gegen eine Straßenbahn fuhr?** *When a coach full of tourists collided with (ran into) a tramcar?*
ein Bus voller Touristen Nowadays **voll** is usually used with **von** after it and then the dative of the noun, or just the form **voll** followed by an undeclined form, or sometimes with the genitive. This last usage is unusual in the spoken language and always sounds rather elevated and pedantic. **Voller** is what might be called a 'frozen' form which has survived and is preferred by some people. It is like a strong adjective agreeing with **Bus.**

37 **ein dritter ist . . . gestorben.** *a third died.*
ist gestorben *Dying* is regarded as a change of state and as such justifies **sein** as auxiliary.

Lektion siebenundzwanzig   Ein Fernseh-interview

Lesson twenty-seven   A television inter-view

What happens

Renate and Franz, having already been interviewed for the newspaper, are taken along to the television studio.

In Part 1 the television reporter talks about the local television news programme. In Part 2 Renate and Franz prepare for the interview. Herr and Frau Le Gras, the accident victims, arrive and invite Renate and Franz to their country house for the weekend. Finally Renate and Franz describe their television experiences to their parents.

New words in this lesson

der Bericht(-e) account, report
der Bildschirm(-e) screen
der Held(-en) hero
der Insasse(-n) car occupant
der Lippenstift(-e) lipstick
der Puder powder
der Sprecher(–) announcer
der Zuschauer(–) spectator, audience

die Aufregung(-en) excitement
die Beruhigungstablette(-n) tranquillizer
die Fernsehsendung(-en) TV broadcast
die Kamera(-s) camera
die Lampe(-n) lamp
die Sendung(-en) broadcast

das Feuer fire
das Landhaus("er) country house
das Kompliment(-e) compliment
das Make-up make-up
das Unglück(-e) accident, mishap

(bekommen) Sie bekamen you got
erscheinen to appear

(sinken) es wäre gesunken it would have sunk
(treten) wir traten we stepped

belohnen to reward
eilen to hurry, to rush
verunglücken to have an accident
wiederholen to repeat
zögern to hesitate

übrig bleiben to remain

allerbest best possible
blaß pale
furchtbar frightful
heutig of today
kommend coming, next
langweilig boring
ohnmächtig unconscious
spannend exciting
stolz proud
tadellos perfect
vergangen last

27

dauernd continuously
ebenfalls also, too
einmalig exceptionally
entsetzlich dreadfully
persönlich personally

so daß so that, with the result that
trotz in spite of

auf on
bei on
innerhalb within

derselbe, dieselbe the same
so etwas such a thing

aus zweiter Hand second-hand
durch Zufall by chance
erst einmal first of all
es gab überhaupt nicht viel zu tun there
  was nothing much to do
etwas Aufregendes something exciting
man sieht es euch nicht an you do not
  show it
ohnmächtig werden to faint
schon längst long since
spät werden to get late
um zu in order to
zu Hilfe kommen to come to one's aid

Notes

Part one

1 **derselbe, von dem** *he* (*the one*) *from whom* **Derselbe**: *the same*
  is frequently used as a demonstrative pronoun (*he/she/they/* etc.,
  or *the one/ones*) before a relative clause. (**Der** declines like the
  definite article and **selbe** like a weak adjective, remember.)

2 **bekamen** *received* This is the imperfect of **bekommen**: *to receive.*

3 **bei der ich als Sprecher oft auch zu sehen bin,** *on which I often*
  appear also as announcer,
  ich ... zu sehen bin: lit. *I am to be seen* **Zu sehen** can mean
  to be seen as well as *to see.* This is a feature of the German
  infinitive which makes phrases like *I* AM TO BE *seen, they* ARE
  TO BE *had* very easy to translate.

4 **Durch Zufall,** *By chance,* **Durch** is used to translate *by the agency*
  of, by means of so long as what follows is not a person. If it
  is followed by a person, the meaning is *through.*

5 **gerade in demselben Augenblick, als** *just at the very moment when*

a **in demselben Augenblick**: *at the same* (*very*) *moment* **Demselben**
  is the dative case.

b **als ... passierte** **Als** in a sense is the completion of the
  comparison, and at the same time introduces a time clause.

6 **so daß einem oft nichts anderes übrig bleibt,** *so that often there is*
  (*remains*) *nothing else for one to do,*

a **so daß**: *with the result that* This is not to be confused with
  damit: *so that,* meaning *in order that.*

214

b einem ... übrig bleibt: *remains for one (to do)* **Einem** is the dative case of **man**: *one.*

7 als langweilige Berichte aus zweiter Hand zu schreiben. *but write boring second-hand reports.* **Als** does NOT introduce a dependent clause here; it is the completion of **nichts anderes.**

Part two

Im Fernsehstudio *In the television studio*

8 Sollten sie es rechtzeitig vom Krankenhaus bis hierher ins Studio schaffen, ja. *Yes, if they should make it in time from the hospital to the studio here.*

sollten sie es ... schaffen This is a new kind of *if* clause, and is the only time (apart from questions and commands) when the verb comes at the very beginning of the sentence. We COULD translate it *Should they...* etc. but that would sound somewhat theatrical. It is called a conditional clause and the verb is, in fact, a subjunctive form identical with the imperfect **sollten.** The subjunctive is used here because it is by no means certain that they WILL make it.

9 Aber ich fürchte, daß es schon zu spät dafür geworden ist. *But I'm afraid it's already (got) too late for that.*

spät ... geworden ist **Spät werden** means *to get late.* **Geworden** is used in its own right here (*become*) and not as any sort of auxiliary.

10 durch deren großen Mut das Leben dreier Menschen gerettet wurde. *by whose great courage the lives of three people were saved.*

a durch *By* with a passive construction is **von** when the English is *by a person,* **durch** when *by a thing.*

b das Leben ... gerettet wurde The singular (**das Leben**) is used in German, so of course the passive auxiliary verb **wurde** is also singular.

c dreier Menschen **Dreier** has a genitive plural ending because there is no **der** word or adjective to show that it is a genitive. This is not done beyond the numeral **drei.** One can, of course, also say **von drei Menschen.**

11 dieselben Fragen, die Sie uns ... stellten, *the same questions (which) you asked us,* **Dieselben** is the accusative plural of **der** plus a weak adjective ending. **Die** is the accusative plural of the relative pronoun.

12   **Wir hätten Ihnen gern … gedankt,** *We would like to have thanked you, (we would gladly have thanked you,)* Once again, the exact translation is complicated by **gern. Wir hätten… gedankt** is a perfect subjunctive form. Note that only the auxiliary changes, and the only change is an Umlaut. You will gradually have come to realize that one of the uses of the subjunctive is expressing actions that MIGHT happen, or MIGHT HAVE happened but did not. This is why it is said to be used in 'unreal' or hypothetical conditions, of which we shall have quite a few more examples.

13   **dafür gedankt, daß Sie unser Leben gerettet haben.** *to have thanked you for saving (having saved) our lives.*
  dafür, daß   This is the only way of saying *for saving (having saved)*. **Für** is an integral part of the verb phrase **danken für** and the whole **daß** clause is its complement. But, as always, **da-** must stand in for the following **daß** clause to complete its own clause. You will be quite familiar with this construction by now (L25, N4).

14   **Wir hätten alle drei tot sein können.** *We could all have been dead.*
  hätten … sein können   This is the subjunctive of **haben** …
  sein können the pattern of the perfect tense of **können** followed by another infinitive. You have already met **hätte … (tun) sollen:** *should have (done)* and **hätte… (tun) können:** *could have (done).* It is quite easy to memorize these constructions, easier than working out the whole pattern on each occasion.

15   **Innerhalb einer halben Minute wäre das Auto gesunken,** *Within half a minute the car would have sunk,*
  a   **innerhalb einer halben Minute**   **Innerhalb:** *inside* (time or place) takes the genitive case.
  b   **wäre das Auto gesunken**   **Sinken** has **sein** as auxiliary in the perfect tense; the subjunctive is required here, as the car did not, in fact, sink; so **wäre** (*would be*) is used as the auxiliary (L26, N26).

16   **und dann wären wir jetzt schon längst tot.** *and then we would have been dead long ago.* There is no **gewesen:** *been* as the English *have been* is equivalent to the German present tense with **schon** and this operates with the subjunctive as well.

17   **Wenn wir nicht gesprungen wären, hätte es ein anderer getan.** *If we hadn't jumped, someone else would have (done it).* Here is an *if* clause in the subjunctive – a conditional clause in the perfect. It is in the subjunctive because it describes events that did not happen. They DID jump and no one ELSE did. The normal rules of word order for **wenn** clauses apply.

18 **daß niemand uns zu Hilfe gekommen wäre.** *that no one would have come to our aid.*

gekommen wäre: *would have come* The auxiliary is **sein** and it must be subjunctive to translate *would have.*

19 **Es müßte eigentlich anders belohnt werden, daß Sie uns trotz des eiskalten Wassers sofort zu Hilfe geeilt sind.** *The fact that you rushed to our aid at once in spite of the ice-cold water – that really ought to be rewarded in another way.*

a **es müßte** **Es** is doing duty for the whole **daß** clause that follows. (If the **daß** clause were placed first in the sentence, the **es** would disappear.) **Müßte** is a subjunctive form of **müssen** (like **könnte, sollte**) and means *ought to* or *should.*

b **trotz des eiskalten Wassers** **Trotz** is followed by the genitive case, though you should be warned that nowadays some people use the dative after it. **Eilen:** *to hurry* has **sein** as auxiliary.

Die Zuschauer *The viewers*

20 **Nun laß sie doch erst mal erzählen, wie es gewesen ist, und was sie alles haben machen müssen!** *Now let them tell us first what it was like and all they had to do!*

a **wie es gewesen ist:** lit. HOW *it was* **Wie** can mean *what . . . like?* as well as *how?*

b **was sie alles haben machen müssen** This is an INDIRECT question, and therefore requires the word order of a dependent clause. If it were a direct question, the word order would be **Was haben sie alles machen müssen?** Compare this with the indirect question and you will see that although **haben** has shifted, the actual sequence of verb phrase elements remains unaltered – AUXILIARY (**haben**), INFINITIVE (**machen**), MODAL (**müssen**). Therefore when a clause with the perfect tense of a modal followed by another infinitive becomes a dependent one, the verbs still cluster at the end, but the SEQUENCE remains the same. An easy way to remember the order is: A-I-M

A = auxiliary I = infinitive M = modal

21 **Wie viele hundert Male werden wir das noch erzählen müssen?** *How many hundreds of times will we have to tell it again?*

a **wie viele hundert Male** Think of **hundert Male** as one unit and of **wie viele** agreeing with it.

  b **werden wir ... erzählen müssen** This is a future with a modal and completing infinitive. Incidentally, note that the order is auxiliary, infinitive, modal.

22 **Ich fand alles schrecklich interessant und aufregend,** *I found it all terribly interesting and exciting,*

  a **Fand** is the imperfect of **finden.**

  b **Aufregend** is the present participle of **aufregen:** *to excite,* used as an adjective.

23 **besonders als wir uns dann endlich vor die Kamera setzen mußten.** *especially when we did at last have to sit down in front of the camera.*

  a **vor die Kamera** This is a good example of an occasion when the accusative is used after **vor** meaning *in front of,* since they move INTO a position in front of the cameras.

  b **als wir uns ... setzen mußten** Here is an imperfect tense of a modal plus the infinitive of a reflexive verb, all within a dependent clause.

24 **Bevor wir ins Studio traten, hustete und nieste er dauernd,** *Before we entered the studio, he kept on coughing and sneezing,*

  a **Traten** is the imperfect of **treten:** *to step.*

  b **hustete und nieste er dauernd** **Dauernd** is the present participle of **dauern** used as an adverb.

25 **so daß ihm erst einmal Hustensaft gegeben werden mußte.** *so that cough mixture had to be given to him first.* This is a dependent clause (**so daß**) containing a passive construction with a modal in the imperfect.

26 **Und sie zitterte vor Aufregung und bekam gleich zwei Beruhigungs-tabletten auf einmal zu schlucken.** *And she was shaking with excitement and immediately got two tranquillizers to swallow at once.*

  a **bekam ... zu schlucken:** lit. *received to swallow* Here it has the sense of *had to swallow.* **Bekam** is the imperfect of **bekommen.**

  b **auf einmal** Here this phrase means *at once (simultaneously).*

27 **Ich wäre bestimmt vor Angst ohnmächtig geworden.** *I would certainly have fainted with fright (nerves).* **ich wäre ... geworden** **Ohnmächtig werden** means *to faint, become unconscious.* Remember **werden** has **sein** as auxiliary, and since it did NOT happen, it is put in the subjunctive.

28 **Auf dem Bildschirm hat man euch jedenfalls nichts davon angesehen.** *On the screen, at any rate, you didn't look anything like that (it didn't show at all).*

29 **Ich war ganz stolz auf euch.** *I was very proud of you.*
    stolz auf: *proud* OF **Stolz** *auf* is used with the accusative.

Part three

Das Make-up   *The Make-up*

30 **heutiges** *today* This is an adjective formed from **heute,** but has
    no English equivalent. We just say *I like your make-up today.*
31 **daß mich der Puder** This is quite a common word order in a
    dependent clause – that is, the object (**mich**) comes before the
    subject (**der Puder**). This happens particularly when the object is a
    pronoun; indeed, the object must be a pronoun for this word
    order. But it is not WRONG to put the subject first.
32 **weil ich in der vergangenen Nacht nicht habe schlafen können.**
    because I wasn't able to sleep last night.
    nicht habe schlafen können (L27, N20b) Statement: **Ich habe
    nicht schlafen können.** Statement within **weil** clause: **Weil ich
    nicht habe schlafen können.** Both have the AIM (auxiliary, infinitive,
    modal) order, but note the position of **nicht** in the dependent
    clause – it precedes the whole verb phrase.

Aufregende Filme   *Exciting films*

33 **habt ihr euch angesehen?** *did you watch?* **Sich ansehen** is more
    active and purposeful than just **sehen. Sehen** can just mean *see,*
    whereas **sich ansehen** means *look at.*
34 **Du solltest ... nicht**   *You shouldn't* (subjunctive)
35 **Du müßtest doch wissen,** *You* SHOULD *know,* **Müßtest** is also
    subjunctive. Here, and in the previous note, you see the **du**
    ending for this subjunctive form **-est** which holds good for any
    verb in this subjunctive form. The difference between **solltest** and
    müßtest in actual use is so unimportant to most people who use
    them, that the two are used indiscriminately by some people.
    Solltest carries a kind of external obligation, a duty imposed on
    one. **Müßtest** implies that the person addressed MUST (in the sense
    of *cannot help but, would have to*) act in a certain way, be in a
    certain state. However, it must be admitted that the latter CAN
    have other meanings, usually clear from the context.

28 Lektion achtundzwanzig   Wochenende auf dem Land

Lesson twenty-eight   Weekend in the country

What happens

This lesson deals with the young people's weekend at the country house of Herr and Frau Le Gras.

In Part 1 Frau Le Gras gives some biographical details. In Part 2 Herr Le Gras drives the young people to his house, they visit a restaurant and Anne Green and Renate talk about the weekend.

New words in this lesson

der Blick(-e) glance, sight, look
der Familienname(-n) surname
der Schneemann("er) snowman
der See(-n) lake
der Übersetzer(-) translator
der Wald("er) wood, forest
der Weinkeller(-) wine cellar
der Zentimeter(-) centimetre

die Feinschmeckerin(-nen) gourmet (female)
die Gastgeberin(-nen) hostess
die Gesellschaft company, party
die Getränkekarte(-n) wine list
die Jugend youth
die Landschaft(-en) scenery, landscape
die Literatur(-en) literature
die Mühe(-n) trouble, difficulty
die Schneeballschlacht(-en) snowball fight
die Speisekarte(-n) menu
die Spezialität(-en) speciality
die Sprache(-n) language

das Deutsch German (language)
das Glatteis slippery surface
das Hochdeutsch standard German

das Italienisch Italian (language)
das Volk("er) people

der Bayer(-n) Bavarian
die Brasilianerin(-nen) Brazilian (female)
die Engländerin(-nen) English woman
der Franzose(-n) Frenchman
die Französin(-nen) French woman
die Japanerin(-nen) Japanese (female)

die Beilage(-n) accompaniment, addition (vegetables)
die Bohne(-n) bean
die Forelle(-n) trout
das Gemüse(-) vegetable
das Gericht(-e) dish
die Hirschkeule(-n) haunch of venison
der Käse(-) cheese
das Kompott(-e) stewed fruit
der Krabbencocktail(-s) shrimp cocktail
die Leberknödelsuppe(-n) soup with liver dumplings
der Nachtisch(-e) dessert
das Obst fruit
die Pellkartoffel(-n) potato in its jacket
die Preiselbeere(-n) cranberry
das Rotkraut red cabbage

220

die russischen Eier Russian eggs
die Salzkartoffeln boiled potatoes
der Sauerbraten(–) stewed pickled beef
die Suppe(-n) soup
die Vorspeise(-n) hors d'oeuvre

(bleiben) er blieb he stayed
bleiben bei to stick to
(bringen) er brachte he brought
(empfehlen) ich empfahl I recommended
(essen) wir aßen we ate
(frieren) es hat gefroren it has frozen
(trinken) wir tranken we drank

bauen to build, make

(einladen) sie luden uns ein they invited
    us
hinuntersteigen to climb (go) down
Schlittschuh laufen to skate

sich (D) ausleihen to borrow
sich verlieben in to fall in love with

international international
jetzig present
russisch Russian
tief deep

dagegen on the other hand
daraus from it

sicher surely
teils partly
unterwegs on the way

als ob as if
als wenn as if
es sei denn unless
es soll gefroren haben there is supposed
    to have been heavy frost
etwas Gutes something good
je eher desto besser the sooner the better
möglichst viel as much as possible
mütterlicherseits on the mother's side
wofür? what (for)?

28

Notes

Part one

1 **und brachte sie, nachdem er sie geheiratet hatte, nach Deutschland.** *and brought her, after he had married her, to Germany.*
a **Brachte** is the imperfect tense of **bringen,** which is one of the
'mixed' group of verbs (internal change plus weak endings).
b **nachdem er sie geheiratet hatte**   This is the pluperfect tense
(auxiliary **sein, haben** in the imperfect) within a dependent clause.
Nachdem is frequently followed by the pluperfect tense.
2 **in meinen jetzigen Mann, einen Franzosen,** *with my present
husband, a Frenchman,*
a **Sich verlieben** *in* + accusative means *to fall in love* WITH.
b **einen Franzosen**   This is accusative, in apposition to **Mann.**
Franzose is a weak noun.
3 **innerhalb von drei Monaten** *within three months*   **Innerhalb von**
is a variation on **innerhalb** with the genitive. There is a general
tendency in spoken German to avoid the genitive when possible;
one way of doing this is to use **von** with the dative instead,

especially when the genitive ending on the following word sounds rather formal (it would have to be **dreier Monate**).

4 **teils hier in Bayern und teils in Lyon.** *part of the time here in Bavaria and the other part (the rest of the time) in Lyons.*
teils ... teils: *partly one thing ... and partly something else*
You met this expression before, but used colloquially (**teils, teils**) meaning *so, so.*

5 **Ich empfahl meinem Mann,... abzuholen,** *I advised my husband to fetch...*
Empfahl is the imperfect of **empfehlen:** *to recommend.* The person TO WHOM something is recommended is in the dative case. In the sense of *advise,* it is completed by **zu** + infinitive.

6 **weil es in der letzten Nacht gefroren haben soll.** *because there is supposed to have been heavy frost (it is supposed to have frozen) during the night.*
gefroren haben soll The verb phrase is in this order because it is within a dependent clause. **Gefroren** is the past participle of **frieren:** *to freeze;* **haben** is the completing infinitive (of the auxiliary required to form the perfect tense); and **soll** means *is supposed to, is to.*

Part two

Auf dem Weg zum Landhaus *On the way to the country house*

7 **Ich wünschte, ich könnte so fließend italienisch wie Deutsch.**
I wish I could speak Italian as fluently as I do German.

a **Ich könnte** is the subjunctive. It is necessary here as the speaker is expressing a wish; what he is wishing is not, by definition, a fact or a reality. The subjunctive expresses the unreal, the unfulfilled, the fictitious or the doubtful. The INDICATIVE (a descriptive word, like SUBJUNCTIVE) describes verb forms used in declaratory statements of fact; it expresses the real, the existing, the factual and the probable. The use of the verb **können** at all here is very idiomatic and requires some explanation. **Ich kann Deutsch** means *I have a knowledge of the German language and can demonstrate some skill in its use.* **Können** used with a language generally implies ability to speak it.

b **italienisch wie Deutsch** These both refer to languages. Why a capital **D** on **Deutsch** and a small **i** on **italienisch?** Let it be admitted at once that while there is never, or rarely, any doubt about using a capital **D** for **Deutsch,** there is dissension in theory and individualism in practice about the initial letter of any language ending in **-isch,** which is felt by some people to be essentially an adjectival or adverbial suffix; these people would only concede an initial capital when the language is used uncompromisingly as a noun, e.g.: **Ihr gutes Portugiesisch hat mich erstaunt.** In speech, of course, the problem simply does not arise, but it is only fair to warn you that you will certainly see both capitals and small letters used in the designation of languages.

28

8 Ja, du sprichst Deutsch, als ob du ein Deutscher wärest. *Yes, you speak German as if you were a German.*

a als ob du ein Deutscher wärest.   This is a dependent clause, introduced by **als ob:** *as if.*

b wärest   This is the subjunctive, because Ned is NOT German. Note that this ending is slightly different from the imperfect form **warst.** The **du** and **ihr** forms of the subjunctive both have this extra **e** in the ending as a rule. (See Appendix **16**).

c ein Deutscher   **Der Deutsche** behaves like **Beamte, Angestellte** etc. in that it is treated as an adjective as far as endings are concerned. It therefore requires the strong ending after **ein.**

9 Wie habt ihr es bloß alle so gut sprechen gelernt? *How on earth did you all learn to speak* (i.e. *master the German language*) *so well?*

sprechen gelernt   **Sprechen lernen** is a CONSTRUCTION like **kennenlernen,** though the two words are much less frequently combined. **Lernen** takes a straight infinitive without **zu,** unless what has been learnt is not so much an activity or skill, but more truths from experience, expressed rather lengthily.

10 Ich selbst spreche außer bayerisch nur Hochdeutsch, *Apart from Bavarian, I myself can only speak standard German,*

a Selbst is only used for *-self* for emphasis. It is unchanging, no matter whether the meaning be *myself, himself, yourself* etc.

b Hochdeutsch: lit. *High German*   **Hoch-** is not qualitative in any sense here. It distinguishes it from Low German (**Plattdeutsch**), which is a different kind of German (spoken in a different area) and which developed along different lines from what we think of as German. The fact that Franz finds **Hochdeutsch** such an effort shows how different the real Bavarian dialect is from the standard language. But it IS a dialect and not a different branch of the Germanic tree, like **Plattdeutsch.** All Bavarians speak **Hochdeutsch** when required and understand **Hochdeutsch,** so you do not have to worry about not being understood in Bavaria. Nowadays, in fact, particularly in Munich, the language used by educated people is more **Hochdeutsch** than Bavarian. Apart from the accent, which many Bavarians do not have, and some colourful idioms, you would find it difficult to differentiate Bavarian from **Hochdeutsch.**

11 **je eher desto besser,** *the earlier* (*sooner*) *the better,* **Je ... desto** translates the English *the ... the* in this idiomatic expression. This phrase is inserted almost in parenthesis into the **daß** clause, and therefore does not affect the word order.

12 **möglichst viel** *as much as possible* **Möglichst** is a superlative form, and coupled with another adverb, is an alternative to the pattern **so ... wie möglich.** It has an overtone of extra urgency which is lacking in the latter expression.

13 **daß man ein Volk nie ganz wird verstehen können,** *that one will never be able to understand a people fully,* **wird verstehen können** This is the auxiliary, infinitive, modal (AIM) pattern, which you use when you have to organize a verb phrase with three such elements within a dependent clause (L27).

14 **es sei denn, man lernt seine Sprache.** *unless one learns their language.*

a **es sei denn** This is a phrase better left without close analysis. It is not particularly common in speech as there are other ways of expressing the same notion, but you have to know it for the odd occasion when nothing else will do. Suffice it to say, as far as form is concerned, that **sei** is a subjunctive form of **sein:** *to be,* though not the same category of subjunctives as you have been learning till now. There is a PRESENT subjunctive and an IMPERFECT subjunctive, or a first and second subjunctive. What you call them does not matter, so long as you know when to use which. The one you already know is the imperfect or second subjunctive and by far the most frequently used of the two; **sei** is the present subjunctive. Note that **es sei denn** is followed by a comma and does not normally affect word order.

b **seine Sprache** It is possible to use **seine** in German because **Volk** is a **das** word and the possessive adjective with singular **das** words is **sein.**

15 **Meine Frau wird Ihnen ... zeigen wollen.** *My wife will want to*

show you... (L28, N13) This is the future tense of **wollen** +
a completing infinitive.

Einladung ins Restaurant „Seeblick" *Invitation to the 'Seeblick'
restaurant*

16 **Was würden Sie gern essen?** *What would you like (to eat)?* This
means the same as **Was möchten Sie gern essen?** and it is not
the first time you have encountered **würden** used in this sense.
It is the imperfect subjunctive of **werden,** and as such, carries a
sense of the future or of intention, as well as of courtesy.

17 **würde ich gern eine Forelle essen.** *I'd like a trout.*
This is the same use of **würde gern essen** as in N16 above.

18 **Wofür haben Sie sich entschieden?** *What have you decided on?*
wofür? Sich entscheiden für means *to decide* ON. You must use
wo for *what?* when it is combined with a preposition (**in, an, zu,
für, auf, über** etc.) which is the last element of a verb phrase
(like **sich entscheiden** *für,* **sich verlassen** *auf,* **sprechen** *über*).

19 **ich hätte gern** *I would/should like* **Ich hätte gern** is an alternative
to **ich möchte gern.** It is often used when ordering in restaurants
or shops.

20 **eine Beilage** *vegetables* This word really means *accompaniment*
or *addition,* but is used almost exclusively as accompaniment
to a main dish, therefore *vegetables.*

21 **sind sehr zu empfehlen.** *are to be highly recommended.* Remember
the infinitive can be used to mean *to be* + past participle, after
zu. This example of this usage is a very common one.

Winterfreuden *Winter pleasures*

22 **daß ihr nicht habt mitkommen wollen.** *that you didn't want to
come.* This is the auxiliary, infinitive, modal order in a dependent clause. Be careful with the position of **nicht** in such
dependent clauses – it must precede the entire verb phrase.

23 **Wir aßen und tranken Küche und Weinkeller leer.** *We ate and
drank larder (kitchen) and cellar bare.*
Aßen is the imperfect of **essen:** *to eat.*

24 **Mir schien es, als wenn ihr nur fünf Minuten weg gewesen wäret.**
It seemed to me as if you'd only been away five minutes.

a **als wenn** This means exactly the same as **als ob.** Both require
the subjunctive and both introduce dependent clauses.

b **weg gewesen wäret** **Weg sein:** *to be away,* requires **sein** as auxiliary in the perfect and pluperfect tenses. And the auxiliary must be in the subjunctive (after **als wenn**). The **ihr** form has an **e** which is not present in the imperfect tense, from which imperfect subjunctives (or second subjunctives) are formed (L28, N8b).

25 **Seid ihr nicht Schlittschuh laufen gewesen?** *Haven't you been skating?/Didn't you go skating?* This kind of verb phrase only occurs with verbs of which the English version could be *to go -ing* (*shopping, dancing, skiing*). It is the infinitive (**Schlittschuh laufen**) plus the past participle of **sein** (**gewesen**).

26 **und stieg . . . ins Dorf hinunter.** *went (climbed) down to the village.* **Stieg** is the imperfect of **steigen.** Words like **hinunter, hinauf** can be used either as separable prefixes or as adverbs like *up* and *down* in English. They are sometimes an integral part of the verb and sometimes not. Compare: *he went down the hill* and *he went down to the village. Down* is indispensable in the first sentence, but could be done without in the second. The fact that such words in German are sometimes joined to the main verb and sometimes written separately (though nearly always retaining the position of a separable prefix) stems from this distinction. If the verb has a direct object (**Ich habe einen steilen Berg** *hinunterfahren* **müssen**), the tendency is to write the prefix or adverb joined to the verb. If an adverbial phrase of place (**ins Dorf**) is the complement of the verb, the tendency is to write the adverb separately. It does not arise in this particular sentence, as **hinunter** is separated here anyway. But you will find examples of both usages in the course.

27 **Wir wären fast stecken geblieben,** *We nearly got stuck*, The subjunctive plus **fast** (or **beinahe**) is used to describe something in the past which NEARLY happened (but did not). *Nearly* + a verb in the past: **wäre/hätte** + **fast** + past participle.

28 **Der blieb mit den beiden Jungen zu Haus,** HE *stayed at home with the two boys,*
Blieb is the imperfect of **bleiben.**

29 **es soll sehr schnell eine Schneeballschlacht daraus geworden sein.** *they say it very soon turned into a snowball fight (it ended up being a snowball fight).*

a **Soll** has the sense of *supposed to, said to* (L28, N6).

b **daraus geworden sein** **Werden aus** means *to become of, turn into, end up as.* **Daraus** – da- refers to the building of the snowman. **Geworden sein** means *to have become.*

226

30 **als Herr und Frau Le Gras uns einluden,** *when Herr and Frau Le Gras invited us,*
Einluden is the imperfect of **einladen**.

31 **dachte ich nicht, daß es so interessant und nett werden würde.**
I didn't think that it would turn out so interesting and pleasant.

a **Werden** has the sense of *develop, turn out* here.

b **werden würde** This is the so-called conditional form – *would* + infinitive in English, **würde** + infinitive in German. Note that: –

 i With **haben, sein** and the modals, the imperfect subjunctive of the verb (e.g. **hätte, wäre, könnte**) is used instead of the version with **würde**.

 ii With weak verbs, the version with **würde** (e.g. **würde lernen**) is preferred. This is because the imperfect subjunctive of weak verbs is identical with the imperfect indicative and the use of **würde** makes the subjunctive obvious.

 iii With other verbs, the imperfect subjunctive is more often associated with an idea of unreality, such as there is after **wünschen** and **als ob,** whereas the version with **würde** has strong future associations and may imply a more realistic possibility. (Renate thought things would turn out, in the future, in a certain way.)

32 **mir würde es auch gefallen, wenn wir noch etwas länger bleiben könnten.** *I would like it too, if we could stay a bit longer.*
wenn wir . . . bleiben könnten This is an *if* (conditional) clause in the subjunctive. Here is a guide to the translation of *could* which has two quite different meanings in English:
could (was/were able): **konnte(n)**
could (would be able): **könnte(n)**
The first is indicative, the second is subjunctive.

Part three

Allein im Schnee   *Alone in the snow*

33 **Nachdem ich einen Kilometer den Berg hinauf gestiegen war,**
After I'd climbed a kilometre up the mountain,
einen Kilometer Distance covered is usually expressed in the accusative.

34 **Sind Sie den weiten Weg ganz allein gelaufen?** *Did you walk all that way alone?*

Gelaufen is the past participle of **laufen**: *to run,* or *to go on foot* and is therefore frequently used to translate *walk.*

35 **Ich wünschte, ich wäre ihn nicht allein gelaufen,** *I wish I hadn't walked it alone,*
ich wünschte This is the subjunctive, although **ich wünschte** can also mean *I wished* (indicative). The following clause is in the pluperfect, and the tendency is to use the imperfect subjunctive in the main clause when the verb in the 'wish clause' contains an imperfect subjunctive form (**wäre**). This is not invariably true, though. *I wish I could...* has two possible versions in German: either **Ich wünsche, ich könnte...** or **Ich wünschte, ich könnte...** You will certainly hear both.

Vorsicht! Glatteis! *Warning! Slippery surface!*

36 **Es sieht aus, als ob Glatteis auf den Straßen läge.** *It looks as if there was (were) ice on the roads.*
Läge: *was (were) lying* is the imperfect subjunctive of **liegen**: *to be lying.* To form the imperfect subjunctive of a strong verb, you take the imperfect indicative (e.g. **lag, gab, ging**), add an Umlaut if possible (**läg-, gäb-, ging-**) and the following endings: –
-e (ich/er läge, gäbe, ginge)
-est (du lägest, gäbest, gingest)
-en (wir/Sie/sie lägen, gäben, gingen)
-et (ihr läget, gäbet, ginget)
The imperfect subjunctive of weak verbs, on the other hand, is identical with the imperfect indicative, hence the preference for the form with **würde** mentioned already (N31).

37 **Müßten wir nicht schon längst am Ammersee sein?** *Shouldn't we have been at the Ammersee long ago?* A perfect tense construction is unnecessary here because of the presence of **schon längst** (L27, N16 **wären wir schon längst tot**: *would* HAVE BEEN *dead long ago*). This has the same effect as **schon lange** on the tense used. **Müßten** is the imperfect subjunctive of **müssen**, of course.

38 **Eigentlich ja, es sei denn, ich bin falsch gefahren.** *Yes, we should, actually, (actually, yes) unless I've taken the wrong road.*
ich bin falsch gefahren The verb is in the INDICATIVE, remember, following **es sei denn**. Falsch + infinitive means *to do something wrong, to make a mistake* in whatever is being done.

Lektion neunundzwanzig Ein Theaterabend

Lesson twenty-nine An evening at the theatre

What happens

Renate wants a last evening out with her parents before they fly back to Brazil.

In Part 1 the booking office clerk talks about her job. In Part 2 the Kühns and the Pfaffingers discuss what kind of entertainment they like best. Renate returns – she has finally managed to buy some tickets – and Herr Kühn tells her something about the opera they are going to see.

New words in this lesson

der **Erfolg**(-e) success
der **Inhalt**(-e) content
der **Kartenkauf**(¨e) buying tickets
der **Kauf**(¨e) buying, purchase
der **Opernführer**(-) opera guide (book)
der **Parkplatz**(¨e) parking space
der **Schweinebraten**(-) roast pork
der **Staat**(-en) state
der **Theaterabend**(-e) evening at the theatre
der **Theaterbesucher**(-) theatregoer

die **Karte**(-n) ticket
die **Kartenverkäuferin**(-nen) ticket-office clerk (female)
die **Laune**(-n) temper, mood
die **Oper**(-n) opera
die **Operette**(-n) operetta
die **Stelle**(-n) place
die **Theaterkasse**(-n) box-office
die **Vorstellung**(-en) performance

das **Ballett**(-s) ballet
das **Publikum** public, audience
das **Radio**(-s) radio
das **Staatstheater**(-) national theatre

das **Stück**(-e) play
das **Unterhaltungsstück**(-e) light comedy
das **Wort**(¨er/-e) word

einiges some things
irgendein one, some, any

(**dürfen**) es **dürfte sein** it might be
(**essen**) ich **äße** I would eat
(**finden**) ich **fände** I would find
(**geben**) es **gäbe** there were (would be)
(**gefallen**) es **gefiele ihr** it would please her
(**gehen**) ich **ginge** I would go
(**halten**) du **hieltest** you thought (would think)
(**kommen**) sie **kämen** they came (were to come)
(**sitzen**) wir **säßen** we would sit
(**trinken**) ich **tränke** I would drink
(**wissen**) ich **wüßte** I would know
(**wollen**) ich **wolle** I wanted (would want)

spielen to play
strömen to rush
(**verkaufen**) sie **habe verkauft** she had sold

29 (ausgehen) wir gingen aus we went out
(would go out)
ausverkaufen (alles sei ausverkauft) to
sell out (everything was/had been sold
out)
(zurückbringen) sie brächten zurück
they brought back (would/should
bring back)
sie seien zurückgebracht worden they
had been brought back
zurückgeben to return, to give back

sich kümmern um to see about
sich zeigen to be revealed

ausverkauft sold out
bestimmt certain, specific
fett fat
zornig angry
da because

je each
womit? how? by what means?
wovon? about what?
zwar well

an eurer Stelle if I were in your place
auch wenn even if
Bescheid wissen to have knowledge of
bravo! well done! good!
es dürfte zwar schwer sein it might well
be difficult
es fällt schwer it proves difficult
es handelt von it is about
etwas ganz anderes something quite
different
immer wieder very often
längere Zeit for some time
um so weniger all the less so
wovon handelt sie denn? what is it about?
zu Hilfe nehmen to make use of

Notes

Part one

1 **Wer in München in die Oper oder in eines der bekannten Theater gehen will,** *Anyone in Munich who wants to go to the opera or to one of the famous theatres,*

a **Wer** is used for *he who, anyone who* and therefore acts as a relative pronoun, so the verb will be at the end of the clause.

b **in eines der bekannten Theater** **Eines** is a pronoun, hence the necessity to distinguish it from **ein,** the indefinite article, which precedes a noun. As usual, distinction is made by means of different endings. The pronoun has 'strong' endings. Compare: **ein Theater:** *a theatre* **eines der Theater:** *one of the theatres* **ein Grund:** *a/one reason* **einer der Gründe:** *one of the reasons.* **Einer/eine/eines** are the nominatives of the pronoun.

2 **muß sich rechtzeitig um Karten kümmern,** *must see about tickets in good time,*
sich ... um Karten kümmern **Sich kümmern um** + accusative means *to see to, worry about, concern oneself with.*

3 **für.alle beim Publikum besonders beliebten Stücke** *for all plays (or musicals) particularly popular with the public*
beim Publikum besonders beliebten This is what is known as the

long adjectival phrase and is a particular feature of the German language. English has to make a relative clause out of this information or put it AFTER the noun (**Stücke**: *plays*) instead of BEFORE it, as in German. It is more common in the written than in the spoken language. The literal translation would be *for all with the public particularly popular plays*. Note how far removed **beliebten** is from **alle,** on which its ending depends. If **alle** is followed by another adjective, that adjective has a weak ending. When several words come between a **der** or an **ein** word and a following adjective, it is difficult for foreigners to carry the correct ending in their heads until they arrive at the adjective. It is therefore to be avoided when possible, but you must be able to recognize the pattern.

4 **Da ich ... bin Da:** *since, as* causes the verb to be placed at the end of the clause.

5 **Das Interesse mancher vorsichtiger Theaterbesucher** *The interest of some careful theatregoers.* **Mancher** is declined like **der.** Followed by another adjective, there is a variety of possibilities. In the singular, a following adjective has a weak ending – **mancher vorsichtige Theaterbesucher** *many a careful theatregoer* (nominative). In the plural, the following adjective can be either weak or strong, but there is a prevailing preference for the strong ending. Hence **vorsichtig*er*** – genitive plural strong ending, matching **manch*er*.**

6 **und sind schnell zornig oder schlechter Laune,** *and soon get angry or ill-humoured,*

a **sind schnell zornig:** lit. *are quickly angry* **Schnell** must often be translated as *soon.*

b **oder schlechter Laune Laune** means *mood, humour.* **Schlecht*er* Laune:** *in a bad mood* (gen.); **gut*er* Laune:** *in a good mood* (gen.).

7 **daß es sich vielleicht lohnen würde,** *that it would perhaps be worth while,*
es sich lohnen würde Lohnen being a weak verb, the imperfect subjunctive is the same as the imperfect indicative, therefore **lohnen *würde*** is preferable.

8 **wenn sie kurz vor Beginn der Vorstellung noch einmal kämen,** *if they come (were to come) back shortly before the beginning of the performance,*
kämen This is the imperfect subjunctive of **kommen.** Starting with the **ich** form of the imperfect, **kam,** add an Umlaut and the

29

same endings as for the imperfect and the result in this case is **kämen,** the imperfect subjunctive. **Kommen würden** would not be incorrect but since subjunctives (imperfect) of strong verbs are immediately recognizable as such, this form is normally used. The subjunctive is required here because an unfulfilled condition is being expressed. If the English translation could be WERE TO *come* and not DID *come,* then it must be the subjunctive in German.

9 da es immer wieder Leute gäbe, *as there would very often be (were very often) people,*

a es gibt: *there is/are* **es gäbe:** *there would be*

b immer wieder: *again and again (always again)*

10 die aus irgendeinem Grund ihre Karte zurückbrächten. *who, for some reason or other, brought back (would bring back) their ticket.*

a irgendeinem You have already encountered other words beginning with **irgend-,** expressing vagueness: **irgendwo, irgend- wie, irgend etwas** etc. **Irgendein** changes exactly like **ein.**

b zurückbrächten The verb is placed at the end because it is a relative clause, and it is subjunctive because it is just a possibility and not a fact. **Bringen,** remember, has an irregular imperfect – **brachte** – and to form the subjunctive, one just adds an Umlaut since the necessary ending is already there.

Part two

Wohin? *Where to go?*

11 ob wir nicht noch einmal mit ihr ausgingen, *if we wouldn't go out with her once more,* **Ausgingen** could be either subjunctive or indicative, but from the context (since he is not talking of the past) we know it must be subjunctive.

12 bevor wir wieder nach Brasilien zurückreisen würden. *before we travelled back to Brazil, (would travel back).* The subjunctive form with **würden** is preferred as **reisen** is a weak verb.

13 Das fände ich schön. *That would be lovely. (I would find that lovely.)* **Fand** is the imperfect of **finden.** Add an Umlaut and the **ich** ending of a weak imperfect (**-e**) and the result is **fände.**

14 Wir könnten uns ein leichtes, deutsches Unterhaltungsstück mit ihr ansehen. *We could go to a light German comedy (musical) with her.* **wir könnten uns ... ansehen:** lit. *we could* LOOK AT The German is more logical, but the idiom is *go to* in English.

15 Ja, das gefiele ihr sicher. *Yes, I'm sure she'd like that.*

gefiele   This is imperfect subjunctive of **gefallen:** *to please.*
No Umlaut is possible with **ie,** so just add **-e** to the imperfect
to form the subjunctive.

16   **Sagtet ihr nicht kürzlich, ihr wäret schon in der Oper oder in so
einem komischen modernen Ballett gewesen?** *Didn't you say
recently you'd been at the opera or one of those peculiar modern
ballets?*
ihr wäret ... gewesen   This episode has happened inasmuch as
it is being referred to in the past and not in the uncertain future,
subject to certain conditions. Why subjunctive? This example
brings you to one of the main uses of the subjunctive in German,
namely in indirect or reported speech. The idea behind the use
of the subjunctive here is that the speaker is reporting something
at second hand and will not be responsible for stating it as
established fact. **Ihr wäret gewesen:** *you* HAD *been* (*but for all I
know you haven't*). Remember the **ihr** form of the imperfect
subjunctive has an **e, -et.**

17   **Wenn ich wählen könnte, ginge ich z.B. ins Platzl.** *If I could
choose, I'd go to the Platzl, for instance.*
ginge ich: *I* WOULD *go*   We know it is subjunctive from the **-e**
ending, and of course, from the context.

18   **wir säßen dort und verstünden kein Wort.** *we would sit there and
wouldn't understand a word.*

a   **wir säßen**   This is the subjunctive of **sitzen:** *to sit.*

b   **verstünden**   This is one of the very few irregular subjunctives in
German. Any verb which has **-stehen** as its second component
has an imperfect subjunctive with **ü** (and not **ä** as one would
expect).

19   **An eurer Stelle äße ich wenigstens** *If I were you* (*in your place*)
I would eat at least
äße ich   This is the imperfect subjunctive of **essen:** *to eat.*

20   **tränke** *I'd drink*   This is the subjunctive of **trinken.**

Der schwierige Kartenkauf   *Complicated ticket buying*

21   **Hätte ich doch nur etwas mehr Geld bei mir gehabt!** *If only I'd
had some more money on me!*
hätte ich nur ... gehabt! This is pluperfect subjunctive – i.e. the
imperfect subjunctive of **haben** + past participle. It is subjunctive
because it is the expression of a wish that cannot be fulfilled.
Any similar expression, usually beginning with *If only I could* ...

If only I had..., apart from questions or commands, is the only other time when a verb can be item one in a sentence – namely in a **wenn** clause when **wenn** is omitted.

22 **Dafür hätte ich keine Karten für „Die Zauberflöte" bekommen können.** *I couldn't have got tickets for 'The Magic Flute' for* THAT. **hätte ich ... bekommen können** This is a perfect subjunctive with a modal verb – hence the two infinitives **hätte(n)**... + infinitive + **können:** *could have* + past participle.

23 **Die Dame an der Kasse sagte, daß alles schon seit Tagen ausverkauft sei,** *The lady in the box-office said that everything had been sold out for days,*
ausverkauft sei Sei is the present (or 'first') subjunctive of **sein** – **ich** and **er** forms. The subjunctive is required here because Renate is reporting what someone else said. In order to arrive at a decision between present and imperfect subjunctive, you must take your mind back to what the original speaker said and use present or imperfect accordingly. Here, she would have said *everything has been sold out for days* (*everything* IS *sold out since days*). She uses a present tense, therefore what she is reported to have said is in the present subjunctive. The present subjunctive is normally formed from the stem. You add to the stem the same endings as you add to form the imperfect subjunctive of strong verbs. The only forms which will be different from the present indicative (if the verb is regular) will be the second (familiar) and third person singular and the second (familiar) plural.

24 **daß aber gerade drei Karten zu je 25 DM zurückgegeben worden seien.** *but that precisely three tickets at 25 marks each had been given back (returned).*
zurückgegeben worden seien This is a perfect passive subjunctive, within a **daß** clause. The auxiliary is in the subjunctive (indirect or reported speech) and is placed at the end; **worden** is the special form of the past participle of **werden** reserved for passive use. Think what the speaker would say: *Three tickets* HAVE *been handed back* – a present tense auxiliary is required.

25 **sie habe eben in derselben Minute die letzten Karten verkauft.** *she had just sold the last tickets that very minute.*
sie habe ... verkauft This is the present subjunctive of **haben,** plus the past participle. The girl would say: *I* HAVE *just sold ...* etc., so the present subjunctive of the auxiliary is required.

26 **ob ich nicht warten wolle.** *if I didn't want to wait.*
wolle This is the present subjunctive (**ich** form) of **wollen.** She would say *Don't you want to wait?* Therefore a present subjunctive is required. However, there is a tendency, in speech particularly, to avoid the present subjunctive ('first' subjunctive) in favour of the imperfect subjunctive, in spite of all the rules.

27 **Falls jemand seine Karten zurückbrächte, könnte ich sie haben.**
In the event of someone bringing back (In case someone should bring back) his tickets, I could have them.
Zurückbrächte is the imperfect subjunctive, and bears out what has been said above. After **falls** (unless a simple present indicative is used) the preference is for the imperfect subjunctive of the verb, or for the infinitive of the verb plus **sollte/n/ – Falls jemand seine Karten zurückbringen sollte.**

Zum Gärtnerplatztheater *To the theatre in the Gärtnerplatz*

28 **Womit sollen wir zum Theater fahren?** *How shall we go to the theatre?*
womit? The word **wo?** can be combined with a preposition to form a question in the same way as it can to form a relative pronoun, provided one is talking about a thing or things and not persons. **Wer?:** *who?* is declined like **der** and you can therefore show the correct case after it (**mit wem? für wen?**). But **was?** cannot be similarly declined, so when it follows a preposition (*with what? by what? for what?* etc.) **wo** is used instead. This does not mean that you will not hear people use **was?** after a preposition, but **wo?** is more correct. (See Appendix 7.)

29 **dürfte zwar schwer sein,** *might well be difficult,*
dürfte ... sein This is the imperfect subjunctive of **dürfen** and is often used to translate *might* or *could.*

30 **an Haltestellen stehen zu müssen, ist kein Vergnügen.** *To have to stand at bus-stops is no pleasure.*
stehen zu müssen When the infinitive of the modal is required, as well as the completing infinitive of the modal, the modal infinitive is placed last, and (as is usually the case) when **zu** is required, it immediately precedes the modal infinitive.

31 **Um so weniger als wir umsteigen müssen.** *All the less so as we have to change.* **Um so** plus a comparative form is idiomatic and means *all the,* e.g.: **um so besser:** *all the better;* **um so mehr:** *all the more (so).*

32 **von Schwabing aus** *from Schwabing* It is necessary to use **aus** in addition to **von** when the meaning is that one starts from the point mentioned and moves (or looks) AWAY from it. There is no way of translating it satisfactorily into English because it just is not considered necessary.

33 **Erinnerst du dich daran,... die Oper ... gehört zu haben?** *Do you remember hearing the opera?*

daran, ... gehört zu haben You are familiar with the use of **da** + a preposition followed by a whole clause (usually a **daß** clause) for which **da** is standing in the main clause. This is the same sort of construction, except that **da** here is standing for an infinitive phrase – **gehört zu haben.** This is possible when there is no change of subject. Otherwise you would require a **daß** clause. *Do* YOU *remember that* YOU *heard* does not require two finite verbs. (i.e. not infinitives or participles). **Gehört zu haben** is really a perfect infinitive (*to have heard*). We say in English *having heard* if we are strictly correct, but *do you remember hearing* is quite acceptable. In German, however, it MUST be a perfect infinitive. It would be impossible to say **Erinnerst du dich daran, die Oper zu hören?**

34 **Vielleicht wüßte ich es wieder, wenn ich die Musik hören würde.** *Perhaps I would know it again if I heard (were to hear) the music.*

a **wüßte ich** This is the imperfect subjunctive of **wissen,** which belongs to the mixed group of verbs having an internal change and adding weak verb endings. To form the subjunctive (imperfect or second) one adds an Umlaut if possible, or else uses the infinitive of the verb with **würde/n.**

b **wenn ich die Musik hören würde** **Hören** being a weak verb, the imperfect subjunctive is indistinguishable from the imperfect indicative, so the infinitive of **hören** with **würde** is preferable.

35 **Das wird nicht ganz leicht sein, ohne daß du deinen Opernführer zu Hilfe nimmst.** *That won't be so easy, without (your) consulting your opera guide.*

a **ohne daß du** The only way of dealing with the phrase *without doing* something, if there has been a change of subject, is with **ohne daß** plus a finite verb. English can manage with participles (*without doing, without* HIS *doing,* MY *doing,* OUR *doing* etc., thus making clear WHO is meant), but in German, unless there is already a finite verb in the sentence which agrees with the person who is meant by the *without doing* phrase, you must use **ohne** + a **daß** clause. Compare:

1 **Das findest du nicht leicht,** *ohne* **deinen Opernführer zu Hilfe** *zu nehmen.*

2 **Das wird nicht leicht sein, ohne daß du deinen Opernführer zu Hilfe nimmst.**

The second sentence has no **du** verb before the **daß** clause; the first one has.

b **zu Hilfe nimmst** **zu Hilfe nehmen**: *to make use of, to consult, to have recourse to.*

36 **Auch wenn ich einiges nicht mehr ganz genau wissen sollte,** *Even if I shouldn't remember some things too well,*

a **einiges** This is a form like **viel***es* or **Verschieden***es,* with a strong neuter ending. It means *some things, a few things.*

b **wissen sollte** This kind of subjunctive phrase with an infinitive and the imperfect subjunctive of **sollen** is favoured in conditional clauses with the sense – *if it should happen that, if things should turn out that, in case it should be that . . .*

c **Wissen** is used here in the sense of *remember* or *recognize.*

Lektion dreißig   Abschied

Lesson thirty   Farewell!

What happens

The day of departure for Herr and Frau Kühn has arrived.

In Part 1 Herr Kühn talks about all he has had to do in the last few days. In Part 2 Frau Kühn and Renate pack, and clean up the flat. Frau Kühn tells Frau Pfaffinger not to spoil Renate and Renate says good-bye to her parents.

New words in this lesson

der **Balkon**(-e) balcony
der **Engel**(–) angel
der **Frühling** spring

der **Haushalt**(-e) household
der **Zuschauerbalkon**(-e) spectators' balcony

die Sonne(-n) sun
die Tischdecke(-n) table-cloth

das Holz(¨er) wood
das Tablett(-s) tray

bringen to take
(denken) er hätte gedacht he would have thought
(finden) wir haben gefunden we've found
(gelingen) es gelang mir I succeeded
scheinen to shine

führen to carry on (conversation)

abfliegen to take off

sich freuen über to be pleased with

froh happy

selbstverständlich self-evident, obvious

recht pretty, very
sowie as well as
voneinander from each other

während while

Abschied nehmen to say good-bye
das liegt daran, daß it results from the fact that
die beiden the two
es ist doch ganz selbstverstandlich that goes without saying
fertig werden mit to get finished with
gute Reise! bon voyage! have a good journey!
ihr seid dran it's your turn
vor längerer Zeit quite a long time ago

Notes

Part one

1 Wer hätte gedacht, daß in den letzten Tagen noch so viel zu tun wäre! *Who would have thought that there would still be so much to do on the last days!*

a wer hätte gedacht This is a perfect subjunctive. The auxiliary has the imperfect subjunctive form. It is subjunctive because he finds it so difficult to believe. In the thinker's mind what actually happened did not seem at all likely. You have met the construction before, and you know that the word *would* nearly always demands a subjunctive in German. This is a useful working rule, but it is not an explanation. An understanding of the kind of situation in which users of a language feel a need for a special set of verb forms is much more important, and is, in the long run, much more helpful than a dependence on word signals. The term SUBJUNCTIVE is classified as a MOOD in language jargon, and this is a very good name for it, since it indicates the speaker's ATTITUDE to what he is saying. Doubt, supposition, uncertainty, unreality all require the subjunctive in German.

b noch so viel zu tun wäre **Wäre** is subjunctive to accord with the subjunctive in the previous clause.

2 hatte ich noch eine lange Korrespondenz sowie einige wichtige Telephongespräche zu führen. **Führen** is used in a particular sense here – *to conduct* or *to carry on*. This verb is used with **Korrespondenz** and **Telephongespräche** where English would simply use *have*.

3 so daß sich unsere schwierige Lage in Rio verbessern dürfte. *so that our difficult situation in Rio might well improve.*

a so daß This is a dependent clause of result. **So daß** may be translated as *so that* but there is a risk of confusion with *so that* meaning *in order that,* which introduces a purpose clause and must be rendered in German by **damit.** It is safer to think of **so daß** as meaning *as a result of which* or *with the result that.*

b Dürfte is a subjunctive of possibility used when something is or can be expected.

4 glauben wir ... gefunden zu haben, *we think we have found,* This perfect infinitive construction (**gefunden zu haben**) is common after **glauben** when there is no change of subject. It could not be used if the sentence were WE *think* HE (or anyone other than *we*) *has found...*

5 schweren Herzens *heavy hearted* This is the literal translation. *Downhearted* or *downcast* would suit quite well here. This is the genitive case, used in certain ready-made phrases to express emotional states or moods. (Compare **guter Laune**: *in a good mood* and **schlechter Laune**: *in a bad mood*) **Herz** is a 'mixed' noun – i.e. it shows characteristics of both strong and weak declensions (See Appendix **8.**) as is shown in the genitive **Herzens.** Since the noun is so obviously genitive, the adjective has the weak form (unlike **guter** in the phrase **guter Laune**).

Part two

Die letzten Stunden *The last hours*

6 mit allem rechtzeitig fertig werden sollen, *are to (are supposed to) get everything done (finished) in time,* mit allem **Allem** is the dative of the pronoun **alles.**

7 Wovon sprichst du? *What are you talking about?*

a sprechen von: *to talk about*

b wovon? *about what?* (L29, N28)

8 daß er uns um elf Uhr abholen würde, *that he would fetch us at eleven o'clock,* würde This is the subjunctive of indirect speech. This is neither unreal nor conditional. Franz has said: **ich werde euch ...**

abholen. Werde changes to **würde** when what he said is later reported.

9 **einem** This is the dative of **man.**

Frau Kühns letzte Ratschläge *Frau Kühn's last words of advice*

10 **muß ihr das immer wieder gesagt werden,** *she must be told repeatedly* (*that must be said to her again and again*), Remember, when using passive constructions, that if the German verb requires the dative (like **sagen**), the subject of the English sentence (**she**) becomes the indirect object (**ihr**) in the German sentence. (See Appendix 15.)

11 **und von selbst nichts tun würde.** *and would do nothing of her own accord.*
    Selbst remains the same, irrespective of the person in question.

12 **Manchmal wünschte ich, du wärest kein so seelenguter Mensch,** *Sometimes I (could) wish you weren't such a kind-hearted soul,*
    wünschte ich, du wärest These are subjunctives because the speaker is voicing a wish which cannot be fulfilled. **Wünschen** is in the subjunctive as well as the verb in the following clause when realization is either extremely unlikely or impossible.

Am Flughafen *At the airport*

13 **jetzt wo der Frühling schon fast gekommen ist,** *now that spring is almost here,*
    jetzt wo **Wo** introduces a kind of relative clause here, the antecedent being **jetzt** (an adverb). **Wo** is used thus when the sense is *at the point in time or space where...*

14 **Das hättet ihr früher wissen müssen.** *You would have had to know that earlier.* This is the perfect subjunctive of **müssen** followed by a completing infinitive and follows the same pattern as the perfect tense of modal verbs. **Können, müssen** and **sollen** are so frequently used in the perfect subjunctive that it is worth trying to memorize the three phrases:
    hätte ... können: *could have*   **hätte ... sollen:** *should have*
    hätte ... müssen: *would have had to*

15 **Jetzt läßt sich nichts mehr daran ändern.** *There's nothing to be done about it now. / Nothing can be done about it now.* **Läßt sich** + infinitive means *can be* + past participle in English.

16 **Ihr seid zuerst mit dem Schreiben dran.** *It's your turn to write first.*
    ihr seid dran This is very idiomatic. It means *it's your move/turn.*

Appendices

1 Articles Demonstratives Adjectives

A The definite article, *der, die, das,* and an adjective.
The demonstrative, *dieser,* and an adjective.

Singular

	masculine	feminine	neuter
Nom.	*der* gute Mann *dieser* alte Film	*die* gute Frau *diese* alte Uhr	*das* gute Kind *dieses* alte Buch
Acc.	*den* guten Mann *diesen* alten Film	*die* gute Frau *diese* alte Uhr	*das* gute Kind *dieses* alte Buch
Dat.	*dem* guten Mann *diesem* alten Film	*der* guten Frau *dieser* alten Uhr	*dem* guten Kind *diesem* alten Buch
Gen.	*des* guten Mannes *dieses* alten Films	*der* guten Frau *dieser* alten Uhr	*des* guten Kindes *dieses* alten Buchs

Plural

	masculine, feminine and neuter
Nom. & Acc.	*die* guten Männer, Frauen, Kinder *diese* alten Filme, Uhren, Bücher
Dat.	*den* guten Männer*n*, Frauen, Kinder*n* *diesen* alten Filme*n*, Uhren, Büchern
Gen.	*der* guten Männer, Frauen, Kinder *diese*.· alten Filme, Uhren, Bücher

Note: Like *dieser* are: *jeder, welcher, solcher*; also *alle* (mostly in the plural).

B The indefinite article, *ein,* and an adjective.
(Only the forms printed in heavy italics differ from declension **A** above.)

Singular

	masculine	feminine	neuter
Nom.	*ein* gro*ßer* Mann	eine schöne Dame	*ein* rot*es* Kleid
Acc.	einen großen Mann	eine schöne Dame	*ein* rot*es* Kleid
Dat.	einem großen Mann	einer schönen Dame	einem roten Kleid
Gen.	eines großen Mannes	einer schönen Dame	eines roten Kleids

Note: Like *ein* are: *kein,* and the possessive adjectives, *mein, dein, sein,*
unser, euer, Ihr, ihr (see Appendix 3).

Plural
The plural forms are the same as for *diese* in **A** above, thus: N. & A.
keine großen Männer; D. keinen großen Männern; G. keiner großen Männer.

C Adjectives *not* preceded by an article, demonstrative, or like word – see **A** and **B** above.

(Only the forms printed in heavy italics differ from the endings of *dieser* above.)

Singular

	masculine	feminine	neuter
Nom.	schwar**zer** Kaffee	kalte Milch	dunkl**es** Bier
Acc.	schwar**zen** Kaffee	kalte Milch	dunkl**es** Bier
Dat.	schwar**zem** Kaffee	kalt**er** Milch	dunkl**em** Bier
Gen.	schwar**zen** Kaffees	kalt**er** Milch	dunkl**en** Biers

Plural

	masculine, feminine and neuter		
Nom. & Acc.	schöne Männer,	Frauen,	Bücher
Dat.	alten Männern,	Frauen,	Büchern
Gen.	großer Männer,	Frauen,	Bücher

EXAMPLES

Nominative

A *Der junge Hoteldiener* holt die Koffer.
Diese schwarze Reisetasche ist zu klein.
Welches kleine Kind hat gerufen?
Sind *alle reichen Verwandten* tot?

B *Ein ausländischer Empfangschef* erwartet uns.
Ist das *Ihre junge Tochter?*
Ein grünes Auto ist nicht schön.
Heute landen *keine anderen Flugzeuge.*

C *Guter Fisch* ist teuer.
Deutsches Essen schmeckt wunderbar.
Das ist *echte Seide* aus Indien.
Mehrere kranke und leidende Menschen wohnen hier.

Accusative (see Lesson 2, note 5b and Appendix 7)

A Ich trinke *solchen starken Tee* nicht gern.
Sie kann *die braune Tasche* nicht finden.
Der Hoteldiener bringt *dieses schwere Gepäck* in Ihre Zimmer.
Die Verkäuferin packt *die beiden Sachen* ein.

B Willst du *meinen hübschen Hut* tragen?
Ich habe *eine große Flasche Wein* zu verzollen.
Wir haben *ein nettes Ehepaar* kennengelernt.
Der Vater grüßt *seine jungen Kinder.*

C Sie trinken *schwarzen Kaffee* und essen *frisches Obst.*
In diesem Restaurant nehme ich immer *kalte Limonade.*
Ich zeige Ihnen *einige historische Bücher.*
Franz hat *viele blaue Pullover.*

Dative (see Lesson 4, note 32 and Appendix 7)

A Ich sitze auf *diesem harten Stuhl.*
  Ihr helft *jeder alten Frau.*
  Sie möchte in *dem neuen Hotel* wohnen.
  Der Zollbeamte antwortet *den anderen Ausländern.*

B Du antwortest *keinem alten Mann.*
  Wir danken *eurer jungen Tochter.*
  Der Polizist hilft *meinem kleinen Kind.*
  Sie schreibt *ihren lieben Eltern.*

C Siehst du den Jungen mit *lockigem Haar?*
  Der Kellner kommt mit *warmer Suppe.*
  Nach *heißem Tee* kann ich nichts mehr essen.
  Sie helfen *armen Menschen* gern.
  Meine Tochter schreibt *einigen reichen Bekannten.*

Genitive (see Lesson 8, notes 1b and 36, and Appendix 7)

A Die Frau *jedes reichen Geschäftsmannes* kauft Parfum.
  Er trägt die Koffer *der schönen Dame.*
  Ich habe den Schlüssel *dieses neuen Autos.*
  Hier sind die Bücher *der beiden Mädchen.*
  Der Preis *aller modischen Taschen* ist zu hoch.

B Der Pullover *meines jungen Sohns* war sehr teuer.
  Das Auto *ihrer reichen Schwester* fährt schnell.
  Das ist der Apfel *eines kleinen Kindes.*
  Trotz *unserer vielen Fragen* antwortet er nicht.

C Das Trinken *starken Tees, eiskalter Milch* und *dunklen Biers* schadet seiner
  Gesundheit.
  Das Leben *mancher kranker Kinder* ist nicht leicht.

2 Comparison of Adjectives and Adverbs

1

	billig	(cheap)	elegant	(elegant)
Comparative + er	billiger	(cheaper)	eleganter	(more elegant)
Superlative + (e)st	billigst-	(cheapest)	elegantest-	(most elegant)

2 Some take an *Umlaut* (single-syllable words):
  jung, jünger, jüngst-; alt, älter, ältest-

3 Words ending in -el, -er, -en drop the e in the comparative:
  dunkel, dunk-ler, dunkelst-; teuer, teu-rer, teuerst-

4 Irregular:

groß	gut	hoch	nah	viel	gern
größer	besser	höher	näher	mehr	lieber
größt-	best-	höchst-	nächst-	meist-	am liebsten (adverb only)

EXAMPLES

Dieser Anzug ist *billig.* Es ist ein *billig*er Anzug. Peter sucht einen *billig*eren
Anzug, aber er kauft den *billig*sten nicht. Eva findet das gelbe Kleid nicht *so
hübsch wie* das weiße. Frau Kühn findet das weiße *genauso hübsch wie* das gelbe,
aber das gelbe paßt ihr *besser.*
Sie läuft *schnell* Ski. Er läuft *schneller.* Ich laufe *am schnellsten.*

3 Possessives

	1st Person	2nd Person		3rd Person		
Singular	my **mein**	your **dein**	your **Ihr**	his its (*masc.*) **sein**	her its (*fem.*) **ihr**	its (*neut.*) **sein**
Plural	our **unser**	your **euer**	your **Ihr**	their (*masc., fem. and neut.*) **ihr**		

Notes: (1) *dein* and *euer* are the familiar forms used with persons addressed as *du* and *ihr*, (see Appendix 4, Personal Pronouns).
(2) For endings see Appendix 1 **B**.

EXAMPLES

Das ist *mein* Koffer, und das ist *meine* Tasche.
Wir haben *unser* Auto nicht hier. Hast du *dein* Auto, Paul? Vielleicht haben Sie *Ihres**, Frau Lenz?
Wollt ihr *eure* Verwandten besuchen?
Die Frau öffnet *ihren* Koffer, und der Mann öffnet *seine* Tasche.
*Pronoun forms, *yours, mine* etc. have strong endings, cf. *dieser*.

4 Personal and Reflexive Pronouns

1 *Personal*	1st person	2nd person		3rd person		
Singular	I/me	you	you	he/him; it	she/her; it	it
Nom. Acc. Dat.	**ich** **mich** **mir**	**du*** **dich** **dir**	**Sie**** **Sie** **Ihnen**	**er** **ihn** **ihm**	**sie** **sie** **ihr**	**es** **es** **ihm**
Plural	we/us	you	you	they/them		
Nom. Acc. Dat.	**wir** **uns** **uns**	**ihr*** **euch** **euch**	**Sie**** **Sie** **Ihnen**	**sie** **sie** **ihnen**		

(*) *du* (singular) and *ihr* (plural) are familiar forms, used when speaking, for example, to children, relatives and close friends.
(**) *Sie* (singular and plural) is the more formal form of address.

EXAMPLES

Ich bin Frau Kühn. Meine Kinder besuchen *mich* oft und helfen *mir*.
Brauchst *du* das Geld, Renate? Es ist für *dich*. Ich gebe es *dir*.
Haben *Sie* einen Brief für mich? Nein, ich habe nichts für *Sie*. Wie geht es *Ihnen* heute?
Wo ist Hans? Ist *er* in Berlin? Wenn ich *ihn* sehe, will ich mit *ihm* sprechen.
Ist der Garten hübsch? Ja, *er* ist hübsch. Haben Sie *ihn* gesehen?

Ist Ihre Freundin nett? Ja, *sie* ist nett. Ich finde *sie* auch schön. Ich schreibe *ihr* eine Postkarte.

Ist die Wohnung neu? Ja, *sie* ist neu. Haben Sie *sie* gesehen?

Kennen Sie das Kind? *Es* hat keinen Bruder. Wir lieben *es*. Mein Sohn spielt oft mit *ihm*.

Das Zimmer ist teuer. Ist *es* schön? Ja, ich finde *es* schön.

Wir wohnen jetzt in München. Wollen Sie *uns* besuchen und mit *uns* ausgehen?

Seid *ihr* morgen frei? Dann sehe ich *euch* also? Ich erkläre *euch* den Weg.

Sind *Sie* die Eltern von Renate und Herbert? Ich freue mich, *Sie* kennenzulernen. Kommt Renate nicht mit *Ihnen*?

Sind die Gäste hier? Nein, *sie* sind nicht hier. Ich erwarte *sie* noch. Eva kommt mit *ihnen*.

Die Zimmer sind billig, aber *sie* haben kein Bad. Nehmen Sie *sie*?

2 *Reflexive*

	ich	du	er, sie, es	wir	ihr	Sie, sie
Acc.	mich	dich	sich	uns	euch	sich
Dat.	mir	dir	sich	uns	euch	sich

EXAMPLES

Ich wasche *mich*. Er wäscht *sich*.

Ich wasche *mir* die Haare. Er wäscht *sich* die Haare.

5 Interrogatives

Who/(to) whom/whose?

Nom. *Wer* kommt? Walter kommt. Walter und Lore kommen.

Acc. *Wen* fragt er? Er fragt diesen Mann. Er fragt die Leute dort.

Dat. *Wem* gibt er den Schlüssel? Dem Gepäckträger. Seinen Gästen.

Gen. *Wessen* Koffer ist das? Das ist der Koffer meines Mannes.

Wessen Taschen sind das? Das sind die Taschen unserer Freunde.

What?

Nom. *Was* ist das? Das ist unser Hotel.

Acc. *Was* trinkt Herr Kühn? Einen Rotwein.

How? *Wie* komme ich zum Rathaus? Sie gehen geradeaus.

Where? *Wo* wohnen eure Eltern? Sie wohnen in Berlin.

Where (to)? *Wohin* fährt dieser Zug? Er fährt nach Köln.

Where from? *Woher* kommt das Flugzeug? Es kommt aus Rio.

How much? *Wieviel* kostet dieses Doppelzimmer? Es kostet 28 DM.

Which? *Welcher* Junge ist dein Kind? Das Kind mit lockigem Haar.

What kind of? *Was für* eine Tasche haben Sie? Eine braune Tasche.

When? *Wann* gehst du ins Kino? Freitagabend.

6 Relative Pronouns

These have the same forms as the definite article (see Appendix 1, Articles) except in the following cases:–
  Genitive: *dessen* (instead of **des**) and *deren* (instead of **der**)
  Dative plural: *denen* (instead of **den**)
EXAMPLES
Ich möchte mit der Verkäuferin sprechen, *die* (who) uns heute bedient hat.
Das ist das Fräulein, *das* (whom) ich als meine Sekretärin angestellt habe.
Der Doktor, *dem* (whom) ich davon erzählte, lachte sich halbtot darüber.
Sind Sie die Eltern, *denen* (to whom) ich ein Rezept für Tabletten geben soll?
Ich suche das Kind, *dessen* (whose) Name auf dem Rezept geschrieben ist.
Wo ist die Dame, *deren* (whose) Kind eine Erkältung hat?
Der Hut, *den* (that/which) ich verloren habe, war mein eigener.
Jetzt haben wir Fasching, *der* (that/which) dieses Jahr besonders lange dauert.
Note: After *nichts, vieles* and *alles* use *was:*
In diesem Geschäft sehe ich *nichts, was* mir gefällt.
Vieles, was ich gekauft habe, war zu teuer.
Alles, was du sagst, ist richtig.

7 Prepositions

1 *Dative* always after: *aus, außer, bei, gegenüber, mit, nach, seit, von, zu*
EXAMPLES
Sie kommen *aus* dem Haus, *aus* der Schule, *aus* den Theatern.
Er wohnt *bei* seinem Bruder.
Sie fahren *mit* dem Auto. Sie fliegt *mit* ihrer Tochter.
Nach vier Stationen steigen Sie aus.
Sie kommen *von* dem Bahnhof. Das ist nett *von* dir.

2 *Accusative* always after: *bis, durch, entlang, für, gegen, ohne, um*
EXAMPLES
Sie gehen *durch* den Park.
Vielen Dank *für* Ihre Auskunft.
Heute essen sie *ohne* ihn zu Mittag.

3 With *accusative* (*Wohin?* Where to?) or *dative* (*Wo?* Where?):
an, auf, hinter, in, neben, über, unter, vor, zwischen
EXAMPLES
Sie hängt ein Bild *an* die Wand./Ich sehe das Bild *an* der Wand.
Er schreibt die Adresse *auf* einen Zettel./Das Geschenk liegt *auf* dem Tisch.
Wir gehen *in* einen Club./Sie bekommen Briefmarken *im* Postamt.
Ich fahre *über* den Platz zum Haus./Die Wohnung liegt *über* meiner Wohnung.
Sie legen Geschenke *unter* den Baum./*Unter* meinem Zimmer wohnt Renate.
Das Auto fährt *vor* das Haus./*Vor* dem Haus ist ein Garten.

4 *Genitive* always after: *statt, trotz, während, wegen*
EXAMPLES
Trotz des eiskalten Wassers springt er ins Wasser.
In München gibt es *während* des ganzen Jahres Feste.
Wir können *wegen* des schlechten Wetters nicht aus dem Bus.

Contracted forms: am = an + dem; *beim* = bei´+ dem; *im* = in + dem; *vorm* = vor + dem; *vom* = von + dem; *zum* = zu + dem; *zur* = zu + der

Prepositions with interrogative (wo-) EXAMPLES:
Wofür hast du Karten gekauft? **Für** eine Oper.
Womit sollen wir fahren? **Mit** dem Auto.
Wovon handelt die Oper? **Vom** Inhalt der Oper erzähle ich dir später.

Prepositions with pronoun (da-) EXAMPLES:
Sie sind auch *dabei.* (beim Weihnachtsfest)
Sie haben nichts *dagegen.* (gegen den Besuch)
Sie freut sich *darauf.* (auf das Skilaufen)

8 Nouns

Formation of plurals

1	-e	der Tag, die Tag*e*; das Flugzeug, die Flugzeug*e*; die Sprachkenntnis, die Sprachkenntnis*se*
2	⸚e	der Platz, die Plätz*e*; die Nacht, die Nächt*e*
3	-er	der Ski, die Ski*er*; das Ei, die Ei*er*
4	⸚er	der Mann, die Männ*er*; das Haus, die Häus*er*
5	⸚	der Bruder, die Brüder
6	-	der Kellner, die Kellner; das Mädchen, die Mädchen
7	-(e)n	der See, die See*n*; das Ohr, die Ohr*en*; die Abteilung, die Abteilung*en*;
8	-nen	die Freundin, die Freundin*nen*
9	-s	der Park, die Park*s*; das Auto, die Auto*s*; die Bar, die Bar*s*

Weak nouns (masculine) – always ending in -(e)n except in Nom. Singular

der Bursche	der Kurfürst	*(nationalities)*	*(foreign loan words)*
Held	Junge	der Finne	der Automat
Herr*	Mensch	der Portugiese	Patient
Kollege	Neffe	etc.	Polizist
Kunde	Zeuge		Student
			Tourist

(*+n *in Singular;* +en *in Plural*)
EXAMPLES
Die Herr*en* erklären dem Jung*en* den Automat*en*.
Der Finne gibt dem Polizist*en* den Paß seines Neff*en*.

Mixed nouns with genitive singular in -ens

Nom.	Acc.	Dat.	Gen.	
der Name	den Namen	dem Namen	des Nam*ens*;	Plur. die Namen
das Herz	das Herz	dem Herzen	des Herz*ens*;	Plur. die Herzen

Verbs (Infinitives) as nouns – always singular and neuter
EXAMPLES
Der Direktor ist gegen *Rauchen.*
Die Schüler gehen zum *Tanzen.*
Sie freuen sich auf das *Wiedersehen.*

Adjectives as nouns
EXAMPLES
Die *Jungen* lieben Sport. Renate gehört zu den *Jugendlichen.* Eva Schultze tut
ihr *Bestes.* Die Kälte im Winter ist das *Schlimmste.* Sie liebt alles *Schwere.*
Renate ißt gern etwas *Gutes.* Es fehlt ihm nichts *Schlimmes.* In München sehen
sie viel *Neues.*

Participles as nouns
EXAMPLES
Frau Kühn unterhält sich mit einer *Mitreisenden.*
Sie arbeitet als *Angestellte* in einem Reisebüro.
Herr Weigandt ist ein *Bekannter* von Frau Rupf.
Herr und Frau Kühn besuchen *Verwandte* in München.

9 Numerals

1 *Cardinal numbers*

0	null	11	elf	22	zweiundzwanzig
1	eins	12	zwölf	23	dreiundzwanzig
2	zwei	13	dreizehn	24	vierundzwanzig
3	drei	14	vierzehn	25	fünfundzwanzig
4	vier	15	fünfzehn	26	sechsundzwanzig
5	fünf	16	sechzehn	27	siebenundzwanzig
6	sechs	17	siebzehn	28	achtundzwanzig
7	sieben	18	achtzehn	29	neunundzwanzig
8	acht	19	neunzehn	30	dreißig
9	neun	20	zwanzig		
10	zehn	21	einundzwanzig		

40	vierzig	70	siebzig	100	hundert	500	fünfhundert
50	fünfzig	80	achtzig	110	hundertzehn	600	sechshundert
60	sechzig	90	neunzig	400	vierhundert	1000	tausend

2 *Nouns: Hunderte* von Fragen, *Tausende* von Mitarbeitern

3 *Ordinal numbers:*

1. Teil – erster Teil	4. viert-	7. siebt-
2. Programm – zweites Programm	5. fünft-	8. acht-
3. Lektion – dritte Lektion	6. sechst-	9. neunt- etc.

4 *Fractions:* ein Drittel der Studenten; ein Viertel vor elf (Uhr);
eine Viertelstunde; ein halbes Jahr; anderthalb Stunden;
zweieinhalb Jahre

10 Time

12.00 Uhr – zwölf Uhr
12.05 – fünf (Minuten) nach zwölf
12.10 – zehn nach zwölf
12.15 – (ein) Viertel nach zwölf/Viertel eins

12.20	– zwanzig nach zwölf/zehn vor halb eins
12.25	– fünf vor halb eins
12.30	– halb eins
12.35	– fünf nach halb eins
12.40	– zehn nach halb eins/zwanzig vor eins
12.45	– (ein) Viertel vor eins/drei V'ertel eins
12.50	– zehn vor eins
12.55	– fünf vor eins
1.00	– ein Uhr
13.18 Uhr	– dreizehn Uhr achtzehn
23.00 Uhr	– dreiundzwanzig Uhr

EXAMPLES

Wie spät ist es? Es ist eine halbe Minute vor neun.
Wieviel Uhr ist es? Punkt zwölf/schon vier Uhr/gleich drei.
Wann kommt er?/*Um wieviel Uhr?* Um fünf/gegen drei.
Wie lange wartete er? Von drei bis sechs/stundenlang.
Wie oft fährt der Zug? Alle fünf Minuten.

11 Present Tense

	to be *sein*	to have *haben*	Strong Verb* *fahren*	Weak Verb *lernen*
ich	*bin*	habe	fahre	lerne
du**	*bist*	hast	fährst	lernst
er, sie, es	*ist*	hat	fährt	lernt
wir	*sind*	haben	fahren	lernen
ihr**	*seid*	habt	fahrt	lernt
Sie**/sie	*sind*	haben	fahren	lernen

Imperatives

du forms	*sei!*	habe!	fahr(e)!	lern(e)!
ihr forms	seid!	habt!	fahrt!	lernt!
Sie forms	seien *Sie!*	haben *Sie!*	fahren *Sie!*	lernen *Sie!*

  * See Appendix 24 for list of Strong Verbs.
  ** See Appendix 4, Personal Pronouns, for use of *du, ihr, Sie* for *you.*

EXAMPLES

Lernen Sie Deutsch? Nein, ich *lerne* Spanisch.
Fahrt ihr oft in die Schweiz? Ja, wir *fahren* jeden Monat nach Zürich.
Kommt er morgen? Nein, er *hat* keine Zeit.
Ist sie in Frankfurt? Nein, sie *ist* nicht in Frankfurt.
Sei pünktlich, Renate! *Habt* Geduld, meine Kinder! *Fahren Sie* langsam!
Wo *wäschst* du *dich?* Ich *wasche mich* im Badezimmer.
Ich *wasche mir* morgen die Haare. *Waschen* Sie *sich* die Haare?
Wasch dich nicht so oft! *Wascht euch! Waschen Sie sich!*

250

Modal Verbs	wollen	sollen	können	müssen	dürfen
ich	will	soll	kann	muß	darf
du	willst	sollst	kannst	mußt	darfst
er, sie, es	will	soll	kann	muß	darf
wir	wollen	sollen	können	müssen	dürfen
ihr	wollt	sollt	könnt	müßt	dürft
Sie, sie	wollen	sollen	können	müssen	dürfen

Mögen is used in the subjunctive to mean *would like*:
ich/er *möchte*, du *möchtest*, wir/Sie/sie *möchten*, ihr *möchtet*.

EXAMPLES

Ich *will* heute nicht ins Kino.
Sollst du sofort nach Haus(e) gehen?
Sie *kann* nicht so viel essen.
Wann *müssen* wir aussteigen?
Ihr *dürft* euch nicht über die Bedienung beschweren.
Sie *möchten* lieber eine Tasse Kaffee trinken.

12 Imperfect Tense

	to be *sein*	to have *haben*	Strong Verbs* *fahren*	*lesen*
ich	war	hatte	fuhr	las
du	warst	hattest	fuhrst	lasest
er, sie, es	war	hatte	fuhr	las
wir	waren	hatten	fuhren	lasen
ihr	wart	hattet	fuhrt	last
Sie, sie	waren	hatten	fuhren	lasen

	Weak Verbs *lernen*	*arbeiten*	Mixed Verbs** *bringen*	Modals*** *wollen*
ich	lernte	arbeitete	brachte	wollte
du	lerntest	arbeitetest	brachtest	wolltest
er, sie, es	lernte	arbeitete	brachte	wollte
wir	lernten	arbeiteten	brachten	wollten
ihr	lerntet	arbeitetet	brachtet	wolltet
Sie, sie	lernten	arbeiteten	brachten	wollten

* See Appendix 24 for list of Strong Verbs.

**	*denken*	*kennen*	*nennen*	*wissen*
ich	dachte	kannte	nannte	wußte

***	*sollen*	*können*	*müssen*	*dürfen*	*mögen*
ich	sollte	konnte	mußte	durfte	mochte

Ich *war* gestern bei meiner Freundin.
Wart ihr schon im Deutschen Museum?
Wir *hatten* eine Party bis Mitternacht.
Von wem *hattest* du Besuch?
Er *schrieb* eine Bewerbung.
Ich *saß* oder *lag* oft im Schnee.
Er *blieb* mit den Jungen zu Haus(e).
Nachts *schliefen* wir so gut wie gar nicht.
Ich *brachte* sie nach Haus(e).
Er *kannte* uns nicht.
Sie *wollten* ein dunkles Bier, nicht wahr?
Warum *mußten* sie zu Haus(e) bleiben?
Sie *fuhren* abends von München *ab* und *kamen* morgens in Berlin *an*.
Die Freundinnen *unterhielten sich* in Ruhe.

13 Perfect Tense

Formed with *haben* or *sein* + *past participle* (see Lesson 11, note 9 and Lesson 13, note 12)

	sein	haben	Strong Verbs	Weak Verbs
Past Participles	*gewesen*	gehabt	*getragen*	*gekauft*
(with sep. prefix)			ein*gelad*en	aus*gefüllt*
(with insep. prefix)			verlor*en*	besuch*t*
(*-ieren* verbs)				kontrollier*t*

Mixed verbs	bringen	denken	kennen	nennen	wissen
Past participles	*gebracht*	*gedacht*	*gekannt*	*genannt*	*gewußt*

EXAMPLES

(haben) Er *hat* keine Zeit *gehabt*.
(sein) Sie *ist* in einem Museum *gewesen*.
(kaufen) Er *hat* eine Kollegmappe *gekauft*.
(eilen) Sie *sind* uns zu Hilfe *geeilt*.
(ausfüllen) Ich *habe* den Meldezettel *ausgefüllt*.
(hereinströmen) Die Kunden *sind* herein*geströmt*.
(sich duzen) Wir *haben uns* sofort *geduzt*.
(tragen) Er *hat* die Koffer *getragen*.
(aussteigen) Wir *sind* aus dem Bus *ausgestiegen*.
(gelingen) Die Rettung *ist* ihnen *gelungen*.
(sich waschen) Du *hast dir* die Hände *gewaschen*.
(kennen) Ich *habe* ihn nicht *gekannt*.
(wissen) Das *habe* ich nicht mehr *gewußt*.

Perfect Tense of Modal Verbs

wollen   Ich *habe* es nicht *gewollt*.
            Hast du ins Theater *gehen wollen*?

sollen	Sie *hat* einen steilen Berg hinunter *gesollt*.
	Sie *hat* pünktlich nach Haus(e) *kommen sollen*.
können	Das *habe* ich nicht *gekonnt*.
	Sie *hat* gut portugiesisch *sprechen können*.
müssen	Er *hat* nach Frankfurt *gemußt*.
	Er *hat* nach Frankfurt *fahren müssen*.
dürfen	Du *hast* nicht ins Kino *gedurft*.
	Wir *haben* zum Fasching *gehen dürfen*.
mögen	Renate *hat* Herrn Martens nicht *gemocht*.

14 Future Tense

Formed with **werden** + *an infinitive*

EXAMPLES

Ich *werde* im Frühjahr zum Skilaufen nach Österreich *fahren*.
Wann *wirst* du uns in München *besuchen?*
Wird der Busfahrer ohne Fräulein Green *abfahren?*
Wird sie *sich* mit ihm *versöhnen?*
Wo *wird* das Konzert *stattfinden?*
Werden wir nicht mit dem Flugzeug nach Berlin *fliegen?*
Ihr *werdet* keine Karten mehr *bekommen*.
Sie *werden sich beeilen* müssen.

15 Passive Voice

Formed with **werden** + *past participle* (see Lesson 16, note 25b)

Present: Ausgezeichnete Arbeitsbedingungen *werden geboten*.
Imperfect: Ich *wurde* von einem Herrn Kühn *angerufen*.
Perfect: Dr. Lodenhuber *ist* uns von meiner Schwägerin *empfohlen worden*.
Future: Der Hin- und Rückflug *wird* von uns *bezahlt werden*.

With modal verb

Present: Sie *wollen* durch das Werk *geführt werden*.
Imperfect: Der Rückflug *sollte* von ihm *gebucht werden*.
Perfect: Ab und zu *haben* das Öl und das Wasser *kontrolliert* und *nachgefüllt werden müssen*.
Future: Der Rückflug *wird* von ihm *gebucht werden müssen*.

Without subject

Im Freizeitzimmer *wird geraucht*.
Wann *wurde* zum letzten Mal *saubergemacht?*

With grammatical subject es

Es *wird* trotzdem *getanzt*.

16 Subjunctive

Subjunctive I – formed from the stem of the infinitive

Infinitive	sein	haben	werden
ich, er, sie, es	*sei*	hab*e*	werd*e*
du	sei*st*	hab*est*	werd*est*
ihr	sei*et*	hab*et*	werd*et*
wir, Sie, sie	sei*en*	hab*en*	werd*en*

Subjunctive II – formed from the imperfect

	sein	haben	werden	müssen*
Imperfect	war	hatte	wurde	mußte
ich, er, sie, es	*wäre*	*hätte*	*würde*	*müßte*
du	*wärest*	*hättest*	*würdest*	*müßtest*
ihr	*wäret*	*hättet*	*würdet*	*müßtet*
wir, Sie, sie	*wären*	*hätten*	*würden*	*müßten*

* *Modals*	müssen	dürfen	können	mögen	wollen	sollen
ich	*müßte*	*dürfte*	*könnte*	*möchte*	*wollte*	*sollte*

EXAMPLES

1 *Indirect speech* – (see Lesson 29, note 16)
Die Kartenverkäuferin sagte, sie *habe* die letzten Karten *verkauft*.
Sie sagte, daß die Karten, die *zurückgebracht worden seien*, gut *wären*.

2 *Expressions of politeness* – (see Lesson 7, notes 22, 23)
Würden Sie so freundlich *sein*, Herrn Schmidt vom Flughafen abzuholen?
Ich *hätte* gern eine Tasse Tee; *könnte* ich mit dem Kellner sprechen?

3 *Expression of unfulfillable wish* – (see Lesson 28, note 7a)
Wärest du doch eine halbe Minute früher dort *gewesen!*
Hätte ich doch nur etwas mehr Geld bei mir *gehabt!*

4 *Comparison ('as if')* – see Lesson 28, notes 8a and 24)
Es sieht aus, als ob Glatteis auf den Straßen *läge*.
Mir schien es, als wenn ihr nur fünf Minuten weg *gewesen wäret*.

5 *Possibility, doubt, unreality* – (see Lesson 29, note 10b)
Wir *hätten* tot *sein können*.
Es *dürfte* schwer *sein*, einen Parkplatz zu finden.

6 *Conditional* – (see Lesson 27, note 17)
Wenn Frau Pfaffinger *wählen könnte, ginge* sie ins Platzl.
Falls jemand Karten *zurückbrächte, könnte* Renate sie *haben*.

17 The Infinitive with and without *zu*

1 The infinitive without *zu* after a) the modal verbs
b) **helfen, hören, sehen, lassen**

a Du *darfst* mit deinem Freund *ausgehen.*
   Der Junge *wollte* einen neuen Pullover *kaufen.*
   Er *hätte* im Schlafzimmer nicht *rauchen sollen.*

b Franz *hilft* das Auto aus dem Wasser *ziehen.*
   Er *hat* das Auto aus dem Wasser *ziehen helfen.*
   Wir *hören* jemanden um Hilfe *rufen.*
   Wir *haben* jemanden um Hilfe *rufen hören.*
   Brigitte *läßt* ihre Bücher oft bei uns *liegen.*
   Lassen Sie mich Ihre Mäntel in die Garderobe *bringen!*
   Ich *habe* meine Haare *färben lassen.*

2 *Zu, um* ... *zu, ohne* ... *zu, statt* ... *zu* and infinitive

EXAMPLES

Hat man versucht, Herrn Kühn in die Maschine *zu stecken?*
Ich freue mich, Sie *kennenzulernen* und das Weihnachtsfest feiern *zu können.*
Ich kam nach München, *um* mir eine neue Stellung *zu suchen.*
Er ging ins Bett, *ohne* etwas *zu essen* und *zu trinken.*
Statt um die Ecke *zu fahren,* ist sie an einem Baum gelandet.

18 Word Order

Verb in Main Clause

Statements: Er *lernt* Deutsch in der Schule.
                  Er *hat* Deutsch in der Schule *gelernt.*
                  Er *muß* Deutsch in der Schule *lernen.*
                  Er *hat* Deutsch in der Schule *lernen müssen.*
With inversion: In der Schule *lernt er* Deutsch.
                  Weil er nach Deutschland will, *lernt er* Deutsch.
Questions: *Lernt er* Deutsch?
                  Warum *lernt er* Deutsch?

Verb in Subordinate Clause

                  Ich glaube, daß er Deutsch *lernt.*
                  Ich glaube, daß er Deutsch gelernt *hat.*
With modal: Ich glaube, daß er Deutsch lernen *muß.*
                  Ich glaube, daß er Deutsch *hat* lernen müssen.
                  Ich glaube, daß er Deutsch *wird* lernen müssen.
Passive: Ich glaube, daß kein Alkohol getrunken *wird.*
                  Ich glaube, daß kein Alkohol getrunken werden *darf.*

19 Co-ordinating Conjunctions

1 These have no effect on word order:
   aber, but   **oder,** or   **und,** and
   denn, for, since **sondern,** but (instead)

Es tut mir leid, *aber* Sie kommen zu spät.

Ich fühle mich froh, *denn* die Konferenz hat sich für mich gelohnt.

Meine Kunden bieten eine Wohnung an, *oder* sie suchen eine.

Mein Haus ist niemals leer, *und* es fehlt mir an nichts.

2 The following cause inversion:

    deshalb, therefore, so   *sonst,* otherwise   *trotzdem,* nevertheless

EXAMPLES

Es ist trockener und fester Schnee, *deshalb* wollen wir spazierengehen.

Beeilt euch, *sonst* werdet ihr naß.

20 Subordinating Conjunctions

These are followed by subordinate clause word order – see Appendix 18.

als, when, than	*daß,* that	(as a result)
als ob, als wenn, as if	*falls,* in case	*solange,* as long as
bevor, before	*nachdem,* after	*soviel,* as far as
bis, until	*obwohl,* although	*während,* while
da, since, as	*seit,* since	*weil,* because
damit, so that,	*sobald,* as soon as	*wenn,* if, when(ever)
in order that	*so daß,* so that,	*wie,* as (*so . . . wie,* as . . . as)

EXAMPLES

Ich fuhr gerade in demselben Augenblick die Isar entlang, *als* es passierte.

Du sprichst Deutsch, *als ob (als wenn)* du ein Deutscher wärest.

Bevor ich nach München kam, war ich bei einem Zahnarzt angestellt.

Da ich viele Länder besucht habe, kenne ich viele Sprachen.

Machen Sie Platz, *damit* der Krankenwagen durch kann.

Ihr wißt doch, *daß* er in einem Studentenheim wohnt.

Nachdem ich alles gekauft hatte, kam ich direkt zu Ihnen.

Seit mein Mann tot ist, lebe ich allein, aber *sobald* ich genug Geld habe, werde
   ich in einem Hotel wohnen, *so daß* ich nicht mehr allein bin.

Während du auf der Bank warst, machten wir die Wohnung sauber.

Sie hat ein rotes Kleid gekauft, *weil* die Farbe ihr paßt.

Wenn Sie langsam fahren, schaffen Sie es vielleicht bis zur Hütte.

21 Relative Clauses

See also Appendix 6, Relative Pronouns and Appendix 18 Subordinate clause
word order.

EXAMPLES

Im Herbst haben wir das Oktoberfest, *das* auf der ganzen Welt bekannt *ist.*

Sind Sie die Dame, *der* ich ein Rezept für Halstabletten geben *soll?*

Doktor Lodenhuber, *dessen* Sprechstundenhilfe ich *bin,* ist praktischer Arzt.

Renate trägt Ketten aus Kaffeebohnen, *die* bis auf den Boden *hängen.*

Es gibt nichts, *was* ich so ungern *tue,* wie früh aufzustehen.

Alles, *was* ein bißchen Phantasie *zeigt,* ist erlaubt.

Ich lief zur Haltestelle, *wo* mir der Bus vor der Nase *wegfuhr.*

22 Indirect Questions

See Appendix 18, Subordinate clause word order

EXAMPLES

Sagen Sie mir bitte, *wo* Sie *wohnen!*
Der Schaffner weiß, *wann* der Zug in Köln *ankommt.*
Sie weiß nicht, *wie lange* sie im Jugendheim arbeiten *wird.*
Christian Riemer fragt, *was* er essen und trinken *soll.*
Renate und Franz sollen erzählen, *was* sie im Fernsehstudio alles *haben* machen müssen.
Sie kann sich nicht vorstellen, *wer* Herrn Martens eingeladen *hat.*
Ich weiß nicht, *warum* er ins Wasser gesprungen *ist.*
Brigitte hat vergessen, *ob* man das Wasser zuerst kochen *muß.*
Renate ist gespannt, *ob* Herbert und Eva sich wieder versöhnen *werden.*

23 Verb Prefixes

Separable

ab-	*fort-*	*hoch-*	*vor-*
an-	*her-*	*mit-*	*vorbei-*
auf-	*herab-*	*nach-*	*weg-*
aus-	*herein-*	*statt-*	*wieder-**
dran-	*herum-*	*übrig-*	*zurück-*
ein-	*herunter-*	*um-**	*zusammen-*
entgegen-	*hinunter-*	*unter-**	

EXAMPLES

Frau Kühn paßt nicht *auf.*
Sie sahen sich seit vielen Jahren zum ersten Mal *wieder.*
Die Verlobung findet morgen abend *statt.*
Der Empfangschef wartet, während du die Formulare *aus*füllst.
Ich weiß nicht, warum er an Ihrem Haus dreimal *vorbei*fuhr.
Der Kellner will die Bestellung *entgegen*nehmen.
Ist es nötig, stundenlang *herum*zustehen und ein Plakat *hoch*zuhalten?
Jemand hat drei Karten zu je 25 DM *zurück*gegeben.
Der Ausländer ist in eine andere Straßenbahn *um*gestiegen.

Certain verbs, such as **kennenlernen** and **spazierengehen** are made up of two joined verb infinitives, the first of which is treated as a separable prefix:
Gehen Sie gern *spazieren?*
Ich möchte in Ihrem schönen Garten *spazieren*gehen.
Gestern hat er einen sehr netten Geschäftsmann *kennen*gelernt.

Inseparable

be-	**ent-**	**ge-**	**unter-***	**wieder-***
emp-	**er-**	**um-***	**ver-**	

Bedienen Sie hier, Fräulein?
Die Angestellte im Reisebüro *empfahl* uns eine Reise mit dem Bus.
Er *erinnerte* sich nicht mehr an seine kleine Schwester.
Der Hund *gehört* diesem Mann hier.
Die Freundinnen *unterhielten* sich in Ruhe.
Er *wiederholte* sein Examen nicht.

* Separable when stressed (e.g. *wieder*kommen – Sie kam *wieder*.)
  Inseparable when unstressed (e.g. wiederholen – Sie *wiederholte* das Wort.)

24 Strong Verbs

Notes

1 These deviate from the weak (regular) verbs only in:
    (i) the *du* and *er* forms of the present, in which there may be a vowel
    change (see Appendix 11):
    ich esse, du *ißt*, er *ißt*, wir essen, ihr eßt, Sie/sie essen;
    (ii) the imperfect, which has a vowel change:
    ich *aß*
    See Appendix 12 (*fahren* and *lesen*) for endings;
    (iii) the past participle, which may have a vowel change and has the
    ending *-en: geboten.*

2 The past participle is used with **haben** (or with *sein* where indicated) to form
the perfect tense.
    EXAMPLES: **Er *hat* die Koffer nach oben *getragen*.**
    Sie *sind* ins kalte Wasser *gesprungen*.

3 Verbs with separable and inseparable prefixes are generally listed under the
main verb. For example, for *aufgeben,* see *geben.* (See Appendix 23.)

Infinitive	Present	Present	Imperfect	Past Participle
beginnen		(er) **beginnt**	(ich/er) **begann**	(er hat) **begonnen**
bieten		**bietet**	**bot**	**geboten**
bitten		**bittet**	**bat**	**gebeten**
bleiben		**bleibt**	**blieb**	**ist geblieben**
empfehlen	(du) *empfiehlst*	*empfiehlt*	**empfahl**	**empfohlen**
essen	*ißt*	*ißt*	**aß**	**gegessen**
fahren	*fährst*	*fährt*	**fuhr**	**ist gefahren**
fallen	*fällst*	*fällt*	**fiel**	**ist gefallen**
finden		**findet**	**fand**	**gefunden**
fliegen		**fliegt**	**flog**	**ist geflogen**
frieren		**friert**	**fror**	**gefroren**
geben	*gibst*	*gibt*	**gab**	**gegeben**
gefallen	*gefällst*	*gefällt*	**gefiel**	**hat gefallen**
gehen		**geht**	**ging**	**ist gegangen**
gelingen		**gelingt**	**gelang**	**ist gelungen**
hängen		**hängt**	**hing**	**gehangen**

Infinitive	Present	Present	Imperfect	Past Participle
halten	(du) *hältst*	(er) *hält*	(ich/er) hielt	(er hat) gehalten
heißen		heißt	hieß	geheißen
helfen	*hilfst*	*hilft*	half	geholfen
klingen		klingt	klang	geklungen
kommen		kommt	kam	ist gekommen
laden	*lädst/ladest*	*lädt/ladet*	lud	geladen
lassen	*läßt*	*läßt*	ließ	gelassen
laufen	*läufst*	*läuft*	lief	ist gelaufen
leiden		leidet	litt	gelitten
lesen	*liest*	*liest*	las	gelesen
liegen		liegt	lag	gelegen
messen	*mißt*	*mißt*	maß	gemessen
nehmen	*nimmst*	*nimmt*	nahm	genommen
rufen		ruft	rief	gerufen
schaffen		schafft	schuf	geschaffen
scheiden		scheidet	schied	geschieden
scheinen		scheint	schien	geschienen
schlafen	*schläfst*	*schläft*	schlief	geschlafen
schließen		schließt	schloß	geschlossen
schreiben		schreibt	schrieb	geschrieben
schwimmen		schwimmt	schwamm	ist geschwommen
sehen	*siehst*	*sieht*	sah	gesehen
sinken		sinkt	sank	ist gesunken
sitzen		sitzt	saß	gesessen
sprechen	*sprichst*	*spricht*	sprach	gesprochen
springen		springt	sprang	ist gesprungen
stehen		steht	stand	gestanden
sterben	*stirbst*	*stirbt*	starb	ist gestorben
tragen	*trägst*	*trägt*	trug	getragen
treffen	*triffst*	*trifft*	traf	getroffen
treten	*trittst*	*tritt*	trat	ist getreten
trinken		trinkt	trank	getrunken
tun		tut	tat	getan
vergessen	*vergißt*	*vergißt*	vergaß	vergessen
verlieren		verliert	verlor	verloren
waschen (sich)	*wäschst*	*wäscht*	wusch	gewaschen
werden	*wirst*	*wird*	wurde	ist geworden
wiegen		wiegt	wog	gewogen
ziehen		zieht	zog	gezogen

25 Mixed Verbs

Infinitive	Present	Present	Imperfect	Past Participle
bringen		(er) bringt	(ich/er) brachte	(er hat) gebracht
denken		denkt	dachte	gedacht
kennen		kennt	kannte	gekannt
nennen		nennt	nannte	genannt
wissen	(du) *weißt*	(ich/er) *weiß*	wußte	gewußt

259

German-English

A

ab *6* from, away from, off
ab und zu *21* now and then, from time to time
abends *7* in the evening
aber *1* but, *9* however
abfahren (-fährt, -fuhr, -gefahren) *9* to leave
die **Abfahrt(-en)** *9* departure
abfliegen (-flog, -geflogen) *30* to take off (aircraft)
abgenommen *23* took off (see abnehmen)
abhalten (-hält, -hielt, -gehalten) *17* to hold (a function)
abholen *7* to collect, *10* to go to meet
abhorchen *24* to listen to (with stethoscope)
das **Abitur** *16* secondary-school leaving examination, ('A' levels)
abnehmen (-nimmt, -nahm, -genommen) *9* to pick up, take off
der **Abschied(-e)** *14* departure, farewell
Abschied nehmen *30* to say goodbye
zum Abschied *14* to say farewell
abstehend *11* sticking out
das **Abteil(-e)** *18* compartment
die **Abteilung(-en)** *8* department
ach so! *4* I see!
acht *2* eight
achte *8* eighth
achtundzwanzig *2* twenty-eight
Achtung! *15* take care!, look out!
achtzehn *5* eighteen
die **Adresse(-n)** *2* address
ah! *1* ah!
ah gut! *1* oh good!
aha! *1* aha! (I see!)
die **Ahnung(-en)** *4* idea
der **Alkohol** *1* alcohol

alle *1* all, *4* every
allein *10* alone
allerbest *27* best possible
allerseits *20* to all (of you)
alles *6* everything
als *7* as, *14* than, *18* when
als ob *28* as if
als wenn *28* as if
also *2* so, therefore
also gut *25* all right then
alt *8* old
die **Alten** *16* old ones
das **Alter** *8* age
die **Älteren** *16* older ones
am = an dem *5* at the, *10* on
der **Amerikaner(–)** *25* American
an *4* at, *7* on, *18* against, *19* up against, *24* in, *25* about
anbieten(-bot, -geboten) *6* to offer
andere *8* other
sich **ändern** *17* to change
anders *11* different(ly)
anderthalb *9* one and a half
die **Anerkennung(-en)** *26* appreciation
anfangen (-fängt, -fing, -gefangen) *7* to begin, start
das **Angebot(-e)** *6* offer
der/die **Angestellte(-n)** *7, 17* employee
angezogen *15* dressed, put on (see anziehen)
die **Angst(¨e)** *14* fear, fright
Angst haben *21* to be afraid
Angst machen *14* to frighten
ankommen (-kam, -gekommen) *3* to arrive
ankommen auf *14* to depend on
das kommt darauf an *14* it depends
die **Ankunft(¨e)** *10* arrival
anlernen *17* to instruct, train
anmelden *7* to book, place
anprobieren *23* to try on
der **Anruf(-e)** *7* call (telephone)
anrufen (-rief, -gerufen) *2* to ring up, telephone
anschließend *12* afterwards

sich (D) ansehen (-sieht, -sah, -gesehen) *15* to watch, *24* to look at
man sieht es euch nicht an *27* you do not show it
anstellen *13* to employ
antworten (auf) *16* to answer
anwesend *26* present
die **Anzeige(-n)** *6* advertisement
(sich) **anziehen (-zog, -gezogen)** *15* to dress (oneself), put on
der **Anzug(⸗e)** *12* suit
der **Apfel(⸗)** *5* apple
der **Apparat(-e)** *9* telephone
der **Appetit** *3* appetite
die **Arbeit(-en)** *4* work
arbeiten *1* to work
der **Arbeiter(-)** *17* worker
die **Arbeitsbedingung(-en)** *22* conditions of work
der **Arbeitsplatz(⸗e)** *8* place of work
die **Arbeitszeit(-en)** *5* working hours
sich **ärgern (über)** *12* to be annoyed, angry (with)
arm *14* poor
die **Art(-en)** *21* type, sort
der **Arzt(⸗e)** *24* doctor (medicine)
praktischer Arzt *24* general practitioner (G.P.)
(wir) **aßen** *28* (we) ate (see **essen**)
auch *1* also
auch wenn *29* even if
auf *1* on, *4* for, *5* at, *13* to, *14* of, *7*, *18* in, *27* on
der **Aufenthalt(-e)** *11* stay, *18* stop
auffallend *23* striking, showy
aufgeben (-gibt, -gab, -gegeben) *5* to send, to hand in
aufhören *5* to finish, *13* give up
aufmachen *3* to open
aufpassen *15* to watch out
etwas **Aufregendes** *27* something exciting
die **Aufregung(-en)** *27* excitement
aufs=auf+das *21* to the
aufstehen (-stand, -gestanden) *23* to get up
aufwachsen (-wächst, -wuchs,

-gewachsen) *22* to grow up
das **Auge(-n)** *8* eye
der **Augenblick(-e)** *6* moment
im Augenblick *6* at the moment
im letzten Augenblick *13* at the last moment
aus *1* from, *8* of, made of, *9* out of, *11* for
ausbilden *17* to train
ausfüllen *2* to fill in
ausgeben (-gibt, -gab, -gegeben) *14* to spend (money)
ausgebildet *17* trained
ausgehen (-ging, -gegangen) *3* to go out
das **Ausgehen** *16* going out
ausgezeichnet *17* excellent
die **Auskunft(⸗e)** *4* information
im Ausland *18* abroad
der **Ausländer(-)** *4* foreigner
ausländisch *16* foreign
ausleihen (-lieh, -geliehen) *21* to hire out
sich (D) **etwas ausleihen** *21* to borrow something
aussehen (-sieht, -gesehen) *10* to look, to appear
außen *19* outside
außer *11* apart from
außerdem *14* besides, also
äußerst *23* extremely
aussteigen (-stieg, -gestiegen) *4* to get off, alight
die **Ausstellung(-en)** *9* exhibition
austrinken (-trank, -getrunken) *25* to empty, drink up
ausverkauft *29* sold out
die **Auswahl(-en)** *8* selection
der **Ausweis(-e)** *2* identity card
sich (D) **etwas ausziehen (-zog, -gezo-gen)** *12* to take something off (i.e. a garment)
das **Auto(-s)** *1* car
der **Automat(-en)** *3* slot-machine
automatisch *4* automatically
der **Automechaniker(-)** *21* motor mechanic

die Autovermietung(-en) 2 car-hire firm

die Autowerkstatt(¨en) 3 garage

B das Bad(¨er) 2 bath(room)

das Badezimmer(–) 6 bathroom

der Bahnhof(¨e) 5 station

bald 6 soon

bis bald! 7 see you soon

der Balkon(-e) 30 balcony

das Ballett(-s) 29 ballet

die Bank(-en) 5 bank

die Bar(-s) 25 bar, counter

das Bargeld 23 cash

bat 24 asked (see **bitten**)

bauen 28 to build, make

der Baum(¨e) 15 tree

der Bayer(-n) 28 Bavarian

bayerisch 11 Bavarian

beantworten 5 to answer

bedienen 8 to serve

die Bedienung(-en) 8 service

sich beeilen 13 to hurry

sich befinden (befand, befunden) 8 to be (situated)

befreundet 18 friendly

der Beginn 17 start

begann 23 began (see **beginnen**)

beginnen (begann, begonnen) 5 to begin

begonnen 17 begun (see **beginnen**)

begrüßen 9 to welcome

die Begrüßung(-en) 1 welcome

behalten (behält, behielt, behalten) 8 to keep

behandeln 24 to treat

bei 4 with, at, 5 by, near, 6 c/o (care of), 11 from, 18 while having, 24 for

bei mir 6 here (at my house)

beide 6 both

die beiden 30 the two

beige 23 beige

die Beilage(-n) 28 accompaniment, addition (vegetables)

beim = bei dem 4 from the, 5 by, near the, 7 with the

das Beispiel(-e) 6 example

zum Beispiel (z.B.) 6 for example (e.g.)

(Sie) bekamen 27 (you) got, (see **bekommen**)

bekannt 22 known, well-known

ist dir bekannt? 14 are you aware? do you know?

der/die Bekannte(-n) 9 acquaintance, friend

bekanntmachen 19 to introduce

die Bekanntschaft(-en) 3 acquaintance

bekommen (bekam, bekommen) 3 to get

beliebt 7 popular

belohnen 27 to reward

bemalen 25 to paint over, colour

das Benzin 21 petrol

bequem 7 comfortable

bereit 22 prepared

der Berg(-e) 14 mountain

die Berghütte(-n) 21 mountain-hut, refuge

der Bericht(-e) 27 account, report

der Beruf(-e) 4 job, profession

von Beruf 4 by profession

die Beruhigungstablette(-n) 27 tranquillizer

berühmt 9 well-known, famous

beschäftigen 13 to occupy, entertain

der Bescheid 6 reply, decision

sagen Sie mir Bescheid 6 let me know

Bescheid wissen 9 to know (how), 29 to have knowledge of

sich beschweren 8 to complain

besetzt 9 engaged

besichtigen 6 to view

die Besichtigung(-en) 6 viewing,

9 sight-seeing
besonders *8* especially
besprechen (bespricht, besprach, besprochen) *17* to discuss
besser *6* better
besser gesagt *14* or rather
gute Besserung! *24* I hope you will soon be well!
best *16* best
am besten *4* best, the best way
das **Beste** *13* best (thing)
bestellen *5* to order
die **Bestellung(-en)** *13* order
bestimmt *4* definite(ly), *10* surely, *29* certain, specific
der **Besuch(-e)** *4* visit, *22* attendance
zu Besuch *4* on a visit
besuchen *7* to visit
der **Besucher(–)** *5* visitor
der **Betrieb(-e)** *7* firm, business
das **Bett(-en)** *17* bed
bevor *23* before
die **Bewerberin(-nen)** *22* applicant (female)
die **Bewerbung(-en)** *22* application
bezahlen *8* to pay
das **Bier** *3* beer
bieten (bot, geboten) *22* to offer
das **Bild(-er)** *9* picture, painting
der **Bilderrahmen(–)** *25* picture-frame
der **Bildschirm(-e)** *27* screen
billig *6* cheap
bin *1* am (see **sein**)
bis *5* until
bis auf *25* down to
bis bald! *7* see you soon!
bis...Uhr *9* by...o'clock
bisher *24* until now
ein **bißchen** *3* a little bit
bist *3* are (see **sein**)
bitte *1* please
bitte schön! *1* please!
bitten (bittet, bat, gebeten) um *13* to ask (for), request
blaß *27* pale
das **Blatt(¨er)** *25* leaf

blau *8* blue
bleiben (blieb, geblieben) *4* to remain, *6* to stay
bleiben bei *28* to stick to
der **Blick(-e)** *28* glance, look
bloß *8* only, I wonder, *19* really, merely
die **Blume(-n)** *8* flower
der **Boden(¨)** *25* floor
die **Bohne(-n)** *28* bean
die **Borte(-n)** *23* trimming
böse *21* angry
die **Boutique(-n)** *14* boutique
brachte *28* brought (see **bringen**)
die **Branche(-n)** *17* branch
die **Brasilianerin(-nen)** *28* Brazilian (female)
brasilianisch *16* Brazilian
(das) **Brasilien** *1* Brazil
brauchen *2* to need, want, *25* to have to
braun *1* brown
bravo! *29* well done, good
breit *23* broad, wide
die **Bremse(-n)** *3* brake
der **Brief(-e)** *5* letter
die **Briefmarke(-n)** *5* stamp
bringen (brachte, gebracht) *2* to bring, to take
das **Brot(-e)** *26* bread
das **Brötchen(–)** *11* roll
die **Brücke(-n)** *26* bridge
der **Bruder(¨)** *2* brother
das **Buch(¨er)** *15* book
buchen *7* to book
bunt *8* multi-coloured
die **Burg(-en)** *15* castle
das **Büro(-s)** *6* office
der **Bursche(-n)** *26* youth, lad
der **Bus(-se)** *7* bus, coach
die **Butter** *11* butter

C das **Café(-s)** *5* café
der **Chauffeur(-e)** *17* driver, chauffeur

der Chef(-s) *17* boss, chief, head
der Clown(-s) *17* clown
der Club(-s) *3* club
der Computer(–) *17* computer
die Couch(-es) *6* couch

D   da *1* there, *29* because, as
dabei *11* through it, *18* there, with us, present
dafür *8* in return for that, *23* instead
dagegen *9* against it, *28* on the other hand
damals *11* at that time, then
die Dame(-n) *1* lady
damit *24* with it, *26* so that, in order that
damit beginnen *17* to begin on (something)
danach *9* afterwards
daneben *17* next to it
dänisch *25* Danish
der Dank *1* thanks
besten Dank! *2* thanks a lot!
vielen Dank *1* thank you very much
danke *1* thank you, *18* nò thank you
danke schön *1* thank you very much
danke vielmals *3* thanks a lot
danken (D) *6* to thank
nichts zu danken *4* that's all right, it's a pleasure
dann *2* then
daran *20* on it, *21* of it
darauf *13* on that
daraus *28* from it
(ich) darf *4* (I) am allowed to (see dürfen)
darüber *13* about that, *24* at it
darum *11* for that reason, *24* for it
darunter *17* under it, as a result of it
das *1* the, that

daß *7* that
dauern *4* to last, to go on for
es dauert so lange *4* it takes such a long time
dauernd *27* continuously
davon *24* of it
dazu *8* in addition, *11* as well, *12* with it, *17* for that
dazwischenkommen *23* to come between, to intervene
die Decke(-n) *26* blanket
decken *11* to lay, set, *24* to cover
dein, deine *3* your
denken (an) (dachte, gedacht) *8* to think (of)
sich (D) denken *17* to think, to imagine
denn *4* then, *6* because, as
es sei denn *28* unless
der *1* the
dergleichen (dgl.) *13* such like
derselbe *27* the same
deshalb *11* therefore, for that reason
deutsch *9* German
das Deutsch *28* German (lang.)
der Deutsche(-n) *1* German person (male)
Deutsche *1* German (people)
(das) Deutschland *1* Germany
der Dezember *6* December
der Dialekt(-e) *11* dialect
dich *3* you (acc.)
dicht *17* thick, dense
dick *23* fat
die *1* the, *2* the (all plural nouns)
der Dienst *5* work (hours on duty)
(der) Dienstag *5* Tuesday
dieselbe *27* the same
dieser *7* this, that
das Ding(-e) *18* thing
vor allen Dingen *21* above all
dir *6* you (dat.)
direkt *4* direct(ly)
der Direktor(-en) *16* headmaster,

principal

die Diskothek(-en) *9* discothèque

doch *1* but, *2* yes, *7* surely

der Doktor(-en) *24* doctor

(der) Donnerstag *5* Thursday

das Doppelzimmer(-) *2* double-room

das Dorf(-̈er) *21* village

dort *1* there

dort drüben *8* over there

dorthin *15* to that place, *22* there

dortig *22* local

drankommen (-kam, -gekommen) *12* to have one's turn

ihr seid dran *30* it's your turn

draußen *1* outside

drehen *12* to curl

drei *2* three

dreijährig *18* lasting three years

dreizehn *5* thirteen

drinnen *11* inside

dritte *3* third

das Drittel(-) *14* third

(da) drüben *17* over there

du *3* you

dumm *12* stupid

der Dummkopf(-̈e) *19* idiot

dunkel *8* dark

dunkler *21* darker

durch *9* through, across *17* round

durchaus nicht *24* absolutely not, by no means

dürfen (darf, durfte, gedurft) *4* be allowed to, may, can (see Appendix 11)

es dürfte sein *29* it might be

die Dusche(-n) *2* shower

sich duzen *13* to say "du" to each other

E

eben *9* for that reason, *11* just

ebenfalls *27* also, too

echt *8* pure, *25* true, real

die Ecke(-n) *12* corner

um die Ecke *15* round the

corner

egal *13* equal

es ist mir egal *13* I don't mind, it's all the same to me

das Ehepaar(-e) *8* married couple

das Ei(-er) *11* egg

eifersüchtig *13* jealous

eigen *15* own

eigentlich *9* actually, really

eilen *27* to hurry, to rush

der Eilzug(-̈e) *18* fast train

ein, eine, ein *1* a, *2* one

der Eindruck(-̈e) *22* impression

einfach *7* easy, simple, simply

die Einfachheit *21* simplicity

einfallen (D) (-fällt, -fiel, -gefallen) *16* to occur (to)

einfarbig *8* of one colour

einige *4* some

einiges *29* some things

der Einkauf(-̈e) *23* purchase

einkaufen *23* to buy

einladen (-lädt, -lud, -geladen) *9* to invite

die Einladung(-en) *10* invitation

die Einleitung(-en) *Intro.* introduction

einmal *15* once

auf einmal *19* all at once, *26* suddenly

nicht einmal *23* not even

einmalig *27* exceptionally

einpacken *8* to wrap up

einrichten *17* to install

eins *1* one

einsteigen (-stieg, -gestiegen) *4* to get on (into)

eintreten (-tritt, -trat, -getreten) *18* to enter

einverstanden *3* agreed

einwerfen (-wirft, -warf, -geworfen) *9* to put in, insert

die Einzelfahrt(-en) *4* single ticket

die Einzelheit(-en) *26* detail, particular

das Einzelzimmer(-) *2* single room

das Eis *2* ice-cream, *15* ice

das Eisbein *12* pig's knuckle

eiskalt *18* cold as ice

das **Eisschießen** *15* curling (game)
elegant *23* elegant
der **Elektrobetrieb(-e)** *22* electrical firm
der **Elektroherd(-e)** *6* electric cooker
elf *5* eleven
die **Eltern (Pl.)** *4* parents
empfahl *28* recommended (see **empfehlen**)
der **Empfangschef(-s)** *2* reception-clerk
empfehlen (-fiehlt, -fahl, -fohlen) *7* to recommend
die **Empfehlung(-en)** *22* recommendation
empfohlen *15* recommended (see **empfehlen**)
das **Ende(-n)** *7* end
zu Ende *7* over
zu Ende bringen *14* to finish
endlich *4* at last
der **Engel(–)** *30* angel
der **Engländer(–)** *25* Englishman
die **Engländerin(-nen)** *28* English woman
entgegennehmen (-nimmt, -nahm, -genommen) *13* to accept, to take (an order)
entlang *4* along
sich **entscheiden für (entschied, entschieden)** *15* to decide in favour of
die **Entscheidung(-en)** *22* decision
sich **entschließen (-schließt, -schloß, -schlossen)** *8* to make up one's mind
sich **entschuldigen bei** *12* to apologize to
sich **entschuldigen lassen** *17* to send one's apologies
entschuldigen Sie! *4* excuse me!
Entschuldigung! *5* excuse me! I beg your pardon!
entsetzlich *27* dreadful(ly)
entweder…oder *6* either…or
er *1* he, it
das **Erdgeschoß(-sse)** *8* groundfloor

ereignisreich *12* eventful
der **Erfolg(-e)** *29* success
sich **erholen** *26* to recover
sich **erinnern (an)** *12, 22* to remember
die **Erkältung(-en)** *24* cold
sich **(D) eine Erkältung holen** *24* to catch cold
erklären *5* to explain
sich **erkundigen nach** *8* to enquire after
erlauben *14* to allow, permit
erledigen *22* to see to, carry out, take care of
ernst nehmen *21* to take seriously
der **Ersatzteil(-e)** *17* spare part
erscheinen (erschien, erschienen) *27* to appear
erst *5* only, just, *18* for the first time
erst einmal *27* first of all
erste *1* first
erwarten *2* to expect
erzählen (von) *12* to tell (*24* about)
die **Erziehung** *16* education
es *1* it
die **Eßecke(-n)** *6* dining-area
das **Essen(–)** *3* meal, *12* food
essen (ißt, aß, gegessen) *3* to eat
gern essen *3* to like eating
das **Eßzimmer(–)** *11* dining-room
die **Etage(-n)** *6* storey
etwa *5* about, approximately
etwas *1* something, anything
noch etwas *3* some more
so etwas *27* such a thing
euch *7* you (acc. and dat.)
euer, eure *7* your
das **Examen(–)** *13* examination
extra *2* extra, additional

266

F   die **Fabrik(-en)** *17* factory
die **Fachkraft(̈e)** *17* skilled worker
die **Fähigkeit(-en)** *22* capability, ability
fahren (fährt, fuhr, gefahren) *1* to drive, *3* to go (in vehicle)
der **Fahrer(-)** *11* driver
der **Fahrgast(̈e)** *4* passenger
die **Fahrkarte(-n)** *7* ticket
der **Fahrplan(̈e)** *18* time-table
der **Fahrschein(-e)** *4* ticket
die **Fahrt(-en)** *4* trip, journey
der **Fall(̈e)** *6* instance, case
auf keinen Fall *13* on no account
auf jeden Fall *6* in any event
fallen (fällt, fiel, gefallen) *21* to fall
falls *23* in case
falsch *18* wrong
die **Familie(-n)** *2* family
der **Familienname(-n)** *28* surname
fanatisch *16* fanatical(ly)
fände *29* would find (see **finden**)
farben *23* coloured
färben *12* to dye
der **Fasching** *25* Carnival
das **Faschingskleid(-er)** *14* fancy dress
fast *4* almost
das **Fechten** *16* fencing
fehlen *15* to be missing
es fehlt an (D) *17* there is a lack of
was fehlt mir? *24* what's wrong with me?
fehlend *17* lacking
der **Fehler(-)** *16* mistake
feiern *10* to celebrate
der **Feiertag(-e)** *25* holiday, festival
die **Feinschmeckerin(-nen)** *28* gourmet (female)
das **Fenster(-)** *6* window
die **Ferien (Pl.)** *21* holidays
die **Ferienzeit(-en)** *21* holiday period

das **Fernamt(̈er)** *7* long distance telephone exchange
das **Ferngespräch(-e)** *7* long-distance call
die **Fernsehsendung(-en)** *27* TV broadcast
das **Fernsehstudio(-s)** *26* TV studio
die **Fernsprechzelle(-n)** *9* call-box
fertig *12* ready, *13* finished
fertig werden *14* to finish
das **Fest(-e)** *20* festival, feast
fest *15* hard, solid, *21* tight
fett *29* fat
das **Feuer** *27* fire
die **Feuerwehr** *26* fire brigade
das **Fieber** *24* temperature, fever
fiel *21* fell (see **fallen**)
die **Figur(-en)** *8* figure
der **Film(-e)** *16* film
finden (fand, gefunden) *5* to find, *16* to think of, *18* to have an opinion about
fing an *26* started (see **anfangen**)
der **Finne(-n)** *16* Finn (male)
die **Finnin(-nen)** *16* Finn (female)
die **Firma (Firmen)** *17* company, firm, factory
der **Fisch(-e)** *3* fish
die **Flasche(-n)** *1* bottle
fleißig *16* hard-working
fliegen (flog, geflogen) *6* to fly
fließend *16* fluent(ly)
flog *19* flew (see **fliegen**)
der **Flug(̈e)** *22* flight
der **Flughafen(̈)** *1* airport
das **Flugzeug(-e)** *1* plane
der **Flur(-e)** *19* hall, corridor
die **Forelle(-n)** *28* trout
die **Form(-en)** *16* form
das **Formular(-e)** *5* form (paper)
der **Fortschritt(-e)** *21* progress
fortsetzen *26* to continue
das **Foto(-s)** *10* photograph
die **Frage(-n)** *5* question
fragen *4* to ask
sich fragen *14* to wonder, (to ask oneself)

Frankfurter *22* of, from Frankfurt

fränkisch *20* Franconian

der **Franzose(-n)** *28* Frenchman

die **Französin(-nen)** *28* French woman

französisch *22* French

die **Frau(-en)** *1* woman, Mrs., wife

das **Fräulein(–)** *1* young lady, Miss

frei *2* free, *7* vacant, *24* available

frei haben *25* to have a holiday (time off from work)

(der) **Freitag(-e)** *3* Friday

die **Freizeit(-en)** *16* spare time, leisure

fremd *4* strange, foreign

die **Fremdsprache(-n)** *8* foreign language

die **Freude(-n)** *24* pleasure

vor Freude *26* with joy

sich **freuen auf** *7* to look forward to

sich **freuen über** *13* to be very pleased about

das **freut mich** *6* I'm glad

der **Freund(-e)** *4* friend

die **Freundin(-nen)** *18* girl-friend

freundlich *4* friendly, *14* kind

frieren (fror, gefroren) *26* to feel cold, *28* to freeze

frisch *18* fresh

der **Friseur(-e)** *12* hairdresser

froh *15* glad, pleased, *30* happy

die **Frucht(ᵘe)** *25* fruit

früh *5* early, in the morning

früher *11* formerly

das **Frühjahr** *7* spring

der **Frühling** *30* spring

das **Frühstück** *2* breakfast

frühstücken *11* to have breakfast

(sich) **fühlen** *20* to feel

(Sie) **fuhren** *22* (you) went (see **fahren**)

führen *6* to lead, *17* to guide, to conduct, *30* to carry on (conversation)

der **Führerschein(-e)** *2* driving-licence

die **Führung(-en)** *9* conducted tour

fünf *2* five

fünfte *5* fifth

fünfzehn *4* fifteen

für *2* for, *12* in

furchtbar *14* terrible, terribly

fürchten *22* to be afraid, fear

der **Fuß(ᵘe)** *4* foot

zu Fuß *4* on foot

der **Fußgänger(–)** *26* pedestrian (male)

der **Fußgängerin(-nen)** *26* pedestrian (female)

der **Fußball(ᵘe)** *16* football

G

gab *21* gave (see **geben**)

die **Galerie(-n)** *12* gallery

der **Gang(ᵘe)** *7* aisle, gangway

der **Gänsebraten** *20* roast goose

ganz *6* completely, *8* entirely, *12* whole, all, *16* really, very

ganz allein *10* all alone

nicht ganz einfach *7* not so easy

ganz genau *7* exactly

ganz leicht *5* quite easy

gar nicht *8* not at all

gar nichts *25* nothing at all

die **Garage(-n)** *21* garage

die **Garderobe(-n)** *13* cloak-room

der **Garten(ᵘ)** *9* garden

der **Gast(ᵘe)** *11* guest

die **Gastgeberin(-nen)** *28* hostess

das **Gebäck** *20* pastries, biscuits

das **Gebäude(–)** *17* building

geben (gibt, gab, gegeben) *3* to give

es gibt *3* there is, there are

gebeten *17* requested, asked (see **bitten**)

das **Gebiet(-e)** *16* field

geblümt *25* flowery

geboren *16* born

geboten *22* offered (see **bieten**)

gedacht *17* thought (see **denken**)

die **Geduld** *9* patience
sich **gedulden** *11* to have patience, wait
gefallen (D) (gefällt, gefiel, gefallen) *6* to please
es gefällt mir *6* I like it
gefiel *21* liked (see **gefallen**)
gefroren *28* frozen (see **frieren**)
gefunden *30* found (see **finden**)
gegen *9* towards, about, *16* against
die **Gegend(-en)** *15* area, district
gegenseitig *18* each other
im **Gegenteil** *18* on the contrary
gegenüber *6* opposite
gehen (ging, gegangen) *3* to go, *11* to work (watches etc.)
es geht ihm schlecht *24* he feels ill
wie geht es Ihnen? *1* how are you?
geholfen *14* helped (see **helfen**)
gehören (D) *4* to belong to
es gehört dazu *21* it's all part of it
gekannt *22* known (see **kennen**)
gekocht *11* boiled
gelang *30* succeeded (see **gelingen**)
gelb *14* yellow
das **Geld** *4* money
die **Gelegenheit(-en)** *15* opportunity
gelingen (D) (gelang, gelungen) *16* to succeed, manage
gelungen *16* succeeded, managed (see **gelingen**)
gemischt *16* mixed
das **Gemüse(-)** *28* vegetable(s)
gemütlich *13* comfortable, pleasant
genannt *21* called
genau *5* exactly
genauso *15* just as
die **Generation(-en)** *21* generation
genommen *14* taken (see **nehmen**)

genug *3* enough
der **Genuß (Genüsse)** *20* treat, enjoyment
das **Gepäck** *1* luggage
der **Gepäckträger(-)** *1* porter
gerade *1* just
geradeaus *5* straight ahead
das **Gericht(-e)** *28* dish
gern *2* with pleasure
gern essen *3* to like (eating)
gern trinken *5* to like (drinking)
herzlich gern *3* with pleasure
das **Geschäft(-e)** *2* business, shop
(etwas) **Geschäftliches** *17* business matters
der **Geschäftsbericht(-e)** *17* business report
die **Geschäftskonferenz(-en)** *17* business conference
der **Geschäftsmann(-leute)** *1* businessman/-men
das **Geschenk(-e)** *8* gift, present
die **Geschichte(-n)** *14* story
geschlossen *23* closed
der **Geschmack** *8* taste
jeder nach seinem Geschmack *25* everybody to his liking
die **Gesellschaft(-en)** *28* company, party
einem Gesellschaft leisten *19* to keep someone company
gesessen *18* been sitting (see **sitzen**)
das **Gesicht(-er)** *11* face
gespannt sein *12* to wonder, be anxious to know
das **Gespräch(-e)** *7* conversation, (telephone) call
ein Gespräch führen *22* to have an interview, talk
gesprochen *14* spoken (see **sprechen**)
gesprungen *26* jumped (see **springen**)
gestern *12* yesterday
gestorben *26* died, dead (see **sterben**)

das Gesuch(-e) *6* request
gesund *18* healthy
die Gesundheit *5* health
gesunken *27* sunk (see **sinken**)
getan *19* done (see **tun**)
das Getränk(-e) *24* drink
die Getränkekarte(-n) *28* wine list
getroffen *19* met (see **treffen**)
getrunken *14* drunk (see **trinken**)
gewesen *13* been (see **sein**)
sich gewöhnen an *16* to get used to
gewöhnlich *4* usual(ly)
geworden *16* got (see **werden**)
gewünscht *29* desired
gewußt *17* known (see **wissen**)
gibt *3* is, gives (see **geben**)
ging *21* went (see **gehen**)
das Glas(⸚er) *2* glass
das Gläschen(-) *13* small glass
glatt *12* straight, smooth, *15* slippery
das Glatteis *28* slippery ice
glauben *6* to think, believe
gleich *3* nearly, any' minute, *6* at once, *10* straightaway
das Glück *18* luck
Glück haben *18* to be lucky
zum Glück *26* luckily, fortunately
glücklich *13* happy
der Glühwein(-e) *20* mulled wine
mein Gott! *19* good heavens!
Gott sei Dank! *17* thank heavens!
gratulieren (D) *13* to congratulate
groß *2* big, great
die Größe(-n) *21* size
die Großeltern (Pl.) *21* grandparents
größte *22* greatest
grün *8* green
der Grund(⸚e) *11* reason, *24* cause
grüßen *7* to greet, give regards to

gurgeln *24* to gargle
der Gürtel(–) *8* belt
gut *1* good, *3* well
guten Abend *6* good evening
guten Morgen *6* good morning
guten Tag *1* good morning, good afternoon, how do you do?
ach du meine Güte! *18* good gracious!
etwas Gutes *28* something good

H das Haar(-e) *8* hair
haben (hat, hatte, gehabt) *1* to have (see Appendix *11*)
halb *3* half
halb eins *3* half past twelve
half *24* helped (see **helfen**)
die Hälfte(-n) *4* half
hallo! *1* hey! I say!
der Hals(⸚e) *24* neck, throat
halt *21* just, simply
halt deinen Mund! *25* hold your tongue!
halten (hält, hielt, gehalten) *15* to stop
halten für *15* to consider, think, deem
die Haltestelle(-n) *4* (bus, tram etc.) stop
die Hand(⸚e) *18* hand
aus zweiter Hand *27* second-hand
die Handarbeit(-en) *13* handicraft and needlework
die Handelsfirma(-firmen) *22* commercial firm
die Handelsschule(-n) *22* college of commerce
es handelt sich (nicht) um *17* it is (not) a question of
es handelt von *29* it is about
der Handschuh(-e) *15* glove
die Handtasche(-n) *18* handbag
hängen (hing, gehangen) *18* to be hanging

270

hängen an (gehängt) *20* to hang (something) on
das hängt davon ab *16* that depends (on)
hart *8* hard
häßlich *11* ugly
hat *1* has (see **haben**)
hatte *8, 11* had (see Appendix 12)
hätten Sie gern? *7* would you like? (see **haben**)
das **Hauptpostamt(̈er)** *5* main post office
das **Hauptwerk(-e)** *17* main factory
das **Haus(̈er)** *6* house
nach Haus *6* home(ward)
zu Haus *3* at home
die **Hausfrau(-en)** *Intro.* housewife
der **Haushalt(-e)** *30* household
das **Haushaltsgerät(-e)** *8* household utensil
die **Hausmeisterin(-nen)** *19* caretaker (female)
die **Haut** *8* skin
das **Heilmittel(-)** *24* remedy, cure
das **Heimweh** *16* home-sickness
heiraten *13* to marry
heiser *24* hoarse
heiß *11* hot
heißen (hieß, geheißen) *1* to be called
das heißt (d.h.) *9* that is (i.e.), *14* that means
heizen *11* to heat
der **Held(-en)** *27* hero
helfen (D) (hilft, half, geholfen) *5* to help
hell *23* light, light-coloured
herabsetzen *23* to lower (price)
der **Herbst** *7* autumn
hereinkommen (-kam, -gekommen) *6* to enter
hereinströmen *23* to stream in
herkommen (-kam, -gekommen) *16* to come here
der **Herr(-en)** *1* Mr., gentleman
mein Herr *1* Sir

herrlich *11* glorious, excellent, delicious
die **Herrschaften (Pl.)** *2* ladies and gentlemen, sir and madam
herumführen *16* to show round
herumstehen (-stand, -gestanden) *17* to stand around
herunterkommen (-kam, -gekommen) *25* to come down
das **Herz(-en)** *13* heart
herzlich *3* heartfelt, sincere
heute *1* today
heute abend *3* this evening
heute nachmittag *5* this afternoon
heutig *27* of today
heutzutage *7* nowadays
hielt *24* considered (see **halten**)
hier *1* here
hierher *11* here, hither
die **Hilfe(-n)** *4* help
erste Hilfe leisten *26* to give first aid
um Hilfe rufen *26* to shout for help
zu Hilfe kommen *27* to come to one's aid
zu Hilfe nehmen *29* to make use of
hilft *5* helps (see **helfen**)
der **Himmel(-)** *30* sky, heaven
du lieber Himmel! *19* good heavens!
um Himmels willen! *12* good heavens!
hinauf *21* up, upwards
der **Hinflug(̈e)** *22* outward flight
hingehen *25* to go (to)
hinten *4* at the back
hinter *6* behind
hinter mir her sein *19* to be after me
hinunter *21* down, downwards
hinuntersteigen (-stieg, -gestiegen) *28* to climb (go) down
die **Hirschkeule(-n)** *28* haunch of venison

historisch *9* historical
hoch *6* high
höchste *22* highest
der Hochbetrieb *21* rush, busy
    season
das Hochdeutsch *28* standard German
    man
hochhalten (-hält, -hielt, -gehalten) *17* to hold up (high)
hochqualifiziert *17* highly
    trained
der Hof(¨e) *3* yard
hoffen *14* to hope
hoffentlich *2* I hope (so)
höflich *4* polite
hohe *15* high
höher *21* higher (see **hoch**)
holen *3* to fetch, *24* to catch
das Holz *30* wood
das Holztablett(-s) *30* wooden tray
hören *6* to hear
hör mal! *19* listen!
der Hörer(–) *9* receiver
der Hosenboden(¨) *21* seat of
    trousers, bottom
die Hosentasche(-n) *26* tröuser
    pocket
so gut wie meine eigene Hosentasche *26* like the back of
    my hand
das Hotel(-s) *1* hotel
der Hoteldiener(–) *2* hotel porter
hübsch *3* smart
hübscher *14* prettier, nicer
der Hund(-e) *4* dog
(das) Hundert(-e) *8* hundred
der Hunger *3* hunger
Hunger haben *3* to be hungry
husten *24* to cough
der Hustensaft(¨e) *24* coughmixture
der Hut(¨e) *23* hat
die Hutabteilung(-en) *23* millinery
    department
die Hütte(-n) *21* hut

I   ich *1* I
die Idee(-n) *8* idea
ihm *5* him (dat.)

ihn *2* him, it
ihnen *5* them (dat.)
Ihnen *1* you (dat.)
ihr *6* you, her (dat.)
ihr, ihre *1* her, *5* their
Ihr, Ihre *1* your
im = in + dem *4* on the,
    5 in the
immer *3* always
immer noch *10* still
in *1* in, *2* on, *7* at
inbegriffen *2* included
die Information(-en) *22* information
der Informationsstand *8* enquiry
    desk
die Inhaberin(-nen) *11* owner,
    proprietress
der Inhalt(-e) *24* sense, meaning,
    29 content, subject
innerhalb (von) *27* within
ins = in + das *3* to the
der Insasse(-n) *27* car occupant
interessant *22* interesting
das Interesse(-n) *16* interest
sich interessieren für *12* to be
    interested in
das Internat(-e) *15* boardingschool
international *28* international
das Interview(-s) *22* interview
inzwischen *13* in the meantime
irgendein *14* some or other,
    29 one, some, any
irgend etwas *17* something,
    anything
irgendwie *13* somehow, in any
    way
irgendwo *11* somewhere
der Irrtum(¨er) *12* error, mistake
ist *1* is (see **sein**)
ißt *3* eats (see **essen**)
der Italiener(–) *16* Italian (male)
das Italienisch *28* Italian (lang.)

J   ja *1* yes, *10* after all
das Jahr(-e) *7* year
die Jahreszeit(-en) *7* season

das Jahrhundert(-e) *12* century
der Januar *9* January
die Japanerin(-nen) *28* Japanese (female)
der Jazzkeller(-) *25* jazz club
je *24* at a time, *29* each
je eher desto besser *28* the sooner the better
oh je! *3* heavens, *21* oh dear!
jedenfalls *25* in any case
jeder *8* every, each, *9* everyone, each person
jedoch *18* however
jemand *9* someone, somebody
jetzig *28* present
jetzt *1* now
die Jugend *28* youth
das Jugendheim(-e) *13* youth centre
der Jugendliche(-n) *13* juvenile, young person
jung *3* young
der Junge(-n) *7* boy, son
die Jüngeren *16* younger ones

K das Kabarett(-s) *13* cabaret
der Kaffee *2* coffee
der Kaffeebaum(⁼e) *25* coffee tree
die Kaffeebohne(-n) *25* coffee bean
kalt *15* cold
die Kälte *24* cold
kam *22* came (see kommen)
die Kamera(-s) *27* camera
der Kanal(⁼e) *15* canal
kann *3* can (see können)
die Kantine(-n) *17* canteen
kaputt *2* out of order
die Karte(-n) *29* ticket
der Kartenkauf *29* buying tickets
die Kartenverkäuferin(-nen) *29* ticket-office clerk (fem.)
die Kartoffel(-n) *3* potato
der Käse(-) *28* cheese
die Kasse(-n) *8* cash-desk, *24* insurance
die Kassette(-n) *Intro.* cassette
der Kauf(⁼e) *29* buying, purchase
kaufen *2* to buy

das Kaufhaus(⁼er) *8* department store
kaum *7* hardly
kein *2* no, not a, none
der Kellner(-) *2* waiter
kennen (kannte, gekannt) *4* to know, be familiar with
sich kennen *11* to know each other
kennenlernen *10* to meet, get to know
die Kerze(-n) *20* candle
die Kette(-n) *25* chain
der Kilometer(-) *21* kilometre
das Kind(-er) *4* child
die Kindergärtnerin(-nen) *13* kindergarten teacher
die Kindheit *18* childhood
das Kino(-s) *3* cinema
klar *12* clear
die Klasse(-n) *16* class, form
das Kleid(-er) *14* dress, article of clothing
klein *6* small, little
das Kleingeld *4* change (money)
klingeln *19* to ring (bell)
klingen (klang, geklungen) *6* to sound
kochen *11* to cook, boil, make
die Kochkunst(⁼e) *12* cookery
der Koffer(-) *1* suitcase
der Kognak(-s) *1* brandy
der Kollege(-n) *1* colleague
die Kollegmappe(-n) *8* briefcase
komisch *22* strange, funny
kommen (kam, gekommen) *1* to come, *15* to get (to)
kommend *27* next, coming
das Kompliment(-e) *27* compliment
das Kompott(-e) *28* stewed fruit
die Konferenz(-en) *17* conference
können (kann, konnte, gekonnt) *3* to be able to (can) (see Appendix *11*)
das Konto (Konten) *23* account
der Kontrolleur(-e) *4* inspector
kontrollieren *21* to control, check

das **Konzert(-e)** *14* concert
der **Kopf("e)** *18* head
  aus dem Kopf *18* from
    memory
der **Körper(–)** *24* body
  am ganzen Körper *24* all over,
    in the whole body
die **Korrespondenz(-en)** *22*
  correspondence
  kosten *2* to cost
  wieviel kosten sie? *2* how
    much are they?
die **Kosten (Pl.)** *22* costs,
  expenditure
das **Kostüm(-e)** *25* fancy-dress
der **Krabbencocktail(-s)** *28* shrimp
  cocktail
der **Krach** *19* noise, din
  krank *24* ill, sick
der **Kranke(-n)** *26* sick person,
  patient
das **Krankenhaus("er)** *11* hospital
die **Krankenversicherung(-en)** *24*
  sickness and accident
  insurance
der **Krankenwagen(–)** *26* ambulance
die **Krankheit(-en)** *24* illness
der **Krieg(-e)** *11* war
  kriegen *11* to get (colloquial)
die **Kritik(-en)** *21* criticism
  kritisieren *25* to criticize
das **Krokodilleder** *8* crocodile
  skin
  krumm *11* crooked
die **Küche(-n)** *6* kitchen
der **Kuchen(–)** *5* cake
sich **kümmern um** *29* to see about,
  to worry about
der **Kunde(-n)** *6* customer
der **Kundendienst(-e)** *17* after-
  sales service
die **Kunst("e)** *9* art
der **Kunststoff(-e)** *8* plastic
der **Kurfürst(-en)** *15* Elector
das **Kursbuch("er)** *18* railway
  guide
  kurz *9* short(ly)

  kürzlich *18* recently
die **Kusine(-n)** *25* cousin (female)

L

  lächeln *26* to smile
  lächelnd *26* smiling
  lachen *24* to laugh
  sich halbtot lachen *24* to split
    one's sides laughing
  lächerlich *17* ridiculous
  lag *21* lay (see **liegen**)
die **Lage(-n)** *6* situation, site
das **Lager(–)** *17* warehouse
die **Lampe(-n)** *27* lamp
das **Land("er)** *6* country
  auf dem Land *6* in the country
  landen *1* to land
das **Landhaus("er)** *27* country
  house
die **Landschaft(-en)** *28* scenery,
  landscape
  lang *11* tall, long
  lange *5* long (time)
  noch lange nicht *9* far from
  länger *14* longer
  langsam *15* slow(ly)
  längst *22* long since
  schon längst *22* for a long time
  langweilig *27* boring
  las *22* read (see **lesen**)
  lassen (läßt, ließ, gelassen) *9*
    to leave, *12* to have some-
    thing done, *16* to let
  machen lassen *12* to have
    (something) done
  tun und lassen, was man will
    25 to do just what one likes
  laufen (läuft, lief, gelaufen) *15*
    to walk, *21* to run
die **Laune(-n)** *29* temper, mood
  laut *19* noisy
das **Leben** *13* life
  leben *11* to live
der **Lebenslauf("e)** *22* curriculum
  vitae, personal record
die **Leberknödelsuppe(-n)** *28* soup
  with liver dumplings
das **Leder** *8* leather

die **Lederhose(-n)** *25* leather trousers

die **Lederwaren (Pl.)** *8* leather articles, goods

leer *11* empty

legen *13* to put

die **Lehre(-n)** *18* apprenticeship

eine Lehre machen *18* to be apprenticed

der **Lehrer(-)** *Intro.* teacher

die **Lehrerin(-nen)** *18* teacher (woman)

der **Lehrling(-e)** *25* apprentice

leicht *5* easy, *24* light

es tut mir leid *5* I am sorry

leiden (litt, gelitten) *17* to suffer, *19* to bear

leidend *24* suffering, ailing

leider *2* unfortunately, *5* I'm afraid

leisten *26* to give, render

sich **(D) leisten** *21* to afford

der **Leiter(-)** *16* head, manager

die **Lektion(-en)** *1* lesson

lernen *21* to learn

lesen (liest, las, gelesen) *6* to read

letzt *13* last

die **Leute (Pl.)** *3* people

lieb *10* dear

die **Liebe** *12* love

lieben *4* to love

lieber *2* rather, preferably, *11* had better

liebst *14* favourite

lief ran (see **laufen**)

die **Lieferzeit(-en)** *17* delivery date

liegen (lag, gelegen) *6* to be (situated), *16* to lie

das **liegt daran, daß** *24* that's because

liegen lassen *13* to leave lying, *23* to forget

der **Liegesitz(-e)** *7* tip-back seat

liest *6* reads (see **lesen**)

der **Lift(-s)** *2* lift

lila(farben) *23* lilac coloured

die **Limonade(-n)** *2* lemonade

die **Linie(-n)** *4* number

links *6* on the left

der **Lippenstift(-e)** *27* lipstick

die **Literatur(-en)** *28* literature

die **Locke(-n)** *8* curl

lockig *8* wavy

sich **lohnen** *11* to be worth it

lokal *17* local

die **Lokalzeitung(-en)** *6* local paper

los! *26* stand back!, away!

also dann los! *15* right, let's go

was war los? *12* what happened? what went wrong?

lösen *4* to buy (ticket)

loswerden *19* to get rid of

(sie) **luden... ein** *28* (they) invited... (see **einladen**)

die **Luft** *18* air

der **Luftdruck** *21* pressure

mit **Luftpost** *5* by airmail

die **Lunge(-n)** *24* lung

lustig *25* funny, gay

M

machen *1* to do, *7* to have, take, *9* to make, go, *19* to give, *25* to cut

ein Examen machen *13* to sit an exam

eine Führung machen *9* to go on a tour

einen Spaziergang machen *9* to go for a walk

das macht nichts *9* never mind

das **Mädchen(-)** *5* girl

das mag *26* it might

(du) **magst** *21* (you) like (see **mögen**)

das **Make-up** *27* make-up

mal *10* sometime, *11* just

jetzt gehen Sie mal! *11* do go!

das **Mal(-e)** *11* time

zum ersten Mal *11* for the first time

man *4* one, you

manch- *13* some, quite a few

manchmal *4* sometimes

der **Mann($\ddot{}$er)** *2* husband, *4* man
das **Männergespräch(-e)** *3* men's talk
der **Mantel($\ddot{}$)** *13* coat
die **Mark** *4* mark (German currency unit)
die **Marmelade(-n)** *11* jam
der **März** *17* March
die **Maschine(-n)** *12* machine
mehr *8* more
nicht mehr *11* no longer
mehr oder weniger *17* more or less
mehrere *8* several
mein, meine, mein *1* my
meinen *20* to think
die **Meinung(-en)** *16* opinion
meiner Meinung nach *16* in my opinion
meist *16* most
meistens *14* mostly, usually
die **Meisterprüfung(-en)** *18* exam. for the title of "master" of a trade
sich **melden** *9* to answer
der **Meldezettel(–)** *2* registration form
die **Mensa (Mensen)** *14* student refectory
der **Mensch(-en)** *11* human being, individual, soul
Menschenskind! *19* good gracious!
messen (mißt, maß, gemessen) *24* to measure, take (temp.)
mich *2* me
das **Mietauto(-s)** *3* hired car
die **Miete(-n)** *6* rent
mieten *2* to hire
der **Mieter(–)** *6* tenant
das **Mietgesuch(-e)** *6* accommodation wanted
mindestens *17* at least
die **Minute(-n)** *4* minute
mir *5* me (dat.)
mit *2* with, *4* by, *7* in, *10* to
der **Mitarbeiter(–)** *17* colleague
mitbringen (-bringt, -brachte, -gebracht) *18* to bring (a present), to bring along
miteinander *18* together, jointly, with each other
mitgehen (-geht, -ging, -gegangen) *25* to go along (with)
mitkommen (-kam, -gekommen) *3* to come along (with)
der/die **Mitreisende(-n)** *18* fellow passenger (traveller)
der **Mittag(-e)** *3* noon
das **Mittagessen(–)** *3* lunch
zu(m) Mittag(essen) *3* for lunch
die **Mitte(-n)** *4* middle, centre
die **Mitternacht** *17* midnight
(der) **Mittwoch** *5* Wednesday
die **Möbel (Pl.)** *18* furniture
möbliert *6* furnished
mochte *23* wanted (see **mögen**)
möchte, möchten *2* would like
die **Mode(-n)** *14* fashion
die **Modenschau(-en)** *14* fashion show
modern *8* modern
modisch *18* fashionable
mögen (mag, mochte) *21* to like, to want to (See Appendix 11)
möglich *6* possible
die **Möglichkeit(-en)** *16* possibility
möglichst viel *28* as much as possible
der **Moment(-e)** *11* moment
Moment mal! *19* just a moment!
der **Monat(-e)** *6* month
im Monat *6* per month
(der) **Montag** *5* Monday
die **Montage(-n)** *17* assembly
morgen *3* tomorrow
morgen früh *3* tomorrow morning
morgens *7* in the morning
die **Mühe(-n)** *28* difficulty
(das) **München** *1* Munich
Münchner *4* of Munich
der **Münchner(–)** *11* person from Munich

der **Mund**(¨er) *24* mouth
das **Museum** (**Museen**) *9* museum
die **Musik** *25* music
die **Musikhochschule**(-n) *14* school of music
müssen (**muß, mußte, gemußt**) *3* to have to (must) (See Appendix **11**)
der **Mut** *26* courage
die **Mutter**(¨) *3* mother
mütterlicherseits *28* on the mother's side

N **na** *4* well
nach *1* to, *4* after, *8* according to, in keeping with
nach oben *2* upstairs
nach rechts *5* to the right
die **Nachbarin**(-nen) *11* neighbour (female)
nachdem *23* after
nachfüllen *21* to refill
nachgehen (-**ging, -gegangen**) *11* to go slow (watch etc.)
nachher *12* afterwards
der **Nachmittag**(-e) *5* afternoon
heute nachmittag *5* this afternoon
nächst *7* next
die **Nacht**(¨e) *2* night
das **Nachthemd**(-en) *25* nightdress
der **Nachtisch**(-e) *28* dessert
nachts *7* by night
der **Nachtzug**(¨e) *10* night train
nah *17* close, near
die **Nähe** *4* neighbourhood, *14* proximity
aus der Nähe *15* from close up
in der Nähe *4* around here
näher *17* closer
nahm took (see **nehmen**)
der **Name**(-n) *2* name
nämlich *7* namely, because, you see
nanu! *11* well, well!
die **Nase**(-n) *11* nose
vor der Nase *23* in front of my nose

naß *13* wet
natürlich *2* of course
neben *6* next to
nebenbei gesagt *25* by the way
der **Neffe**(-n) *11* nephew
nehmen (**nimmt, nahm, genommen**) *2* to take
nein *1* no
nennen (**nannte, genannt**) *13* to call, to name
nett *4* nice(ly)
neu *6* new
das **Neujahr** *21* New Year (1st of January)
neulich *14* recently
neun *2* nine
nicht *1* not
nicht mehr *11* no longer
nicht wahr? *1* isn't it? wasn't it? haven't you? etc.
nichts *1* nothing
nichts mehr *3* nothing more
nichts zu danken *4* that's all right, pleasure
nie *3* never
noch nie *15* never (yet)
niedrig *17* low
niemals *11* never
niemand *9* no one, nobody
niesen *24* to sneeze
nimmt *3* takes (see **nehmen**)
nirgends *13* nowhere
noch *2* still, *14* also
noch ein bißchen *3* a little more
noch einmal *3* again
noch etwas *3* some more, *10* something else
noch immer und überall *16* no matter where or when
noch mehr *6* even more
noch nicht *3* not yet
noch vor *9* before
was noch? *24* what else?
normal *24* normal
die **Norwegerin**(-nen) *25* Norwegian (female)
nötig *11* necessary
der **November** *7* November

die **Nummer(-n)** *2* number
nun *7* now, *12* well
nur *2* only
die **Nuß (Nüsse)** *20* nut

O   **ob** *12* whether, if
oben *8* upstairs, *25* at the top,
   above
dort oben *26* up there
von oben bis unten *25* from
   top to bottom
Herr **Ober!** *5* waiter!
oberst *17* top, highest
das **Obst** *28* fruit
obwohl *13* although
der **Ochs(-en)** *23* ox
oder *2* or
oder aber *26* or else
offiziell *25* official(ly)
öffnen *5* to open
oft *3* often
ohne *2* without
ohne weiteres *22* readily, easily
ohnmächtig *27* unconscious
das **Ohr(-en)** *11* ear
der **Oktober** *9* October
das **Oktoberfest** *25* October beer
   festival
das **Öl(-e)** *21* oil
der **Onkel(–)** *5* uncle
die **Oper(-n)** *29* opera
die **Operette(-n)** *29* operetta
der **Opernführer(–)** *29* opera guide
   (book)
in Ordnung *1* that's fine
das **Ortsgespräch(-e)** *9* local call
(das) **Ostern** *21* Easter

P   **ein paar** *2* a few
packen *9* to pack
(die) **Pädagogik** *10* education
die **Panne(-n)** *21* break-down
das **Parfum(-s)** *1* perfume
der **Park(-s)** *5* park
parken *8* to park
der **Parkplatz(¨e)** *17* car-park,
   29 parking space
die **Party(-s)** *19* party

der **Paß (Pässe)** *1* passport
der **Paßbeamte(-n)** *1* immigration
   officer, passport official
passen (D) *6* to suit, *14* to fit
passen zu *8* to go with
passend *22* suitable
passieren *12* to happen
die **Paßkontrolle** *1* immigration,
   passport control
der **Patient(-en)** *24* patient
die **Pause(-n)** *19* break, rest
die **Pellkartoffel(-n)** *28* potato in
   its jacket
die **Pension(-en)** *10* guest house
die **Person(-en)** *7* person
der **Personalausweis(-e)** *2* identity
   card
der **Personenzug(¨e)** *18* local
   train
persönlich *27* personal(ly)
die **Perücke(-n)** *12* wig
der **Pfennig(-e)** *4* penny (smallest
   unit of German currency)
pfui! *12* shame!
die **Phantasie(-n)** *25* imagination
das **Plakat(-e)** *17* poster
der **Platz(¨e)** *2* seat, *4* room,
   space, *19* square
plötzlich *19* sudden(ly)
die **Polizei** *26* police
die **Polizeiwache(-n)** *26* police station
der **Polizist(-en)** *5* policeman
die **Portion(-en)** *3* helping
(das) **Portugal** *22* Portugal
der **Portugiese(-n)** *16* Portuguese
   person (male)
die **Portugiesin(-nen)** *16* Portuguese person (female)
portugiesisch *16* Portuguese
   (language)
das **Porzellan** *8* china,
   porcelain
das **Postamt(¨er)** *5* post office
der **Postbeamte(-n)** *5* post office
   clerk
die **Postkarte(-n)** *5* post card
praktisch *22* practical(ly)

der Preis(-e) 8 price
die Preiselbeere(-n) 28 cranberry
der Preisunterschied(-e) 21 difference in price
preiswert 2 cheap
primitiv 21 primitive
privat 17 personal, private
die Privatschule(-n) 16 private school
das Problem(-e) 12 problem
der Professor(-en) 14 professor
prost! 3 cheers! your health!
das Protokoll(-e) 26 record, report
zu Protokoll nehmen 26 to make out an official report
prüfen 14 to examine, 21 to check
(die) Psychologie 10 psychology
das Publikum 29 public, audience
der Puder(-) 27 powder
der Pullover(-) 3 pullover, sweater
der Puls(-e) 24 pulse
der Punkt(-e) 26 point, dot
Punkt 12 Uhr 26 on the stroke of 12
pünktlich 10 on time

R das Radio(-s) 29 radio
der Rand(-er) 23 brim
das Rathaus(-er) 4 town hall
der Ratschlag(-e) 25 advice, piece of advice
rauchen 3 to smoke
rechnen mit 24 to reckon on, to bargain for
die Rechnung(-en) 8 bill, invoice
recht 30 pretty, very
recht haben 18 to be right
wenn es euch recht ist 9 if it's all right with you
rechts 5 on the right
nach rechts 5 to the right
rechtzeitig 17 on time
die Rede(-n) 21 words, talk
nicht der Rede wert 21 not worth mentioning
regelmäßig 5 regularly

der Regen 24 rain
regnen 13 to rain
der Reifen(-) 21 tyre
reinigen 12 to clean
die Reinigung(-en) 12 cleaner's, cleaning
die Reise(-n) 7 journey
gute Reise! 30 bon voyage! have a good journey
das Reisebüro(-s) 7 travel agency
der Reiseführer(-) 9 guide
reisen 7 to travel
der Reisepaß(-pässe) 1 passport
die Reisetasche(-n) 1 travelling-bag
die Reparatur(-en) 21 repair
die Reparaturwerkstatt(-en) 17 repair shop
der Reporter(-) 26 reporter
reservieren 13 to book, reserve
die Reservierung(-en) 2 reservation
die Residenz(-en) 15 residence
das Restaurant(-s) 2 restaurant
retten 26 to save
der Retter(-) 26 rescuer
die Rettung(-en) 26 rescue
das Rezept(-e) 24 prescription
richtig 1 right, 11 properly
die Richtung(-en) 4 direction
rief (an) 24 rang (up) (see anrufen)
die Riesenportion(-en) 12 giant helping
riesig 7 immensely, 17 huge
der Ring(-e) 13 ring
rot 8 red
das Rotkraut 28 red cabbage
der Rotwein(-e) 19 red wine
der Rückflug(-e) 22 return flight
die Rückkehr 19 return
rufen (rief, gerufen) 2 to call
in Ruhe 18 undisturbed
die Ruhepause(-n) 7 break, pause
ruhig 6 quiet
rund 8 round
die Rundfahrt(-en) 9 round trip, tour

russisch *28* Russian
russische Eier *28* Russian eggs

S   die Sache(-n) *2* thing
der Saft(⁼e) *8* juice
sagen *6* to say
sah *21* saw (see sehen)
die Sahne *2* cream
die Saison(-s) *7* season
der Salat(-e) *3* salad
die Salzkartoffeln *28* boiled
   potatoes
(der) Samstag *5* Saturday
saß *21* sat (see sitzen)
satt *16* satisfied
saubermachen *21* to clean
sauer *26* sour, bitter
der Sauerbraten(-) *28* stewed
   pickled beef
das Sauerkraut *12* sauerkraut,
   pickled cabbage
die Schachtel(-n) *3* packet
es ist schade! *6* it is a pity
schaden (D) *5* to harm
schaffen (schuf, geschaffen) *16*
  to create, accomplish
wir haben es geschafft *13* we
  have made it
der Schaffner(-) *4* conductor,
  18 guard
die Schallplatte(-n) *Intro.* record
der Schalter(-) *5* counter
sich schämen *12* to feel ashamed
das Scheckbuch(⁼er) *23* cheque
  book
die Scheibe(-n) *11* slice, piece
der Schein(-e) *4* (bank) note
scheinen (D) (schien, geschienen)
  17 to seem, appear
scheinen (schien, geschienen)
  30 to shine
schenken *12* to give (as a present)
schicken *5* to send
das Schiff(-e) *7* boat
schlafen (schläft, schlief, geschlafen) *6* to sleep
der Schlafsack(⁼e) *21* sleeping bag
das Schlafzimmer(-) *6* bedroom

schlank *8* slim
schlecht *3* bad
es geht ihm schlecht *24* he is
  not well
ihr wird schlecht *7* she gets sick
schlief *24* slept (see schlafen)
schließen (schloß, geschlossen)
  4 to close
schlimm *6* bad
nicht so schlimm! *20* don't
  worry
nichts Schlimmes *24* nothing serious
das Schlimmste *21* worst
der Schlittschuh(-e) *15* ice-skate
Schlittschuh laufen *15* to skate
schloß *26* closed (see schließen)
das Schloß (Schlösser) *14* palace,
  castle, *19* lock
schlucken *24* to swallow
der Schluß *13* end
zum Schluß *13* finally
der Schlüssel(-) *2* key
der Schlußverkauf(⁼e) *23* sale
schmecken *3* to taste
der Schmerz(-en) *24* pain
schmücken *20* to decorate
schmutzig *12* dirty
der Schnee *15* snow
die Schneeballschlacht(-en)
  28 snowball fight
die Schneekette(-n) *21* non-skid
  chain
der Schneemann(⁼er) *28* snowman
die Schneiderin(-nen) *18* dressmaker
schneien *15* to snow
schnell *7* soon, *10* fast, quickly
die Schnellstraße(-n) *17* clearway
der Schnupfen(-) *24* cold, sniffles
die Schokolade(-n) *11* chocolate
das Schokoladeneis *2* chocolate
  ice-cream
schon *2* already, *4* certainly
das schon *4* of course,
  that is possible
schon gut *11* that's fine
schon immer *18* always

schon längst *22* for a very long time
schon wieder *14* again
schön *1* nice, beautiful
der Schrank(¨e) *18* cupboard
der Schreck *26* fright
schrecklich *12* terribly
schreiben (schrieb, geschrieben) *6* to write
die Schreibkraft(¨e) *18* typist
die Schreibmaschine(-n) *22* typewriting, typewriter
der Schulbesuch(-e) *16* visit to a school
die Schuld *21* fault
die Schule(-n) *16* school
der Schüler(-) *16* pupil
die Schülerin(-nen) *16* schoolgirl
der Schuljunge(-n) *12* schoolboy
schwach *23* weak
der Schwager(-) *5* brother-in-law
die Schwägerin(-nen) *11* sister-in-law
schwarz *1* black
schwedisch *25* Swedish
der Schweinebraten(-) *29* roast pork
die Schweiz *21* Switzerland
schwer *4* hard, *7* difficult, *24* heavy, *26* serious
schwerfallen (D) (-fällt, -fiel, -gefallen) *14* to be difficult
die Schwester(-n) *3* sister
das Schwesterchen(-) *12* little sister
schwierig *4* difficult
die Schwierigkeit(-en) *18* difficulty
das Schwimmbad(¨er) *16* swimming pool
schwimmen (schwamm, geschwommen) *26* to swim
das Schwimmen *16* swimming
schwitzen *24* to sweat, perspire
sechs *2* six
sechzig *5* sixty
der See(-n) *28* lake
seelengut *11* kindhearted

das Segeln *16* sailing
sehen (sieht, sah, gesehen) *3* to see, look
die Sehenswürdigkeit(-en) *9* sight
sehr *2* very, *10* very much
sehr gern *3* with great pleasure
sehr gut *1* very well
seid *6* are (see sein)
die Seide(-n) *8* silk
seiden *8* silk
das Seidentuch(¨er) *8* silk scarf
sein (ist, war, gewesen) *1* to be (See Appendix 11)
sein, seine *2* his, its
seit *7* for, since
die Seite(-n) *15* side
seither *11* since then
die Sekretärin(-nen) *18* secretary
selb- *19* same
selber *14* oneself
selbst *2* self (myself, himself etc.)
selbständig *22* independent
selbstverständlich *3* of course, *30* self-evident, obvious
selten *3* seldom, rare(ly)
das Semester(-) *10* term
die Sendung(-en) *27* broadcast
das Service(-) *8* set (of crockery)
setzen *6* to put, place
sich setzen *11* to sit down
sicher *8* certainly, *28* surely
Sie *1* you
sie *1* they, *2* them
sie *1* she, it, *2* her
sieben *2* seven
siebte *7* seventh
siebzehn *2* seventeen
sieht *3* sees, looks (see sehen)
sind *1* are (see sein)
das Singen *13* singing
sinken (sank, gesunken) *26* to sink
die Sirene(-n) *26* siren
die Sitzbank(¨e) *6* bench-type seat
sitzen (sitzt, saß, gesessen) *7* to sit
der Ski(-er) *21* ski

der **Skikurs** *21* ski course
das **Skilaufen** *7* skiing
der **Skilehrer**(–) *21* ski instructor
so *4* so
eine so *8* such a
so daß *27* so that, with the
result that
sobald *11* as soon as
sofort *1* at once
sogar *18* even
der **Sohn**(ᵘe) *7* son
solange *24* as long as
solch- *12* such
sollen *3* to be to (ought)
(See Appendix **11**)
ich soll *8* I should
der **Sommer** *7* summer
sondern *5* but
die **Sonne**(-n) *30* sun
sonnig *6* sunny
(der) **Sonntag** *5* Sunday
sonst *11* in other respects,
otherwise, *13* or else
die **Sorge**(-n) *17* trouble, worry
soviel *7* as far as
so...wie... *11* as...as...
sowie *30* as well as
sowieso *18* anyway
sowohl...als auch... *22*
both...and...
(die) **Soziologie** *10* sociology
sozusagen *17* so to speak
(das) **Spanien** *22* Spain
der **Spanier**(–) *16* Spaniard (male)
die **Spanierin**(-nen) *16* Spaniard
(female)
spannen *21* to tighten
spannend *27* exciting
Spaß machen *19* to joke
es macht Spaß *4* I enjoy it
viel Spaß! *25* have fun!
spät *17* late
wie spät ist es? *3* what time is
it?
spätestens *9* at the latest
spazierengehen (-ging, -gegan-
gen) *15* to go for a walk
der **Spaziergang**(ᵘe) *9* walk

die **Speisekarte**(-n) *28* menu
die **Spezialität**(-en) *28* speciality
spielen *29* to play
das **Spielen** *13* play
der **Sport** *16* sport(s)
die **Sportart**(-en) *16* type of sport
der **Sportler**(–) *16* athlete, sportsman
die **Sprache**(-n) *28* language
die **Sprachkenntnis**(-se) *17* knowledge of the language
die **Sprachlehrerin**(-nen) *11*
language teacher (female)
sprang *26* jumped (see **springen**)
sprechen (**spricht, sprach, gesprochen**) *4* to speak, *19* to
talk
der **Sprecher**(–) *27* announcer
die **Sprechstundenhilfe**(-n) *24*
receptionist
spricht *4* speaks (see **sprechen**)
springen (**sprang, gesprungen**)
26 to jump
der **Staat**(-en) *29* state
das **Staatstheater**(–) *29* national
theatre
die **Stadt**(ᵘe) *4* town
der **Stadtbummel**(–) *3* stroll (in
the town)
die **Stadtmitte**(-n) *4* town centre
der **Stadtplan**(ᵘe) *26* street map
der **Stadtteil**(-e) *26* district (of
town or city)
der **Stand**(ᵘe) *8* stall, stand
stand *22* stood (see **stehen**)
stark *23* great(ly), strong
die **Station**(-en) *4* stop
statt *9* instead of
stattfinden (-findet, -fand, -ge-
funden) *7* to take place
stecken *12* to put, *19* to stick
stecken bleiben *17* to get stuck,
21 to break down
stecken lassen *19* to leave
(sticking in)
stehen (**stand, gestanden**)
4 to stand, to be

stehenbleiben (-blieb, -geblie-
ben) *19* to stay, to stop

steil *21* steep

die Stelle *29* place

an eurer Stelle *29* if I were in
your place

stellen *12* to put, to stand

die Stellung(-en) *22* position, job

die Stenographie *22* shorthand

sterben (stirbt, starb, gestorben) *26* to die

die Stewardeß(-essen) *7* hostess

der Stiefel(–) *15* boot

der Stil(-e) *15* style

das stimmt *8* that's true

stirbt *26* dies (see sterben)

der Stock *2* floor, storey

der Stoff(-e) *23* material

stolz *27* proud

stören *18* to inconvenience,
to disturb

stört es Sie? *18* do you mind?

die Straße(-n) *15* street, road

die Straßenbahn(-en) *4* tram,
tramway

die Straßenbahnfahrt(-en) *4* tram
journey

das Straßenbahnsystem(-e) *4* tram
system

der Strom *6* electricity (current)

strömen *24* to pour, *29* to rush

das Stück(-e) *4* coin, piece,
29 play

der Student(-en) *10* student

das Studentenheim(-e) *7* student
hall of residence

studieren *10* to study

das Studium (Studien) *14* study

der Stuhl(ᵈe) *8* chair

die Stunde(-n) *6* hour

stundenlang *17* for hours

stündlich *26* every hour

die Suche *14* search

suchen *6* to look (for)

die Suppe(-n) *28* soup

T der Tabak *1* tobacco

das Tablett(-s) *30* tray

die Tablette(-n) *24* tablet

tadellos *27* perfect

der Tag(-e) *7* day

guten Tag! *1* good morning,
good afternoon

die Tageszeit(-en) *7* time of day

täglich *6* daily

tagsüber *7* during the day

tanken *21* to refuel

der Tankwart(-e) *21* garage
attendant

die Tante(-n) *9* aunt

tanzen *16* to dance

das Tanzen *16* dancing

die Tasche(-n) *8* bag

die Tasse(-n) *5* cup

tat *24* did (see tun)

tätig sein *11* to work

das Tauchen *16* diving

(das) Tausend(-e) *17* thousand

das Taxi(-s) *9* taxi

der Techniker(–) *17* technician

technisch *22* technical

der Tee *5* tea

der Teil(-e) *1* part

zum größten Teil *22* for the
most part

teils *28* partly

teils, teils *6* fairly good, so-so

das Telegramm(-e) *5* telegram

das Telephon(-e) *2* telephone

das Telephonbuch(ᵈer) *9* telephone directory

telephonieren (D) *7* to telephone

die Temperatur(-en) *24* temperature

das Tennis *16* tennis

teuer *6* expensive

die Textilabteilung(-en) *8* "textiles" department

das Theater(–) *9* theatre

der Theaterabend(-e) *29* evening
at the theatre,

der Theaterbesucher(–) *29* theatregoer

die Theaterkasse(-n) *29* box-office

tief *28* deep

tiefer *19* below, lower

der ,**Tintenfischkeller**' *25*   **U**
   'Cuttlefish Cellar'
der **Tisch**(-e) *2* table
die **Tischdecke**(-n) *30* table-cloth
der **Tischler**(–) *18* carpenter
der **Tischlermeister**(-) *18* master carpenter
der **Toast**(-s) *11* toast, *13* health
der **Toaster**(–) *11* toaster
die **Tochter**(∺) *1* daughter
   todmüde *8* dead tired
die **Toilette**(-n) *6* W.C.
das **Tonband**(∺er) *Intro.* tape
das **Tonsignal**(-e) *9* pip (telephone)
der **Topf**(∺e) *11* pot
   tot *11* dead
der **Tourist**(-en) *4* tourist
   tragen (**trägt, trug, getragen**)
    2 to carry, *3* to wear,
    22 to meet (costs)
(wir) **tranken** *28* (we) drank (see
    trinken)
der **Transport**(-e) *26* transportation
   auf dem Transport *26* on the way
(wir) **traten** *27* (we) stepped (see
    treten)
   treffen (**trifft, traf, getroffen**)
    11 to meet, *22* to take
    (decision)
sich **treffen** (**trifft, traf, getroffen**)
    11 to meet each other
der **Treffpunkt**(-e) *23* meeting-
    place
die **Treppe**(-n) *25* stairs
   treten (**tritt, trat, getreten**)
    26 to step, go
   trifft *11* meets (see **treffen**)
   trinken (**trank, getrunken**)
    2 to drink
das **Trinkgeld**(-er) *12* tip
   trocken *15* dry
   trotz *27* in spite of
   trotzdem *14* in spite of it
   trug *23* wore (see **tragen**)
das **Tuch**(∺er) *8* scarf
   tun (**tut, tat, getan**) *13* to do
die **Tür**(-en) *3* door
das **Turnen** *16* P.T., gymnastics
   typisch *12* typical

   über *7* about, *9* across,
    through, *18* via, *19* on top
    of, over
   überall *13* everywhere
   überhaupt *21* at all, *25* after
    all
   überhaupt nicht *9* not at all
   übermorgen *6* the day after
    tomorrow
   übernächst- *10* the next but
    one
die **Überraschung**(-en) *11* surprise
   überrascht *22* surprised
der **Übersetzer**(–) *28* translator
   üblich *16* usual
   übrig *17* remaining, other,
    21 left
   übrig bleiben *27* to remain
   übrig haben *21* to have left
    over
   übrigens *11* by the way
   Uhr *2* o'clock
die **Uhr**(-en) *5* clock, watch
das **Uhrengeschäft**(-e) *5* watch-
    maker's
   um *12* by (the amount of),
    to the extent of, *15* round,
    24 for
   um zu *27* in order to
   um... Uhr *5* at... o'clock
die **Umgebung**(-en) *16* surround-
    ings
der **Umsatz**(∺e) *17* turnover
   umsteigen (**-stieg, -gestiegen**)
    4 to change (bus etc.)
   unangenehm *19* unpleasant
   unbedingt *23* whatever
    happens, at all costs, *24*
    come what may, necessarily,
    without fail
   und *1* and
   und dergleichen (**u. dgl.**) *13*
    and the like
   und so weiter (**usw.**) *8* and so
    on (etc.)
   unerwartet *11* unexpected
der **Unfall**(∺e) *26* accident
   unfreundlich *22* unpleasant

ungeduldig *23* impatient
ungefähr *14* about, approximately
ungern *23* unwillingly, reluctantly
das **Unglück(-e)** *27* accident, mishap
unglücklich *25* unfortunate, unsuccessful, unhappy
die **Universität(-en)** *10* university
unmöbliert *6* unfurnished
unmodern *23* old-fashioned
uns *2* us
unser, unsere *2* our
Unsinn! *26* nonsense!
unten *8* downstairs, *25* at the bottom, below
unter *6* under
unter uns *17* between ourselves
unterhalten (unterhält, unterhielt, unterhalten) *17* to entertain
sich **unterhalten** *11* to talk, converse
das **Unterhaltungsstück(-e)** *29* light comedy
der **Unterschied(-e)** *8* difference
unterwegs *28* on the way
unvernünftig *24* foolish, unreasonable
unzufrieden *21* discontented
der **Urlaub** *1* holiday
auf Urlaub *1* on holiday

V der **Vater(⁼)** *3* father
sich **verabreden** *22* to make an appointment
die **Verabredung(-en)** *9* appointment
sich **verabschieden** *11* to say goodbye, take one's leave
verantwortungsvoll *22* responsible
verbessern *22* to improve
verbieten (verbietet, verbot, verboten) *16* forbid, prohibit
verboten *16* forbidden, prohibited (see **verbieten**)
verdienen *18* to earn, *26* to deserve
vergangen *24* past, *27* last
vergessen (-gißt, -gaß, -gessen) *9* to forget
vergißt *9* forgets (see **vergessen**)
das **Vergnügen** *5* delight, pleasure
viel Vergnügen! *25* have a good time!
verheiratet *11* married
sich **verheiraten** *18* to get married
verkaufen *23* to sell
die **Verkäuferin(-nen)** *8* sales girl
der **Verkaufsingenieur(-e)** *Intro.* sales engineer
der **Verkehr** *17* traffic
verlangen *22* to demand
verlassen (-läßt, -ließ, -lassen) *7* to leave
sich **verlassen auf** *22* to rely on
sich **verlieben in** *28* to fall in love with
verlieren (verlor, verloren) *13* to lose
sich **verloben (mit)** *10* to become engaged (to)
die **Verlobung(-en)** *7* engagement
verloren *23* lost
vermieten *6* to let
der **Vermieter(-)** *6* landlord
die **Vermittlung(-en)** *7* operator
sich **verrechnen** *12* to miscalculate
sich **versammeln** *23* to rally, assemble
verschieden *8* various
verschreiben (verschrieb, verschrieben) *24* to prescribe
sich **versöhnen** *12* to patch up a quarrel
die **Versöhnung(-en)** *20* reconciliation
versorgen *7* to look after, *11* to provide
verstehen (verstand, verstanden) *3* to understand
sich **verstehen** *10* to get on
(wir) **verstünden** *29* (we) would

understand (see **verstehen**)

der **Versuch(-e)** *21* attempt

versuchen *12* to try

verunglücken *27* to have an accident

der **Verunglückte(-n)** *26* casualty, victim

die **Verwaltung(-en)** *17* administration

der, die **Verwandte(-n)** *3* relative

verzollen *1* to declare

der **Vetter(-n)** *11* cousin (male)

viel *2* much

viele *6* many

vielleicht *6* perhaps

vielmals *10* very much

vielseitig *22* varied

vier *2* four

vierhundert *6* four hundred

vierte *4* fourth

zu viert *16* in a group of four, as a foursome

das **Viertel(–)** *5* quarter

drei Viertel sechs *13* quarter to six

die **Viertelstunde** *4* quarter of an hour

das **Volk(¨er)** *28* people

voll *24* full

vom = von + dem *10* off the

von *1* of, *2* from, *10* off, *12* by

von jetzt ab *13* from now on

voneinander *30* from each other

vor *3* in front of, *6* ago, *9* before

vor einer Stunde *6* one hour ago

vor Freude *26* with joy

vorbei *26* past, over

vorbeifahren *17* to drive past

vorbereiten *18* to prepare

die **Vorbereitung(-en)** *3* preparation

vorgehen (-ging, -gegangen) *11* to go fast (watch etc.)

vorgestern *15* the day before yesterday

vorher *9* before

vorhin *17* a short while ago

vorig *11* last, previous

der **Vormittag(-e)** *5* morning

vorn *4* in front, at the front

Vorsicht! *4* look out! be careful!

vorsichtig *25* careful

die **Vorspeise(-n)** *28* hors d'oeuvre

vorstellen *4* to introduce

sich (D) **vorstellen** *12* to imagine

die **Vorstellung(-en)** *10* introduction, *29* performance

vorübergehend *24* temporarily

W der **Wagen(–)** *2* car

wählen *8* to choose, *9* to dial

während *9* in the course of, during, *30* while

wahrscheinlich *12* probably

der **Wald(¨er)** *28* wood, forest

die **Wand(¨e)** *18* wall

wann? *3* when?

die **Ware(-n)** *23* goods

wäre *7* would be (see **sein**)

(wir) **waren** *9* (we) were (see **sein**)

warm *11* warm

warten auf *4* to wait for

das **Wartezimmer(–)** *24* waiting-room

warum? *7* why?

was? *1* what?

was für ein? *6* what sort of?

(sich) **waschen** *18* to wash (oneself)

sich (D) (etwas) **waschen** *18* to wash (a part of oneself)

das **Wasser** *21* water

wechseln *4* to change

weder...noch *23* neither... nor

der **Weg(-e)** *5* way, *15* path

weg *6* gone, *15* away

wegen *9* because of

wegfahren (-fährt, -fuhr, -gefahren) *19* to go (drive) away

weggehen (-ging, -gegangen) *24* to leave, to go away

weh tun (D) *24* to hurt
weich *12* soft
(das) Weihnachten *8* Christmas
an Weihnachten *14* at Christmas
frohe Weihnachten! *20* Happy Christmas!
zu Weihnachten *8* for Christmas
der Weihnachtsbaum("e) *20* Christmas tree
das Weihnachtsfest(-e) *18* Christmas festivities
weil *11* because
der Wein(-e) *1* wine
der Weinkeller(-) *28* wine-cellar
(ich) weiß *5* (I) know (see wissen)
weiß *14* white
weit *2* far
welche *16* some, any
welcher? *7* which?
die Welt *16* world
wem? *4* to whom?
wen? *2* whom?
wenig *3* little, *20* few
um so weniger *29* all the less so
wenigstens *21* at least
wenn *6* when, if
wer? *1* who?
werden (wird, wurde, geworden) *7* to get, *24* to become
das Werk(-e) *17* works, factory
die Werkskantine(-n) *17* factory canteen
die Werkstatt("en) *3* workshop
wert *21* worth
wessen? *8* whose?
das Wetter *7* weather
wichtig *13* important
wie? *2* what?, *6* how?
wie *5* like, *7* as
wieder *7* again
immer wieder *29* very often, again and again
wiederholen *14* to take again, *27* to repeat

wiedersehen (-sieht, -sah, -gesehen) *10* to meet again
das Wiedersehen *3* reunion
auf Wiedersehen *2* goodbye
wiegen (wog, gewogen) *5* to weigh
wieviel? *2* how much?
wie viele? *5* how many?
will *3* want (see wollen)
willkommen in...! *3* welcome to...!
der Winter *7* winter
der Wintersport *15* winter sport(s)
wir *1* we
wird *7* gets, becomes (see werden)
wirken *23* to have an effect
wirklich *3* really
wissen (weiß, wußte, gewußt) *5* to know (a fact)
wo? *1* where?
die Woche(-n) *7* week
das Wochenende(-n) *16* weekend
wofür? *28* for what?
woher? *9* where from?
wohin? *3* where to?
wohl *14* probably, *26* well (in good health)
sich wohl fühlen *16* to feel at ease
wohnen *1* to live, *4* to stay
die Wohnung(-en) *6* flat, apartment
die Wohnungssuche *6* flat (house) hunting
der Wohnungsvermittler(-) *6* housing agent
die Wohnungsvermittlung(-en) *6* housing agency
das Wohnzimmer(-) *6* living-room
wollen (will, wollte, gewollt) *2* to want, *3* to want to (see Appendix **11**)
womit? *29* how? by what means?
das Wort("er /-e) *29* word
wovon? *29* about what?
kein Wunder! *24* no wonder!
wunderbar *3* wonderful

sich **wundern** *8* to be surprised
der **Wunsch**("e) *13* wish
wünschen *11* to wish, *13* hope
wurde *21* (see **werden**)
würden (Sie)? *17* would (you)?
(see **werden**)
wußte *21* knew (see **wissen**)

Z **zahlen** *4* to pay
der **Zahnarzt**("e) *24* dentist
sich **zanken** *12* to quarrel
zehn *2* ten
der **Zehnmarkschein**(-e) *4* ten
Mark note
zeigen *5* to show
sich **zeigen** *29* to be revealed
die **Zeit**(-en) *2* time
höchste Zeit *22* high time
längere Zeit *29* for a consid-
erable time
die **Zeitschrift**(-en) *14* magazine
die **Zeitung**(-en) *6* newspaper
der **Zentimeter**(-) *28* centimetre
die **Zentralheizung**(-en) *2* central
heating
das **Zentrum (Zentren)** *6* centre
die **Zeremonie**(-n) *13* ceremony
der **Zettel**(-) *6* note, slip of paper
der **Zeuge**(-n) *26* witness
das **Zeugnis**(-se) *22* certificate
ziehen (zieht, zog, gezogen)
21 to pull
ziemlich *4* rather, fairly, quite
die **Zigarre**(-n) *1* cigar
die **Zigarette**(-n) *1* cigarette
das **Zimmer**(-) *2* room
die **Zimmerreservierung**(-en)
2 reserving a room
die **Zitrone**(-n) *5* lemon
zittern vor *24* to shiver with
(sie) **zogen** *26* (they) pulled (see
ziehen)
zögern *27* to hesitate
der **Zollbeamte**(-n) *1* customs
officer
die **Zollkontrolle** *1* customs control

zornig *29* angry
zu *1* to, *7* at, *10* with, *11* on
zu *6* too
der **Zucker** *2* sugar
zueinander *25* together, to
each other
zuerst *5* first
der **Zufall**("e) *22* coincidence
durch Zufall *27* by chance
zufrieden *6* content
der **Zug**("e) *7* train
der **Zugführer**(—) *4* driver
(tram/train)
zukünftig *12* future
zum = zu dem *4* to the
zur = zu der *4* to the
zurück *4* back
**zurückbringen (-brachte, -ge-
bracht)** *29* to bring back
**zurückgeben (-gibt, -gab, -ge-
geben)** *29* to give back
zurückgebracht *29* brought
back (see **zurückbringen**)
zurückgehen (-ging, -gegangen)
21 to go back, to return
zusammen *3* together
**zusammenfallen (-fällt, -fiel,
-gefallen)** *19* to collapse
der **Zuschauer**(—) *27* spectator,
audience
der **Zuschauerbalkon**(-e)
30 spectators' balcony
zuverlässig *22* reliable
zwanzig *5* twenty
zwar *11* it is true, *13* actually,
really, *29* well
zwei *2* two
zweieinhalb *22* two and a half
zweimal *7* twice
zweistündig *9* lasting two
hours
zweite *2* second
zwischen *8* between
zwölf *3* twelve

English-German

A

a ein, eine
ability die Fähigkeit(-en)
to be able to können
about (**concerning**) über; (**approximately**) ungefähr, etwa; (**towards**) gegen
about that darüber
it is about es handelt von
above (**aloft**) oben; (**over**) über
above all vor allen Dingen
abroad im Ausland
absolutely not durchaus nicht
to accept entgegennehmen
accident der Unfall("e), das Unglück(-e)
to have an accident verunglücken
accommodation wanted das Mietgesuch(-e)
accompaniment (**vegetables**) die Beilage(-n)
to accomplish schaffen
according to nach
account das Konto (Konten)
account (**report**) der Bericht(-e)
on no account auf keinen Fall
acquaintance die Bekanntschaft(-en); (**person**) der/die Bekannte(-n)
across (**over**) über; (**through**) durch
actually eigentlich, zwar
in addition dazu
additional extra
address die Adresse(-n)
administration die Verwaltung(-en)
advertisement die Anzeige(-n)
advice der Ratschlag("e)
to afford sich (D) leisten
to be afraid fürchten, Angst haben
I'm afraid. . . leider. . .
after nach; hinterher; nachdem
to be after me hinter mir her sein
after-sales service der Kundendienst(-e)
afternoon der Nachmittag(-e)
good afternoon guten Tag
this afternoon heute nachmittag
afterwards danach, anschließend, nachher

again noch einmal, wieder, schon wieder
against gegen, an
against it dagegen
age das Alter
one hour ago vor einer Stunde
a short while ago vorhin
agreed einverstanden
ah! ah!
to come to one's aid zu Hilfe kommen
ailing leidend
air die Luft
by airmail mit Luftpost
airport der Flughafen("）
aisle der Gang("e)
alcohol der Alkohol
to alight aussteigen
all alle; (**whole**) ganz
all alone ganz allein
after all überhaupt, ja
all right in Ordnung
all right then also gut
if it's all right with you wenn es euch recht ist
at all überhaupt
not at all überhaupt nicht, gar nicht
that's all right nichts zu danken
to all (**of you**) allerseits
to allow erlauben
to be allowed to dürfen
almost fast
alone allein
along entlang
already schon
also auch, noch, außerdem, ebenfalls
although obwohl
always immer, schon immer
ambulance der Krankenwagen(-)
American der Amerikaner(-)
and und
angel der Engel(-)
angry böse, zornig
announcer der Sprecher(-)
to be annoyed, angry with sich ärgern über
to answer beantworten, sich melden, antworten (auf)

to be anxious to know gespannt sein
any welche, irgendein
in any case jedenfalls
in any event auf jeden Fall
anything etwas, irgend etwas
anyway sowieso
in any way irgendwie
apart from außer
apartment die Wohnung(-en)
to send one's apologies sich entschuldigen lassen
to apologize to sich entschuldigen bei
to appear erscheinen; **(seem)** scheinen
appetite der Appetit
apple der Apfel(ˮ)
applicant (female) die Bewerberin(-nen)
application die Bewerbung(-en)
appointment die Verabredung(-en)
to make an appointment sich verabreden
appreciation die Anerkennung(-en)
apprentice der Lehrling(-e)
to be apprenticed eine Lehre machen
apprenticeship die Lehre(-n)
approximately ungefähr
area die Gegend(-en)
around here in der Nähe
arrival die Ankunft(ˮe)
to arrive ankommen
art die Kunst(ˮe)
as als; **(because)** denn; **(like)** wie
as...as so... wie
as if als ob, als wenn
to feel ashamed sich schämen
to ask fragen
to ask for bitten um
to ask oneself sich fragen
to assemble sich versammeln
assembly die Montage(-n)
at an, auf, bei, in, zu
at ... o'clock um ... Uhr
athlete der Sportler(–)
attempt der Versuch(-e)
attendance der Besuch(-e)
audience die Zuschauer (Pl.)
aunt die Tante(-n)
automatically automatisch
autumn der Herbst
available frei

away weg; los!
are you aware? ist dir bekannt?

B
back zurück
at the back hinten
bad schlecht, schlimm
bag die Tasche(-n)
balcony der Balkon(-e)
ballet das Ballett(-s)
bank die Bank(-en)
bar die Bar(-s)
to bargain for rechnen mit
bath das Bad(ˮer)
bathroom das Badezimmer
Bavarian (male) der Bayer(-n)
Bavarian bayerisch
to be sein
to be familiar with kennen
to be (obliged/supposed) to sollen
to be (situated) liegen, sich befinden
to be (standing) stehen
bean die Bohne(-n)
to bear leiden
because weil, da, nämlich; **(for)** denn
because of wegen
to become werden
bed das Bett(-en)
bedroom das Schlafzimmer(–)
beer das Bier
before vor; bevor; **(previously)** vorher
to begin beginnen, anfangen
to begin on (something) damit beginnen
behind hinter
beige beige
to believe glauben
to belong to gehören (D)
below unter; unten
belt der Gürtel(–)
bench die Sitzbank(ˮe)
besides (also) außerdem
best am besten, best; das Beste
best possible allerbest
better besser
had better (preferably) lieber
between zwischen
between ourselves unter uns
big groß

bill die Rechnung(-en)
fancy biscuits das Gebäck
a little bit ein bißchen
bitter sauer
black schwarz
blanket die Decke(-n)
blue blau
boarding-school das Internat(-e)
boat das Schiff(-e)
body der Körper(-)
in the whole body am ganzen Körper
to boil kochen
boiled gekocht
bon voyage! gute Reise!
book das Buch(-er)
to book buchen, reservieren; anmelden
boot der Stiefel(-)
boring langweilig
born geboren
to borrow sich (D) etwas ausleihen
boss der Chef(-s)
both beide
both... and ... sowohl...als auch...
bottle die Flasche(-n)
bottom der Hosenboden(-)
at the bottom unten
boutique die Boutique(-n)
box-office die Theaterkasse(-n)
boy der Junge(-n)
brake die Bremse(-n)
branch (commercial) die Branche(-n)
brandy der Kognak(-s)
Brazil Brasilien
Brazilian brasilianisch
Brazilian (female) die Brasilianerin(-nen)
bread das Brot(-e)
break die Ruhepause(-n), die Pause(-n)
to break down stecken bleiben
breakdown die Panne(-n)
breakfast das Frühstück(-e)
to have breakfast frühstücken
bridge die Brücke(-n)
briefcase die Kollegmappe(-n)
brim der Rand(-er)
to bring bringen
to bring along mitbringen
to bring back zurückbringer
broad breit

broadcast die Sendung(-en)
brother der Bruder(-)
brother-in-law der Schwager(-)
brown braun
to build bauen
building das Gebäude(-)
bus der Bus(-se)
business der Betrieb(-e), das Geschäft
(-e); -matters (etwas) Geschäftliches
business conference die Geschäftskonfe-
renz(-en)
businessman der Geschäftsmann(-leute)
business report der Geschäftsbericht(-e)
busy season der Hochbetrieb
but aber, doch, sondern
butter die Butter
to buy kaufen, einkaufen
to buy (ticket) lösen
buying der Kauf(-e)
buying tickets der Kartenkauf
by bei, mit, von
by (the amount of) um
by... o'clock bis... Uhr

C
cabaret das Kabarett(-s)
red cabbage das Rotkraut
café das Café(-s)
cake der Kuchen(-)
call (telephone) der Anruf(-e)
local call das Ortsgespräch(-e)
to call rufen; (to name) nennen
call-box die Fernsprechzelle(-n)
called genannt
to be called heißen
camera die Kamera(-s)
can können; (be allowed to) dürfen
canal der Kanal(-e)
candle die Kerze(-n)
canteen die Kantine(-n)
capability die Fähigkeit(-en)
car das Auto(-s), der Wagen(-)
hired car das Mietauto(-s)
car-hire firm die Autovermietung(-en)
car park der Parkplatz(-e)
care of (c/o) bei
careful vorsichtig
be careful! Vorsicht!

caretaker die Hausmeisterin(-nen) (fem)
carnival der Fasching
carpenter der Tischler(-)
to carry tragen
to carry out erledigen
in case falls
cash das Bargeld
cash-desk die Kasse(-n)
cassette die Kassette(-n)
castle die Burg(-en), das Schloß
  (Schlösser)
casualty der Verunglückte(-n)
to catch cold sich (D) eine Erkältung holen
cause der Grund(¨e)
to celebrate feiern
centimetre der Zentimeter(-)
centre das Zentrum(Zentren), die Mitte(-n)
century das Jahrhundert(-e)
ceremony die Zeremonie(-n)
certain bestimmt
certainly schon, sicher
certificate das Zeugnis(-se)
chain die Kette(-n)
non-skid chain die Schneekette(-n)
chair der Stuhl(¨e)
by chance durch Zufall
change(money) das Kleingeld
to change
(exchange, alternate) wechseln;
(bus, train, etc.) umsteigen;
(undergo change) sich ändern
chauffeur der Chauffeur(-e)
cheap preiswert, billig
to check kontrollieren, prüfen
cheers! prost!
cheese der Käse(-)
cheque book das Scheckbuch(¨er)
chief der Chef(-s)
child das Kind(-er)
childhood die Kindheit
china das Porzellan
chocolate die Schokolade(-n)
to choose wählen
Christmas (das) Weihnachten
Christmas festivities das Weihnachts-
  fest(-e)
Christmas tree der Weihnachtsbaum(¨e)
at Christmas an Weihnachten

for Christmas zu Weihnachten
Happy Christmas frohe Weihnachten
cigar die Zigarre(-n)
cigarette die Zigarette(-n)
cinema das Kino(-s)
class die Klasse(-n)
to clean reinigen, saubermachen
cleaners, cleaning die Reinigung(-en)
clear klar
clearway die Schnellstraße(-n)
to climb (go) down hinuntersteigen
cloak-room die Garderobe(-n)
clock die Uhr(-en)
close, closer nah, näher
to close schließen
from close up aus der Nähe
closed geschlossen
article of clothing das Kleid(-er)
clown der Clown(-s)
club der Club(-s)
coach der Bus(-se)
coat der Mantel(¨)
coffee der Kaffee
coffee bean die Kaffeebohne(-n)
coffee tree der Kaffeebaum(¨e)
coin das Stück(-e)
coincidence der Zufall(¨e)
cold kalt; die Kälte; (illness) die Er-
  kältung(-en), der Schnupfen(-)
cold as ice eiskalt
to collapse zusammenfallen
colleague der Kollege(-n)
to collect abholen
college of commerce die Handels-
  schule(-n)
to colour bemalen
of one colour einfarbig
coloured farben, bemalt
to come kommen
to come along (with) mitkommen
to come between dazwischenkommen
to come down herunterkommen
to come here herkommen
come what may unbedingt
light comedy das Unterhaltungsstück(-e)
comfortable bequem; (cosy) gemütlich
coming kommend
commercial firm die Handelsfirma (-en)

292

company die Firma(Firmen), die Gesellschaft(-en)

to keep someone company einem Gesellschaft leisten

compartment das Abteil(-e)

to complain sich beschweren

complete(ly) ganz

compliment das Kompliment(-e)

computer der Computer(–)

concert das Konzert(-e)

to conduct führen

conducted tour die Führung(-en)

conductor der Schaffner(–)

conference die Konferenz(-en)

to congratulate gratulieren(D)

to consider halten für

content der Inhalt(-e)

content zufrieden

to continue fortsetzen

continuously dauernd

on the contrary im Gegenteil

to control kontrollieren

conversation das Gespräch(-e)

to converse sich unterhalten

to cook kochen

electric cooker der Elektroherd(-e)

cookery die Kochkunst(¨e)

corner die Ecke(-n)

round the corner um die Ecke

correspondence die Korrespondenz(-en)

corridor der Flur(-e)

to cost kosten

costs die Kosten (pl.)

cosy gemütlich

couch die Couch(-es)

to cough husten

cough-mixture der Hustensaft(¨e)

counter der Schalter(–); die Bar(-s)

country das Land(¨er)

in the country auf dem Land

country house das Landhaus(¨er)

married couple das Ehepaar(-e)

courage der Mut

of course natürlich, selbstverständlich, das schon

in the course of während

cousin (male) der Vetter(-n)

cousin (female) die Kusine(-n)

to cover decken

cranberry die Preiselbeere(-n)

cream die Sahne

to create schaffen

criticism die Kritik(-en)

to criticize kritisieren

crocodile skin das Krokodilleder

crooked krumm

cup die Tasse(-n)

cupboard der Schrank(¨e)

cure das Heilmittel(–)

to curl drehen

curl die Locke(-n)

curling das Eisschießen

curriculum vitae der Lebenslauf(¨e)

customer der Kunde(-n)

customs control die Zollkontrolle

customs officer der Zollbeamte(-n)

'Cuttlefish Cellar' der ‚Tintenfischkeller‘

D

daily täglich

to dance tanzen

dancing das Tanzen

Danish dänisch

dark dunkel

darker dunkler

daughter die Tochter(¨)

day der Tag(-e)

dead tot

dear lieb

oh dear! oh je!

December der Dezember

to decide in favour of sich entscheiden für

decision die Entscheidung(-en)

to declare verzollen

to decorate schmücken

deep tief

definite(ly) bestimmt

delicious herrlich

delight das Vergnügen(–)

delivery date die Lieferzeit(-en)

to demand verlangen

dense dicht

dentist der Zahnarzt(¨e)

department die Abteilung(-en)

departure die Abfahrt(-en); der Abschied(-e)

on departure zum Abschied
that depends on das kommt darauf an, das hängt davon ab
to deserve verdienen
desired gewünscht
dessert der Nachtisch(-e)
detail die Einzelheit(-en)
to dial wählen
dialect der Dialekt(-e)
to die sterben
difference der Unterschied(-e)
difference in price der Preisunterschied(-e)
different(ly) anders
difficult schwierig
to be difficult schwerfallen (D)
anything difficult alles, was schwierig ist
difficulty die Schwierigkeit(-en), die Mühe(-en)
din der Krach
dining-area die Eßecke(-n)
dining-room das Eßzimmer(-)
direct(ly) direkt
direction die Richtung(-en)
dirty schmutzig
discontented unzufrieden
discothèque die Diskothek(-en)
to discuss besprechen
dish das Gericht(-e)
diving das Tauchen
to do machen, tun
doctor der Doktor(-en), der Arzt(⁼e)
dog der Hund(-e)
door die Tür(-en)
dot der Punkt(-e)
double-room das Doppelzimmer(-)
down hinunter
down to bis auf
downstairs unten
dreadful(ly) entsetzlich
dress das Kleid(-er)
to dress (oneself) (sich) anziehen
dressmaker die Schneiderin(-nen)
to drink trinken
drink das Getränk(-e)
to drive fahren
to drive past vorbeifahren
driver der Fahrer(-), der Chauffeur(-e)

train driver der Zugführer(-)
driving-licence der Führerschein(-e)
dry trocken
during während
during the day tagsüber
to dye färben

E
each jeder
each other gegenseitig
each person jeder
to each other zueinander
with each other miteinander
ear das Ohr(-en)
early früh
to earn verdienen
easiest am einfachsten
easily ohne weiteres
Easter (das) Ostern
easy leicht, einfach
not so easy nicht ganz einfach
quite easy ganz leicht
to eat essen
education die Erziehung, Pädagogik
to have an effect wirken
egg das Ei(-er)
eight acht
eighteen achtzehn
eighth achte
either... or entweder...oder
Elector der Kurfürst(-en)
electricity der Strom
elegant elegant
eleven elf
anything else? sonst noch etwas?
or else sonst, oder aber
something else noch etwas
what else? was noch?
to employ anstellen
employee der/die Angestellte(-n)
empty leer
to empty (drink up) austrinken
end das Ende(-n), der Schluß
engaged besetzt
to become engaged to sich verloben mit
engagement die Verlobung(-en)
Englishman der Engländer (-)

English woman die Engländerin(-nen)
enjoyment der Genuß (Genüsse)
enough genug
to enquire after sich erkundigen nach
to enter hereinkommen, eintreten
to entertain unterhalten
entirely ganz
error der Irrtum(-er)
especially besonders
even sogar
even if auch wenn
not even nicht einmal
in the evening abends
good evening guten Abend
this evening heute abend
eventful ereignisreich
every jeder, alle (Pl.)
everyone jeder
everything alles
everywhere überall
self-evident selbstverständlich
exactly genau, ganz genau
examination das Examen(-)
secondary-school leaving examination, ('A' levels) das Abitur
exam for the title of 'master' of a trade die Meisterprüfung(-en)
to sit an exam. ein Examen machen
to examine prüfen
example das Beispiel(-e)
for example zum Beispiel (z.B.)
excellent ausgezeichnet
exceptionally einmalig
excitement die Aufregung(-en)
exciting spannend
something exciting etwas Aufregendes
excuse me! Entschuldigung! entschuldigen Sie!
exhibition die Ausstellung(-en)
to expect erwarten
expenditure die Kosten (pl.)
expensive teuer
to explain erklären
to the extent of um
extra extra
extremely äußerst
eye das Auge(-n)

F
face das Gesicht(-er)
factory die Fabrik(-en), die Firma (Firmen), das Werk(-e)
main factory das Hauptwerk(-e)
factory canteen die Werkskantine(-n)
to faint ohnmächtig werden
fairly ziemlich
fairly good teils, teils
to fall fallen
to fall in love with sich verlieben in
family die Familie(-n)
famous berühmt
fanatical(ly) fanatisch
fancy dress das Faschingskleid(-er), das Kostüm(-e)
far weit
as far as soviel
far from noch lange nicht
to say farewell zum Abschied
fashion die Mode(-n)
fashion show die Modenschau(-en)
fashionable modisch
fast schnell
fat dick, fett
father der Vater(-)
fault die Schuld
favourite liebst
fear die Angst(-e)
to fear fürchten
feast das Fest(-e)
to feel (sich) fühlen
to feel at ease sich wohl fühlen
to feel cold frieren
he feels ill es geht ihm schlecht
fencing das Fechten
festival, feast das Fest(-e), der Feiertag(-e)
to fetch holen
fever das Fieber(-)
few paar, wenig
field das Gebiet(-e)
fifteen fünfzehn
fifth fünfte
figure die Figur(-en)
to fill in ausfüllen
film der Film(-e)
finally zum Schluß
that's fine schon gut, in Ordnung ●

to find finden
to find satisfaction in Freude haben an
to finish aufhören, fertig werden, zu
　Ende bringen
finished fertig
Finn (male) der Finne(-n)
Finn (female) die Finnin(-nen)
fire das Feuer(–)
fire brigade die Feuerwehr
firm der Betrieb(-e), die Firma (Firmen)
electrical firm der Elektrobetrieb(-e)
first erste, zuerst
to give first aid erste Hilfe leisten
for the first time erst
first of all erst einmal
fish der Fisch(-e)
to fit passen (D)
five fünf
flat die Wohnung(-en)
flight der Flug(¨e)
outward flight der Hinflug(¨e)
return flight der Rückflug(¨e)
to flock in hereinströmen
floor der Stock, der Boden(¨)
flower die Blume(-n)
flowery geblümt
fluent(ly) fließend
to fly fliegen
food das Essen(–)
foolish unvernünftig
foot der Fuß(¨e)
on foot zu Fuß
football der Fußball(¨e)
for für, auf, zu, seit, aus, bei, um
for it darum
for that dazu
forbid verbieten
foreign fremd, ausländisch
foreign language die Fremdsprache(-n)
foreigner der Ausländer(–)
forest der Wald(¨er)
to forget vergessen, liegen lassen
form die Form(-en)
form (paper) das Formular(-e)
form (class) die Klasse(-n)
formerly früher
fortunately zum Glück
four vier

four hundred vierhundert
as a foursome zu viert
fourth vierte
Franconian fränkisch
of, from Frankfurt Frankfurter
free frei
to freeze frieren
French französisch
Frenchman der Franzose(-n)
French woman
　die Französin(-nen)
fresh frisch
Friday (der) Freitag(-e)
friend der Freund(-e), der Bekannte(-n)
friendly befreundet, freundlich
fright die Angst(¨e), der Schreck
to frighten Angst machen
frightful(ly) furchtbar
from aus, von, ab, bei
from it daraus
in front vorn
in front of vor
fruit die Frucht(¨e), das Obst
stewed fruit das Kompott(-e)
full voll
have fun! viel Spaß!
funny komisch, lustig
furnished möbliert
furniture die Möbel (pl.)
further up höher hinauf
future zukünftig

G
gallery die Galerie(-n)
gangway der Gang(¨e)
garage die Garage(-n), die Autowerk-
　statt(¨en)
garage attendant der Tankwart(-e)
garden der Garten(¨)
to gargle gurgeln
gay lustig
generation die Generation(-en)
gentleman der Herr(-en)
German deutsch
German (male) der Deutsche(-n)
German (language) das Deutsch
German (people) Deutsche
standard German das Hochdeutsch

Germany Deutschland
to get (receive) bekommen; **(become)**
  werden; **(obtain)** kriegen
to get off aussteigen
to get on/in einsteigen
to get on well sich gut verstehen
to get to kommen nach/zu
to get up aufstehen
gift das Geschenk(-e)
girl das Mädchen(–)
girl-friend die Freundin(-nen)
to give geben
to give (as a present) schenken
to give back zurückgeben
to give up (stop) aufhören
I'm glad das freut mich
glad, froh
glance der Blick(-e)
glass das Glas(¨er)
small glass das Gläschen(–)
glorious herrlich
glove der Handschuh(-e)
to go gehen
to go (in vehicle) fahren
to go along (with) mitgehen
to go away wegfahren
to go back zurückgehen
to go fast (watch etc.) vorgehen
to go on for dauern
right, let's go! also, dann los!
to go out ausgehen
to go slow (watch, clock etc.) nachgehen
to go (to) hingehen
to go with passen zu
going out das Ausgehen
gone weg
ah good! ah gut!
good gut
good! bravo!
good gracious! ach du meine Güte!,
  Menschenskind!
something good etwas Gutes
good-bye auf Wiedersehen
to say good-bye sich verabschieden,
  Abschied nehmen
goods die Ware(-n)
roast goose der Gänsebraten(–)

gourmet (female) die Feinschmeckerin
  (-nen)
grand-parents die Großeltern (pl.)
great (large) groß; **(strong)** stark
greatest größst-
green grün
to greet grüßen
ground-floor das Erdgeschoß (Erd-
  geschosse)
in a group of four zu viert
to grow up aufwachsen
guard der Schaffner(–)
guest der Gast(¨e)
guest house die Pension(-en)
guide der Reiseführer(–)
to guide führen
gymnastics das Turnen

H

hair das Haar(-e)
hairdresser der Friseur(-e)
half halb; die Hälfte(-n)
half past twelve halb eins
hall der Flur(-e)
student hall of residence das Studenten-
  heim(-e)
hand die Hand(¨e)
on the other hand dagegen
like the back of my hand so gut wie
  meine eigene Hosentasche
handbag die Handtasche(-n)
handicraft die Handarbeit(-en)
to hang (something) hängen an
to be hanging hängen
to happen passieren
what happened? was war los?
whatever happens unbedingt
happy glücklich, froh
hard hart, fest; **(difficult)** schwer
hardly kaum
hard-working fleißig
to harm schaden (D)
hat der Hut(¨e)
to have haben
to have to müssen, brauchen
to have breakfast frühstücken
to have knowledge of Bescheid wissen
to have one's turn drankommen

to have something done machen lassen
he er
head der Kopf("e); der Leiter(–),
  der Chef(-s)
headmaster der Direktor(-en)
health die Gesundheit; der Toast
your health prost
healthy gesund
to hear hören
heart das Herz(-en)
heartfelt herzlich
to heat heizen
central heating die Zentralheizung(-en)
heaven der Himmel(–)
heavens! oh je!
good heavens! mein Gott!, du lieber
  Himmel!, um Himmels willen!
thank heavens! Gott sei Dank!
heavy schwer
to help helfen (D)
help die Hilfe(-n)
to shout for help um Hilfe rufen
helping die Portion(-en)
giant helping die Riesenportion(-en)
her ihr, ihre; sie, ihr
here hier; (to this place) hierher
here (at my house) bei mir
hero der Held(-en)
to hesitate zögern
hey! hallo!
high hoch, hohe
higher höher
higher up höher hinauf
highest höchst, oberst
highly trained hochqualifiziert
him ihn; ihm
to hire mieten
to hire out ausleihen
his sein, seine
historical historisch
hoarse heiser
to hold abhalten
hold your tongue! halt deinen Mund!
to hold up hochhalten
holiday der Urlaub, der Feiertag(-e)
holidays die Ferien (pl.)
to have a holiday frei haben
on holiday auf Urlaub

holiday period die Ferienzeit(-en)
at home zu Haus
home(ward) nach Haus
home-sickness das Heimweh
to hope hoffen
I hope (so) hoffentlich
hors d'œuvre die Vorspeise(-n)
hospital das Krankenhaus("er)
hostess die Stewardeß(-ssen), die Gast-
  geberin(-nen)
hot heiß
hotel das Hotel(-s)
hotel porter der Hoteldiener(–)
hour die Stunde(-n)
every hour stündlich
for hours stundenlang
house das Haus("er)
household der Haushalt(-e)
housewife die Hausfrau(-en)
household utensil das Haushaltsgerät(-e)
house-hunting die Wohnungssuche
housing agency die Wohnungsvermitt-
  lung(-en)
housing agent der Wohnungsvermitt-
  ler(–)
how? wie?
how are you? wie geht es Ihnen?
how do you do? guten Tag
how long? wie lange?
how many? wie viele?
how much? wieviel?
how much are they? wieviel kosten sie?
however jedoch, aber
huge riesig
human being der Mensch(-en)
hundred das Hundert(-e)
to be hungry Hunger haben
hurrah hurrah
to hurry sich beeilen, eilen
to hurt weh tun (D)
husband der Mann("er)
hut die Hütte(-n)

I
I ich
ice das Eis
ice-cream das Eis
chocolate ice-cream das Schokoladeneis

idea die Idee(-n), die Ahnung(-en)
identity card der Ausweis(-e), der Personalausweis(-e)
idiot der Dummkopf(⸚e)
if wenn; (**whether**) ob
ill krank
he feels ill es geht ihm schlecht
illness die Krankheit(-en)
imagination die Phantasie(-n)
to imagine sich (D) vorstellen
immense(ly) riesig
immigration die Paßkontrolle
immigration officer der Paßbeamte
impatient ungeduldig
important wichtig
impression der Eindruck(⸚e)
to improve verbessern
in in, mit, für, auf, an, zu
incidentally nebenbei
included inbegriffen
to inconvenience stören
independent selbständig
individual der Mensch(-en)
information die Auskunft(⸚e), die Information(-en)
insert einwerfen
inside drinnen
inspector der Kontrolleur(-e)
to install einrichten
instance der Fall(⸚e)
instead dafür
instead of statt
to instruct anlernen
insurance die Kasse(-n)
sickness and accident insurance die Krankenversicherung(-en)
interest das Interesse(-n)
to be interested in sich interessieren für
interesting interessant
international international
to intervene dazwischen kommen
interview das Interview(-s), das Gespräch(-e)
into in
to introduce vorstellen, bekanntmachen
introduction die Vorstellung(-en)
invitation die Einladung(-en)
to invite einladen

invoice die Rechnung(-en)
isn't it? (wasn't it?) nicht wahr?
it es, sie, er; ihn
Italian (male) der Italiener(–)
Italian (language) das Italienisch
its sein, seine

J
jam die Marmelade(-n)
January der Januar
Japanese (female) die Japanerin(-nen)
jazz club der Jazzkeller(–)
jealous of eifersüchtig auf
job (occupation) der Beruf(-e); (**position**) die Stellung(-en)
to joke Spaß machen
journey die Fahrt(-en), die Reise(-n)
have a good journey gute Reise!
with joy vor Freude
juice der Saft(⸚e)
to jump springen
just gerade, eben, mal, halt
just as genauso
juvenile der Jugendliche(-n)

K
to keep behalten
key der Schlüssel(–)
kilometre der Kilometer(–)
kind freundlich
kindergarten teacher (female) die Kindergärtnerin(-nen)
kindhearted seelengut
kitchen die Küche(-n)
to know (person/place) kennen; (**fact**) wissen
to know each other sich kennen
to get to know kennenlernen
to know (how) Bescheid wissen
do you know? ist dir bekannt?
let me know sagen Sie mir Bescheid
known bekannt
pig's knuckle das Eisbein

L
there is a lack of es fehlt an (D)
lacking fehlend
lad der Bursche(-n)

ladies and gentlemen die Herrschaften
lady die Dame(-n)
lake der See(-n)
lamp die Lampe(-n)
to land landen
landlord der Vermieter(–)
landscape die Landschaft(-en)
language die Sprache(-n)
knowledge of the language die Sprach-
  kenntnis(-se)
language teacher (female) die Sprach-
  lehrerin(-nen)
to last dauern
last letzt; (past) vorig, vergangen
at last endlich
lasting three years dreijährig
late spät
to laugh lachen
to split one's sides laughing sich halbtot
  lachen
to lay (a table) decken; (put) legen
to lead führen
leaf das Blatt (¨er)
to learn lernen
at least mindestens, wenigstens
leather das Leder
leather articles, goods die Lederwaren
leather trousers die Lederhose(-n)
to leave lassen, verlassen
to leave (depart) abfahren, weggehen
to leave lying liegen lassen
left over übrig
on the left links
leisure die Freizeit(-en)
lemon die Zitrone(-n)
lemonade die Limonade(-n)
all the less so um so weniger
lesson die Lektion(-en)
to let lassen; (property) vermieten
letter der Brief(-e)
to lie liegen
life das Leben
lift der Lift(-s)
light leicht; (in colour) hell
like wie
to like mögen, gern haben
how do you like? wie finden Sie?
I like it es gefällt mir

to like drinking gern trinken
to like eating gern essen
would like möchte, möchten
everybody to his liking jeder nach seinem
  Geschmack
and the like und dergleichen (u. dgl.)
lilac coloured lila(farben)
lipstick der Lippenstift(-e)
listen! hör mal!
listen to (with stethoscope) abhorchen
literature die Literatur
little klein; (not much) wenig
a little more noch ein bißchen
to live wohnen, leben
living-room das Wohnzimmer(–)
local lokal, dortig
lock das Schloß (Schlösser)
long lang; (time) lange
as long as solange
long-distance call das Ferngespräch(-e)
long-distance telephone exchange das
  Fernamt(¨er)
longer länger
no longer nicht mehr
look der Blick(-e)
to look sehen, ansehen; aussehen
to look after versorgen
to look at sich (D) ansehen
to look for suchen
to look forward to sich freuen auf
look out! Vorsicht!, Achtung!
to lose verlieren
lost verloren
love die Liebe
to love lieben
low niedrig
to lower (price) herabsetzen
luck das Glück
luckily zum Glück
to be lucky Glück haben
luggage das Gepäck
lunch das Mittagessen(–)
for lunch zu(m) Mittag(essen)
lung die Lunge(-n)

M
machine die Maschine(-n)
made of aus

we have made it wir haben es geschafft
magazine die Zeitschrift(-en)
to make machen, bauen
to make (tea, coffee etc.) kochen
to make out an official report zu Protokoll nehmen
make-up das Make-up
to make up one's mind sich entschließen
man der Mann("er)
manage (to) gelingen (zu)
manager der Leiter(-)
many viele
March der März
mark (German currency unit) die Mark
married verheiratet
to get married sich verheiraten
to marry heiraten
material der Stoff(-e)
that doesn't matter das macht nichts
may (be allowed to) dürfen
me mich; mir
meal das Essen(-)
meaning der Inhalt(-e)
by no means durchaus nicht
by what means? womit?
in the meantime inzwischen
to measure messen
motor mechanic der Automechaniker(-)
to meet treffen; **(get to know)** kennenlernen
to meet (costs) tragen
to meet again wiedersehen
to meet each other sich treffen
to go to meet abholen
meeting place der Treffpunkt(-e)
from memory aus dem Kopf
not worth mentioning nicht der Rede wert
men's talk das Männergespräch(-e)
menu die Speisekarte(-n)
merely bloß
middle die Mitte(-n)
midnight die Mitternacht
it might das mag
it might be es dürfte sein
millinery department die Hutabteilung(-en)
do you mind? stört es Sie?
I don't mind es ist mir egal

never mind das macht nichts
minute die Minute(-n)
to miscalculate sich verrechnen
mishap das Unglück(-e)
Miss das Fräulein(-)
to be missing fehlen
mistake der Irrtum("er), der Fehler(-)
mixed gemischt
modern modern, heutig
moment der Augenblick(-e), der Moment(-e)
any moment jeden Augenblick
at the last moment im letzten Augenblick
at the moment im Augenblick
just a moment Moment mal!
Monday (der) Montag
money das Geld
month der Monat(-e)
per month im Monat
mood die Laune(-n)
more mehr
even more noch mehr
nothing more nichts mehr
some more noch etwas
more or less mehr oder weniger
morning der Vormittag(-e)
good morning guten Tag, guten Morgen
in the morning morgens
most meist
mostly meistens
mother die Mutter(")
on the mother's side mütterlicherseits
mountain der Berg(-e)
mountain hut die Berghütte(-n)
mouth der Mund("er)
Mr. (der) Herr(-en)
Mrs. (die) Frau(-en)
much viel; **very much** vielmals, sehr
multicoloured bunt
Munich (das) München
of Munich Münchner
person from Munich der Münchner(-)
museum das Museum (Museen)
music die Musik
school of music die Musikhochschule(-n)
must müssen
my mein, meine

N

name der Name(-n)
namely nämlich
near bei
nearby in der Nähe
nearly fast, gleich
necessarily unbedingt
necessary nötig
neck der Hals(-e)
to need brauchen
needlework die Handarbeit(-en)
neighbour (female) die Nachbarin(-nen)
neighbourhood die Nähe
neither...nor weder...noch
nephew der Neffe(-n)
never nie, niemals
never (yet) noch nie
new neu
newspaper die Zeitung(-en)
New Year (1st of January) das Neujahr
next nächst, kommend
next to neben
next but one übernächst
next to it daneben
nice schön; hübsch
nice(ly) nett
night die Nacht (-e)
by night nachts
nightdress das Nachthemd(-en)
nine neun
no nein; (not a/not any) kein, keine
nobody niemand
noise der Krach
noisy (loud) laut
no matter where or when noch immer
und überall
none kein, keine
nonsense Unsinn!
noon der Mittag(-e)
no one niemand
normal normal
Norwegian (female) die Norwege-
rin(-nen)
nose die Nase(-n)
in front of my nose vor der Nase
not nicht
not at all gar nicht
note der Zettel(-)

(bank) note der Schein(-e)
nothing nichts
nothing at all gar nichts
November der November
now jetzt, nun
now and then ab und zu
nowadays heutzutage
nowhere nirgends
number die Nummer(-n); die Linie(-n)
nut die Nuß (Nüsse)

O

obvious selbstverständlich
occupant (car) der Insasse(-n)
to occupy beschäftigen
to occur (to) einfallen (D)
to occur einfallen (D)
o'clock Uhr
October der Oktober
of von, aus
of it davon
off (from) von; (away) ab
offer das Angebot(-e)
to offer anbieten, bieten
office, das Büro(-s)
officially offiziell
often oft
very often immer wieder
oh good! ah gut!
oil das Öl(-e)
old alt
older ones die Älteren
old-fashioned unmodern
on auf, an, zu, in
on that/it darauf, daran
once einmal
at once sofort, gleich
all at once auf einmal
one eins; (a person) man; (any) irgendein
one and a half anderthalb
oneself selber
only nur, bloß; erst
to open aufmachen, öffnen
opera die Oper(-n)
opera guide (book) der Opernführer(-)
operator die Vermittlung(-en)
operetta die Operette(-n)
opinion die Meinung(-en)

in my opinion meiner Meinung nach
opportunity die Gelegenheit(-en)
opposite gegenüber
or oder
order die Bestellung(-en)
to order bestellen
in order that damit
in order to um zu
other andere, übrig
otherwise sonst
our unser, unsere
out of aus
out of order kaputt
outside draußen, außen
over vorbei, zu Ende
all over (the body) am ganzen Körper
to have left over übrig haben
over there dort drüben
own eigen
owner (proprietress) die Inhaberin(-nen)
ox der Ochs(-en)

P
to pack packen
packet die Schachtel(-n)
pain der Schmerz(-en)
to paint over bemalen
painted bemalt
painting das Bild(-er)
palace das Schloß (Schlösser)
pale blaß
local paper die Lokalzeitung(-en)
I beg your pardon! Entschuldigung!
parents die Eltern (pl.)
park der Park(-s)
to park parken
parking space der Parkplatz(¨e)
part der Teil(-e)
for the most part zum größten Teil
it's all part of it es gehört dazu
particular die Einzelheit(-en)
partly teils
party die Party(-s), die Gesellschaft(-en)
passenger der Fahrgast(¨e)
fellow passenger (traveller) der/die Mit-
    reisende(-n)
passport der Reisepaß (Reisepässe)
passport control die Paßkontrolle(-n)

passport officer der Paßbeamte(-n)
past vorbei; (last) vergangen
pastries das Gebäck
to patch up a quarrel sich versöhnen
path der Weg(-e)
patience die Geduld
to have patience sich gedulden
patient der Patient(-en), der Kranke(-n)
pause die Ruhepause(-n)
to pay zahlen, bezahlen
pedestrian (male) der Fußgänger(–)
    (female) die Fußgängerin(-nen)
penny der Pfennig(-e)
people die Leute (pl.), das Volk(¨er)
perfect tadellos
performance die Vorstellung(-en)
perfume das Parfum(-s)
perhaps vielleicht
permit erlauben
person die Person(-en)
personal privat
personal(ly) persönlich
to perspire schwitzen
petrol das Benzin
photograph das Foto(-s)
to pick up abnehmen
picture das Bild(-er)
picture frame der Bilderrahmen (–)
piece das Stück(-e), die Scheibe(-n)
piece of advice der Ratschlag(¨e)
it is a great pity es ist sehr schade
to that place dorthin
to place (trunk calls etc.) anmelden
plane das Flugzeug(-e)
plastic der Kunststoff(-e)
play das Stück(-e); (playing) das Spielen
to play spielen
pleasant (cosy) gemütlich
please bitte
please! bitte schön!
to please gefallen (D)
pleased froh
to be very pleased about sich freuen über
to be pleased with sich freuen über
I should be pleased es soll mir recht sein
pleasure das Vergnügen, die Freude(-n)
it's a pleasure nichts zu danken
with pleasure gern, herzlich gern

303

with great pleasure furchtbar gern, sehr gern
point der Punkt(-e)
police die Polizei
police station die Polizeiwache(-n)
policeman der Polizist(-en)
polite höflich
poor arm
popular beliebt
porcelain das Porzellan
roast pork der Schweinebraten(–)
porter der Gepäckträger(–)
Portugal (das) Portugal
Portuguese (language) portugiesisch
Portuguese person der Portugiese(-n), die Portugiesin(-nen)
position die Stellung(-en)
possible möglich
that is possible das schon
as much as possible möglichst viel
possibility die Möglichkeit(-en)
post-card die Postkarte(-n)
post office das Postamt(¨er)
main post office das Hauptpostamt(¨er)
post office clerk der Postbeamte(-n)
poster das Plakat(-e)
pot der Topf(¨e)
potato die Kartoffel(-n)
potato in its jacket die Pellkartoffel(-n)
boiled potatoes die Salzkartoffeln
pouring strömend
powder der Puder(–)
practical praktisch
general practitioner (G.P.) praktischer Arzt
preferably lieber
preparation die Vorbereitung(-en)
to prepare vorbereiten
prepared bereit
to prescribe verschreiben
prescription das Rezept(-e)
present (gift) das Geschenk(-e)
present anwesend, dabei; jetzig
pressure (air) der Luftdruck
pretty hübsch; (very) recht
previous vorig
price der Preis(-e)
primitive primitiv

principal der Direktor(-en)
private privat
probably wahrscheinlich, wohl
problem das Problem(-e)
profession der Beruf(-e)
by profession von Beruf
professor der Professor(-en)
progress der Fortschritt(-e)
to prohibit verbieten
properly richtig
proud stolz
to provide with versorgen
proximity die Nähe
psychology (die) Psychologie
P.T. das Turnen
public das Publikum
to pull ziehen
Pullover der Pullover(–)
pulse der Puls(-e)
pupil der Schüler(–)
purchase der Einkauf(¨e), der Kauf(¨e)
pure echt
to put (stand) stellen; (lay) legen; stecken, setzen
to put in einwerfen
to put on (clothes) anziehen

Q

to quarrel sich zanken
quarter das Viertel(–)
quarter of an hour die Viertelstunde(-n)
quarter to six drei Viertel sechs
question die Frage(-n)
it is a question of es handelt sich um
quiet ruhig
quite ganz; (fairly) ziemlich
quite a few manch-

R

radio das Radio(-s)
railway guide das Kursbuch(¨er)
rain der Regen
to rain regnen
to rally sich versammeln
rarely selten
rather ziemlich; (preferably) lieber
to read lesen

readily ohne weiteres
ready fertig
real echt
really wirklich, ganz, eigentlich
reason der Grund($\ddot{}$e)
for that reason deshalb, darum, eben
receiver der Hörer(–)
recently neulich, kürzlich
reception clerk der Empfangschef(-s)
receptionist die Sprechstundenhilfe(-n)
to reckon on rechnen mit
to recommend empfehlen
recommendation die Empfehlung(-en)
reconciliation die Versöhnung(-en)
record das Protokoll(-e), die Schallplatte
to recover sich erholen
red rot
student refectory die Mensa (Mensen)
to refill nachfüllen
to refuel tanken
to give regards to grüßen
registration form der Meldezettel(–)
regularly regelmäßig
relative der/die Verwandte(-n)
reliable zuverlässig
reluctantly ungern
to rely on sich verlassen auf
to remain bleiben; **(be left over)** übrig bleiben
remaining übrig
remedy das Heilmittel(–)
to remember sich erinnern (an)
rent die Miete(-n)
repair die Reparatur(-en)
repair shop die Reparaturwerkstatt($\ddot{}$en)
to repeat wiederholen
reply (decision) der Bescheid
report das Protokoll(-e), der Bericht(-e)
reporter der Reporter(–)
request das Gesuch(-e)
to request bitten
rescue die Rettung(-en)
rescuer der Retter(–)
reservation die Reservierung(-en)
to reserve reservieren
reserving a room die Zimmerreservierung(-en)
residence die Residenz(-en)

in other respects sonst
responsible verantwortungsvoll
rest die Pause(-n)
to rest (lie) liegen
restaurant das Restaurant(-s)
it results from the fact that das liegt daran, daß
with the result that so daß
return die Rückkehr
to return zurückgehen
in return for that dafür
reunion das Wiedersehen
to be revealed sich zeigen
to reward belohnen
to get rid of loswerden
ridiculous lächerlich
right richtig
to be right recht haben
on the right rechts
to the right nach rechts
ring der Ring(-e)
to ring (bell) klingeln
to ring up anrufen
road die Straße(-n)
roll das Brötchen(–)
room das Zimmer(–); **(space)** der Platz($\ddot{}$e)
single room das Einzelzimmer(–)
round rund; **(around)** um, durch
to run laufen
rush der Hochbetrieb
to rush eilen, strömen
Russian russisch

S
sailing das Segeln
salad der Salat(-e)
sale der Schlußverkauf($\ddot{}$e)
sales engineer der Verkaufsingenieur(-e)
sales girl die Verkäuferin(-nen)
same selb
the same derselbe, dieselbe, dasselbe
it's all the same to me es ist mir egal
satisfied satt
Saturday (der) Samstag
to save retten
I say! hallo!
to say sagen

to say "du" to each other sich duzen
scarf das Tuch(¨er)
silk scarf das Seidentuch(¨er)
scenery die Landschaft(-en)
school die Schule(-n)
school attendance der Schulbesuch(–)
schoolboy der Schuljunge(-n)
schoolgirl die Schülerin(-nen)
private school die Privatschule(-n)
screen der Bildschirm(-e)
search die Suche
season die Saison(-s), die Jahres-
    zeit(-en)
seat die Sitzbank(¨e), der Platz(¨e)
seat of trousers der Hosenboden(¨)
tip-back seat der Liegesitz(-e)
second zweite
second-hand aus zweiter Hand
secretary die Sekretärin(-nen)
I see! ach so!, aha!
to see sehen
to see about sich kümmern um
to see to erledigen
to seem scheinen
seldom selten
selection die Auswahl(-en)
self (myself, himself etc.) selbst
to sell verkaufen
to send schicken; (hand in) aufgeben
to send one's apologies sich entschuldi-
    gen lassen
serious schwer
to serve bedienen
service die Bedienung(-en)
after sales service der Kundendienst
set (crockery) das Service(-s)
to set (table) decken
seven sieben
seventeen siebzehn
seventh siebte
several mehrere
shame! pfui!
she sie
to shine scheinen
to shiver with zittern vor
shop das Geschäft(-e)
short(ly) kurz
shorthand die Stenographie

to show zeigen
to show round herumführen
shower die Dusche(-n)
showy auffallend
shrimp cocktail der Krabbencock-
    tail(-s)
sick krank
she gets sick ihr wird schlecht
sick person der/die Kranke(-n)
side die Seite(-n)
sight die Sehenswürdigkeit(-en), der
    Blick(-e)
sight-seeing die Besichtigung(-en)
silk die Seide(-n); seiden (adj.)
simple, simply einfach, halt
simplicity die Einfachheit
since seit
long since längst
since then seither
sincere herzlich
singing das Singen
to sink sinken
Sir mein Herr
Sir and Madam die Herrschaften (pl.)
siren die Sirene(-n)
sister die Schwester(-n)
little sister das Schwesterchen(–)
sister-in-law die Schwägerin(-nen)
to sit sitzen
to sit (down) sich setzen
site die Lage(-n)
situation die Lage(-n), die Stellung(-en)
six sechs
sixth sechste
sixty sechzig
size die Größe(-n)
skate der Schlittschuh(-e)
to skate Schlittschuh laufen
ski der Ski(-er)
ski course der Skikurs(-e)
ski instructor der Skilehrer(–)
ski-ing das Skilaufen
skilled worker die Fachkraft(¨e)
skin die Haut
sky der Himmel(–)
to sleep schlafen
sleeping bag der Schlafsack(¨e)
slice die Scheibe(-n)

slim schlank
slip of paper der Zettel(–)
slippery glatt
slippery ice das Glatteis
slot machine der Automat(-en)
slow(ly) langsam
small klein
smart hübsch
to smile lächeln
smiling lächelnd
to smoke rauchen
smooth glatt
to sneeze niesen
sniffles der Schnupfen(–)
snow der Schnee
to snow schneien
snowball fight die Schneeball-
   schlacht(-en)
snowman der Schneemann("er)
so also
and so on, etc. und so weiter (usw.)
so, so teils, teils
so that (in order that) damit; (as a result)
   so daß
sociology (die) Soziologie
soft weich
sold out ausverkauft
solid fest
some einige, manch-; welch-
some more noch etwas
some (or other) irgendein
some things einiges
somebody jemand
somehow irgendwie
someone jemand
something etwas
something good etwas Gutes
something or other irgend etwas
sometime mal
sometimes manchmal
somewhat etwas
somewhere (or other) irgendwo
son der Junge(-n), der Sohn("e)
soon bald
as soon as sobald
see you soon! bis bald!
the sooner the better je eher desto
   besser

I am sorry es tut mir leid
sort die Art(-en)
what sort of? was für ein?
to sound klingen
soup die Suppe(-n)
soup with liver dumplings die Leber-
   knödelsuppe
sour sauer
space der Platz("e)
Spain Spanien
Spaniard (female) die Spanierin(-nen)
Spaniard (male) der Spanier(–)
spare part der Ersatzteil(-e)
spare time die Freizeit(-en)
to speak sprechen
so to speak sozusagen
speciality die Spezialität(-en)
specific bestimmt
spectator der Zuschauer(–)
spectators' balcony der Zuschauer-
   balkon(-e)
to spend (money) ausgeben
in spite of trotz
in spite of it trotzdem
sport(s) der Sport
type of sport die Sportart(-en)
sportsman der Sportler(–)
Spring das Frühjahr, der Frühling
square der Platz("e)
stairs die Treppe(-n)
stamp die Briefmarke(-n)
stand der Stand("e)
to stand stehen; (put) stellen
to stand around herumstehen
stand back! los!
start der Beginn
to start anfangen
State der Staat(-en)
station der Bahnhof("e)
stay der Aufenthalt(-e)
to stay (reside) wohnen; (remain)
   bleiben, stehenbleiben
steep steil
to step treten
to stick stecken
to stick to bleiben bei
sticking out abstehend

still immer noch, noch
stop die Station(-en), der Aufenthalt(-e)
stop (bus, tram etc.) die Haltestelle(-n)
to stop halten, stehenbleiben
department store das Kaufhaus(⸗er)
storey die Etage(-n)
story die Geschichte(-n)
straight (of hair) glatt
straight ahead geradeaus
straightaway gleich
strange fremd; (odd) komisch
to stream in hereinströmen
street die Straße(-n)
street map der Stadtplan(⸗e)
striking auffallend
on the stroke of 12 Punkt 12 Uhr
stroll (in the town) der Stadtbummel(–)
strong stark
to get stuck stecken bleiben
student der Student(-en)
study das Studium (Studien)
to study studieren
stupid dumm
style der Stil(-e)
subject matter der Inhalt(-e)
to succeed gelingen (D)
success der Erfolg(-e)
such solch-
such a eine so
such a thing so etwas
such like dergleichen (dgl.)
sudden(ly) plötzlich, auf einmal
to suffer leiden
suffering leidend
sugar der Zucker
suit der Anzug(⸗e)
to suit passen (D)
suitable passend
suitcase der Koffer(–)
summer der Sommer
this summer in diesem Sommer
sun die Sonne(-n)
Sunday (der) Sonntag
sunny sonnig
surely doch, bestimmt, sicher
surname der Familienname(-n)
surprise die Überraschung(-en)
surprised überrascht

to be surprised sich wundern
surroundings die Umgebung(-en)
to swallow schlucken
to sweat schwitzen
sweater der Pullover(–)
Swedish schwedisch
to swim schwimmen
swimming das Schwimmen
swimming pool das Schwimmbad(⸗er)
Switzerland die Schweiz
T
table der Tisch(-e)
tablecloth die Tischdecke(-n)
tablet die Tablette(-n)
to take nehmen, bringen; (temperature) messen
to take again (exam.) wiederholen
to take a holiday Urlaub machen
take care! Achtung!
to take care of (deal with) erledigen
to take off abnehmen; (plane) abfliegen
to take one's leave sich verabschieden
to take place stattfinden
to take seriously ernst nehmen
to take something off (i.e. a garment) sich (D) etwas ausziehen
to take (an order) entgegennehmen
it takes such a long time es dauert so lange
talk das Gespräch(-e), die Rede(-n)
to talk sprechen; (converse) sich unterhalten
to have a talk ein Gespräch führen
men's talk das Männergespräch(-e)
tall lang
tape das Tonband (⸗er)
taste der Geschmack
to taste schmecken
to my taste nach meinem Geschmack
taxi das Taxi(-s)
tea der Tee
teacher (man) der Lehrer(–)
teacher (woman) die Lehrerin(-nen)
technical technisch
technician der Techniker(–)
telegram das Telegramm(-e)
telephone das Telephon(-e), der Apparat(-e)

to telephone telephonieren, anrufen
telephone directory das Telephon-
buch("er)
to tell (about) erzählen (von)
temper die Laune(-n)
temperature das Fieber(-); die Tempe-
ratur(-en)
temporarily vorübergehend
ten zehn
tenant der Mieter(-)
tennis das Tennis
term das Semester(-)
terrible(ly) furchtbar, schrecklich
textiles department die Textilabtei-
lung(-en)
than als
thanks der Dank
to thank danken (D)
thank you danke
no thank you danke
thank you very much danke schön, vielen Dank
thanks a lot! besten Dank! danke vielmals!
that das, dieser; daß
that's because, das liegt daran, daß
that is, i.e. das heißt (d.h.)
that means das heißt (d.h.)
the der, die, das
theatre das Theater(-)
evening at the theatre der Theater-
abend(-e)
national theatre das Staatstheater(-)
theatregoer der Theaterbesucher(-)
their ihr, ihre
them sie; ihnen
then dann; (at that time) damals; (in
that case) denn
there dort, da; (to that place) dorthin
there is, there are es gibt
therefore also, deshalb
they sie
thick dicht
thing die Sache(-n), das Ding(-e)
to think glauben, halten für, sich (D)
denken, meinen, finden
to think (of) denken (an)
third dritte, das Drittel(-)

thirteen dreizehn
this dieser, diese
as though als ob
thousand (das) Tausend(-e)
three drei
throat der Hals("e)
through durch, über
through it (thereby) dabei
Thursday (der) Donnerstag
ticket der Fahrschein(-e), die Karte(-n)
single ticket die Einzelfahrt(-en)
ticket-office clerk (fem.) die Karten-
verkäuferin(-nen)
tight fest
to tighten spannen
time die Zeit(-en); (occasion) das Mal(-e)
at a time je
at that time damals
at what time? um wieviel Uhr?
for a very long time schon längst
for some time längere Zeit
for the first time zum ersten Mal
from time to time ab und zu
have a good time viel Vergnügen
high time höchste Zeit
on time rechtzeitig, pünktlich
time of day die Tageszeit(-en)
to have time off frei haben
what time is it? wie spät ist es?
timetable der Fahrplan("e)
tip das Trinkgeld(-er)
dead tired todmüde
to in, nach, zu, auf
toast der Toast
toaster der Toaster(-)
tobacco der Tabak
today heute
of today heutig
together zusammen, miteinander, zueinander
tomorrow morgen
the day after tomorrow übermorgen
tomorrow morning morgen früh
too zu; (also) auch, ebenfalls
top oberst
at the top oben
on top of über
from top to bottom von oben bis unten

tour die Rundfahrt(-en)
to go on a tour eine Führung machen
tourist der Tourist(-en)
towards gegen
town die Stadt(⁼e)
town centre die Stadtmitte(-n)
town hall das Rathaus(⁼er)
traffic der Verkehr
to train anlernen, ausbilden
train der Zug(⁼e)
fast train der Eilzug(⁼e)
local train der Personenzug(⁼e)
night train der Nachtzug(⁼e)
trained ausgebildet
tram(way) die Straßenbahn(-en)
tranquillizer die Beruhigungstablette(-n)
translator der Übersetzer(–)
transportation der Transport(-e)
to travel reisen
travel agency das Reisebüro(-s)
travelling-bag die Reisetasche(-n)
tray das Tablett(-s)
wooden tray das Holztablett(-s)
treat der Genuß (Genüsse)
to treat behandeln
tree der Baum(⁼e)
trimming die Borte(-n)
trip die Fahrt(-en)
round-trip die Rundfahrt(-en)
trouble die Sorge(-n)
trouser pocket die Hosentasche(-n)
trout die Forelle(-n)
true echt
it is true zwar
that's true das stimmt
to try versuchen
to try on anprobieren
Tuesday (der) Dienstag
it's your turn ihr seid dran
to have one's turn darankommen
turnover der Umsatz(⁼e)
TV broadcast die Fernsehsendung(-en)
TV studio das Fernsehstudio(-s)
twelve zwölf
twenty zwanzig
twenty-eight achtundzwanzig
twenty-six sechsundzwanzig
twice zweimal

two zwei
two and a half zweieinhalb
the two die beiden
type (sort) die Art(-en)
typewriter die Schreibmaschine(-n)
typical typisch
typist die Schreibkraft(⁼e)
tyre der Reifen(–)

U

ugly häßlich
uncle der Onkel(–)
unconscious ohnmächtig
under unter
under it darunter
to understand verstehen
undisturbed in Ruhe
unexpected unerwartet
unfortunate unglücklich
unfortunately leider
unfurnished unmöbliert
university die Universität(-en)
unless es sei denn
unpleasant unangenehm, unfreundlich
unreasonable unvernünftig
unsuccessful unglücklich
until bis
until now bisher
unusual selten
unwillingly ungern
up, upwards hinauf
up there dort oben
upstairs nach oben, oben
us uns
to make use of zu Hilfe nehmen
to get used (to) sich gewöhnen (an)
usual üblich, gewöhnlich
usual(ly) gewöhnlich, meistens

V

vacant frei
in vain vergeblich
varied vielseitig
various verschieden
vegetable(s) das Gemüse(–)
vegetables (with main dish) die Beilage(-n)
haunch of venison die Hirschkeule(-n)
very sehr, ganz, recht

via über
victim der Verunglückte(-n)
to view besichtigen
viewing die Besichtigung(-en)
village das Dorf("er)
visit der Besuch(-e)
on a visit zu Besuch
to visit besuchen
visit to a school der Schulbesuch(-e)
visitor der Besucher(–)

W
to wait for warten auf
to wait sich gedulden, warten auf
waiter der Kellner(–)
waiter! Herr Ober!
waiting-room das Wartezimmer(–)
walk der Spaziergang("e)
to walk laufen
to go for a walk spazierengehen, einen
  Spaziergang machen
wall die Wand("e)
to want wollen; brauchen
to want to mögen
war der Krieg(-e)
warehouse das Lager(–)
warm warm
to wash waschen
to have a wash sich waschen
to wash (a part of oneself) sich (D) etwas
  waschen
watch die Uhr(-en)
to watch sich (D) ansehen
to watch out aufpassen
water das Wasser
wavy lockig
way der Weg(-e)
by the way nebenbei gesagt, übrigens
on the way unterwegs, auf dem
  Transport
the best way am besten
W.C. die Toilette(-n)
we wir
weak schwach
to wear tragen
weather das Wetter
Wednesday (der) Mittwoch
week die Woche(-n)

weekend das Wochenende(-n)
to weigh wiegen
welcome die Begrüßung(-en)
welcome to...! willkommen in...!
to welcome begrüßen
I hope you will soon be well! gute Besserung!
well gut; na, nun
well (in good health) wohl, gesund
very well sehr gut
well, well! nanu!
well done! bravo!
as well dazu
as well as sowie
well-known berühmt, bekannt
wet naß
what? was?, wie?
for what? wofür?
when(?) wann? wenn, als
where? wo?
where from? woher?
where to? wohin?
whether ob
which? welcher, welche, welches?
while während
while having bei
white weiß
who? wer?
whole ganz
whom? wen?
to whom? wem?
to whom wem
whose? wessen?
why? warum?
wide breit
wife die Frau(-en)
wig die Perücke(-n)
window das Fenster(–)
wine der Wein(-e)
wine list die Getränkekarte(-n)
mulled wine der Glühwein(-e)
red wine der Rotwein(-e)
wine cellar der Weinkeller(–)
winter der Winter
winter sports der Wintersport
wish der Wunsch("e)
to wish wünschen
with mit, bei, zu

with it damit, dazu
within innerhalb (von)
without ohne
without fail unbedingt
witness der Zeuge(-n)
woman die Frau(-en)
to wonder gespannt sein
no wonder kein Wunder!
I wonder ich frage mich nur; bloß
wonderful wunderbar
wood das Holz; (forest) der Wald(¨er)
word das Wort(¨er)
work die Arbeit(-en), das Werk(-e)
work (hours on duty) der Dienst
to work arbeiten, tätig sein
to work (watches etc.) gehen
condition of work die Arbeits-
    bedingung(-en)
place of work der Arbeitsplatz(¨e)
worker der Arbeiter(–)
working hours die Arbeitszeit(-en)
workshop die Werkstatt(¨en)
world die Welt
worry die Sorge(-n)
to worry about sich kümmern um
don't worry! nicht so schlimm!
the worst das Schlimmste
worth wert
not worth mentioning nicht der Rede
    wert

to be worth it sich lohnen
to wrap up einpacken
to write schreiben
wrong falsch
what's wrong with him was fehlt ihm?
what was wrong? was war los?

Y

yard der Hof(¨e)
year das Jahr(-e)
lasting three years dreijährig
yellow gelb
yes ja; doch
yesterday gestern
the day before yesterday vorgestern
not yet noch nicht
you du, Sie; dich; dir, Ihnen
you (pl. form) ihr; euch
you (one) man
you see nämlich
young jung
young lady das Fräulein(–)
young one der Junge(-n)
young person der Jugendliche(-n)
younger ones die Jüngeren
your dein, deine; euer, eure; Ihr, Ihre
youth (lad) der Bursche(-n); die Jugend
youth centre das Jugendheim(-e)